D0407682

# THE GERMAN MIND OF
# THE NINETEENTH CENTURY

# THE
# GERMAN MIND
# OF THE
# NINETEENTH
# CENTURY

*A Literary & Historical Anthology*

*Edited by*

## Hermann Glaser

CONTINUUM • New York

Published in German under the title *Soviel Anfang war nie*
*Deutscher Geist im 19. Jahrhundert. Ein Lesebuch.*
© 1981 Carl Hanser Verlag München Wien.

English translation copyright © 1981
by The Continuum Publishing Corporation,
18 East 41st Street, New York, N.Y. 10017.

*Printed in the United States of America*

Library of Congress Cataloging in Publication Data

The German mind of the nineteenth century.

Bibliography: p.
1. German literature—19th century. 2. Germany—
Intellectual life. I. Glaser, Hermann.
PT1136.G47     083     80-29402
ISBN 0-8264-0041-8
ISBN 0-8264-0044-2 (pbk.)

Grateful acknowledgment is made to the following for permission to use excerpts from these translations, reprinted by permission of the publishers:

From *Iphigenia in Tauris* by J. W. v. Goethe, translated by Charles E. Passage. Copyright © 1963 by Frederick Ungar Publishing Co., Inc.

From *Hymns to the Night* by Novalis (v. Hardenberg), translated by Charles E. Passage. Copyright © 1960 by The Bobbs-Merrill Co., Inc.

From *Lectures on the Philosophy of World History* by G. W. F. Hegel, translated by H. B. Nisbet. Copyright © 1975 by Cambridge University Press.

From *Dearest Father* by Franz Kafka. Copyright © 1954 by Schocken Books Inc.

From *Critique of Hegel's Philosophy of Right* by Karl Marx, edited by J. O'Malley. Copyright © 1970 by Cambridge University Press.

From *The Notebooks of Malte Laurids Brigge* by Rainer Maria Rilke, translated by M. D. Herter Norton. Copyright © 1949 by W. W. Norton & Company, Inc. and renewed 1977 by M. D. Herter Norton. Reprinted by permission of W. W. Norton & Company, Inc.

From *Parerga and Paralipomena* by Arthur Schopenhauer, translated by E. F. J. Payne. Copyright © 1974 by Oxford University Press.

From *The World as Will and Representation* by Arthur Schopenhauer, translated by E. F. J. Payne. Copyright © 1969 by Dover Publications, Inc.

From *Stories of Three Decades* by Thomas Mann, translated by H. T. Lowe-Porter. Copyright © 1936 and renewed 1964 by Alfred A. Knopf, Inc.

From *Basic Writings of Nietzsche* by Friedrich Nietzsche, edited and translated by Walter Kaufmann. Copyright © 1966, 1967, 1968 by Random House, Inc.

From *Faust,* by Johann Wolfgang von Goethe, a Norton Critical Edition, translated by Walter Arndt, edited by Cyrus Hamlin. Copyright © 1976 by W. W. Norton & Co., Inc.

Grateful acknowledgment is made for permission to translate the following works from the original German:

Georg Heym, "Der Gott der Stadt," Verlag Heinrich Ellermann, Munich; Jakob van Hoddis, "Weltende," Verlag der Arche, Peter Schifferli, Zurich; Arthur Schnitzler, from *Jugend in Wien,* Fritz Molden Verlag, Munich; August Stramm, "Patrouille" and "Wache," Limes Verlag, Munich; Hugo von Hofmannsthal, *Ein Brief,* S. Fischer Verlag, Frankfurt; Gottfried Benn, "Mann und Frau gehen durch die Krebsbaracke" and *Hirne,* Klett-Cotta Verlag, Stuttgart; Stefan George, "Entrückung," Helmut Küpper, Stuttgart.

# CONTENTS

# Titanism • Suspending the World      103

# FOREWORD

When New York's Metropolitan Museum of Art, in the spring of 1980, opened its new André Meyer Gallery, dedicated to a permanent exhibit of masterpieces of nineteenth-century European painting, leading critics expressed their high regard for this excellent collection, but noted that German contributions to the art of this period were nearly absent. Thus, the Metropolitan Museum's special exhibition devoted to German painting of the nineteenth century to take place from May 2 to July 5, 1981, is a welcome event.

To complement the exhibition and to stimulate interest in nineteenth-century Germany, Goethe House New York–German Cultural Center, in cooperation with renowned institutions and museums in New York and in Germany, is mounting a program that will explore some of the intellectual currents and cultural trends of that period. Throughout 1981 there will be exhibitions, lectures, symposia, theatrical productions, and films, under the program title "Germany in the Nineteenth Century—Cultural Aspects of an Age."

In *The German Mind of the Nineteenth Century*, texts from various fields represent an age which in many ways influenced and shaped the world we live in today. As this volume impressively makes clear, one cannot reduce such a rich century to a single common denominator. An examination of its often contradictory tendencies and phenomena will surely sharpen our view of the greatness and beauty, as well as the failings, of the epoch, and perhaps aid us in understanding aspects of our own situation.

Special thanks are due to Editor Hermann Glaser for compiling this anthology and providing it with comprehensive introductions that set forth and explain the prevalent patterns of thought of the period; and to the Carl Hanser Verlag, Munich and The Continuum Publishing Corporation, New York, for their preparation of the German and English-language editions respectively.

May this book find many readers on both sides of the Atlantic, readers who want to learn more about our common heritage.

CHRISTOPH WECKER, DIRECTOR
Goethe House New York

## Acknowledgments

This reader was suggested by Christoph Wecker, Director of the Goethe House New York. He also provided advice and help in the inception of this volume, especially the English-language edition. I wish to express my keen gratitude to him and to Burkhart Kroeber of the editorial staff of Hanser Verlag. I would also like to thank Nina Morris-Farber of the publishing staff at The Continuum Publishing Corporation, and Martha Humphreys for her excellent translations of my introductory essays and biographical material.

# INTRODUCTION

Hegel states in the preface to his *Fundamentals of the Philosophy of Right* that when "philosophy paints gray on gray, a form of life has become old and can merely be recognized but not rejuvenated by gray on gray—the owl of Minerva only starts its flight at the break of dawn." Hegel's conceptual edifice comes at the end of one epoch and introduces a new one. He completed his *Phenomenology of the Spirit* in 1806, during the night prior to the battle of Jena and Auerstedt that ushered in Napoleon's victory over Prussia. Hegel completes and suspends the Enlightenment; he is bound up with the Romantic feeling of the world and creates a system that provides the basis for the epoch of Realism.

The Rococo and the Enlightenment had aged. With Romanticism a spiritual attitude and a philosophy came into being that sought to assist the force of feeling to a breakthrough. The German classics, on the other hand, attempted sensuously to disclose the realm of thought, to comprehend the "world spirit" via its concrete expressions and phenomena. Political and economic turmoil upset the individual as well as society. People hoped for "progress," but conservatism tried to stop the clock. The Biedermeier period took refuge in a flight within that proclaimed "cheerfulness based on melancholy." The rise of Realism occurred in the middle of the century; the world of ideas was to be set right side up and theory to be replaced by action. Karl Marx stated in his *Critique of Hegel's Philosophy of Right* that it was necessary to portray every sphere of German society as the *partie honteuse* of German society. "These petrified relations must be compelled to dance by playing them their own tune! People must be given courage by being taught to be terrified of themselves." The course of reality permitted recognition only of the beginnings of such a dynamic force, but much of what was placed in motion proved at least intrinsically to be an important legacy of the era, both a fund and a fundament of "another Germany."

1

The reality of Germany, which still existed in the first half of the nineteenth century only as an idea, had to be painted gray on gray. But from the twilight, not least of all from the twilight over defeated Prussia, arose the real utopia of a united nation that with the wars of liberation seemed to approach the goal of its longing.

Germany had disintegrated into petty states and was vegetating economically, politically, and socially. It offered a picture of gray on gray. Then industrialization belatedly set in with vehemence. By 1871 "it had been achieved!"—the second German Reich had become a great European power.

The picture of reaction and restoration was gray on gray. But the achievements of the liberal revolutions of the nineteenth century, particularly of the year 1848, could no longer be banished from consciousness. Along with the reforms following the Prussian renaissance after 1807, the "civilian state" had been manifested as a possibility.

The light of morning emerging in this manner from the evening twilight has altogether a duplicitous, iridescent, irritating brilliance—the wars of liberation and the Romantic movement that supported them turned into chauvinism and epigonal arrogance. Dreams became nightmares. The powerful were not anointed with democratic oil and they did not understand the signs of the enlightened spirit. Republican consciousness came to a halt. The second German Reich admittedly satisfied the longing for unity but not for freedom. Friedrich Nietzsche spoke of the extirpation of the German spirit in favor of the German Reich.

"The spirit of the people exists for itself as a genus; herein lies the possibility that the universal contained in this existing appears as the opposite. Its negative aspects are expressed in it; thinking is elevated above immediate action." (Hegel) From the standpoint of thought elevating itself, nineteenth-century Germany was to a large extent unreal; i.e. unreasonable. The negative aspect of the spirit of the people was expressed and it erupted. Grillparzer spoke of the fact that the route of German humanity led via nationality to bestiality. Thinking, however, soared beyond such malaise and beyond "direct action." The German spirit, only slightly sicklied by the German nonspirit, conceived a world that proved to be a utopian counterworld. Hölderlin's formulation, "Never were there so many beginnings," characterizes the German spirit of the nineteenth century. It was a century of revolutions and radical changes, of condemnations and eruptions, of evolutions and revolutions. But it was also a century in which abysses opened up that became more and more dizzying, dangerous, uncanny.

But the topic of this book is not German reality; the topic is the German mind or spirit of the nineteenth century. The issue is the "universal" that manifested itself as the opposing force in the existing spirit of the people. One can altogether say it shone forth. Until today. Now more than ever. The universalism of German thought in the nineteenth century is an achievement that can be neither lost nor renounced.

> The universal aspect is the demand of the moment and of our anxious heart; and the thought of the honor of mankind, the word humanity, has long ceased to be the most extensive participation, a "weak rule of behavior" at which "our feelings evaporate and fade away." Precisely this comprehensive feeling is what is necessary, all too necessary; and if mankind as a whole fails to focus on itself, on its honor, and on the mystery of its dignity, it is not only morally but physically lost.

The man in whose honor Thomas Mann spoke these words, Friedrich Schiller (on the 150th anniversary of his death), incorporated and anticipated in his thinking the tragic antinomy of Germany's development in the nineteenth century. What Schiller anticipated, namely, was the "aesthetic State," by which he meant the "place" for the whole of *Humaniora*—the place for the union of substantiality and formality in the "drive to play," the place for the unfolding of the "beautiful soul." Schiller's thought anticipated that this aesthetic State could exist only in appearance, hence only as a model. "Here, therefore, in the realm of aesthetic appearance, is fulfilled the ideal of equality that the enthusiast would so much like to see realized in essence."

The fact that "the essence" was so little realized in the Germany of the nineteenth century, that the essence was so little turned right side up, was so little transformed from ideality into reality, does not justify having a low estimate of what did exist as "aesthetic appearance"; the principle of ideality must not be burdened with the accusation of not being followed by the reality principle. The fact that the classics remained extremely ineffective does not speak against them. All the worse for reality!

The legacy of the era—of the German nineteenth century—consisted in the fact that the "completion of the thoughts of the past" remained possible for the future, since precisely such thoughts had already been thought and hence could be rethought.

> It will then be shown that the world has long owned the dream of a thing of which it must merely possess consciousness in order to really possess it. It will be shown that what is at issue is not a large hyphen between past and future; at issue is the completion of the thoughts of the past. Ultimately

it will be shown that mankind does not initiate any new work; what it does is to accomplish its old work with consciousness.

Thus wrote Karl Marx to Arnold Ruge in September 1843.

This book does not report on the failure in the completion of thoughts past; its intention is to show a conceptual world, as such, in its relation to the moment—namely, in the form of selected documents by German poets, philosophers, publicists, historians, natural scientists, and artists. The texts in this reader are conceived as pieces of a mosaic—their composition is intended to indicate the picture of a "thing" of which it is merely necessary to be conscious in order to really possess it. In doing so, only the contours of the "thing" can be shown; the volume contains a portrayal neither of German literature nor of German philosophy; a portrayal neither of German music nor of German art; it is neither a spiritual nor a cultural history of Germany. Above all, it does not provide another portrait of German reality. Reality—facts, dates, events, trends of a century that is in equal measure fatal and laden with opportunity—is to a large extent omitted. (The background of the period is, however, indicated in the introduction to each chapter.) The far greater concern is to make clear something of what Hegel meant by the "world spirit" and the "universal in the existing," which also proved to be a contribution of the nineteenth-century German spirit to the world spirit.

The "universal" is developed from the texts in four *leitmotifs* with multifarious variations:

- Withdrawal—Dreaming the World
- Titanism—Suspending the World
- Concerning Horror and Flourishing—Justifying the World
- Errors and Confusions—Observing the World.

With the advent of and since the Romantic period, whatever could be conveyed about both the inner and the external world by exorbitance, by exiting from the world, by transcendence, by exceeding the world, by insight and by inspection was "performed." The capacity to dream—withdrawal both as a waking dream and a turning toward the "heaven of the night," both as yearning hope and as nightmare—characterizes an important motif of the German spirit of the nineteenth century.

The strength for "suspending," or titanism, indicates another motif: constituting the world from the spirit, in particular from the spirit of

philosophy. That is, thinking of the whole and attempting to comprehend the whole, behind the flight of appearance, ("And neither time nor
force will ever alter / Intrinsic form, evolving as it lives," as Goethe states
in "Primal Orphic Words"). The titanism of music also portrayed the
world as will and idea. Titanism let a counterworld of tones, a world
composition, be sounded.

Justifying the world, the third motif, means juxtaposing green to gray,
hope to despair, affirmation of life to infathomability. Support meant immanence—that it is not possible to exit from the world. Grass grows
everywhere. Cheerfulness is based on melancholy. Despite chaos, to be
happy under the sun in the moment.

Errors and confusions, as the fourth motif, focuses on the role of observing, on the capacity for release, of being able to exit. To describe the
transitory and thereby oneself "going over" as if nothing had happened.
The Romantic dream, titanic thinking, realistic perseverance, all end in
dispassionate resignation.

Each of these *leitmotifs* is traced in separate texts through the entire
nineteenth century. The chronology, or the ordering into epochs, recedes
in favor of the intention of showing the "basic melody" of that century.
"Romantic" and "Realistic" are therefore understood less as characterizations of temporal data than as characterizations of extratemporal existential givens. These givens are the issue in all the excerpts, and conceptual
states and moods are stressed by headings that intimate the value accorded
the separate element within the entire texture.

Each main part of the book is preceded by a *leitmotif;* each section is
preceded by an interpretive introduction to the variants on the *leitmotif.*
The introductory comments to the excerpts provide the necessary details
for understanding both author and text.

To disclose the spiritual locus of the nineteenth century with the greatest possible vividness (which is why we have preferred poetic texts in their
symbolic concentration) is the purpose of this volume. The contribution
of the German spirit to the world spirit was noteworthy and deserves
respect. "The poet will love the Fatherland as a human being and citizen,
but the Fatherland of his poetic energy and effectiveness is the good, the
noble, and the beautiful, which is bound to no particular province and to
no particular country and which is grasped and formed where the poet
finds it. The poet in this repect resembles the eagle that hovers over
countries with a free glance, indifferent whether the hare on which it
plummets is running in Prussia or in Saxony." So Goethe said to Ecker-

mann shortly before his death. And in the same conversation he stated, "Watch out, the politician will devour the poet."

The nineteenth century permits the "task of pride." And it evokes the task of mourning about the fact that it simply was as Goethe, with reference here to poets, predicted. The world spirit removed itself from the spirit of the people; the spirit of the people prepared its own decline. "The appearance of the infection has its various forms—and in such a way that ruin breaks out from within, desires are unleashed, the single entity seeks its contentment, hence the substantial is not given its due and is destroyed. Separate interests rend the forces, fortunes in themselves, that formerly were devoted to the whole. Thus the negative appears as ruin from within to differentiate itself." (Hegel) This "negative from within" is admittedly no longer the topic of this reader, which deals with the German spirit and not with its perversion into the nonspirit, or even into the antispirit.

# WITHDRAWAL

# DREAMING
# THE WORLD

*The brightness of the Enlightenment is replaced by Romanticism's longing for the night. Feeling comes to the fore. The unconscious plays a large role; truth is sought in the dream, in the realm beyond reason. At a time when (at the beginning of the nineteenth century) industrialization introduced great economic and social upheavals in other countries, German poets, thinkers, and artists "withdrew" from immediate reality. In their thoughts of the night they had the "dream of a thing" but not the consciousness of it.*

*In addition to fantasies of the night, in which it is possible to transpire in pleasure and suffering, there is an ideal landscape of antiquity. The commitment to the Apollonian spirit attempts, through the device of a backward-oriented utopia, to gloss over the misery of a fragmented nation, a nation that exists as such only in longing. Blessed are the times when the gods still reigned, where the reference to "actuality" has no place. Idealism is a cerebral creation—reality remains suspended. Withdrawal from the earthly also includes an appreciation of the "subterranean," which is experienced as the Dionysian. The hope for an earthly paradise assumes the most various forms. The appearance of an intact, senseful, ordered world is sentimentally summoned. Love provides relief from the downward pull of gravity; the cheerfulness of Indian summer permits passions to be transformed into maturity; a self-contained society tames self-seeking individualism.*

*Everything admittedly remains "fictitious." The dreamed world is nonetheless a wealth of "what has been anticipated." It is full of "essences" that can be turned upside down—if some day there is a desire to do so.*

# THOUGHTS OF THE NIGHT

The spiritual landscape of the Enlightenment is presented as a brightly illuminated, transparent sphere; the sun of reason standing at the zenith and casting few shadows on the clear contours of the surface. What lies beyond the horizon of thought is of less interest.

The Baroque artist, feeling delivered up to heavenly and satanic powers, to pleasures of the senses and to anxiety about life, drew on the basic situation of conflict. These tensions abated in the eighteenth century. The human being in the era of the Enlightenment strives for harmonious, life-affirming balance; the perceived task is to plan in the "here and now," to act and be happy. To some extent, such faith in the world means switching from the vertical, purposeless glance that is directed upward to a horizontal glance, perceiving the world to be broad and large and beautiful. The world is made subservient to the human being. The world is conceived as a setting for the construction of "everything conceivably useful, beneficial, and life-promoting; for institutions and equipment for the refinement, relief, and heightening of existence; for Babylonian towers that soar toward heaven to ensnare its secret. That is, the world is conceived as an immeasurably broad and inexhaustibly rich field of operation for the activation and increase of the forces of an entirely autonomous, pure reason that shies away from nothing and cannot be disappointed by anything." (Egon Friedell)

In the Baroque period the world was experienced through the senses—impulsively, instinctively, intuitively. The world, a dusky and infathomable fragment, remained in chaos. The person of the Enlightenment uses *ratio,* gaining insight and an overview and seeing the effectiveness of rules and laws that imply order. "If we see a broken bone, a piece of flesh from an animal, or a branch torn from a plant, we are confronted with disorder. The diligent anatomist, on the other hand, who recognizes the relationship of such fragments to the whole and who understands their

11

structure will be able to understand their inherent purposefulness. Thus it is, too, with our judgment about the world." So said Gottfried Leibniz (1646–1716), for whom the world was entirely comprised of monads (elementary particles) which, ordered within themselves from the lowest to the *ultima ratio rerum,* or to God himself, are independent but simultaneously are the reflection of the universe. A world created, moved, and animated by God—an ordered, harmonious world—that could only be the best of all possible worlds.

Leibniz's philosophy, which emerges from such a theodicy, culminates in the sentence: "This highest wisdom, now connected with a no less infinite goodness, could only choose the best. For just as lesser evil is a kind of good, so is a lesser good a kind of evil when confronted with a larger good: and there would be something to report in the action of God if it were possible to do it better. And just as in mathematics, as soon as there is neither maximum nor minimum, there is altogether nothing excellent. Everything becomes the same or, if that is not possible, nothing at all can come about. Then it is possible to say, concerning complete wisdom, which is not less ordered than mathematics, that if there were not a best (optimum) world among the possible worlds, then God would not have produced any world."

Along with the discovery of reason, recognition was given to the value of the person and of individuality. The human being as a spiritual creature feels himself to be the crown of creation. The Enlightenment, wrote Immanuel Kant, "is the human being's departure from his self-imposed immaturity. Immaturity is the lack of ability to use one's own reason without the guidance of another. This immaturity is self-imposed when the cause of it is not from a deficiency of reason but from a deficiency of resolution and courage to use one's reason without the guidance of another. *Sapere aude!* Have the courage to use your own reason! is therefore the motto of the Enlightenment." The spiritual landscape of the Enlightenment is ordered in many different ways. There is a flat country cultivated by a utilitarian thinking of touching simplicity. The popular Enlightenment is entirely committed to the "common" man, who is to be instructed and led toward the good, suspending the trivial in the simple. "It is necessary only to address the person reasonably, and one will be astonished at how quickly the person understands it," stated Matthias Claudius in the *Wandsbeck Messenger,* one of the "moral newspapers" published by him between 1771 and 1775. This paper sought, through the use of reason, heart, feeling, and prankishness, to provide assistance in the adversities of life.

The spiritual landscape of the Enlightenment similarly knows the dramatic "exaggeration"; the peak of contention, the abysses of anxiety; yet such polarities between the star-strewn heaven and the categorical imperative are endured with the help of an obsessive belief in reason as the force making possible the recognition of truth. The human being is only truly a person when he thinks; and when he thinks, he is entirely human. Gotthold Ephraim Lessing, in his work entitled *The Education of Humankind* (1780) stated, "the era of completion will certainly come about when the person, the more convinced his reason is of an ever-better future, will not find it necessary to draw on this future, for whatever reasons, for his actions, since he will do good because it is good and not because arbitrary rewards have been placed upon the good that will sooner fix and strengthen his shifting gaze to recognize the inner, better rewards of it. The era of a new, eternal Evangelium promised in the basic books of the new alliance will certainly come."

The attitude of the early nineteenth century is quite different. Certainty yields to intimation, the horizons vanish, the shadows become immeasurable; people turn more toward the mysterious than to the clarified (enlightened). Even with all the doubts, struggles, and anxieties; the Enlightenment referred to a fixed place in this world. Transcendence provided the foundation for immanence; the human as a reasonable being was the focus of the world. Withdrawal means a change of position—nowhere is there a firm footing; support and attitude turn into movement and ambivalence. Withdrawal means not so much seeing the world as it is but rather fantasizing, imagining, and presuming the world. Withdrawal means a transitory consciousness—the dream is life, and life is a dream. Withdrawal is the Romantic consciousness; the consequence is that in all things there is a magical note that can be made to sound even though it often enough cannot be understood. Withdrawal as portrayed by the Romantic consciousness conceives, presents, even performs the external as an interiority. Subject and subjectivity, introspection and introversion, alternate with an enlightened, objectifying turning toward the world. In our mind "everything is related in the most singular, most pleasurable and lively manner. The most alien things come through *one* place, *one* time," states Novalis. Signs, codes, hieroglyphs of the mind are all reality. The universal secret should at least be conjured, if not solved, by the magical word. "Thinking is only a dream of feeling, a dream of a vanished feeling." Poetry, or inspiration, is "one and everything."

This tender, ethereal, supernatural, poetic capacity for entering into the spirit of things—this highest sensibility—this overalert sentimentality, is not disclosed in broad daylight; the magic of fantasy requires the nighttime. "I turn away toward the holy, unutterable, secretive night." The belief in the "heaven of the night" characterizes the German spirit at the beginning of the nineteenth century. Withdrawal, fantasizing the world, takes place in thoughts of the night—i.e., in thoughts and feelings of passion, resignation, euphoria—and of horror. The person who escapes bright day and plunges into the visionarily perceived magical realm of the night experiences it as the supernatural, love-drunk, death-drunk night, but also as life-supporting darkness, mother of the light, primordial reason of all things. In the night lie redemption, liberation, and union with the beloved; love and blessedness are present. At the same time, night anticipates the apocalypse. The texts that illuminate the turn toward the mysteriousness of night show darkness in the most varied wealth of contrasting shadings. Novalis's thoughts of the night, the *Hymns to the Night* (1) manifest the impulse both toward love and toward death. The night is both the wedding night and the night of death. The ancient Greek world, as the eternal feast of the gods and of people, still completely belonged to the terrestrial world of the day; with Christ the night becomes actual (eternal) life. The night of death opens the gates to real being.

Heinrich Heine wrote in a letter to Karl August Varnhagen von Ense, in 1846, that the "new race" would enjoy and assert itself in the visible.

> We, the elderly, bowed humbly before the invisible, chased after shadow kisses and fragrances of blue flowers, renounced and wept, and were perhaps happier than those tough gladiators who went so proudly to death in battle. The thousand-year Reich of the Romantic has an end; I myself was its last king of fable, and abdicated.

The two souls in the breast of the Romantic—the one transitory, intuitive, with great depth of feeling, and addicted to the night; the other critical, satirical, ironic-sarcastic (that also constantly heartens and encourages the awakening or else withdraws before completely vanishing in the darkness) is expressed poetically by Heine in a particularly consummate manner. "O Death, It is the Chill of Night" (2) is a poem of resignation, of euphoria (of cheerfulness before the end); the day's misery has disappeared in the longing for death. Life's force of gravity, sickness (imprisonment in the "mattress grave") is lulled away in the dream song. Night is sweet and addictive. "Yes, my body is very sick," wrote the poet in the already-cited letter to Varnhagen von Ense, "but my soul has suffered little; a weary flower, it is a little bent but by no means faded and is still firmly rooted in the truth of love." Heine's song of the night proves to be a poetic highpoint of romantic withdrawal, of dreamlike longing for the world experienced and written in the consciousness of the questionability of romantic transcendence. It is stated in Heine's *Confessions,* after he has dealt the deadliest blows to the meaning of German Romantic poetry,

> I myself was again overcome by an endless longing for the blue flower in the dreamland of Romanticism, and I seized the enchanted lute and sang a song in which I gave myself over to all the blessed exaggerations, to all manner of moonlight intoxication, to all the flourishing, formerly beloved flight of madness. I know it was "the last free forest song of the Romantic" and that I am its last poet.

Within poems having the same motifs (2), Eichendorff represents the dream feeling of German Romanticism in a particularly pure manner. The soul spreads its wings and flies off into unimagined distance. While in Eichendorff the soul feels protected within the Christian cosmos, in Heine it is homeless. The panorama of Eichendorff's landscape, which is drawn with few strokes as part of a lyrical cosmogony, is that of a pacified world. The earth itself starts to dream, although in an attitude of exorbitance. Heine's dream world is no longer one of a happy sense of the night; rather, it produces disquiet through "excessive nightness." It is permeated with leftovers of the day and is inspired by the drug of illusion. Protected from the bitterness of awakening only by not reawakening.

In Mörike's poem "At Midnight," the Romantic subject is again included in a new form of objectivity. Day and night are "balanced out"; the poem turns to the night, but it is a portrayal that includes the "day just past." Consciousness of reality is not abandoned; at midnight the scale again tips toward the (new) morning. The slumber song comes to an end. Thoughts of the night are experienced with composure. Romantic elements in the metaphor are restrained with "classical strictness." These are the verses of a Romantic poet in the era of realism.

Similarly, in the world of Annette von Droste-Hülshoff (2), thoughts of the night do not result in "abandonment to the mystery of the night." During the hours of the night she is particularly sensitive. The day has brought alertness; the night brings no reassurance. Delicate nerves register a dense succession of impressions that are provided with caesuras by the beats of the clock. The realistic turning toward the world cannot be eluded in the nocturnal setting. The world is not fantasized but is registered; one no longer believes in the heaven of the night. The ambivalence of night—anxiety about falling asleep as well as about remaining awake; anxiety about not reawakening as well as about the weariness of the day. The ambivalence of the half-awake state.

In the metaphor the poet entwines her thoughts of the night with the "products" of the light of day—with the first attempts at photography by the French painter J. M. Daguerre (1787–1851). In a general sense, these verses mark the demarcation where thoughts of the night turn into a new consciousness of the day; where Romanticism is replaced by Realism. From the night no longer experienced asleep but awake there emerges an attitude of consciousness that transforms withdrawal from the world into turning-toward-the-world. When Alexander von Humboldt reported about Daguerre's discovery on January 7, 1839, in a letter to Duchess Friederike von Anhalt-Dessau, he wrote:

> The word "curiosity" has a higher and nobler meaning when it indicates a turn of mind that is animated not merely by ideas but is characterized by desiring a larger form for intelligence. Objects that express themselves in inimitable fidelity, light forced by the art of chemistry to leave enduring traces within a few minutes and to circumscribe clearly even the most delicate parts of contours—to see all this magic (admittedly without color) produced within eight to ten minutes in our Northern zone on a clear, sunny day, probably within two to three minutes in the transparency of the air of Egypt with its abundance of tropical light, certainly speaks incontrovertibly for reason and the power of imagination.

The "photographic look" of the new epoch is that of rational curiosity but no longer of enlightened optimism. The realistic feeling for life does not exclude the Romantic dream; the dream world is strewn with images of reality that emerge at night as marginal situations. Even the *Nightwatches of Bonaventura* (3) proves to be an arsenal of social critique, a toying with the night. The average person's vices and weakness, concealed by night, are unmasked during the "last night" (the "final judgment") that is summoned and simulated by the nightwatchman. The darkness holds no magical song. Utter despair and desperate anxiety engulf the sinners; the last hour seems at hand.

Such a nightmare, which in Bonaventura's nightwatch is laced with realistic details, becomes an existential vision in Jean Paul. While the night in Novalis's work was actual being, in Jean Paul it discloses the possibility of nonbeing. Night is the night of worlds, the night of emptiness in which Christ proclaims the death of God (4).

In contrast, though, Novalis's *Dream of the Blue Flower* (5) is entirely wish-fulfillment, a dream of longing. Despite the presence of many forms of withdrawal, the world is neither bypassed nor forgotten. When Heinrich, the hero of the novel [*Green Henry*], "intoxicated by rapture and yet aware of every impression," swims toward the blue flower, he is suddenly awakened by his mother's voice and finds himself in his parents' parlor "that was already gilded by the morning sun." "He was too delighted to be bothered by this disturbance; on the contrary, he wished his mother a friendly 'good morning' and responded to her hearty embrace. 'You slugabed,' said the father. 'How long have I already been sitting here filing. For your sake, I was not permitted to hammer; your mother wanted to let her dear son sleep. I also had to wait for breakfast. You wisely are in the teaching profession of the world, for which we stay awake working. Even a diligent scholar, I have heard, must use the help of the night to study the great works of the wise forefathers.' " The father, who continues to work busily, states that dreams are froth but that he respects the son's "dream work." Both conversations to some extent become a dialogue between the principles of withdrawal and of reality. Both sides are justified in the discourse. The dream world and the world of reality are balanced out in the focus of a Romantic text; both forms of existence are so justified.

Even where the Romantic consciousness's thoughts of the night are present and utterly romantic, the withdrawal from the world is never complete. If it were complete, it would not be withdrawal. It is axiomatic that the same applies to the dream. The ongoing force of darkness emerges from the tension between reality and irreality. Karl Marx wrote to Arnold Ruge in September 1843 (see also Introduction, above) that their slogan must be "reform of the consciousness not by dogmas but by analysis of the mythical consciousness, which is unclear to itself, regardless of whether it is now manifested religiously or politically. It will then be shown that the world has long been in possession of the dream of a thing of which it need only possess consciousness to possess it in reality. It will be shown that at issue is not a large hyphen between past and future but the completion of the past's thoughts." That was written, according to Ernst Bloch's interpretation of this quotation, by "the least abstract conceptualizer of a better life, the most concrete critic of every 'idea' that emerges subjectively as wishful thinking, objectively as a castle in the air." The "dream of a thing" consistently appears in Marx mainly as an anticipatory dream that has been clouded and impeded by conditions. The "awakened" does not attempt to bargain down the dream content but rather attempts to illuminate it and make it viable. The dream as a time for wishing is an a priori.

The thoughts of the night that characterize the German spirit, especially at the beginning of the nineteenth century, determine and conceal, in their withdrawal from the world, an emerging new perspective on the world; they portray an intellectual achievement that, by removing itself from reality, conceives and anticipates new realities. The content of the "dream pieces" is often vague, elusive, not directly comprehensible; but by turning toward a world that is not of this world, the pieces create a possibility of consciousness that, so to speak, points from an "unusual" (exceptional) position via the dream of the night to the route toward the waking dream, toward the "dream in a forward direction." The "dream of a thing" was possessed, even though, as shown by German history of the nineteenth century, it was not realized.

## (1) Belief in the heaven of the night

NOVALIS, Hymns to the Night

It was the conviction of Friedrich von Hardenberg, who was born in 1772 and called himself Novalis, that truth must be sought at the source, i.e., in the soul. The inner world is more real than the outer world. He replaced a conceptual *Weltanschauung* by belief in the heart's strength of intuition. Novalis, who had studied law and worked as an assessor in a saltworks, believed the world should be romanticized. "In this way, the original meaning is rediscovered. This procedure is still entirely unknown. I romanticize it by imbuing the commonplace with an elevated meaning, the ordinary with a mysterious appearance, the familiar with the dignity of the unfamiliar, the finite with an infinite appearance." Novalis's extraordinary sensitivity channeled all impressions into a comprehensive metaphysical realm, and he was the most universal of the Romantic poets. His longing for death increased after the death of his fiancée, Sophie von Kühn, whom he loved passionately. *Hymns to the Night* was printed in 1800 in *Athenaeum,* a journal published by Friedrich Schlegel, that provided a forum for the young Romantics. Novalis died in 1801.

What living man and sense-endowed loves not, above all the wonders of space spread out around him, the universally gladdening Light with its colors, its rays and waves, its gentle omnipresence as awakening day? As inmost soul of life it is breathed by the giant-realm of the restless stars and floats dancing in its azure flood; it is breathed by the glittering, everlastingly reposeful stone, by the sensuous, suckling plant, and by the wild, ardent, multiform beast; but above all by the glorious stranger with the thoughtful eyes, the hovering gait, and the gently closed, rich-toned lips. As a king of earthly nature it summons every force to uncounted transformations, conjoins and resolves infinite alliances, hangs its heavenly image about every earthly being. Its presence alone reveals the wondrous splendor of the Kingdoms of the world.

Aside I turn to the holy, ineffable, mysterious Night. Far below lies the world, sunken in a profound pit: waste and solitary is its place. Through the strings of the heart wafts deep sadness. I seek, as drops of dew, to subside and to blend with ashes. Distances of memory, desires of youth, dreams of childhood, the brief joys and futile hopes of the whole of long life, come in gray raiment like evening mists after the sun's setting. In other realms the Light has pitched its joyous tents. Might it never return to its own children who with the faith of innocence abide its coming?

What is it wells thus suddenly full of premonition beneath my heart and swallows down the soft air of sadness? Dost thou take pleasure in us also, dark Night? What dost thou hold underneath thy mantle that with unseen power affects my soul? Precious balm sheds from thy hand, from the cluster of poppies. Thou dost uplift the heavy wings of the soul. Dimly, inexpressibly, we feel ourselves moved: a grave countenance I see, startled with gladness, which gently and reverently inclines toward me and amid infinitely tangled locks reveals the mother's lovely youth. How paltry and childish seems now the Light to me! How comforting and blessed the day's departure! It was, then, only because the Night estranged thy servants from thee that thou didst sow the breadths of space with gleaming spheres to proclaim thy omnipotence, thy return in the times of thy withdrawal? More heavenly than these flashing stars seem to us the infinite eyes which the Night has opened within us. They see further than the palest of those countless hosts; without need of the Light they penetrate the depths of a loving heart, a feat which fills a higher realm with unutterable delight. Praise be unto the world's queen, the high herald of sacred worlds, the fostering nurse of blessed love! She sends thee to me, tender Beloved, lovely sun of the Night. I wake now, for I am thine and mine: thou hast proclaimed to me the Night as life and made me human. Consume my body with spirit-fire that I may ethereally commingle more intensely with thee and that the bridal night may last then forever.

Must morning ever return? Does the power of things earthly never end? Unholy activity consumes the heavenly descent of the Night. Will the secret sacrifice of love never burn eternally? Apportioned to the Light was its time, but timeless and spaceless is the Night's dominion. Eternal is the duration of sleep. Holy sleep! make not too seldom glad the Night's consecrated ones in this earthly day-labor. Only fools mistake thee and know of no sleep save that shadow which in that twilight of the true Night thou dost cast compassionately upon us. They feel thee not in the golden flood of the grapes, in the almond tree's wondrous oil, and in the brown juice of the poppy. They know not that it is thou who hoverest about the tender maiden's bosom and makest of the womb a heaven: they guess not that out of old stories thou dost step forth to open the skies, bearing the key to the dwelling-places of the blessed, silent messenger of infinite mysteries.

Once, as I shed bitter tears, as in sorrow dissolved my hopes melted away, and I stood lonely by the barren mound which in narrow and dark room hid away the form of my life—lonely as none before was ever lonely, goaded by unspeakable dread, bereft of strength, no more than a thought of wretchedness—as I gazed about there for help, incapable of moving forward, nor yet backward either, and clung to fleeting extinguished life with infinite yearning—then, out of blue distances, from the pinnacles of my old blessedness, there came a twilight shudder, and all at once the bond of birth broke the Light's fetters. Fled was earthly splendor, and with it my grief. Condensed, sadness flowed away into a new and unfathomable world. Thou Night-inspiration, slumber of heaven, didst come over me: the region gently rose aloft and over the region hovered my released and newborn spirit. The mound became a cloud of dust and through the cloud I beheld the transfigured features of my Beloved. In her eyes reposed eternity; I grasped her hands, and my tears became a glittering chain that could not be wrenched asunder. Millennia passed off into the distance, like storms. Upon her neck I wept ecstatic tears unto the new life. It was my first and only dream, and since then only have I felt everlasting, immutable faith in the heaven of the Night and in its Light, the Beloved.

TRANSLATED BY CHARLES E. PASSAGE

## (2) Of the day that was today

JOSEPH VON EICHENDORFF, "Moonlit Night"

Joseph Carl Benedikt Freiherr von Eichendorff was born in 1788 in Castle Lubowitz near Ratibor (which at that time was Austrian Upper Silesia). The idyllic life there, gilded by childhood recollections, seemed to him all his life to be the essence of the most beautiful existence. "The garden of Lubowitz: actions and trees secretly tell the young poet stories, which he must then communicate further." The poet joined the Romantic movement while studying in Heidelberg. He was fascinated by the folk song's quiet piety, simplicity, connection with nature, and mood. Longing for the paradise of childhood, tireless longing for the distant, and a conservative Christian religiosity characterize Eichendorff's poetry. He died in 1857 after having worked for years in the service of the Prussian state.

It was as if the moonlight
Had softly kissed the earth,
Who blossomed into midnight
With dreams of love and mirth.

The fields were touched by zephyrs
Which caused the spikes to sigh,
The forest sang in murmurs
And star-bright was the sky.

And then my being left me
On outspread wings to roam,
Flew o'er the silent country
As if it flew back home.

TRANSLATED BY ADRIAN DEL CARO

EDUARD MÖRIKE, "At Midnight"

As the artistic pastor of Cleversulzbach (Württemberg) Eduard Mörike (1804–1875) was by no means merely a Biedermeier protagonist of the idyllic who watered his flowers, took snuff, drank coffee, observed the "old weathervane," lay in the grass, and dreamed up poems. His novel, *Painter Nolten,* in many respects autobiographical, makes clear the extent to which his work was determined by very exciting youthful experiences, especially his love for a vagrant (Peregrina). The forces of being that both attract and repel us are incomprehensible. "What is beautiful, though, seems blessed in itself." "World piety" permitted the poet to enjoy the moment and to find support in immanence.

The night has calmly dropped her pall,
Leans dreaming on the mountain wall,
Her eye beholds the golden scale of time
At balance in a revery sublime;
      The fountains are splashing more playfully,
      They sing to the night time in secrecy
          Of the day,
Of the day that was today.


The never changing lullaby,
She does not heed its ancient sigh;
She heeds instead the azure of the heights,
The level yoke of passing days and nights.
      But always the fountains maintain the last word,
      In slumber their watery music is heard
          Of the day,
Of the day that was today.

TRANSLATED BY ADRIAN DEL CARO


HEINRICH HEINE, "O Death, It is the Chill of Night"

"Poetry, however much I loved it, was for me always a holy toy or a consecrated tool for heavenly purposes. But you should place a sword on my casket, for I was always a brave soldier in the war of mankind's liberation." Thus Heinrich Heine characterizes his poetic existence. Devoted to Romanticism, he was at the same time a realist with a keen eye on the era and the world. Born in 1797, the son of a Jewish businessman in what was then Duesseldorf, Heine was apprenticed while living with a rich uncle in Hamburg. The poet experiences the emancipation of the Jews—the certificate of baptism is the almost indispensable ticket to social status. After studying at various universities and traveling, Heine went into political exile in Paris even before the 1835 edict of the German Confederation that banned all the writings of the Young German authors with whom he identified. During a long illness he wrote, "Two consolations remained for me—my French wife and the German muse." Heine died in 1856.


O death, it is the chill of night,
But life is like the sultry day.
Now darkness falls, I'm sleepy,
The day has consumed my might.

Rising over my head is a tree,
There sings the youthful nightingale;
She sings of loving only,
In my dream she sings to me.

TRANSLATED BY ADRIAN DEL CARO

ANNETTE VON DROSTE-HÜLSHOFF, "A Night Awake"

Annette von Droste-Hülshoff (1797–1848) was born in an old palace in Westphalia. Although she grew up in a happy family circle, she was deeply disturbed by signs of the dissolution of the nobility. She had a passionate nature and seemed inclined to prefer eccentric characters. Her friendship with the author Levin Schücking became of particular importance for her. As a "young noblewoman" she led a conventional life in terms of class and morals. Her poetry often reveals untrammeled power, suggesting that she is a "later sister of the Sibyl."

How hot and heavy sank the sun
And from the burning waves a host
Of mists arose, that drove and spun
This starless night toward my coast!—
I hear a distant step again—
The clock strikes *ten*.

Not yet has every creature gone to rest,
The last of bedroom doors creaks on its hinges;
The cautious fitchet on his nightly quest
Creeps through the gable rafters, halts and cringes.
The drowsy heifer's head droops to her chest
And in the stall the weary gelding twinges,
He paws and snorts, till sleep's narcotic balm
Has soothed the restless flank and made him calm.

Intoxicating lilac scent
Drifts through my window's open crack,
Where swarming branches represent
A ghostly dance in gray on black.
Weak I am, and weak the times!—
*Eleven* chimes.

O strange condition mixed of wake and sleep,
Are you the curse of fragile nerves or blessing?—
This dew-kissed night its wakefulness will keep
I feel the darkness, cool as mist, caressing
And soft upon my cheek, while curtains sweep
From swaying rods, receding now, now pressing,
And there the plastered wall's heraldic crest
Writhes snakelike, coiled in dim unrest.

How blood is dancing in my brain!
A rustling haunts the roofing thatch,
And in the dusk it stirs and fain
Would turn the key within the latch,
While—there! the hanging clock awakes!
And *midnight* breaks.

Was that a sound of ghosts? As weak and faint
As crystal roused by gentle touch to humming,
And from the lilacs rises now a plaint
Like muted sobs, a long and mournful thrumming,
Then sweeter, as if under tears' constraint
A bashful love were here succumbing;—
O Nightingale, that is no wakeful song,
But such as souls released in dream prolong.

That rumbling once more from the rocks!
The turret's crumbling fragments fall,
A screeching owl dryly mocks;
And then a sudden summer squall
Bends low the grove, is past and done.
The clock strikes *one*.

The heavy cloud now eddies, climbs, and rolls;
And like a lamp from ancient mounded barrows
The moon sails forth upon the shoals,
A silver gondola through bluewashed narrows;
Among the lilac leaves gleam sparks like coals;
And the pale shaft of light shoots milk-white arrows
To trace designs of restless line and plane,
The window's image, on my counterpane.

Now I would like to sleep, to sleep,
To rest beneath the moon's pale eye,
While lilac bushes watch do keep
And whisper still their lullaby,
To slumber here the whole night through;—
The clock strikes *two*.

And ever clearer grows the lovely song,
The charming laughter, while upon my ceiling
Gray shapes, like pictures by Daguerre, now throng
And flee with arrow's speed, alive and reeling.
I seem to see fair ringlets, loose and long,
A pair of eyes like glowworms now revealing.
The eyes grow moist with tears, grow blue and mild,
And at my feet there sits a lovely child.

It turns to me with eager eye,
A heartfelt joy beams from its face;
A playful hand is lifted high,
Withdrawn again with laughing grace;—
The cock crows once! O harsh decree!
The clock strikes *three*.

How I did start!—dear image, you have fled
And taken with you all the night's sweet dreaming.
The faint first light swells drear around my bed,
Extinguishing the lilacs' dewy gleaming.
The moon's once silver shield has rusted red.
With anxious murmurs now the woods are teeming,
And from the barn I hear the muffled cheep
Of swallows grown uneasy in their sleep.

A swarm of doves takes drunken flight,
Describing circles in the yard.
The cock again dispels the night
And rouses now the dog on guard.
I hear the creaking of a door—
The clock strikes *four*.

Then in the east it blazes up—ah dawn!
It rises higher, higher and enhances
With morning glow the forest, heath, and lawn,
Awakes a flood of birdsong with its glances.
The hawk ascends, through hay the scythe is drawn,
Toward the wood the hunter's horn advances,
And like a glacier sinks the land of dreams,
Subsiding in the fire of these beams.

TRANSLATED BY SHARON JACKIW

## (3) The trump of the false Judgment Day

### The Nightwatches of Bonaventura

The anonymous *Nightwatches of Bonaventura* (probably written by Ernst August Friedrich
Klingemann, 1777–1831), published in 1804, assumes a counterposition to the religiously expectant Baroque and to the rationally affirmative Enlightenment. A poet, who,
ironizing the "creative hours" of the night, has become a nightwatchman, narrates his life
in sixteen installments of exciting confessions, including observations of other people's
lives. As a bitterly disappointed idealist, he behaves as if he were a grim prankster who
sees behind the facades of human vanity and unmasks man's mendacity. In the end the
titanic questioner hears a threefold nothing sounded at his father's grave: "I don't see you
any more, Father. Where are you? Upon contact everything disintegrates into ashes, only
a handful of dust is still lying on the ground, and a few well-fed worms crawl past like
moral eulogizers who have overeaten at the funeral repast. I scatter this handful of paternal
dust into the air and it remains—nothing! Over there on the grave there still stands the
seer and embraces—nothing! And the echo in the charnel house one last time calls out—
nothing!"

What would I not give to be able to tell my tale as straightforwardly
and coherently as other honorable protestant writers and journalists, who
grow fat and rich in doing so and exchange their golden thoughts for
golden realities! But I simply have not the gift, and my short simple tale
of murder has cost me enough sweat and tears, and still looks amply
checkered and confused.

I was unfortunately already spoiled in my boyhood years, so to speak
in the very bud, for just as other young scholars and promising youths
devote themselves to growing ever more knowledgeable and wiser, so did
I on the contrary always have an especial preference for wildness. And so
I tried to cultivate within myself a state of absolute disorder, simply to

do as our dear Lord did in first perfecting a good and total chaos, from which at some later time I might, if it seemed desirable, put together a tolerable sort of world. —Indeed, it seems to me in occasional over-wrought moments as if the human race had made a botch even of chaos and had been premature with its imposition of order, which explains why nothing can ever come to occupy its rightful place, and as if our Creator should take steps as soon as possible to blot out and destroy this world as a system that has come to grief.

Ah, this *idée fixe* of mine has caused me enough damage! Once it almost cost me even my office as night watchman, in that it occurred to me during the last hour of the century to conjure up a semblance of the Judgment Day and to cry out Eternity in the streets instead of Time, which roused many gentlemen, both clergy and laity, in terror from their pillows and caused them great embarrassment, because they were not pre-pared to meet it so unexpectedly.

The scene was comical enough at this trump of the false Judgment Day, a scene in which I played the single dispassionate observer, while all the others had to serve as ardent actors. —Oh, it should have been seen, the hustling and bustling among all those poor mortals. The aristocracy ran anxiously hither and yon and tried still to range itself in proper order before its Lord God. A crowd of judicial wolves and others of that ilk tried to change their skins and transform themselves in their despair into sheep, here dispensing generous pensions to the widows and orphans who raced about in torments of fear, there publicly admitting the unjust ver-dicts of the past and promising to repay, immediately after the conclusion of the Judgment Day, the stolen sums by means of which they had made beggars of the poor devils. Many such bloodsuckers and vampires de-nounced themselves as worthy of hanging and beheading and urged that these sentences be hurriedly carried out here below, in order to avoid the punishment meted out by Higher Authority. The proudest man in the land stood humble for the first time and almost groveling, his crown in his hand, and with much bowing and scraping urged a ragged fellow to take precedence, because it seemed to him that a general equality might well be fast approaching.

Official positions were vacated, honors and decorations stripped away by the hands of their unworthy possessors. The pastors of souls made solemn promises to give their flocks in future, in addition to good words, a good example, if the good Lord would only rest content for now with these fresh resolutions.

Oh, how can I describe how the people on the stage before me ran here and there in their fear, praying and cursing and wailing and howling, and how every mask on this great inflated ball dropped from the true countenance beneath, so that one discovered kings in beggars' garments and weaklings in the armor of knights and in almost every instance a contrast between clothes and man.

It pleased me that their excessive fear long prevented their noticing the delay in the dispensation of divine criminal justice, so that the whole population had time to uncover all its virtues and vices and to bare itself before me, its last fellow citizen. The single stroke of genius was executed by a satirical fellow who long since had decided for reasons of ennui not to enter into the new century. Now, in the last hour of the old one, he decided to see if dying for a moment might still be possible in this neutral moment between death and resurrection, in order that he would not have to depart for eternity without more ado, taking with him all the great burden of his boredom with life.

TRANSLATED BY SHARON JACKIW

## (4) The abyss of the universe

JEAN PAUL, Flower, Fruit and Thorn Arrangements, or Married Life, Death and Wedding of the Public Defender F. St. Siebenkäs

Jean Paul (Johann Paul Friedrich Richter, 1763–1825) states in his *Primer of Aesthetics* that the idyll transforms the dissonance of suffering into euphony—"a hard, long, thorny ladder on the rose tree finally leads past softer thorns to some blossoms." The idyll is the epic portrayal of "utter happiness within limitations." If the infinite world is measured and related to the finite, laughter, marked by both pain and greatness, comes into being. In this sense, Jean Paul was both a humorist and the author of idylls (as in *The Life of the Merry Schoolmaster Maria Wuz in Auenthal*). Jean Paul's poetry describes both the cloistered and secure life and the transport of flight into the spheres. The poetic cosmos of his novels is characterized by an abundance of action, situations, complications, fantasies, observations, information (drawn from a box of memos), and especially by feelings. The experience of chaos and of total existential anxiety is expressed in poetically formed, apocalyptic nightmares. The novel *Siebenkäs* was written in 1796–97.

When one is still a child one hears tell that at midnight, when our sleep approaches our very soul and darkens even our dreams, the dead rouse themselves (from their sleep) and gather in the churches to mimic the worship service of the living. Then one is seized by a horror of death on account of the dead, and in the lonely hours of the night one averts one's eyes from the long windows of the silent church and fears to scrutinize their iridescence, to see if it is merely reflected moonlight.

Childhood's terrors, even more than its charms, resume their wings and colors in our dreams and play like fireflies in the small night of the soul. Do not crush these fluttering sparks! Leave us even our dark and painful dreams, the penumbra that sets reality in bolder relief! And wherewith could one replace those dreams that transport us from the tumult at the bottom of the waterfall to the quiet heights of childhood, where the stream of life, a mirror of heaven, draws tranquilly through its little plain toward its precipices?

Once on a summer evening I lay on a hillside in the sun and slept. And I dreamed that I awoke in the churchyard. The grinding gears of the tower clock, just striking eleven, had wakened me. I searched the night sky for the sun, believing that an eclipse had covered it with the moon. All the graves were open, and the iron doors of the charnel house were opened and closed by invisible hands. Along the walls fled shadows cast by no one, and other shadows moved erect in the empty air. In the open coffins only the children still slept. A gray, oppressive fog hung in great folds in the sky, enclosed within a giant shadow like a net, which drew it ever closer together, ever denser and hotter. Above me I heard the distant rumble of avalanches; below me the first tremor of a vast earthquake. The church swayed from side to side, rent by two persistent and discordant tones within, which struggled together and tried in vain to resolve themselves in harmony. From time to time a gray shimmer flitted past the windows, and then the lead and iron melted in this shimmer and ran down the walls. The net of fog and the trembling earth drove me into the temple, in front of whose portal two gleaming basilisks brooded in two poisonous hedges. I walked among unknown shadows that bore the imprint of all the centuries. All the shadows stood around the altar, and their breasts throbbed and pounded as if they were hearts. Only one corpse, which had just been buried in the church, lay still on its pillow without a pounding breast, and in its smiling countenance one could read a blissful dream. But when I, a living being, entered, the corpse awoke and smiled no longer. With effort it slowly raised one eyelid, but there was no eye within, and in the throbbing breast was a wound instead of a heart. It raised high its hands and folded them for prayer; but its arms stretched ever longer and detached themselves from the body, and the hands fell folded at its side. High up in the vault of the church hung the clock face of Eternity, on which there were no numbers, and which was its own clock hand; only a black finger pointed at it, and the dead believed they read Time there.

And now a tall and noble figure descended from the heights to the altar with incomparable pain, and all the dead shouted, "Christ Jesus! Is there no God?"

The figure, "There is none."

Each shadow shuddered now, not only its breast, but throughout its length, and one after the other they were torn asunder by this trembling.

Christ Jesus continued to speak. "I walked through the worlds, I ascended into the suns and flew with the galaxies through the barren wastes of heaven; but there is no God. I descended as far as existence casts its shadow and looked down into the abyss and called 'Father, where are You?' But I heard only the eternal storm that is commanded by no one, and the shimmering rainbow of living beings stood without a sun to create it and dripped into the abyss. And when I lifted my eyes to the boundless world to see the divine Eye, the world looked upon me from an empty, bottomless eye socket; and eternity brooded on the chaos and chewed it over and over, like a great ruminating beast. —Howl on, discords, shatter the shadows with your shrieks, for He is not!"

The pale shadows dispersed as the white glaze formed by frost dissolves in a warm breath, and everything was empty. Then the dead children, having awakened in the churchyard, came into the temple and threw themselves down before the tall figure at the altar, a sight terrible for the heart, and said, "Jesus! have we no Father?" —And he answered with streaming tears, "We are all orphans, I and you, we are without Father."

Then the discordant tones wailed more violently—the quaking walls of the temple parted—and the temple and the children sank into the depths—and the whole earth and the sun followed after—and the entire universe in all its immensity sank before our eyes—and far above, on the very peak of boundless nature, stood Christ Jesus and looked down into the universe, which lay punctured by a thousand suns, as if he were looking down into a mine dug in everlasting night, a mine in which the suns flickered like miners' lamps and the galaxies were like veins of silver.

And when Christ saw the thronging press of the worlds, the torch dance of those starry will-o'-the-wisps and the coral reefs of beating hearts, and when he saw how one celestial orb after another poured out its gleaming souls into the sea of the dead, as a firework scatters swimming sparks upon the waves, then he, the greatest of finite beings, lifted his eyes to the void and to the empty vastness, and cried out, "Stark, silent Void! Cold, eternal Necessity! Mad Chance! Are you known to yourselves? When will you destroy the universe and me? —Chance, do you yourself know when you sweep with hurricane force through the snow storm of the stars and extinguish one sun after another in your passing? —How alone is everyone in the wide grave of the universe! I have no one beside me but myself—O Father! O Father! Where is your boundless breast, that I might rest upon it? —O if each of us is his own father and creator, why can we not also be our own angel of death?

"Is that still a man here beside me? Poor one! Your little lives are but the sighs of Nature, or only their echoes—a concave mirror throws its light down into the dust clouds made of the ashes of the dead on your earth, and gives rise to you, dim and swaying images. —Look down into the abyss, above which those ash clouds move—mists full of worlds rise from the sea of the dead. The future is a rising mist, and the present is a gathering cloud. Do you recognize your earth?"

Here Christ looked down, and his eyes filled with tears, and he said, "Ah, I was once on that earth: then I was still happy, then I had still my infinite Father and gazed still gladly from the mountains into the boundless heavens and pressed my pierced breast to His healing image and said still in the bitterness of death, 'Father, take Your son from his bleeding husk and lift him to Your heart. . . .' O, you fortunate and more than fortunate inhabitants of earth, you believe Him still. Perhaps your sun will set now, and you will fall to your knees among blossoms, glory and tears, lifting high your blissful hands and calling into the open heavens with thousands of tears of joy: You know even me, Unending One, and all my wounds, and after death You will receive me and heal them all. . . . You unfortunates, you are not healed after death. When a wretched being lays his wounded body in its grave, there to sleep against the beautiful day of his awaking in truth, goodness and joy, he awakes in a stormy chaos, in everlasting night—and no morning comes and no healing touch and no eternal Father! —Mortal beside me, if you still live, worship Him now, or you will have lost Him forever."

And as I fell down and looked into the shining structure of the universe, I saw the lifted coils of the giant serpent of eternity, which had laid itself around the cosmos—and the coils dropped, and the serpent seized the universe doubly round—then wound itself a thousand times around all of nature—and pressed the worlds together—and crushed the endless temple to a small cemetery chapel—and everything grew narrow, dark, constrained—and an immeasurably prolonged pealing of bells began to sound the final hour of time and to splinter the universe . . . when I awoke.

My soul wept with joy that it could worship God again, and the joy and the weeping and the faith in Him were my prayer. And when I woke, the sun glowed low behind full, purple fields of grain and cast a peaceful reflection of its evening color on the little moon that rose without a dawning in the east, and between heaven and earth a glad and transitory world stretched its short wings and lived, as I did, in the eyes of our eternal Father; and from all of nature around me streamed tranquil music, like distant evening bells.

TRANSLATED BY SHARON JACKIW

## (5) The dream of the blue flower

NOVALIS, Heinrich von Ofterdingen

The twenty-year-old Heinrich von Ofterdingen, in the novel of the same name written by Novalis (published posthumously in 1802), is at home with his parents in Eisenach. In a dream he sees the "blue flower," an uncanny blossom that inclines toward him, disclosing in its depths a girl's tender face. "Agitated by the dream face of the blue flower, the symbol of poetry and love as a force and the soul of the world, Heinrich immediately leaves his Thuringian hometown to go to Augsburg. The people he meets on this journey represent classes and areas of the world, nature, and history that he as a budding poet must know. In Augsburg he is instructed in the art of poetry by Klingsohr, and is bound to the spirit of poetry by Klingsohr's daughter Mathilde, the longed-for beloved." (Wolfdietrich Rasch)

Gradually the youth Heinrich became lost in sweet fantasies and fell asleep. At first he dreamed of boundless distances and wild, unknown regions. He traversed seas with incomprehensible ease; he saw strange animals; he lived with many kinds of people, now in war, in wild tumult, now in peaceful huts. He fell into captivity and direst need. All sensations rose within him to an unprecedented fullness. He lived out an endlessly varied life; died and came back again, loved most passionately, and then was separated eternally from his beloved. Toward morning, as dawn was breaking, things grew calmer in his soul, and the images clearer, firmer. It seemed as if he were walking alone through a dark forest. Only rarely did daylight glimmer through the green net. Soon he came to a gorge that rose steeply. He had to clamber over mossy rocks, which rushing water had long ago torn down. The higher he climbed, the thinner the forest became. Finally he reached a small meadow lying on a slope of the mountain. Behind the meadow rose a high cliff, at the foot of which he glimpsed an opening that seemed to be the beginning of a passageway carved into the rock. The path, level and comfortable, led him along for a while and then opened out; from here a bright light came shining toward him at a distance. Upon entering, he became aware of a powerful jet climbing to the ceiling of the cavern, as if from a fountain, and burst up above into countless sparks that collected down below in a large basin; the jet gleamed like flaming gold; not the faintest sound could be heard, a sacred silence surrounded the splendid dumb show. He approached the basin, which rippled and trembled with endless colors. The walls of the cave were coated with this fluid, which was not hot, but cool, and from the walls cast only a subdued bluish light. He dipped his hand into the basin and moistened his lips. It was as if a spirit's breath transfixed him, and he felt utterly strengthened and refreshed. An irresistible desire to bathe seized him; he undressed and stepped into the basin. It was as if a twilight cloud were enveloping him; a heavenly sensation suffused him; blissfully ardent, countless thoughts strove to merge within him; new, hitherto unseen images arose that also flowed together and became visible beings around him, and every wave of the lovely elements nestled like a tender bosom against him. The flow seemed like a stream of charming girls who turned corporeal the instant they touched the youth.

Intoxicated with delight, and yet conscious of every impression, he swam slowly with the current that flowed from the basin into the rocks. A sort of sweet slumber befell him, in which he dreamed indescribable events, and from which another illumination awakened him. He found himself on a soft lawn at the edge of a spring that bubbled up into the air and there seemed to be consumed. Dark blue rocks with dark veins rose up at some distance; the daylight that surrounded him was brighter and gentler than ordinary daylight, and the sky was dark blue and wholly pure. But what most attracted him was a tall, light blue flower that stood next to the spring and touched him with its broad, gleaming leaves. All around it grew countless flowers of all colors, and the most exquisite fragrance filled the air. He saw nothing but the blue·flower, and gazed at it long with unnamable tenderness. Finally, when he was about to approach it, the flower began to move and to change; the leaves gleamed even more and pressed against the growing stem, the flower bent toward him, and the petals formed a broad blue collar in which a delicate face hovered. His sweet astonishment grew with the strange transformation, when suddenly his mother's voice awakened him and he found himself in his parents' room, which the morning sun had already touched with gold. He was too delighted to be vexed by this disturbance; indeed, he wished her good morning and returned her cordial embrace.

"You sleepyhead," his father said. "How long have I been sitting here, filing. On account of you I haven't been able to hammer anything; your mother wanted to let her dear son sleep. I've had to wait for my breakfast, too. How smart of you to choose the student's life, for which we have to rise and work. Yet an able scholar, as I have heard said, must also make use of his nights to study the works of his great predecessors."

"Dear father," Heinrich answered, "do not be vexed by my oversleeping, which you are not used to my doing. At first I could not fall asleep, and then I had many restless dreams, until at last a charming dream occurred that I will not soon forget, and that seems to me as if it were more than just a dream."

"Heinrich dear," his mother spoke, "you must have lain down on your back, or your mind was straying at vespers. You look quite strange, too. Eat and drink, revive yourself."

His mother left the room; his father worked busily on, and said: "Dreams are bubbles, no matter what you learned gentlemen think of that, and you would do well to turn away from such useless and harmful things. The times are past when divine visions paired up with dreams, and we cannot and will not comprehend how those chosen men felt of whom the bible tells. Dreams must have been made of other stuff then, just as were human affairs.

"In the age of the world we are living in now, immediate concourse with the heavens no longer takes place. The old stories and writings are the only source through which we are granted knowledge of the supernatural world, to the extent we need any; and instead of those express revelations, the Holy Ghost now speaks to us indirectly through the minds of knowing and well-disposed men, and through the way of life and the destinies of pious people. I have never been much impressed by pictures of our miracles today, and I have never believed those great deeds that our clergy tells us about in them. But whoever wants to may credit them; far be it from me to sway someone in his belief."

"But, dear father, for what reason are you opposed to dreams, whose strange transformations and light, delicate nature must so surely enliven our reflections? Is not every dream, even the most confused, a unique phenomenon that, without thinking of divine providence, is a significant rent in the mysterious curtain that falls into our inner being with a thousand folds? In the wisest books one finds countless stories of dreams of credible people, and just remember the dream that the revered court chaplain related to us recently, and that seemed so remarkable even to you.

"But even without these stories, how amazed you would be if you had dreamed for the first time in your life, and you would surely not let yourself be dissuaded of the wondrousness of an occurrence that has simply become everyday! Dreams seem to me to be a bulwark against the regularity and ordinariness of life, the free refreshment of a fettered imagination that tosses about all the images of life, and interrupts the constant earnestness of adults with a cheerful child's game. Without dreams we would surely age sooner and so, even though not as given immediately from above, dreams can be considered as a divine boon, a friendly companion on the pilgrimage to the Holy Grave. The dream I dreamed last night is surely no ineffectual coincidence in my life, for I feel it meshing into my soul like a broad wheel and driving it on with a mighty turn."

TRANSLATED BY RALPH R. READ

# APOLLONIAN DIONYSIAN

In the German classics, man in his resemblance to God appears as the highest of the natural living creatures; as the "beautiful soul" having a claim on freedom and humanity. Goethe and Schiller, in particular, uniquely appropriate, enrich, form, and complete what had been thought and felt before them—Lessing's thoughts on progress, Klopstock's belief in creativity, Wieland's striving for harmony, Herder's consciousness of humanity. They imbue the idea and the ideal with sensuous form in their poetry and philosophy. They overcome the predominant ethical rigor of Kant, and with the "beautiful soul" achieve the reconciliation of the dualism of duty and inclination. The schism is not suppressed, though; it is suspended in something more elevated.

Idea and life, hope and anxiety, life and death, freedom and compulsion, happiness and suffering, peace and war, form and content, art and reality are opposites that profoundly determine Friedrich Schiller's dualistic view of life. He is repeatedly concerned with the cleavage between mind and matter, between moral self-determination and enslavement by the sensual world. He repeatedly asks how it is possible that the glorious, free, "enthusiastic spirit" is chained to the "rigid, unchangeable clockwork of a mortal body." Dialectical progression characterizes Schiller's work in its entirety—the spherical illumination of the idea and of ideals is juxtaposed to the downward pull of gravity of the terrestrial. Tending at times optimistically toward the thesis, at other times pessimistically toward the antithesis, he strives for a synthesis and for the conquest of mortal inadequacy by approaching the world of ideas. In doing so, one of his key concepts is freedom—freedom from the compulsion of sensuousness and corporeality—which appears in the form of beauty, charm, grace, and articulations of impulse to play. Gravity is then suspended, and man no longer feels the burden of matter. In "The Ideal and Life" he states, "Only the body owns those powers / That weave dark fate; /

36

But free of every temporal power / The companion of blessed natures / Wanders above in the poet's halls, / Godly the form among Gods."

In *On the Aesthetic Education of Man,* Schiller writes that "through beauty" we enter "the world of ideas but, it should be noted, without thereby leaving the sensual world."

Entirely committed to the individual, as well as to details, Goethe seeks the primordial type, the archetype, the reference point in the flight of appearances. For him, type and metamorphosis are pivotal concepts. Nature eternally creates new forms; what was there was not yet there; what was does not return; everything is new, yet everything is old: "The thousandfold mixture of this flowery abundance / Around the garden confuses you, beloved . . . / All forms are similar, and none resembles the other; / Thus the choir intimates a secret law, a holy riddle . . ."

Law and demon are juxtaposed. Man's moral task of striving for completeness emerges from the tension between passion and control, caprice and moderation, genius and limitation. Goethe's "Primal Orphic Words" summons the cosmos of the classical view of man: demon—the coincidental, love, need, hope (6).

By drawing on antiquity, the nineteenth-century German spirit sought to comprehend and master the contrasts and contradictions of human existence under the rubric "Apollonian-Dionysian." In the same manner that Friedrich Schiller describes in his epic poem "The Walk," the human race's route from nature to civilization, from anarchy to control of our basic drives by commandments and laws that are freely and gladly accepted and internalized—in the same manner, the classic writers were altogether preoccupied with conveying "well-being in civilization." Their successors—from Hölderlin, Joseph von Eichendorff, and Conrad Ferdinand Mayer to Friedrich Nietzsche and Thomas Mann—repeatedly used, as a model for the present and future, a world that was removed to an ideally typical manifestation of antiquity. Longing for a mankind still close to divine origins was the goal both of Apollonian sublimity, which "over-looks" the world, and of Dionysian descent, which becomes one with the world in its depths.

Novalis describes Apollonian mankind in the fifth hymn to the night: cheerful people; the ocean's dark, green depth was a goddess's lap; a flourishing people revelled in the crystal grottos; rivers, trees, flowers, and animals had human intelligence; poured by conspicuous youth, the wine tasted sweeter; the grapes bore God; "a loving, motherly goddess growing up in abundant golden garb; the holy intoxication of love a sweet service of the most beautiful woman of the gods; an eternally colorful festivity of children of heaven and earth-dwellers; life rustled like spring through the centuries." But this world was transitory—the gods vanished with their retinue, nature stood lonely and lifeless and bound in strict proportion by an iron chain and by the sterile numeral. The immeasurable abundance of life disintegrated into dark words as if into dust and nothingness.

Day becomes night, but the poet finds in the night a new (other-worldly) sense of life. At this point the Apollonian-Dionysian is transcended to become the Romantic-Christian, just as in other Romantic poets "classicality," the longing for Greece, is repeatedly allied with Christian-medieval, Nordic-mystical elements. The portrayal of the Apollonian-Dionysian, topographically "anchored" in the Greek and Roman-Italian landscape, can hardly be understood in terms of the indicative; it is almost always to be understood in terms of the subjunctive, as if such beauty of a transported world were possible. Access to the Apollonian realm is through the soaring dream, to the Dionysian, by descent. This "as-if" also characterized especially the moment of the idyll, the hour when the god Pan is asleep; when the cheerfulness of afternoon's calm comes over people—until "panic" breaks out again. Friedrich Schiller believed the danger to be that the true idyll, when the abyss was nearby, might become the false idyll, and this would mean that, left entirely to himself, the person would doze off upon a padding of platitude—and the idyll would degenerate into permanent, egocentric slumber. The nineteenth century proved Schiller's concern to be correct.

Hölderlin's poetry moves between the Apollonian and the Dionysian realms and the "true idyll." Blessed genius aloft in the light, on the gentle terrain of blissful spirits. Yet man is given no resting place (7). Hölderlin makes the passionate attempt of conveying to the ego a new kind of security in the form of a pantheistic disintegration of self within an aorgic world characterized by the dualism of constancy and transitoriness, life and death. He is a poet of panic, an Orpheus who sounds the lament for man's transitoriness, a singer of the self-imposed task. (To be one with everything that is alive, to return in blessed self-forgetfulness into the universe of nature, is the apex of thoughts and pleasures; is the holy mountain height, the place of eternal rest.)

Withdrawal is the leitmotiv of the classical educational ideals referred to in *Humaniora*. The person placed in the "pedagogical province" will be enabled to mature to a complete being. But the work on oneself necessary to do so, work which can ultimately only liberate one from the cocoons enclosing the stages of development, is determined by the strength of one's will. Such an educational ideal as that found in Wilhelm von Humboldt's *Fragments of an Autobiography* (8), is a dream that was seldom realized in the actuality of the nineteenth and twentieth centuries. For example, in the German humanistic *Gymnasium,* it was suspected that the essence of being human included the capacity for transforming oneself into a beautiful soul. This belief deteriorated, however, in the face of disciplinary measures characterized by taboos and repressive norms. When Friedrich Nietzsche, at the end of the nineteenth century, enters the land of education (in *Thus Spake Zarathustra*), he is overcome by horror. The classical cultural legacy appears as "scarecrows." "All eras and peoples peer colorfully from your veils; all customs and beliefs speak colorfully with your gestures. If the veils and shawls and colors and gestures were removed, just enough would be left over for scaring birds. Truly I myself am the frightened bird that once saw you naked and without color; and I flew away when the skeleton waved signs of love to me." The "dreams of the era" had become unbelievable.

The dream of humanity as presented, for example, in Goethe's *Iphigenia in Tauris* (9) had no real successor. External drapery was more important than inner substance. Seeking the country of the soulful Greeks, Iphigenia proves to be a "sublime form clad in antique clothing." Anselm von Feuerbach's painting marks the line of demarcation where the dream of humanity turns into humanity staged with movable props (10).

The palpable manner in which Heinrich Schliemann, using pick and shovel, concretely pursued the dream of classical Greece, dumped, so to speak, German classicism's idealistic, humanitarian, ethereal flight onto the soil of archaeology (11). The excavation of fragments from the debris of time replaced the entire poetic animation of a distant Apollonian-Dionysian world. Of course the torsos then became part of a bourgeois fetishism of civilization. Imitations of ancient works of art were proudly displayed on the console. Here in the realm of *kalokagathia* (physical and spiritual completeness, "beauty-goodness" as the educational ideal of ancient Greece) was another expression of the conviction "it has been achieved." Passionate but sublimated humaneness became nationalistic philistinism adorned with an aesthetic facade.

The clarity of Apollonian "formality" that radiates from such poems as "Nänie" (12), "Roman Fountain" (13), "Archaic Torso of Apollo" (14), "Transport" (15) was replaced by a goldsmithing mentality that settled into formalism. The emphasis in art on withdrawal became an alibi for not having to participate in the world and for being able to dispense with compassion. The dream world of ancient perfection included in the polar-ity of the Apollonian-Dionysian miscarried to become affirmative civilization:

> In its essentials it is idealistic. It responds to the need of the isolated individual with universal humanity, to physical misery with the beauty of the soul, to external enslavement with inner freedom, to brutal egoism with the virtuous realm of duty. If all these ideas at the time of the militant rise of the new society had a progressive character that pointed beyond the achieved organization of existence while the bourgeoisie was stabilizing its dominance, they appear to an increasing extent in the service of the suppression of the discontented masses and of merely justifying self-exaltation: they conceal the physical and psychic decay of the individual. (Herbert Marcuse)

For the Romantic, two works of Friedrich Schlegel, *On the Study of Greek Poetry,* 1797, and the *Holiness of Beautiful Games and the Freedom of the Representational Arts,* correctly characterized genuine Greek antiquity. For the barbarian, however, beauty in itself was not enough. "For crude as well as for refined non-Greeks, art is merely a slave of sensuousness or of reason. A portrayal can become important and interesting for such an audience only through strange, rich, new, and unusual content, only through a lascivious subject. The Romantic Joseph von Eichendorff interprets Greek antiquity in this non-Greek sense in "Marble Statue" (16). Spiritual Christianity and Greek antiquity are juxtaposed. The young poet Florio, torn between two friends symbolizing the redemptive and the demonic forces of poetry, comes under the magic spell of a marble statue of Venus that he encounters in a park as he is leaving the inn (near Lucca) for a walk. The "rigidified antiquity," the remote garden of Venus, emblem of sensuous jeopardy of the human (W. Rehm), exerts a seductive fascination. Florio is able to liberate himself from the spell; he is freed of his infatuation in the bright morning; in Bianca, the embodiment of pure love, he experiences his life's destiny.

This novella is paradigmatic in its creation, though under an ominous threat, of the Dionysian aspects of Greek antiquity—deception, melancholy, and enchantment. The motifs of Tannhäuser and of Tristan's longing for love are sounded. According to Nietzsche, dream and intoxication led to the essence of Greek art. "Prophecy" is mystery; in this sense Apollo is also Dionysian. Under the spell of the Dionysian not only is the alliance between human beings again sealed; alienated, antagonistic, or subjugated nature also celebrates its feast of reconciliation with its lost son, the human being (17). Dionysus' chariot, harnessed to a panther and to a tiger, is showered with flowers and wreaths. The Dionysian spirit is best comprehended by transforming Beethoven's "Ode to Joy" into a painting and giving the imagination free reign when the millions miserably sink into the dust. The suffering from the reality principle, so strongly characteristic of Nietzsche's life and work, is overcome by ecstasy, which is capable of "overplaying" tragic individuation. For Nietzsche, music—especially the music of Richard Wagner—means withdrawal from existential suffering and is the highest pleasure. It is certainly intoxication followed by sobering up (Wagner the seducer!).

The gravity of life, sickness, physical disintegration vanish, as in Thomas Mann's *Tristan* when the "Eleusinian call of the mysteries of music" is sounded (18). The slave is now a free man; all rigid, hostile barriers that have been placed between people by need, arbitrariness, or "impertinent fashion" now disintegrate. "Singing and dancing, the human being now expresses himself as a member of a higher community; he has forgotten speaking and walking and is about to fly up into the air as he dances." (Nietzsche) But the precipice lies directly ahead.

### (6) Intrinsic form, evolving as it lives

JOHANN WOLFGANG VON GOETHE, "Primal Orphic Words"

Johann Wolfgang von Goethe (1749–1832) wrote the poem "Primal Orphic Words" in 1820. As chamber music, in comparison with the powerful symphony *Faust,* these verses represent the quintessence of Goethe's life and of a creative output that is without parallel in breadth, profundity, and inwardness. "There has never been a poet of his caliber of such overwhelming wisdom; none who conducted and completed his life in such an exemplary manner, there was never such a charming artist . . . He had the mission of creating a new style at every stage of his life—indeed, it might almost be said, a new style of each new work. Admittedly, his productivity is even based on this need. He was only able to remain mute or at any moment to be original in such a protean manner that we are tempted to believe that nothing human was alien to him and that there was no situation, no perplexity, no hope, no enchantment, no gloominess that would not be illuminated, cleansed, and transfigured by Goethe's words." (Emil Staiger)

### Genius

As on the day that lent you to the world
The sun and planets stood in salutation,
Forthwith you flourished on and ever onward
According to the law effective when you started.
You *must* be so; you cannot flee your selfhood.
Thus have the sybils and the prophets stated,
And neither time nor force will ever alter
Intrinsic form, evolving as it lives.

### The Accidental

But stringent limits pleasantly are circled
By an inconstant, near and with us changing.
You grow, not lonely, but among companions,
And likely function as another would.
In life soon all is over—, soon expires.
It is a trifle, and one trifles through it.
Swift, unannounced, the years have come full circle;
The trusting lamp awaits the flame that kindles.

### Love

This too will come!—It plunges from the heavens
To where it once had swung from ancient waste.
Approaching close on airy wings it hovers.
Around the brow and breast along the vernal day.
It seems to flee, from fleeing then returning;
Then comes the weal in woe, such sweet alarm.
Full many a heart drifts in the universal;
The noblest dedicates itself to one.

### Constraint

So once again it is as stars had wished it:
The law and the condition; and all will
Is merely wanting, just because we ought to.
When will confronts, discretion keeps quite still.
The stern demands adapts to will and whimsy,
The best belov'd is banished by the heart.
So at long last we have apparent freedom,
And are confined far more than at the start.

### Hope

Yet of this border, of this brazen wall
The most vexatious gate is unsecured.
What matter if it be unyielding stone!
For lightly and unfettered One emerges
From out the clouds, the fog, the shower of rain;
By it made wingéd, we are elevated.
You know it well, it roves through all the zones—
One flap of wings—and to our rear lie eons!

TRANSLATED BY MINETTA ALTGELT GOYNE

## (7) Blindly from hour to hour

FRIEDRICH HÖLDERLIN, "Hyperion's Fate Song"

Friedrich Hölderlin was born in 1770 and was insane when he died in 1843. He was both moved and menaced by the Romantic exuberance of feeling. Eternal being was intensified to heightened visibility in the form of Greek gods. "To him these gods were immediate religious reality; but he experienced them simultaneously with the consciousness that this was a personal and lonely religious experience no longer shared in his era by any community; hence although the gods are real and eternal, they remain 'removed' from the world of his era." The elegiacal sadness about something lost, about a great, luminous, filled existence as shown in the portrayals of antiquity gives rise to the certainty that the gods could one day again be present. "For they rule unaltered in nature; they are in the ether and the sea, as once they were and always will be. Thus the vision of a future day of the gods, a renewal of existence in the familiar world is juxtaposed to that glorification of ancient Greece. The expectation of a new realization of the proximity of the gods, of an approaching rebirth of life in the Fatherland is repeatedly proclaimed in Hölderlin's late work." (Wolfdietrich Rasch)

> You stroll up there in the light
> On cushioned surface, blissful genii!
> Brilliant breezes of gods
> Gently caress you,
> As with her fingers the harpist
> Touching holy strings.
>
> Fateless, like suckling infants
> Sleeping, the Heavenly breathe;
> Chastely preserved
> In diffident bud,
> Their spirits are made
> To blossom forever,
> And blesséd their eyes
> Gaze with a silent
> Eternal serenity.
>
> We, though, are fated
> Never to have an abode:
> Wasting, falling,
> The suffering people,
> Blindly from hour to hour
> Like water cascading
> From cliff to cliff dropping
> A year at a time into limbo.

TRANSLATED BY MINETTA ALTGELT GOYNE

## (8) Perfect self-possession

WILHELM VON HUMBOLDT, Fragments of an Autobiography

The "beautiful soul" was by no means a "coincidence" for Wilhelm von Humboldt (1767–1835) whose unhappy, bleak childhood led him to meticulous self-observation. He had to achieve the "beautiful soul" mainly by being an autodidact. He is guided in his autobiography by the difference "between the symbolic in the human being and in the individual and also by what is present only as a gloss of reality." "It is not at all my intention to dwell on or to return to myself. I merely use myself, as the most familiar creature, as the starting point for the world. I will therefore concern myself primarily with subjects that I have observed or with which I have been occupied in my life—i.e., nature, art, science in all its branches, specifically history and languages, countries, nations, external conditions, affairs of state, people." Therewith is circumscribed the universalism of a thinker who, based on financial independence, set himself the task of engaging in, observing, judging, and dealing with life. Humboldt's position in the Prussian Ministry of the Interior was that of state councilor and director of the section on public worship and education. He achieved reform in the school system with the beginnings of the humanistic Gymnasium, and he founded Berlin University in an effort to replace to the state through intellectual strength what it has lost in external power. As Minister of State and Ambassador to Vienna he was successful in 1813 in persuading Metternich to abandon his policy of mediation and to join the alliance of Prussia and Russia against France. He was not merely a person of the *humaniora* but a tough, sarcastically superior, and keen diplomat and negotiator. This was demonstrated repeatedly in subsequent years at international conferences.

Since my twelfth year when, wholly on my own initiative, I first trained myself in it and until now when I still do not neglect its practice, self-control has never had a purpose other than itself. I did not conquer my passions to be virtuous; I did not master their outbursts to get through life with greater ease; I was driven by no purpose to pursue one thing to the exclusion of all else, by no enthusiasm which, by singling out one idea crushes all others. But I have had a horror of becoming involved in the world and have always felt the need to stand free of it, as one that views and examines it. It was only natural to believe that only the most absolute self-control could afford me the point outside the world I required. There is also this: what I consider truly noble in man lies in the sobriety which honors the pure inner will. It was classical antiquity which first awakened these concepts within me, and to which they subsequently attached me forever. I began with the pure concept of the Stoics, to will because one wills. But my self-control and my stepping back from the world are something altogether different from the ascetic extirpation of desire or the eremitic withdrawal from worldliness. I do not hesitate to give rein to desire and recognize a great and beneficient productive power in pleasure, even in what many would call unbridled.

But some feelings such as wrath, hatred and vengefulness, whose satisfaction does no more for man than that he relieves himself of their blazing intensity, I was either a stranger to or deliberately rid myself of. If they can be justified and are salutary in their consequences, it is either only in those in whom the pure concept of justice, separated from hatred or bitterness, would be too weak or where they produce effects for which the mind of even the strongest has sufficient power only in these, its illnesses. In such cases, man takes on the quality of a natural force which I admire and do not disapprove of but which I do not care to adopt. As regards the world, I have always tried to know and see as much of it as possible instead of divorcing myself from it, and only wished to become a stranger to it while in its very midst. For to grasp the world in its individuality and totality is precisely my striving and the end to which the rule of the will is directed. That rule has a negative and a positive side. Conquering pain, dispensing with pleasures and even overcoming needs and taming one's desires are the easiest and most common accomplishments and belong on the negative side. But over its entire range—and I never thought of it differently—the rule of the will demands unremitting circumspection which always sees things soberly and always unconditionally determines which sentiments to admit or what it proposes to do in the outside world. It therefore consists in the recognition of the true and the doing of what is right, or at least of what is consistent. For that reason, it is quite false to believe that this control has something to do with an innate coldness or weak desires. Such weakness only makes easier the exercise of the lesser part of self-control, the mere taming of the passions. But circumspection, when it is to become productive of truth and right, needs a power of its own that flows from the pure part of the soul. The absence of fear, or courage at least, is connected with self-control. Because courage never was an instinct in me, I can be certain that I possess every kind of it at every moment. What is positive in self-possession I did not acquire until late. I would like to divide this aspect also into two parts. One is the capacity to solve to a significantly satisfactory degree every specific intellectual or practical task, provided it does not lie too far outside one's talents or practice. When I was young I was altogether incapable of this. I could almost never accomplish something because I so desired; what I needed was a mood over which I had no control. Thus even a letter became burdensome and I could never have produced a verse or a rhyme. Only when I was in Rome and had completed the translation of the *Agamemnon,* and in business transactions later, did I wrest this capacity from my nature, and then to no inconsiderable degree. Nowadays I can do pretty much what I wish or circumstances demand along these lines. The other kind of positive self-possession has to do with actions and the implementation of plans that demand time. It was not until I had been married for some years that the reading of I don't remember what biography made this clear to me. At that time, several years before my service, I firmly resolved to seek employment and to achieve the highest I would be capable of, and so I did. Later, I succeeded in similar accomplishments in both my private and my public life. But my way is not just as unremitting and direct pursuit but goes much deeper and tries to force the nature of things themselves. Very often, and for an extended time, I do not advance myself visibly but have my purpose constantly before me: to prepare the soil from which my purpose must emerge as though ordained by the very nature of things, attend to every auspicious moment, choose the proper one, and then act with indefatigable zeal. I do not let myself be discouraged by any momentary failure but turn it to advantage to come closer to my goal. In addition to the eye and the skill, which merely handle the mechanical execution, most is due to an untiring effort and a high degree of indifference to success. It is incredible what combining these two elements can accomplish. Most people fail in their plans because they are too concerned with success and weary too easily in their struggle to achieve it. In conclusion, I still must determine whether I have what people call "character." The simple answer is this: not a trace of it as a natural endowment but when I wish it, I have it to the highest degree. Even when there are no difficulties, I go back on statements, intentions, plans, methods to implement them, and make changes even when the resistance I encounter is small. And generally, I have a tendency to give in to others as regards externals, which comes largely from my own security that inside I will remain as I wish to be. But when there is the will, it would be difficult to find a more iron obstinacy than mine for it is rare that someone should be as profoundly convinced that no external consequence whatever can prevail against the rigor of an idea. But I rarely employ this unshakable unyieldingness because I know that it is a usable weapon only infrequently. The distinctiveness of my self-possession thus lies in its suppleness. It does not rigidly and pedantically serve so-called higher ends and I in turn possess it as I wish.

Quite weighty and not easily refutable criticisms can be raised as to my understanding and the quality of my intellectual powers. I have no speed and ease whatever by which I might grasp the various relations of things and ideas to each other, and this both when intermediate links are missing, and when the conclusions are obvious. In affairs, I get the better of this failing only by industry, by looking into things and by consulting with others, and here the strictest attention has become second nature. I lack any capacity of guessing, combining, divining, have never learned to play any card game even tolerably well, and was never any good at philological criticism. It is surprising how this shortcoming harms me in my life as a diplomat. There is nothing that will make up for it; at best, I can hide it more or less well. I am not at all inventive, and things present themselves to me as order rather than multiplicity, which is the reason that even in my writing and speaking there is a certain monotony that means I often even repeat the same words. At best, a certain abundance of ideas abruptly forms a coherent whole in my mind but there is no ready flow. Much too rarely do I have the certainty of knowing the truth, and I easily waver between two sets of ideas so that I invariably feel that the one I just decided against is the better one. I have never been convinced, nor have I ever observed others truly to believe, that I had a genuine capacity for taking up synthetic metaphysics. I was certainly not born to be a poet and my imagination is alternately overwhelmed by the dryness of my intellect or overcome by what I feel. In my childhood and until I attend a course of lectures by the philosopher Engel and even there at first, I was considered slow and not especially favored by nature, particularly as compared to my brother Alexander. Fortunately no one notices this or ascribes it to other causes, but in society and worldly affairs I still have occasional vacuous, silly and simpleminded moments which, considering what they are, last much too long. Yet I cannot say that my intellectual powers have declined with advancing age; on the contrary, they developed and grew. But it certainly remains true that my mind was originally slow, lacking in versatility and liveliness, and this is still the case. Worse, I did not nourish it enough. I have read incredibly little and still take no pleasure in it. I know very few things with any certainty, much less than the world believes, and have spent a great deal of time with very mechanical studies which did little for the mind. So much for accusations and shortcomings.

TRANSLATED BY MICHAEL SHAW

## (9) Let there be truth between us

JOHANN WOLFGANG VON GOETHE, Iphigenia in Tauris

"Just devilishly human" is how Goethe described his drama *Iphigenia in Tauris,* conceived in 1776 and published in its final version in 1786–87. Iphigenia, the daughter of Agamemnon, is threatened with being sacrificed by her father and his supporters in response to a divine command. She is saved by Diana and abducted to Tauris. There she serves as priestess to the goddess and has the opportunity of achieving much good and eliminating human sacrifice. But her homesickness ("in her soul seeking the country of the Greeks") persists. King Thoas of Tauris wants to win Iphigenia as his wife. She tries to dissuade him by all manner of excuses, ultimately by admission of her tarnished background. Two foreigners are then taken prisoner who, at the command of Thoas—angry at Iphigenia's refusal—are to be brought by the priestess to the goddess and sacrificed. It turns out that the two Greeks are in fact Iphigenia's brother, Orestes, and his friend Pylades. Orestes had murdered Clytemnestra, his mother, and her lovers. Since that time he has been insane. He can free himself from the curse that is on him only by bringing back to Greece "the sister who is living against her will in the shrine on the shores of Tauris." He misunderstands the oracle, believing that what is meant by reference to his sister is the statue of Diana, Apollo's sister, which is in Tauris. The siblings recognize each other. Initially Iphigenia complies and assists in the planned robbery, but ultimately she cannot bring herself to deceive Thoas, who has treated her like a daughter. She admits the deception to him and persuades him to let them all leave in peace.

IPHIGENIA (*after a silence*):
Do men alone, then, have the right to do
Unheard of feats? Can only men clasp things
Impossible to their heroic bosoms?
What is termed great? What lifts to awe the souls
Of minstrels as they tell their oft-told tales,
Except what bravest men began with chances
Unlikely of success? He who by night
Stole up alone upon the enemy,
Then as an unexpected flame seized on
The sleepers and raged in among the wakers
And finally, as hard-pressed by the wakened
He fled on foemen's horses, but with booty,—[2]
Shall he alone be praised? Or he alone
Who, spurning roads of safety, boldly went
A-roaming through the mountains and the forests
To clear the highwaymen out of a district?[3]
Is nothing left for us? Must gentle woman
Renounce her innate right, turn wild and fight

Against wild men, and wrest from you the right
Of swords like Amazons who take revenge
In blood for their oppression? Back and forth
In my heart ebbs a daring enterprise;
I cannot help but meet with great reproach,
And even with dire harm, if I should fail;
Yet on your knees, ye gods, I lay it, and
If you are true, as you are said to be,
Then show it by your help and glorify
Truth through me!—Yes, I confess, O king,
A secret fraud is being perpetrated.
You will in vain ask for those prisoners;
For they have gone—gone searching for their friends
Who with their ship are waiting by the shore.
The elder one, who was afflicted here
But who has now been cured—he is Orestes,
My brother, and the other one is his
Devoted friend since childhood, Pylades
By name. Apollo sends them here from Delphi
With his divine command to carry off
Diana's statue and to bring his sister
Back to him there, in recompense for which
He promises deliverance to the man
Stained with his mother's blood and hounded by
The Furies. To your hands I thus entrust
Both remnants of the house of Tantalus.
Destroy us—if you *can*.

THOAS:         You think the rough
And barbarous Scythian will hear the voice
Of truth and human decency that Atreus
The Greek would not hear?

IPHIGENIA:        All men hear it, born
Beneath whatever sky they may, and through
Whose bosoms flows the fountainhead of life [4]
Pure and unhindered.—What are you devising,
O king, in silence deep within your soul?
If it is our destruction, kill me first!
For now that there is no deliverance left
For us, I realize the ghastly peril

Into which I over-hastily
And wilfully have plunged my !oved ones. Ah!
They will stand bound before me. With what looks
Can I take farewell of my brother then,
Whose murderess I am? O, I can never
Again look into his beloved eyes!

THOAS:     How the deceivers with their artful falsehoods
Have cast their nets about the head of one
Long cloistered and who readily lent ear
To their desires!

IPHIGENIA:          No, no, O king! I could
Have been deceived, but these are loyal men
And true. And if you find them otherwise,
Then leave them to their fate and send me off
To exile as a punishment for folly
Upon the bleak shore of some craggy island.
But if this man is my so long-besought
And much-loved brother, then release us; be
Kind to the brother as well as the sister.
My father died because of his wife's guilt,
And she died from her son. The final hope
Of Atreus' line now rests with him alone.
Let me with pure heart and pure hand go over
The sea and purify our family.
You will stand by your word!—If to my people
Return were ever possible, you swore
To let me go. It now is possible.
A king will not, like vulgar men, consent
Out of embarrassment just to be rid
One moment of the suppliant; nor will
He promise for contingencies he hopes
Will not arise. He feels his full worth only
When he can gladden those who wait in hope.

THOAS:     Impatiently, as fire contends with water
And, hissing, seeks extermination of
Its enemy, so does the anger in
My bosom show resistance to your words.

IPHIGENIA:     O let your mercy, circled round about
With joy and praises and thanksgiving shine

Upon me like the steady altar-flame.

THOAS:   How often has this strain brought me to calm!

IPHIGENIA:   O, offer me your hand in sign of peace.

THOAS:   You ask a great deal in so short a time.

IPHIGENIA:   To do good things does not require reflection.

THOAS:   It does! for sometimes out of good comes evil.

IPHIGENIA:   O, it is doubt that turns good into evil.

Do not reflect; grant as your feelings prompt you.

TRANSLATED BY CHARLES E. PASSAGE

## (10) Tall figure in a classical robe

ANSELM FEUERBACH, A Legacy

"Who better serves his fatherland, the person who has the courage to say the truth, or the person who covers the most conspicuous shortcoming with a patriotic lie? In my art I have offered my Fatherland much that is cheerfully instructive. It did not respond and favored other arts." The painter who wrote these words became a favorite artist of the educated middle class only after his death, especially with his painting *Iphigenia*. Anselm Feuerbach's work, according to Hermann Uhde-Bernays, writing in 1910, stands for itself in its own temple, "preserved from the challenging glances of the ordinary crowd, accessible only to people inclined to comprehend in the rhythmic arrangement and harmonious quiet of the artistic impression the significant beauty of artistic life and the artistic act."

Feuerbach, born in 1829, was a painter of sentimental formalism. In his art the ugly and the truly pitiable are excluded or, as the case may be, stylized away. He died in 1880, alone in an inn in Venice.

May 1861

That ancient story will not leave me in peace. To be sure, man's heart is forever longing and seeking expression. But that's not what I meant to say. Rather, the sculptor Cardwell has used his tailor's art to make me a Greek gown, and now I have found a model who is not a bad Iphigenia. If you could only see the tall figure in her classical robe! When I first saw her I shrank back startled, thinking that a statue by Phidias was standing before me. Such things cannot be achieved in a hurry; it is a matter of time for observation. Where will I ever find that again?

A large Iphigenia already exists, sketched during a hail storm after much searching. And a second one is on hand, quite different, but just as significant. Let's imagine ourselves in this situation: The first, dressed all in white, is leaving the forest and pauses at the sight of the ocean. Instantly she wins our hearts. Quite ordinary people have asked me whether I didn't think she was about to speak. The second is leaning on a column, lost in contemplation of the ocean, thinking of her distant homeland.

But for the present these sketches have been put aside, since I have too great a variety of poses and would like to take only that which exhausts the situation. I can send you a half dozen studies.

The Pietà has also been put aside. Man cannot serve two masters. Besides, I have made considerable progress on this picture; it is complete in my head, down to the last brush stroke. It's always that way when a thought arises directly from intuition. I saw the Maria, and the other figures joined her later. It is turning into a delicately beautiful picture.

June 1861

Now the Iphigenia riddle is solved. The feeling that we call longing requires physical repose. It implies self-absorption, self-indulgence, letting oneself go.

In a moment of intuition the picture was born. Not Eurypidean, not Goethean either, but simply Iphigenia sitting on the beach and "seeking the land of the Greeks with her soul." And what else should she be doing?

February 1862

At the end of the month the large picture will be ready to send.

Up to now I have put aside all cares, insofar as possible, and thus I have succeeded in transplanting the figure in its full simplicity, without any sentimentality (which was certainly unknown to the Greeks, and which is the stumbling block that causes such themes to fail nowadays). So this is a picture after my own heart. What will now become of it I don't know. I have no hopes of a buyer, but first of all it is to be sent home. This picture too is a sacrifice on the altar of art. It is the greatest and best that I have painted up to now. Should I really send my Iphigenia? She requires good eyes and warm hearts.

Recently my life was in danger. An unruly horse ran away with me, so that I covered an hour's journey in a few minutes. On a bridge I was able to rein in the horse and brought it back at a walk. It felt strange later coming into the studio where the large picture stands: Iphigenia—white, entirely white—looking out at the ocean. . . .

TRANSLATED BY MARGARET WOODRUFF

## (11) In the land of Odysseus

HEINRICH SCHLIEMANN, Ithaca, the Peloponnese, and Troy

Heinrich Schliemann, who justly boasted of having discovered a new world for archaeology, "was a genuine representative of his century. The story of his life competes with any Victorian novel. He was born in Mecklenburg-Schwerin in 1822, the son of a Protestant pastor. Oppressed in his youth by poverty that recalled Dickens's portrayals of his milieu, Schliemann rose in the business world through dedication to his goal and by hard work. His travels around the world led to fame and success, but also to a tragic marriage. Ultimately, he found happiness and fulfillment at the side of a beautiful Greek woman, thirty years his junior, who shared his love for Homer and Greek antiquity. Not only is Schliemann a classic example of those great amateur scholars of the nineteenth century who, often without academic training, contributed to revolutionizing scientific research, but he also incorporates the entire scale of middle-class attitudes and behavior: capitalistic entrepreneurial spirit, the drive to speculate, zeal for building, enthusiasm for technological progress (he was fascinated by trains, bridge construction, and steamboats, not to mention the telegraph), blowing his own horn, moral laxity for the sake of success, and an unshatterable trust in his own abilities." (Leo Deuel) Schliemann died in 1890.

It was finally possible to realize the dream of my life, to visit the setting of the events in which I have been so deeply interested. I set out in April 1868 and went via Rome and Naples to Corfu, Cephalonia and Ithaca. One by one, I visited the regions where living, poetic memories of antiquity are still evident . . .

At six in the morning on the sixth of July, I arrived in Corfu, the capital of the island of the same name. I stayed on the island for two days, traveling around the countryside.

Antiquity unanimously witnesses that Corfu is the island Scheria or the land of the Phaeacians that Homer wrote about. . . . Tradition describes a large river, called the "Cressida Spring," which flows from the west and empties into the Kalichiopulos Sea. This river is said to be the one on whose bank Nausicaa and her handmaidens washed their clothes and where they welcomed Odysseus.

This daughter of King Alcinous is one of the most noble characters ever portrayed by Homer. The simplicity of her manner always worked its extraordinary magic on me. No sooner had I landed on Corfu than I rushed to visit the place that had been the setting of one of the most moving scenes in the *Odyssey*.

My guide led me to a mill one kilometer from the mouth of a small river. From there I was forced to go on foot. But I had scarcely taken a hundred steps when I ran into trouble. Irrigation canals, which were too wide to jump across, had been dug on the right and the left sides of the river. In addition, the fields lay partly under water. But these difficulties only increased my desire to push on. I undressed down to my shirt and left my clothes in the care of my guide. In this fashion I walked along the small river, often up to my chest in water, and through the mud of the canals and flooded fields. Finally, after half an hour of this difficult trek, I saw two large, awkwardly carved stones which tradition designates as the washing place for the inhabitants of the old city of Corcyra. This is also the place where Nausicaa and her handmaidens were washing their clothes when they welcomed Odysseus. The surroundings match Homer's description exactly, because Odysseus landed at the mouth of the river. Nausicaa and her handmaidens came to the washing troughs by the river. . . . These troughs must have been located close to the sea because right after Nausicaa and her handmaidens washed their clothes they spread them out to dry on the pebbles along the seashore. Thereupon, they bathed, anointed themselves, ate, and played ball. The princess, throwing the ball to one of her handmaidens, missed her target. The ball fell into the rapidly flowing river; the girls shrieked loudly and awakened Odysseus.

From this we learn that the spot in the bushes near the mouth of the river where Odysseus camped was right next to the washing troughs and the bank of the river where the girls played ball.

No doubt remains that this is the river that Homer described, since it is the only river near the old city. Actually there is only one other river on the whole island but that is twelve kilometers from the old city of Corcyra. In antiquity there was doubtlessly a road from the old city to the washing troughs. Now the fields are all cultivated and no trace of this road remains. For eleven francs I rented a small sailboat to take me to Ithaca. Unfortunately the wind was against us so we were constantly forced to tack. As a result, it took six hours for a trip which, with a more favorable wind, could have easily been made in one. Finally, at eleven o'clock that night, we alighted at the little harbor of St. Spiridon, on the southern side of Mt. Athos, and entered the old kingdom of Odysseus.

I confess that, in spite of being tired and hungry, I felt a boundless joy at being in the fatherland of the hero whose adventures I have read again and again with the most lively interest.

I was very fortunate to meet the miller Panagis Asproieraka as I got out of the boat. For four francs he rented me a donkey to carry my luggage while he served as my cicerone until we got to Vathy, the capital city. When he heard that I had come to Ithaca to begin archaeological explorations, the miller spoke of my plans with animated approval and, as we went along, told me all about Odysseus' adventures from beginning to end. The ease with which he told this story made it clear to me that he had already told the same story a thousand times. The zeal with which he told me about the glorious deeds of the king of Ithaca was so great that he would not let me interrupt him. In vain I asked him: Is this Mt. Athos? Is this the Phorkys' harbor? On which side is the Nymphs' Grotto? Where is Laertes' field . . . ? All of my questions went unanswered. The way was long but the miller's story was long as well. When we finally crossed the threshold of his home in Vathy at half after midnight, he had just reached the underworld along with the souls of the suitors, led by Mercury.

I congratulated him heartily for having read and remembered Homer's poems so well, and for being able to retell the main events of the twenty-four cantos of the *Odyssey* so fluently in modern Greek. To my great amazement he replied that not only did he not know the old Greek language, but he could neither read nor write modern Greek. He knew Odysseus' adventures only from tradition. To the question of whether everyone on Ithaca knew this tradition or if only his family knew it, he replied that in fact his family was the guardian of this tradition. No one on the island knew the story of the great king as well as he; everyone else had merely a vague idea of what it was all about.

TRANSLATED BY FREDERICK D. BOGIN

## (12) Lament on the lips of the beloved

FRIEDRICH SCHILLER, "Nänie"

When Friedrich Schiller succumbed to his severe illness in 1805, Goethe wrote in his "Epilogue to the Bell": "For behind him as mere appearance/lay that which limits us, the common." And ten years after his friend's death, Goethe added another stanza that closes "He shines before us like a comet disappearing,/ mixing infinite light with his own light."

All his life Schiller felt himself committed to the education of mankind. He was consumed by this lofty task with all the passion and splendid emotion of which his unchanging youthfulness was capable. His pedagogical mission went hand in hand with the demand that the most exalted and important task of art should consist in promoting humanity, in the commitment to human freedom, and an effort toward the realization of these ideals.

Born in 1759 in Marbach, the son of a lieutenant, Schiller had a difficult life. Although his father had planned for him to study theology, he was commanded by Duke Karl

Eugene to attend the school for the military and civil service at Castle Solitude, where he first studied law and subsequently medicine after the school was moved to Stuttgart. The boy suffered in the "soul factory and slave plantation," as it was called by Schubart. Nonetheless he found time for his own work. Anonymously inserted as a motto for his first drama, *The Robbers,* were the words, *in tyrannos* ["against tyrants"]. The elements of fury, hatred, revenge, ecstasy, and sensitivity that had petrified in the era of *Storm and Stress* were again expressed in vital gestures—almost every sentence was an indictment against the existing order, a document of the times. After years of flight, the poet found some peace at the University of Jena in 1789, when at Goethe's instigation he was appointed professor of history. Yet economic difficulties and illness remained with him. "From the cradle of my spirit until now when I write this," Schiller states in his response to the Danish government for having granted him an honorary stipendium for three years, "I have struggled with fate, and since the time that I have been able to value intellectual freedom I have been condemned to do without it."

Schiller's "heroic formalism," which for him was the expression of a sublime attitude (for materiality is overcome in the "drive toward form" and gravity of life is mastered), is expressed in his poem "Nänie." According to Thomas Mann in his "Essay on Schiller" (1955), Schiller cannot be accused of aestheticism. "Work on the spirit of the nation, on its morality and education, its spiritual freedom, its intellectual *niveau* that placed it in a position to preserve [the idea] that others living under various historic presuppositions, under a different system of ideas and with different social justice are also human beings; work on mankind for whom propriety and order, justice and freedom are desired instead of mutual defamation, wanton lies, and venomous hate—this is not flight from reality into the idly beautiful: it is service that preserves life, it is the will to cure life by spiritual liberation from anxiety and hatred."

Beauty also must perish! It masters both men and immortals,
    But does not pierce the brazen breast of the stygian Zeus.
Once only did ardor soften the ruler of shadows,
    And just at the threshold, sternly, he called back his gift.
Aphrodite will not soothe the wound of the beautiful youngster,
    So horribly gouged by the boar in his delicate flesh.
Nor will the immortal mother rescue her heavenly hero,
    When he, falling at the gates of Scaeus, fulfills his fate.
But she rises from the sea with all the daughters of Nereus,
    And begins the lament of her glorified son.
Look you! The gods are now weeping, all the goddesses weeping,
    That beauty should perish, that perfection should die.
To be a lament on the lips of the beloved is glorious also,
    For what is common sinks downward to Orcus unheard.

TRANSLATED BY GEORGE F. PETERS

## (13) Classical form

CONRAD FERDINAND MEYER, "The Roman Fountain"

The poetry of Conrad Ferdinand Meyer (1825–1898) manifests an outspoken sense of "scenery" and "gesture." Meyer proves to be the first actual symbolist in German poetry. Image and feeling interact to achieve valid meaning. His poetry is primarily inspired by visual art and landscapes. "Musicality recedes behind the extremely dense, balanced, and terse pictorial and tectonic elements. The conscious achievement of such tectonic-symbolic imagist poems, culminating in the "Roman Fountain," is not immediately compelling but rather preserves the relationship of the work of art and of the imperturbable onlooker in a manner quite different from the song or from the Goethean monologue of feeling." (Heinz Otto Bürger)

Upshoots the stream and falling fills
The marble basin's rounded bowl,
Which, brimming over, downward spills,
And fills the second basin whole;
The second gives, with surging swell,
The third its flood, until it crests,
And each bowl takes and gives as well,
    And flows and rests.

TRANSLATED BY GEORGE F. PETERS

## (14) You must put your life in order

RAINER MARIA RILKE, "Archaic Torso of Apollo"

Rainer Maria Rilke (1875–1926) has been called "Orpheus in the world of the masses." What was fascinating about him was his weakness, the stylized sensitivity that led to an incredible degree of veneration of the poet by all who perceived a special strength in "the endurance of anxiety." The feeling of being exposed permeates Rilke's work. Repeatedly an attempt is made to find support in the quest for the divine, in making visible the world beyond. "For remaining is nowhere," as it is stated in the first "Duino Elegy" (1923). In such abandonment or existential "being hurled," the task was to strengthen being-there while "singing" (just as Orpheus)—to gain strength in creating poetry and to gain strength by commitment to the rigors of form versus the pull of nothingness. Klopstock provided a caption, highest emotion, for his own era, which was in quest of a new world of feeling. Similarly Rilke became the apostle of the highest aesthetic refinement at a moment when the epoch to which he belonged was just preparing to regress into the worst barbarism. The artistic existence culminating in the nineteenth century found its last and most sublime climax in Rilke. "He wrote the verse that my generation will never forget: 'Who speaks of winning—survival is everything!' " (Gottfried Benn)

We never knew his body's marvelous crown,
in which the eyes were growing. All the same
his torso glows like a candelabra's flame,
in which his vision, at the most turned down,


endures and shines. Or else his breast's curved force
could not blind you, and in the gentle flowing
of his loins a smile would not be going
to that same center, his conception's source.


Or else this stone would stand deformed and small
under the shoulders' diaphanous fall,
not glistening like fur on beasts of prey;


and would not burst out all along its border
like a star: for all the while his torso's play
is watching you. You must put your life in order.

TRANSLATED BY GEORGE F. PETERS


## (15) Turbulent rushing

STEFAN GEORGE, "Transport"


A magnificence of style, formality, often admittedly consisting merely of "gesture" and pose, is demonstrated in the work of Stefan George (1868–1933). It emerged even before World WarI and praises the poet as the hero, as the "lofty human being," juxtaposed to the hectic industrial world, the mindless masses, and middle-class pettiness. As the proclaimer of a "new realm," George celebrates "incandescence and mystery" in which aesthetic questions decidedly took precedence over content. The "new nobility" he sought was ultimately only a further intensification of the portrayal of the human being that emerged from the classic German writer's principle of formality, which admittedly was increasingly trivialized in the course of decades, ultimately to embellish aesthetically—for example, as decorative *art nouveau*—the middle classes' flight from social responsibility. What is remarkable about George's paradigmatic distance from reality, according to Ferdinand Lion, is the consistency with which he rejects the "machine-produced hustle and bustle" and ascends "from nothingness into the most extreme freedom" in order to affect the Germans "in an exemplary manner by his attitude and to warn them insistently by poems, oracular intimations, and commands."

I feel the air from a different planet.
I see in the gloom how faces are paling
Which a moment ago turned toward me in kindness.

And trees and pathways I loved are now fading
Till I know them no more and You radiant
Beloved shadow—teller of my torment—

Are now extinguished fully in deeper blazes
In order to delight with a solemn shudder
Succeeding the frenzy of strife-filled turmoil.

Dissolving in tones · I am circling · weaving
With unfounded thanks and unnameable praises
Surrendering myself to the almighty breathing.

Through me passes a turbulent rushing
In rapturous reverence where fervently crying
Thrown down in the dust praying women are pleading.

I watch then as curtains of mist are rising
In a cloudless clearing open and sun-filled
Which enfolds only on farthest mountainous inclines.

As white and as soft as whey the ground trembles . . .
I climb across awesome abysses
Above the last cloud I feel myself swimming

In an ocean of crystalline brilliance—
Of the sacred fires I am but an ember
Of the sacred voice I am but an echo.

TRANSLATED BY GEORGE F. PETERS

## (16) Dazed and melancholy rapture

JOSEPH VON EICHENDORFF, The Marble Image

In the novella *The Marble Image* (1819) the young nobleman Florio strays into a magical garden. In a shimmering palace he encounters a beguiling marble statue transformed into a woman to whom he is in danger of succumbing. He saves himself from the confusion by a prayer: "God, don't let me go astray in this world!" Christian self-control triumphs over heathen sensuality. Maria endures against Venus.

Thus he finally decided to return to the pond and hastily set out on the same path he had taken the night before.

But how different everything now looked there! Cheerful people were busily rushing to and fro in the vineyards, gardens and roadways; children were quietly playing on the sunny lawns in front of those same cottages which, the night before, had struck him as frightening, sleeping sphinxes beneath the nightmarish trees. The moon shone distant and pale in the clear sky; in the forest countless birds were singing in happy confusion. He now could not even conceive of how he could have been so overcome by a strange fright here.

After a while he noticed, however, that while absorbed in thought he had taken a wrong turn. He carefully looked around him and then uncertainly went at first back and then ahead again. The more fervidly he searched, the more foreign and completely different everything looked.

He had been thus wandering around for some time. The birds had already fallen silent, the circle of hills became ever stiller, the rays of the noonday sun scorchingly shimmered across the entire area beyond, which seemed to be slumbering and dreaming beneath a sultry veil of heat. Presently he unexpectedly came upon a wrought-iron gate, through the finely gilded bars of which he could see a lovely large garden. A current of refreshingly cool and fragrant air blew over the exhausted Florio from within. The gate was not locked; he quickly opened it and walked in.

Tall rows of beech trees greeted him there with their welcome shade, in which golden birds now and then swooped like falling blossoms while strange, large flowers, the likes of which Florio had never seen, dreamily nodded their yellow and red heads in the light breeze. Countless fountains, on which golden balls were bobbing, splashed in unison in the vast solitude. Between the trees he could see shimmering in the distance a magnificent palace with tall, slender pillars. Not a soul was to be seen anywhere; a profound silence reigned. Only now and then did a nightingale awaken to sing as if almost sobbing in its slumber. In amazement, Florio observed the trees, fountains and flowers; it seemed to him that all this had long since been submerged, and that the stream of time was flowing over him in light, clear waves, with only the garden spread out below him, transfixed and enchanted, dreaming of the life past.

He had not proceeded very far when he heard the tones of a lute, at times louder, at times softly disappearing beneath the splashing of the fountains. He stopped and listened; the sound came ever closer, until suddenly in the still colonnade a tall, slender woman of wondrous beauty stepped out from between the trees, walking slowly and without looking up. On her arm she carried a splendid lute, decorated with pictures in gold, on which, apparently deeply absorbed in thought, she struck occasional chords. Her long golden hair fell in copious curls over her nearly naked, blindingly white shoulders and down her back. Her long, flowing sleeves, seemingly woven out of snow-blossoms, were fastened with ornate golden clasps. Her beautiful body was enveloped in a sky-blue dress embroidered at the edges with colorfully glowing, marvelously entwined flowers. Just then a bright ray of sun broke through an opening in the colonnade and shone directly on the radiant figure. Florio experienced a profound shock—he recognized unmistakably the traits, the figure of the beautiful Venus statue he had seen the night before at the pond. She, however, commenced to sing, without noticing the stranger:

> Why must you, Spring, awaken me once more?
> With every ancient longing reoccurring,
> Across the land a wondrous wind is stirring;
> It sweetly sends its shivers through my core.
>
> A thousand songs receive the radiant mother,
> Who, young again, with bridal wreath stands glowing;
> The woods would speak, and lulling streams are flowing,
> While swimming naiads sing to one another.
>
> I see the rose escape its green bud's swelling,
> And how the amorous breezes gently weaving
> To Spring's mild air their blushing warmth are bringing.
>
> So thus you call me, too, to leave my dwelling—
> And I must smiling enter Spring though grieving,
> In longing lost amidst the fragrant ringing.

This singing, she walked away, at times disappearing in the foliage, at times reappearing, ever more distant, until he finally lost sight of her completely in the vicinity of the palace. Now it was suddenly still again; only the trees and fountains were murmuring as before. Florio stood still, lost in vivid dreams; it seemed to him that he had long known the beautiful lute player but had forgotten and lost track of her amidst the distractions of his life; as if she were now drowning in melancholy among the splashing fountains and ceaselessly beckoning him to follow her.

Profoundly moved, he hurried farther into the garden, toward the place where she had disappeared. There beneath the ancient trees he came upon the ruins of a wall, upon which here and there beautiful carvings were still visible. Stretched out beside the wall on fragments of marble stones and capitals, between which tall grass and luxurious flowers had grown up, a man lay sleeping. Amazed, Florio recognized the knight Donati. But his features seemed strangely altered in sleep; he looked like he was dead. A sudden shudder ran through Florio at the sight. He violently shook the sleeping man. Slowly Donati opened his eyes, and his initial look was so strange, vacant and wild that Florio was properly horrified. At the same time, half awake and half asleep, he mumbled several mystifying words which Florio did not understand. Once he had finally fully come to his senses, he quickly jumped up and looked at Florio with what seemed to be great amazement. "Where am I?" Florio hastily asked; "Who is the noble lady living in this beautiful garden?" "How did you get into this garden?" Donati gravely asked by way of response. Florio briefly related the course of events, whereupon the knight fell into deep thought. The youth then urgently repeated his previous questions, and Donati responded, preoccupied, "The lady is a relative of mine, rich and powerful; her estate is spread throughout the land—You will find her at times here, at times there—Occasionally she stays in the town of Lucca." Florio took these hastily spoken words curiously to heart, for now what had previously only fleetingly occurred to him became ever clearer; namely, that he had seen the lady somewhere before during his earlier youth, although he was by no means able to remember anything exactly.

Having walked rapidly, they had in the meantime unknowingly reached the gilded wrought-iron gate of the garden. It was not the same one through which Florio had previously entered. In amazement he looked around him at the strange landscape; far beyond the fields the towers of the city gleamed in the bright sunlight. Donati's horse stood hitched to the gate, snorting and pawing the earth.

Florio now timidly expressed his desire to see the beautiful mistress of the garden again in the future. Donati, who up to this point had still been absorbed in thought, seemed only now to come to his senses. "The lady," he said with his usual, measured politeness, "will be happy to make your acquaintance. Today, however, we would be disturbing her, and I, too, am called home on urgent business. Perhaps I will be able to pick you up tomorrow." And thereupon he took leave of the youth with polite words, mounted his horse, and had soon disappeared into the hills.

Thus lost in thought Florio continued on his way, until he unexpectedly came upon a large pond surrounded by high trees. The moon, which was just rising over the tree tops, clearly illuminated a marble statue of Venus standing on a pedestal so close to the water's edge that it appeared as if the goddess had just emerged from the waves and was now, herself entranced, observing in the drunken mirror of the water's surface the image of her own beauty reflected among the stars shining up from the bottom. Several swans were silently gliding in uniform circles about the statue; a quiet rustling stirred the trees all around.

Florio stood watching as if rooted in place, for the statue reminded him of a beloved he had long sought and now suddenly recognized, like a wondrous flower grown up out of the awakening spring and dreamy solitude of his earliest youth. The longer he watched, the more it seemed to him that the statue was slowly opening its soulful eyes, that the lips were trying to form a greeting, that life was spreading its warmth like a lovely song throughout her beautiful limbs. Overcome with a dazed and melancholy rapture he kept his eyes closed for a long time.

When he looked up again, everything seemed to have suddenly changed. The moon shone strangely from between the clouds, a stronger wind was stirring up dark waves across the pond, and from out of an infinite stillness the Venus statue looked at him almost frighteningly with her stony, hollow eyes. A never-before experienced feeling of horror overcame the youth and, faster and faster, without pausing, he hurried away through the gardens and vineyards toward the quiet town; for even the rustling of the trees now struck him as clearly intelligible whispering, and the tall, ghostly poplars seemed to be reaching after him with their lengthy shadows.

Thus visibly distraught he reached the inn. His friend was still lying at the doorstep sleeping and started up in fright as Florio rushed past him. Florio, however, quickly slammed the door behind him, and only after he had reached his room upstairs did he breathe freely again. He paced up and down for a long time before calming himself. Then he threw himself onto the bed and finally fell into a troubled, dream-filled sleep . . .

TRANSLATED BY GEORGE F. PETERS

## (17) Dream and intoxication

FRIEDRICH NIETZSCHE, The Birth of Tragedy
(or, Hellenism and Pessimism)

In the *Twilight of the Idols* Friedrich Nietzsche stated he had always been protected by the psychologist within himself from such "lofty simplicity," actually a *niaiserie allemande,* as sniffing out "beautiful souls," "golden means," and other Greek perfections and from admiring in them some quiet greatness, ideal attitude, or high simplicity. "I saw their strongest instinct, the will to power; I saw them trembling before the irrepressible force of this drive; I saw all their institutions as growing from measures whose purpose was to protect each other against their internal explosive substance." *The Birth of Tragedy* (1872) was his first reevaluation of all values: "In doing so, I again stand on the ground from which my desire and ability grow—I, the last disciple of the philosopher Dionysus—I, the teacher of the eternal return."

Nietzsche, the son of a Protestant pastor, was born in 1844. In 1869 he became professor of classical philology in Basel; and in 1879 an independent author. In Turin in 1880 he became insane. When he died in 1900, he left behind "the most comprehensive diary of a soul, the most open confession, the most merciless journal (merciless even to the point of lack of shame) that was ever written. From *The Birth of Tragedy* until the convolutions of the eighties: a sum of self-interpretations. This is not a philosophy that is being developed; it is a person speaking his mind, initially as an aesthete, then as a scientist, ultimately as a prophet." (Walter Jens)

With the advent of Nietzsche the German spirit had a thinker who suffered from his era and who articulated his suffering passionately and ecstatically. This was a German who hated Germany; a man reared in middle-class prudishness who was made neurotically delicate by women; a man consuming himself in anxiety, committing himself to force out of his weakness, knowing how to sublimate suffering by knowledge. "The contrasts to which he was subject, the contrast of aesthetic-religious and social-ethical impulses, substantial and functional values is the conflict of our era, and in some way we all must go through it. No philosopher can be of more support, provide better protection against lack of restraint and weakliness, everything that is only half and mean! Admittedly no one makes life so difficult for us." (Theodor Lessing)

We shall have gained much for the science of aesthetics once we perceive not merely by logical inference, but with the immediate certainty of vision, that the continuous development of art is bound up with the *Apollonian* and *Dionysian* duality—just as procreation depends on the duality of the sexes, involving perpetual strife with only periodically intervening reconciliations. The terms Dionysian and Apollonian we borrow from the Greeks, who disclose to the discerning mind the profound mysteries of their view of art, not, to be sure, in concepts, but in the intensely clear figures of their gods. Through Apollo and Dionysus, the two art deities of the Greeks, we come to recognize that in the Greek world there existed a tremendous opposition, in origin and aims, between the Apollonian art of sculpture, and the nonimagistic, Dionysian art of music. These two different tendencies run parallel to each other, for the most part openly at variance; and they continually incite each other to new and more powerful births, which perpetuate an antagonism, only superficially reconciled by the common term "art"; till eventually, by a metaphysical miracle of the Hellenic "will," they appear coupled with each other, and through this coupling ultimately generate an equally Dionysian and Apollonian form of art—Attic tragedy.

In order to grasp these two tendencies, let us first conceive of them as the separate art worlds of *dreams* and *intoxication*. These physiological phenomena present a contrast analogous to that existing between the Apollonian and the Dionysian. It was in dreams, says Lucretius, that the glorious divine figures first appeared to the souls of men; in dreams the great shaper beheld the splendid bodies of superhuman beings; and the Hellenic poet, if questioned about the mysteries of poetic inspiration, would likewise have suggested dreams and he might have given an explanation like that of Hans Sachs in the *Meistersinger:*

> The poet's task is this, my friend
> to read his dreams and comprehend.
> The truest human fancy seems
> to be revealed to us in dreams:
> all poems and versification
> are but true dreams' interpretation

The beautiful illusion of the dream worlds, in the creation of which every man is truly an artist, is the prerequisite of all plastic art, and, as we shall see, of an important part of poetry also. In our dreams we delight in the immediate understanding of figures; all forms speak to us: there is nothing unimportant or superfluous. But even when this dream reality is most intense, we still have, glimmering through it, the sensation that it is *mere appearance:* at least this is my experience, and for its frequency—indeed, normality—I could adduce many proofs, including the sayings of the poets.

Philosophical men even have a presentiment that the reality in which we live and have our being is also mere appearance, and that another, quite different reality lies beneath it. Schopenhauer actually indicates as the criterion of philosophical ability the occasional ability to view men and things as mere phantoms or dream images. Thus the aesthetically sensitive man stands in the same relation to the reality of dreams as the philosopher does to the reality of existence; he is a close and willing observer, for these images afford him an interpretation of life, and by reflecting on these processes he trains himself for life.

It is not only the agreeable and friendly images that he experiences as something universally intelligible: the serious, the troubled, the sad, the gloomy, the sudden restraints, the tricks of accident, anxious expectations, in short, the whole divine comedy of life, including the inferno, also pass before him, not like mere shadows on a wall—for he lives and suffers with these scenes—and yet not without that fleeting sensation of illusion. And perhaps many will, like myself, recall how amid the dangers and terrors of dreams they have occasionally said to themselves in self-encouragement, and not without success: "It is a dream! I will dream on!" I have likewise heard of people who were able to continue one and the same dream for three and even more successive nights—facts which indicate clearly how our innermost being, our common ground, experiences dreams with profound delight and a joyous necessity.

This joyous necessity of the dream experience has been embodied by the Greeks in their Apollo: Apollo, the god of all plastic energies, is at the same time the soothsaying god. He, who (as the etymology of the name indicates) is the "shining one," the deity of light, is also ruler over the beautiful illusion of the inner world of fantasy. The higher truth, the perfection of these states in contrast to the incompletely intelligible everyday world, this deep consciousness of nature, healing and helping in sleep and dreams, is at the same time the symbolical analogue of the soothsaying faculty and of the arts generally, which make life possible and worth living. But we must also include in our image of Apollo that delicate boundary which the dream image must not overstep lest it have a pathological effect (in which case mere appearance would deceive us as if it were crude reality). We must keep in mind that measured restraint, that freedom from the wilder emotions, that calm of the sculptor god. His eye must be "sunlike," as befits his origin; even when it is angry and distempered it is still hallowed by beautiful illusion. And so, in one sense, we might apply to Apollo the words of Schopenhauer when he speaks of the man wrapped in the veil of *māyā:* "Just as in a stormy sea that, unbounded in all directions, raises and drops mountainous waves, howling, a sailor sits in a boat and trusts in his frail bark: so in the midst of a world of torments the individual human being sits quietly, supported by and trusting in the *principium individuationis.*" In fact, we might say of Apollo that in him the unshaken faith in this *principium* and the calm repose of the man wrapped up in it receive their most sublime expression; and we might call Apollo himself the glorious divine image of the *principium individuationis,* through whose gestures and eyes all the joy and wisdom of "illusion," together with its beauty, speak to us.

In the same work Schopenhauer has depicted for us the tremendous *terror* which seizes man when he is suddenly dumfounded by the cognitive form of phenomena because the principle of sufficient reason, in some one of its manifestations, seems to suffer an exception. If we add to this terror the blissful ecstasy that wells from the innermost depths of man, indeed of nature, at this collapse of the *principium individuationis,* we steal a glimpse into the nature of the *Dionysian,* which is brought home to us most intimately by the analogy of intoxication.

Either under the influence of the narcotic draught, of which the songs of all primitive men and peoples speak, or with the potent coming of spring that penetrates all nature with joy, these Dionysian emotions awake, and as they grow in intensity everything subjective vanishes into complete self-forgetfulness. In the German Middle Ages, too, singing and dancing crowds, ever increasing in number, whirled themselves from place to place under this same Dionysian impulse. In these dancers of St. John and St. Vitus, we rediscover the Bacchic choruses of the Greeks, with their prehistory in Asia Minor, as far back as Babylon and the orgiastic Sacaea. There are some who, from obtuseness or lack of experience, turn away from such phenomena as from "folk-diseases," with contempt or pity born of the consciousness of their own "healthy-mindedness." But of course such poor wretches have no idea how corpselike and ghostly their so-called "healthy-mindedness" looks when the glowing life of the Dionysian revelers roars past them.

Under the charm of the Dionysian not only is the union between man and man reaffirmed, but nature, which has become alienated, hostile, or subjugated, celebrates once more her reconciliation with her lost son, man. Freely, earth proffers her gifts, and peacefully the beasts of prey of the rocks and desert approach. The chariot of Dionysus is covered with flowers and garlands; panthers and tigers walk under its yoke. Transform Beethoven's "Hymn to Joy" into a painting; let your imagination conceive the multitudes bowing to the dust, awestruck—then you will approach the Dionysian. Now the slave is a free man; now all the rigid, hostile barriers that necessity, caprice, or "impudent convention" have fixed between man and man are broken. Now, with the gospel of universal harmony, each one feels himself not only united, reconciled, and fused with his neighbor, but as one with him, as if the veil of *māyā* had been torn aside and were now merely fluttering in tatters before the mysterious primordial unity.

In song and in dance man expresses himself as a member of a higher community; he has forgotten how to walk and speak and is on the way toward flying into the air, dancing. His very gestures express enchantment. Just as the animals now talk, and the earth yields milk and honey, supernatural sounds emanate from him, too: he feels himself a god, he himself now walks about enchanted, in ecstasy, like the gods he saw walking in his dreams. He is no longer an artist, he has become a work of art: in these paroxysms of intoxication the artistic power of all nature reveals itself to the highest gratification of the primordial unity. The noblest clay, the most costly marble, man, is here kneaded and cut, and to the sound of the chisel strokes of the Dionysian world-artist rings out the cry of the Eleusinian mysteries: "Do you prostrate yourselves, millions? Do you sense your Maker, world?"

TRANSLATED BY WALTER KAUFMANN

## (18) Sweet night of love

THOMAS MANN, Tristan

Elegy on the middle class, critique of the middle class: these complex themes are united in the works of Thomas Mann (1875–1955). He was certainly of the conviction that humanity was the "German middle, the beautiful-human of which our best have dreamed." Thomas Mann used this "pathos of the middle" for the first time in 1901 when he portrayed the German middle class in *Buddenbrooks.* In his congratulatory speech for Thomas Mann's eightieth birthday Herman Hesse expressed Mann's ambivalence toward the middle class, the contradictory "simultaneity" of attraction and repulsion, sarcasm and sympathetic love, as follows: "What first called my attention to you, impressed me, and caused me to reflect were your middle class virtues, the diligence, patience and tenacity with which you applied yourself. They were middle class, Hanseatic virtues, and the less I could boast of them myself, the more they impressed me. This self-discipline and this constant, faithful dedication would have sufficed to assure you of my esteem. But more is required for love. And it was your un-middle-class liberated characteristics that won my heart—your noble irony, your keen sense of play, your courage to uprightness and to affirmation of their middle-class problems. And, not least, your pleasure as an artist in experiment and daring, in play with new forms and devices of art."

The story *Tristan* (published in 1903 in a collection of novellas under the Ibsen slogan, "To write is to sit in judgment of oneself") takes place in the Infried Sanatorium. In an atmosphere of disease and decadence, representatives of the middle class and the artistic class meet. The wholesaler Klöterjahn brings his delicate, sensitive wife, Gabriele, a kind of *femme-enfant* who has succumbed to a disease of the trachea since the birth of their child, to the sanatorium. There Gabriele encounters the writer Spinell, a conflict-ridden type who hopes to gain inner peace and recuperate. He persuades Gabriele to play the piano. During a patients' sledding party, she and Spinell stay behind and she performs excerpts from the piano score of Wagner's *Tristan and Isolde*. After this her condition deteriorates. Gabriele dies, as Spinell expresses it, "proudly and blissfully from beauty's lethal kiss." In this novella Thomas Mann criticizes both bourgeois materialistic dullness as well as the artistic aestheticism that is hostile to life. He shows the tension between an art that is alienated from life and a middle class that acts without reflecting, either disdaining art or using it merely as a facade.

"Well, then, in God's name, I will play one," said she. "But only one—do you hear? In any case, one will do you, I am sure."

With which she got up, laid aside her work, and went to the piano. She seated herself on the music-stool, on a few bound volumes, arranged the lights, and turned over the notes. Herr Spinell had drawn up a chair and sat beside her, like a music-master.

She played the Nocturne in E major, opus 9, number 2. If her playing had really lost very much then she must originally have been a consummate artist. The piano was mediocre, but after the first few notes she learned to control it. She displayed a nervous feeling for modulations of timbre and a joy in mobility of rhythm that amounted to the fantastic. Her attack was at once firm and soft. Under her hands the very last drop of sweetness was wrung from the melody; the embellishments seemed to cling with slow grace about her limbs.

She wore the same frock as on the day of her arrival, the dark, heavy bodice with the velvet arabesques in high relief, that gave her head and hands such an unearthly fragile look. Her face did not change as she played, but her lips seemed to become more clear-cut, the shadows deepened at the corners of her eyes. When she finished she laid her hands in her lap and went on looking at the notes. Herr Spinell sat motionless.

She played another Nocturne, and then a third. Then she stood up, but only to look on the top of the piano for more music.

It occurred to Herr Spinell to look at the black-bound volumes on the piano-stool. All at once he uttered an incoherent exclamation, his large white hands clutching at one of the books.

"Impossible! No, it cannot be," he said. "But yes, it is. Guess what this is—what was lying here! Guess what I have in my hands."

"What? she asked.

Mutely he showed her the title-page. He was quite pale; he let the book sink and looked at her, his lips trembling.

"Really? How did that get here? Give it me," was all she said; set the notes on the piano and after a moment's silence began to play.

He sat beside her, bent forward, his hands between his knees, his head bowed. She played the beginning with exaggerated and tormenting slowness, with painfully long pauses between the single figures. The *Sehnsuchtsmotiv,* roving lost and forlorn like a voice in the night, lifted its trembling question. Then silence, a waiting. And lo, an answer: the same timorous, lonely note, only clearer, only tenderer. Silence again. And then, with that marvellous muted *sforzando,* like mounting passion, the love-motif came in; reared and soared and yearned ecstatically upward to its consummation, sank back, was resolved; the cellos taking up the melody to carry it on with their deep, heavy notes of rapture and despair.

Not unsuccessfully did the player seek to suggest the orchestral effects upon the poor instrument at her command. The violin runs of the great climax rang out with brilliant precision. She played with a fastidious reverence, lingering on each figure, bringing out each detail, with the self-forgotten concentration of the priest who lifts the Host above his head. Here two forces, two beings, strove towards each other, in transports of joy and pain; here they embraced and became one in delirious yearning after eternity and the absolute. . . . The prelude flamed up and died away. She stopped at the point where the curtains part, and sat speechless, staring at the keys.

But the boredom of Frau Spatz had by now reached that pitch where it distorts the countenance of man, makes the eyes protrude from the head, and lends the features a corpse-like and terrifying aspect. More than that, this music acted on the nerves that controlled her digestion, producing in her dyspeptic organism such *malaise* that she was really afraid she would have an attack.

"I shall have to go up to my room," she said weakly. "Goodbye; I will come back soon."

She went out. Twilight was far advanced. Outside the snow fell thick and soundlessly upon the terrace. The two tapers cast a flickering, circumscribed light.

"The Second Act," he whispered, and she turned the pages and began.

What was it dying away in the distance—the ring of a horn? The rustle of leaves? The rippling of a brook? Silence and night crept up over grove and house; the power of longing had full sway, no prayers or warnings could avail against it. The holy mystery was consummated. The light was quenched; with a strange clouding of the timbre the death-motif sank down: white-veiled desire, by passion driven, fluttered towards love as through the dark it groped to meet her.

Ah, boundless, unquenchable exultation of union in the eternal beyond! Freed from torturing error, escaped from fettering space and time, the Thou and the I, the Thine and the Mine at one forever in a sublimity of bliss! The day might part them with deluding show; but when night fell, then by the power of the potion they would see clear. To him who has looked upon the night of death and known its secret sweets, to him day never can be aught but vain, nor can he know a longing save for night, eternal, real, in which he is made one with love.

O night of love, sink downwards and enfold them, grant them the oblivion they crave, release them from this world of partings and betrayals. Lo, the last light is quenched. Fancy and thought alike are lost, merged in the mystic shade that spread its wings of healing above their madness and despair. "Now, when deceitful daylight pales, when my raptured eye grows dim, then all that from which the light of day would shut my sight, seeking to blind me with false show, to the stanchless torments of my longing soul—then, ah, then, O wonder of fulfillment, even then I am the world!" Followed Brangäna's dark notes of warning, and then those soaring violins so higher than all reason.

"I cannot understand it all, Herr Spinell. Much of it I only divine. What does it mean, this 'even then I am the world'?"

He explained, in a few low-toned words.

"Yes, yes. It means that. How is it you can understand it all so well, yet cannot play it?"

Strangely enough, he was not proof against this simple question. He colored, twisted his hands together, shrank into his chair.

"The two things seldom happen together," he wrung from his lips at last. "No, I cannot play. But go on."

And on they went, into the intoxicated music of the love-mystery. Did love ever die? Tristan's love? The love of thy Isolde, and of mine? Ah, no, death cannot touch that which can never die—and what of him could die, save what distracts and tortures love and severs united lovers? Love joined the two in sweet conjunction, death was powerless to sever such a bond, save only when death was given to one with the very life of the other. Their voices rose in mystic unison, rapt in the wordless hope of that death-in-love, of endless oneness in the wonder-kingdom of the night. Sweet night! Eternal night of love! And all-encompassing land of rapture! Once envisaged or divined, what eye could bear to open again on desolate dawn? Forfend such fears, most gentle death! Release these lovers quite from need of waking. Oh, tumultuous storm of rhythms! Oh, glad chromatic upward surge of metaphysical perception! How find, how bind this bliss so far remote from parting's torturing pangs? Ah, gentle glow of longing, soothing and kind, ah, yielding sweet-sublime, ah, raptured sinking into the twilight of eternity! Thou Isolde, Tristan I, yet no more Tristan, no more Isolde. . . .

All at once something startling happened. The musician broke off and peered into the darkness with her hand above her eyes. Herr Spinell turned round quickly in his chair. The corridor door had opened, a sinister form appeared, leant on the arm of a second form. It was a guest of Einfried, one of those who, like themselves, had been in no state to undertake the sleigh-ride, but had passed this twilight hour in one of her pathetic, instinctive rounds of the house. It was that patient who had borne fourteen children and was no longer capable of a single thought; it was Frau Pastor Höhlenrauch, on the arm of her nurse. She did not look up; with groping step she paced the dim background of the room and vanished by the opposite door, rigid and still, like a lost and wandering soul. Stillness reigned once more.

"That was Frau Pastor Höhlenrauch," he said.

"Yes, that was poor Frau Höhlenrauch," she answered. Then she turned over some leaves and played the finale, played Isolde's song of love and death.

How colorless and clear were her lips, how deep the shadows lay beneath her eyes! The little pale-blue vein in her transparent brow showed fearfully plain and prominent. Beneath her flying fingers the music mounted to its unbelievable climax and was resolved in that ruthless, sudden *pianissimo* which is like having the ground glide from beneath one's feet, yet like a sinking too into the very deeps of desire. Followed the immeasurable plenitude of that vast redemption and fulfillment; it was repeated, swelled into a deafening, unquenchable tumult of immense appeasement that wove and welled and seemed about to die away, only to swell again and weave the *Sehnsuchtsmotiv* into its harmony; at length to breathe an outward breath and die, faint on the air, and soar away. Profound stillness.

They both listened, their heads on one side.

"Those are bells," she said.

"It is the sleighs," he said. "I will go now."

He rose and walked across the room. At the door he halted, then turned and shifted uneasily from one foot to the other. And then, some fifteen or twenty paces from her, it came to pass that he fell upon his knees, both knees, without a sound. His long black coat spread out on the floor. He held his hands clasped over his mouth, and his shoulders heaved.

She sat there with hands in her lap, leaning forward, turned away from the piano, and looked at him. Her face wore a distressed, uncertain smile, while her eyes searched the dimness at the back of the room, searched so painfully, so dreamily, she seemed hardly able to focus her gaze.

The jingling of sleigh-bells came nearer and nearer, there was the crack of whips, a babel of voices.

TRANSLATED BY H. T. LOWE-PORTER

# THE EARTHLY PARADISE

Friedrich Schiller wrote the letters *On the Aesthetic Education of Man* (19) in 1793, under the influence of the French Revolution. The poet welcomed the revolution as the liberation of mankind but condemned it as the perversion of the human. In his letters he states that each individual person has within himself the natural disposition and destiny to become a pure, idealistic human being. To harmonize with his unchanging unity in all its variations is the great task of the person's existence. Schiller imparts political-practical relevance to this sentence by continuing:

> This more or less clearly recognizable human being is represented in each subject by the State, which is the objective and also the canonic form that attempts to unify the diversity of subjects. Two different ways, however, can be conceived by which the temporal human being encounters the human being in the idea—hence as many as the State can assert in the individuals: either by the suppression of the empirical person by the pure human being, by the State's supression of individuals, or by the individual's becoming the State, thus enabling the temporal human being to become the human being in the idea.

Schiller's conception of the State, far removed from reality in its abstraction, is embodied in the "aesthetic State." In it, everything, even the "serving tool," is a free citizen who has the same rights as the noblest citizen, and reason, which forcefully bends to its purposes the patient masses, must here request their concurrence. This passage constitutes a central theme of the conceptual landscape of a transported world. Schiller then states, "Thus here, in the realm of aesthetic appearance, is fulfilled the ideal of equality that the fanatic would so much like to see realized in essence."

The greatness of German idealism was simultaneously its weakness. The aesthetic state where the temporal human being coincides with the human being in the idea is a state of "appearance," a state of "pre-seeming"; it is not real, and anyone who truly desires it is a fanatic.

"Actuality" is altogether present in the biographies of the poets and philosophers. But in their intellectual works "only" the "dream of a thing" is present. To fantasize the world means not to register the world in its reality. While *Sturm und Drang* addressed itself critically to its own era and society, the texts in the present work that are ordered under the heading "withdrawal" provide examples of a political and social aloofness. Even someone like Friedrich Schiller, who suffered particularly from feudal tyranny in his lifetime, hardly refers at all to the historical era in his poetry and philosophical writings. The earthly paradise is placed in an intellectually and spiritually stimulating aesthetic, ideal landscape, but it is a landscape without actuality. The great tenacity of social forces in Germany during the first half of the nineteenth century (where, unlike elsewhere in Western Europe, the nobility displayed extraordinary vitality in political leadership while the bourgeoisie remained behind as a possible elite, industrialization slowly got started, and where restoration and reaction became strongly entrenched following the euphoria of the Wars of Liberation) contributed significantly to the endurance of the "spiritual realm," largely pure superstructure, without reference to the political, social, and economic infrastructure. In an astonishing manner, the unfolding of moral forces was completely detached from real-life conditions. In this withdrawn world there is neither suffering from war nor social anxiety, neither epidemics of illnesses nor economic failure. Everything is at rest; nowhere and at no time is there is any movement. To be sure, the idea of utopia sometime and somewhere is implied. Heinrich Heine, who himself fantasized the world but also continually explored its reality, expressed disdain: "And if you were forbidden everything, don't be too gloomy; after all, you have Schiller and Goethe, so go to sleep. What else do you want?"

For the classical and Romantic eras and even into the late Biedermeier period, withdrawal determined the basic theme of the lost paradise that had to be rediscovered. At the beginning of the nineteenth century two historical epochs, antiquity and the Christian Middle Ages, were primarily cited as the paradisiacal epochs. The artist, who needed historical moorings, perceived in both eras an ideal situation of the unity of life, the essence of a truly artistic civilization—in a word, the esthetic State. Both the paradise of antiquity and that of the Middle Ages contain an artistic profession of faith in the primordial.

The dreams of a golden age are hence both conservative and revolutionary in origin. They are dreams of a forward-oriented and of a backward-oriented utopia—dreams of the

> . . . active appropriation of the world, of inactive pleasure, recollections of a peaceful state of nature and of visions clearly characterized by sympathy for a civilizing community. The socialistic utopias laud the actively planned achievement of human happiness. The subjective dreams of happiness are content with arbitrary, individual abandon; their escape worlds imitate the legendary excesses of antiquity. The devotees of a belief in reason hope for an enlightened rebirth of an old, untroubled condition of mankind. Their opponents, repelled by the bustle of civilization, seek the natural, basic existence of exotic worlds. Conjuring belief in the past according to preference—antiquity, the Middle Ages, or the Renaissance—the spokesmen of the present proclaim the actively acquired, classless paradise of mankind. (Werner Hofmann)

Utopian features are predominant even where portrayals of an "earthly paradise" are provided with a political background. There was a cosmopolitan attitude, yet Europe was commanded to participate in a religious vision (as in Novalis). The resulting "Catholicity" was admittedly alien to everything dogmatic and moral.

> Novalis sees the guarantor of peace in Europe in the recognition of a common religious conviction rather than in the rational idea of a balance of power favored by the politicians of enlightened absolutism, as indicated in the following passage: "Does it not seem to him that the revolutionary is like Sisyphus? He has now attained the maximum equilibrium and the heavy burden is already rolling down the other side. It will never remain on top unless held afloat at that height by the magnetism of heaven." Novalis altogether has an eye for the historical developments of his era as well as for the deficiencies of political solutions offered for the guidance of the hopeless development: "The old and the new worlds," he states, "are set upon battle; the inadequacy and deficiency of the institutions of the state have thus far been revealed in dreadful phenomena. . . . It is not possible to make peace among fighting powers; all peace is mere illusion, merely an armistice; from the standpoint of the cabinet members, no unification of a shared consciousness is conceivable." He prescribed religion as the cure for a sick Europe: "Only religion can reawaken Europe and assure the peoples." The contours of the new religion were already emerging, according to Novalis. Novalis prefers his religious concept, which remains vague, to be understood more in terms of poetry or theology than as an immediate pragmatic solution to political problems. Hence his speech ends with a reference to sometime as the beginning of the new religion: "Do not ask when and

again when. Just have patience—the heavenly era of eternal peace will come; the time must come when the new Jerusalem will be the capital of the world." (Paul Michael Lützeler)

This eschatalogical, expectant mood of exaltation is symptomatic of the withdrawal that characterizes the longed-for earthly paradise. So, too, the paintings of Caspar David Friedrich. Even their dramatic, dangerous scenes appear singularly serene and ethereal. In its details, the paradise offers an altogether terrestrial appearance, but this terrestriality is "located" in no real time and in no real space.

The route to paradise seems long, but the enthusiasm becomes tenuous over the long stretches before the last chapter in the history of the world can be written. Allowance is made for the cunning of the idea. "Paradise is locked and the cherub is behind us; we must make the journey around the world and see whether there is perhaps an opening from the rear," as it is stated in Heinrich von Kleist's essay *On the Marionette Theater* (20). Kleist's earthly paradise consists of a new form of inner self-assurance; it is a place of personal totality where charm and grace are no longer menaced by a reflecting consciousness. The marionette is no longer the symbol of the mechanical and inhuman. On the contrary, it is the essence of an unconsciously natural behavior, a mythical code for self-contained existence.

And everything is good, which mainly means security in love (21). Blessedness, consecration, being available for one another, a passion that raises itself to ecstatic heights, a glowing eros oscillating between corporeality and spirituality constitutes paradisiacal hope (22). And ultimately, "paradise" means senseful order, a community whose preindustrial guild and family structures reflect complete harmony. "Order" is the basic pattern of Adalbert Stifter's novel, *Indian Summer* (23), not order, though, in the sense of rigid, prescribed conditions but as an utterly sublime and intelligible structure for action, as an absolutely ritualistic activity of exchange, of accommodation to one another, of sacrifice, of presentation. "The doors were open so it was possible to look through all the rooms. The objects were appropriate, the walls were decorated with numerous paintings, books were in glass cases, musical instruments were available and flowers were appropriately placed on stands. Through the windows could be seen the nearby landscape and the distant mountain range." Such a view as this—of the landscape through doors, rooms, windows—is comparable to a geometrical composition in which separate elements merge into each other in harmonious transparency. The crystalline structure is not subject to any Baroque deviation, and the frequently monotonous linearity is unvarying. Yet the glow of reassurance is the reflection of flickering unrest: panicky summer is turning into autumnal chill. The radiation of passion is transfigured by fall. The extensions of feelings are arranged into a cheerful spectrum by the prism of reflection, passion "catches itself" by ordering itself into the lattice-work of custom and morality. Compelling desires are figuratively quieted; impetuosity strengthens itself for support and takes root as self-control. Movement is restricted. External events show what is to be understood by "agitated peace" and "peaceful movement":

> Mathilde stood up and made a friendly bow toward us. The others did so, too, and so did we toward Mathilde and the others. Afterwards people sat down again . . . People slowly moved forward, remained standing first here, then there, observed this and that, conferred, then moved on, dividing into groups and then uniting again . . . I saw her shimmering forth among the others in her light blue silk dress, then again I did not see her, and then I saw her once again. Then the shrubbery concealed her completely.

All these figurations, apart from their initially sentimental or priggish-sounding stiffness, must be read structurally, so to speak. They are patterns of order in which the people "harvest" their feelings and passions, attitudes and efforts, disappointments and sufferings, and restylize them into composure. These figurations reflect man's attempt to limit and thereby protect himself, to find support in the face of chaos, to become at home in what has been cultivated, furnished, and parcelled out; ceremoniousness contains and bears form; the external enactment of politeness somehow implies respect for the uniqueness of the other person.

In two areas above all, objectivity and nature, the effort toward security becomes clear: both areas are the expression of the simple life that finds support in the innocence of things and in vegetative reality. Hebbel's rebuke to Stifter in an epigram, ". . . that you might excellently convey the small, nature wisely withheld the larger from you . . . ," fails to recognize that the small always refers to the large and that existence always refers to being. By the careful and cultivated daily use of things, the objects are recognized in their particularity and uniqueness, and their essence, which is in contrast to their superficial usage, becomes clear. The issue is a process of discerningly taking possession of things, a process of seeking essence and truth in objects.

If only we were in order ourselves, we would have much more pleasure in the things of this earth. But if an excess of wishes and desires is present in us, we never listen to anything else and are unable to comprehend the innocence of things outside ourselves. Unfortunately we consider it important if objects of our passion are at issue and unimportant if the objects of our passion are not involved, whereas the reverse can often be the case.

Nature is a particularly important realm for paradisiacal projections and fixations. In *Indian Summer* (23) nature is portrayed as the geometry of the garden, the chessboard pattern for the cultural landscape. It is shown against the background of marginal zones of elementary and chaotic force such as the mountain range. A medley of fields, forests, and meadows, dairies, white church steeples, streets that run through the greenery like bright stripes, clouds, mountains, the atmosphere of landscapes both by day and night, dawn and twilight, appear under the omen of an atmospheric clarity and transparency as they might be shown under a cloudless sky after a cleansing storm. The garden is the space where the vegetative and rational, culture and nature, enter into a calming alliance; the figuration of the garden as a formed content is the human being's game with nature. Trees, bushes, plants are ordered into a model of pleasingness. The view from the highest place in the garden provides both a closeup and a look into the distance, while the birds that live in the garden underline the spherical and idyllic characteristics:

> Finally we had reached the highest spot, and with it also the end of the garden. Beyond the garden, the ground sloped off gently. At this site was a very large cherry tree, the largest tree of the garden, perhaps the largest fruit tree in the vicinity. Around the trunk of the tree was a wooden bench before which were four small tables pointing toward the four directions, so it was possible to rest here and look at the surroundings or read or write. From this spot it was possible to look toward all directions of the sky. I now remembered precisely that I had probably seen this tree from the highway and from other places on my wanderings. It had appeared to me like a splendid dark point that crowned the highest place in the region. On clear days it must be possible from this point to see the entire mountain range in the south.

Such a point that discloses the horizontal, the cheerfulness of existence, is vertically anchored in the fundament of melancholy. For all efforts to become at home in what has been cultivated and furnished, in order to conquer time by distorting its course through uniformity and repetitions—all these efforts cannot prevent the figurations that offer security from turning brittle and allowing transitoriness to seep into the model of order. This is what makes *Indian Summer* a heroic attempt at the "nonetheless, or in-spite-of" (and the detailed description of the spiritual and real landscape that occurs in this novel is supposed to altogether characterize the earthly paradise of a withdrawn world!). The brilliance of late blooming is allied with resignation, as shown in the poetic picture of the roses.

For the person situated in time there is only one expectancy of being at home. The images of the earthly paradise present such an option concretely and sensuously. In this sense, Stifter felt a kinship with Goethe; and, in fact, *Wilhelm Meister's Years of Wandering,* one of Goethe's later works, takes place in the garden landscape of the humane in which man's progression to humanity takes place. Wilhelm Meister's son Felix has the opportunity of practicing all the arts in the "pedagogical province." He is also trained there in the three forms of respect that, in Goethe's view, to some extent reveal the ethical basis of the earthly paradise: respect for what is above us; respect for what is below us; respect for those who are with us ("now he stands straight and boldly, not selfishly apart; only in alliance with his peers does he resist the world").

Wilhelm Meister starts as an acting student and ends as a doctor. He separates himself from the bourgeoisie to return to the bourgeoisie via his paternity and the "group of craftsmen." But he is now protected against every form of philistinism by the route he took, which included many false turns. "Education" is the transformation of the individual into a member of a community. Such an ideal of society is specifically projected onto America, to which the "Society of Craftsmen" wishes to emigrate (24). Goethe gave his work the subtitle, "The Renouncers," an expression of his awareness that a new epoch of world history was dawning in America in which the absolute freedom of the individual was given its decisive limitation in the right of the community to life, happiness, and prosperity. That is, the new epoch meant a renunciation of individualism, which included the release of new energy and accomplishment for a changed goal.

The route to the earthly paradise took an entirely different direction than that portrayed by the images of the ideal landscape. Paradise had to be opened by the suffering of revolution, the efforts of evolution, and by the filthy work of reform. But without the visions of a withdrawn world, the forces of the real will toward change would probably not have found their direction.

The social movements of the nineteenth century were arched over by the hope for an earthly paradise where the division of labor, hence the contradiction between the interest of the separate individual or individual family and the community interest of all individuals associated with one another is overcome. The division of work, according to Karl Marx, offers the first example that, as long as people are in an unformed society— hence as long as the split between special and mutual interests exists, as long as activity is therefore not voluntary but is divided unsystemati- cally—the person's own activity will make in him an alien, opposing power; this power will subjugate him instead of the reverse. As soon as a start has been made in the division of labor, each person has a definite and exclusive area of activity that is imposed upon him and from which he cannot escape. He is and must remain a hunter, fisherman, shepherd, or critical critic, if he does not wish to lose the means to life. Under communism, on the other hand, where each person does not have an exclusive area of activity but can train in any field of his choosing, society regulates general production, thus making it possible "to do this today, to do that tomorrow, to hunt in the morning, to fish in the afternoon, to breed animals in the evening, to criticize after the meal just as I please without ever becoming a hunter, fisherman, shepherd, or critic." This is how even Karl Marx, the systematic thinker who set out to teach fear to idealism and action to the interpretive philosopher, resorts at the peak of his criticism of "German ideology" to a "fantasized" image of earthly paradise, both signaling and propagating withdrawal.

## (19) The aesthetic State

FRIEDRICH SCHILLER, On the Aesthetic Education of Man, in a
Series of Letters

The philosophical-aesthetic work entitled *On the Aesthetic Education of Man, in a Series of Letters* was written by Friedrich Schiller in 1793 and published in 1795. Drawing on, but in distinction to, the ideas of Immanuel Kant, Schiller attempted in this theory of the beautiful to locate art within the cultural development of mankind. The point of departure is a critique of the era's materialism: "Now, however, need dominates and bends oppressed mankind under its tyrannical yoke. Profit, the great idol of the time, is to be striven for by all forces, revered by all talents. The intellectual merit of art cannot tilt this crude scale and, robbed of all encouragement, vanishes from the century's noisy marketplace." The reasonable State can be prepared and politics ennobled by training the capacity for sensitivity, the central task of art. In doing so, aesthetic appearance as play has nothing to do with deception. Appearance explicitly renounces all claim on reality. The aesthetic State is the vanishing point in a twofold sense: via idealistic effort it achieves distance from a world that is completely dominated by materiality; and the aesthetic state is the goal of a utopia that some day may be capable of realizing man's potential of being totally the "playing person," a possibility already "pre-apparent" in the beautiful.

Amid the frightful realm of untrammeled forces and amid the sacred realm of laws, the aesthetic urge for education builds—unperceived—a third, cheerful realm of play and appearance, in which it releases man from the fetters of all circumstances and frees him of everything known as compulsion, in the physical as well as the moral sense.

Whereas, in the dynamic State of rights, man encounters man as a force and restricts his activities—whereas, in the ethical State of duties, he confronts him with the majesty of law and shackles his intentions, only as form is he permitted to appear in the aesthetic State, to encounter man as an object of free play in a context of beauty. To give freedom by means of freedom is the fundamental law of this realm.

The dynamic State can make society possible only by taming nature with nature; the ethical State can make society (morally) necessary only by subordinating the individual will to the general; the aesthetic State alone can make society real by carrying out the will of the whole through the nature of the individual. Even though need impels man into society, and reason plants social principles in him, beauty alone can impart a social character to him. Good taste alone brings harmony into society, because it implants harmony in the individual. All other forms of perceiving divide man, because they are based exclusively either on the sensual or the intellectual part of his being; only perceiving beautifully makes an entirety of him, because the two sides of his nature must agree in order to become one. All other forms of communication divide society, because they relate exclusively either to private receptiveness or private completeness of the individual members, and thus to that which distinguishes man from man; only a beautiful communication unites society, because it relates to that which is common to all.

We enjoy the pleasures of the senses only as individuals, without the species inherent within us participating; therefore we cannot extend our sensual pleasure to a general one, because we cannot universalize our individuality. We enjoy the pleasures of cognition only as a species, and by carefully removing every trace of the individual from our judgment: thus we cannot render our pleasures of reason general, because we cannot exclude that trace of the individual from the judgment of others as we can from our own. Beauty alone do we enjoy as individuals and as a species alike; that is, as representatives of the species. That which is sensual and good can only render one happy, since it is based upon appropriateness, which always entails some sort of exclusion; this can result in only one-sided happiness, because the personality does not take part in it. Absolute good can only bring happiness under conditions that cannot be generally presumed: for truth is only the price of renunciation, and only a pure heart believes in pure will. Beauty alone makes the whole world happy, and every creature forgets its limitations as long as it experiences the magic of beauty.

No domination, no sovereign rule, is tolerated where good taste reigns and the realm of beautiful appearance is enlarged. This realm extends upward to the point where reason dominates with absolute necessity and all matter ceases. It extends downward to where the natural impulse in blind necessity holds sway, and form has not yet begun; indeed, even at these extreme boundaries, where it is deprived of law-giving power, good taste nevertheless cannot be robbed of its power of completion. Antisocial desire must relinquish its selfishness, and whatever is pleasant, which otherwise tempts only the senses, must cast its net of grace over the spirit as well. Duty, the stern voice of Nature, must alter its reproaching formula that only resistance justifies, and honor willing Nature with a more noble confidence.

From the mysteries of science, good taste leads knowledge out under the open sky of public spirit and transforms the property of the schools into the common property of all human society. In his region, even the most powerful genius must relinquish his grandeur and descend trustingly to the mentality of a child. Power must let itself be bound by the three Graces, and the defiant lion must obey the bridle of Amor. In recompense it spreads its soothing veil over the physical need that in its naked form insults the dignity of free spirits, and conceals from us the degrading relationship with matter in a lovely illusion of freedom. Thus granted wings, even creeping art-for-hire rises from the dust, and, touched by the staff of good taste, the shackles of serfdom drop from the lifeless as well as from the living. In the esthetic State, everything, even a useful tool, is a free citizen with rights equal to those of the noblest, and reason, which bends the patient masses forcefully to its purpose, must here ask them about their role. Here, therefore, in the realm of esthetic appearance, the ideal of equality if fulfilled, which the enthusiast would so like to see realized in its essence. And if it is true that good conduct ripens earliest and most perfectly in the proximity of thrones, then here too one would have to recognize the hand of providence, which often seems to confine man to reality, only in order to drive him into an ideal world.

But does such a State of beautiful appearance exist, and where is it to be found? It exists in every finely tuned soul according to need; in actuality, though, one might find it, like the pure Church and the pure Republic, only in a few exclusive circles, where not the insipid imitation of foreign customs but rather inherent, beautiful Nature guides conduct, where man passes through the most complicated situations with bold simplicity and calm innocence, and finds it necessary neither to offend the freedom of others in order to assert his own, nor to cast away his dignity in order to display grace.

TRANSLATED BY RALPH R. READ

## (20) About the new state of innocence

HEINRICH VON KLEIST, On the Marionette Theater

Shortly before committing suicide, Heinrich von Kleist wrote to his cousin Maria von Kleist: "Oh, I assure you I am completely happy. I kneel down morning and night and pray to God, something I never was able to do. In my life, the most tortured life any person has ever lived, I can now be grateful if it is compensated by the most magnificent and debauched of all deaths." (He shot himself on November 21, 1811, in Wannsee near Berlin.) In a letter to his stepsister Ulrike, to whom he felt extremely close, he states: "The truth is that there was no help for me on earth." Kleist, born in 1777, was supposed to maintain his family's military tradition by becoming a soldier. The demands of that career were not in accord with his artistic temperament, and all his life he sought in his writing to overcome the split in his existence, the contradiction between the senuous and the reasonable world, between feeling and reason. "He himself experiences a crisis of consciousness that reflects the assailability of modern man and which at the same time lends decisiveness to the poetic word. The person's certainty and feeling perceives itself delivered up to an existence that cannot be comprehended, and subsequently experiences its tragic menace. This situation of the person recurs in his relationship to language, since only in speaking does the person have control over himself and the possibility of participating in his past existence." (Paul Böckmann)

The essay on the marionette theater (1810) attempts to clarify the relationship of life to being and to create a new openness toward fateful certainty.

One evening in M., where I was spending the winter of 1801, I met Mr. C. in a public park. He had recently been hired as the principal dancer at the opera and was enjoying immense popularity with the audiences.

I told him that I had been surprised to see him several times in a marionette theater that had been erected in the marketplace to entertain the populace with short dramatic burlesques interspersed with songs and dance.

He assured me that the pantomime of the puppets brought him much satisfaction and let it be known quite clearly that a dancer who wanted to perfect his art could learn a thing or two from them.

From the way in which he expressed himself, I could tell that it wasn't something he had just now thought up, so I sat down next to him to find out the reasons for such a remarkable claim.

He asked me if I hadn't, in fact, found some of the dance movements of the puppets, particularly of the smaller ones, very graceful.

I could not deny this. A group of four peasants dancing the rondo to a quick beat could not have been painted more delicately by Teniers.

I inquired about the mechanism of these figures. How was it possible to manipulate the individual limbs and extremities in the rhythm of movement or dance without having a myriad of strings on one's fingers?

He answered that I shouldn't imagine each limb as individually positioned and moved by the operator during various moments of the dance.

Each movement, he said, had its center of gravity: it would suffice to control this within the puppet; the limbs, which are only pendulums, follow mechanically of their own accord—without further help.

He added that this movement is very easy; whenever the center of gravity is moved in a *straight line,* the limbs describe *curves.* Often, when shaken in a rather haphazard manner, the entire puppet moves with a kind of rhythm which resembles dance.

This observation seemed to me to shed some light on the enjoyment he claimed to get from the marionette theater. But I was far from guessing the inferences which he would later draw from it.

I asked him if he thought that the operator who controlled these puppets would himself have to be a dancer or at least have some idea of the beauty in the dance.

He replied that if a job is mechanically simple, it doesn't follow that it can be done entirely without sensitivity.

The line which the center of gravity has to follow is indeed quite simple and in most cases, he believed, straight. In the cases in which it is curved, the law of its curvature seems to be at least of the first or at most of the second order; even in the latter case the line is only elliptical, a form of movement of the body's extremities (because of the joints) which is most natural, so this hardly demands great talent on the part of the operator.

But, seen from another point of view, this line could be something very mysterious, for it is nothing other than the *path taken by the dancer's soul;* and he doubted if this could be achieved unless the operator transposed himself into the marionette's center of gravity; that is to say, the operator *dances.*

I replied that the job of the operator had been presented to me as something done without sensitivity, somewhat like turning the handle of a barrel organ.

"Not at all," he answered. "In fact, there is a rather ingenious relationship between the movement of his fingers and the movements of the attached puppets, somewhat like that of numbers to their logarithms or the asymptotes to the hyperbola."

And yet he believed that even the last trace of human volition to which he had referred could be removed from the marionettes, that their dance could be transferred completely to the realm of mechanical forces and that it could be produced, as I had thought, by turning a handle.

I expressed my astonishment at the attention he was paying this species of an art form intended for the masses. It wasn't only that he thought a greater development possible; he himself seemed to be occupying his time with it.

He smiled and said he was confident that if a craftsman were to make a marionette according to his specifications, that he could perform a dance with it which neither he nor any other skilled dancer of his time, not even Vestris herself, could equal.

I said nothing and looked down at the ground. Then he said, "Have you ever heard of those artificial legs made by English craftsmen for those unfortunate individuals who have lost their limbs?"

I said that I hadn't seen anything of this kind.

"That's too bad," he replied, "because if I tell you that these unfortunate people can dance with them, I fear you won't believe me. What am I saying—dance? The range of their movements is rather limited, but those they can perform are executed with a calmness, ease and grace which amazes any thinking observer."

I said, somewhat lightly, that he had, of course, found his man. A craftsman who could make such a remarkable limb could surely construct an entire marionette according to his specifications.

As he lowered his eyes, somewhat perplexed, I asked, "What are the specifications you are thinking of presenting to his artistic skill?"

"Nothing," he answered, "that isn't to be found here as well: symmetry, flexibility, lightness—but of a higher degree; and particularly a natural arrangement of the centers of gravity."

"And what advantage would this puppet have over living dancers?"

"Advantage? First of all a negative one, my dear friend; and that is that it would never behave *affectedly*. For affectation appears, as you know, when the soul (*vis motrix*) can be found at some point other than the center of gravity of movement. Because the operator controls only this point with the wire or thread, all the other limbs are what they should be: dead, mere pendulums, governed only by the law of gravity—an excellent quality hard to find in most of our dancers.

"Take, for example, P., the one who dances Daphne," he continued. "Pursued by Apollo, she turns to look at him. Her soul seems to be in the small of her back; she bends as if she's going to break, like a naiad after the school of Bernini. Or look at young F., who dances Paris. When he stands among the three goddesses and offers the apple to Venus, his soul is located (and it is a fright to perceive) in his elbow.

"Such mistakes are unavoidable," he said, "now that we have eaten from the Tree of Knowledge. But Paradise is locked and the cherubim behind us; we have to travel around the world to see if it is perhaps open again somewhere at the back."

I laughed. Certainly, I thought, the human spirit can't be in error when it doesn't exist. But I could see that he had more to tell me and asked him to continue.

"In addition," he said, "these puppets have the advantage of being practically weightless. The inertia of matter, that property most resistant to the dance, does not affect them, for the force which raises them into the air is greater than the one which draws them to the ground. What would our dear G. give to be sixty pounds lighter, or if a weight of this size came to her aid while she performed her entrechats and pirouettes? Puppets, like elves, need the ground only so that they can touch it lightly and renew the momentum of their limbs through this momentary delay. We need it to rest on, to recover from the exertions of the dance, a moment which is clearly not part of the dance. We can only do our best to make it as inconspicuous as possible."

I said that, regardless of how cleverly he might present his paradoxes, he would never make me believe that a mechanical puppet could be more graceful than the human body.

He said that it would be impossible for man to come anywhere near the puppet. Only a god could equal inanimate matter in this respect; and here is the point where the two ends of the circular world meet.

My wonderment increased, and I didn't know what to say to such extraordinary claims.

It seemed, he said as he took a pinch of snuff, that I had not read the third chapter of the book of Genesis carefully enough; if a man wasn't familiar with that first period of all human development, it would be difficult to discuss the later ones, not to mention the final one.

I told him that I was well aware of how consciousness could disturb the natural grace of man. Before my very eyes one of my young acquaintances had lost his innocence, all because of a chance remark, and had never again, in spite of all conceivable efforts, been able to find his way back to its paradise. But what conclusions, I added, can you draw from that?

He asked me to which incident I was referring.

About three years ago, I related, I was at the baths with a young man who at the time was remarkably graceful in all respects of his education. He was about fifteen years old, and only faintly could one see in him the first traces of vanity—as a result of the favor shown him by women. It just so happened that in Paris we had seen a statue of a young boy pulling a thorn from his foot; the cast of the statue is well known and can be found in most German collections. Now, just as my young friend was lifting his foot on to a stool to dry it, he was reminded of the statue while he looked into a tall mirror; he smiled and told me what he had discovered. I had, in fact, noticed the same thing at the same moment. But—I don't know if it was to test the security of his grace or to provide a salutary counter to his vanity—I laughed and said that he must be seeing things! He blushed and raised his foot a second time in order to show me, but the attempt failed as anyone might have suspected it would. Somewhat confused, he raised his foot a third time and then a fourth; he raised it probably ten times: in vain! He was unable to reproduce the movement—what am I saying? The movements he made were of such a comical nature that I could barely contain my laughter.

From that day, beginning at that very moment, an inconceivable change came over the young man. He stood in front of the mirror for days. One attraction after the other left him. Like an iron net, an invisible and incomprehensible power enveloped the free play of his gestures. After a year had passed, nothing remained of the grace which had previously given pleasure to those who saw him. There's a man still alive who was a witness to that strange and unfortunate event. He can confirm it, just as I have described it, word for word.

"At this juncture," said Mr. C. amiably, "I have to tell you another story, and you'll easily see how it fits in here.

"While on my way to Russia, I spent some time on the estate of a Livonian nobleman, Mr. von G., whose sons were just then passionately interested in fencing. The elder in particular, who had just come back from the university, was somewhat of a virtuoso. One morning when I was in his room he offered me a rapier. We parried, but it just so happened that I was better than he. His passion caused him to be confused. Almost every thrust I made found its mark, and finally his rapier flew into the corner of the room. As he picked it up, he half-jokingly, half-irritatedly, said that he had met his master. But then he added that there was a master for everyone and everything and that now he intended to lead me to mine. His brother laughed loudly and called out, 'Go ahead, go down to the stall!' Together they took me by the hand and led me out to a bear that their father, Mr. von G., was raising on the farm.

"Somewhat astounded I walked up to the bear. He was standing on his hind legs, his back against the post to which he was chained, his right paw raised ready for a battle. He looked me straight in the eye. That was his fighting posture. I wasn't sure if I was dreaming, since I was standing face to face with such an opponent. 'Go ahead, attack,' said Mr. von G. 'See if you can hit him!!' When I had recovered somewhat from my surprise, I lunged at him with my rapier. The bear moved slightly and warded off my thrust. I tried to mislead him by feinting thrusts, but the bear did not move. I attacked him again with all the skill at my command. I most certainly would have left my mark on a human breast, but the bear moved only slightly and warded off my thrust. I now felt the same as had the young Mr. von G. The bear's seriousness robbed me of my composure. I alternately thrust and feinted; sweat poured off me: all in vain! He not only averted my thrusts like the finest fencer in the world, but made no move when I feinted to deceive him. This was something that no fencer in the world could equal. He stood, his paw still raised for battle, his eye fixed on mine as if he could read my soul in it, and when my thrusts were not meant seriously, he didn't move.

"Do you believe this story?"

"Of course," I said, applauding joyfully. "I'd believe it from any stranger, it's so probable! And all the more so from you!"

"Now, my dear friend," said Mr. C., "you have everything you need to understand my argument. We see that in the organic world, as reflection grows darker and weaker, grace emerges more brilliantly and commandingly. But just as the section drawn through two lines suddenly appears on the other side of a point after passing through infinity, or just as the image in a concave mirror turns up before us again after having moved off into the endless distance, so too grace itself returns when knowledge has gone through an infinity. Grace appears purest in that human form which has either no consciousness or an infinite one, that is, in a puppet or in a god."

"Therefore," I said somewhat bewildered, "we would have to eat again from the Tree of Knowledge in order to return to the state of innocence?"

"Quite right," he answered. "And that's the last chapter in the history of the world."

TRANSLATED BY CHRISTIAN-ALBRECHT GOLLUB

## (21) And all was right with the world

JOSEPH VON EICHENDORFF, Memoirs of a Good-for-Nothing

Joseph von Eichendorff's novella *Memoirs of a Good-for-Nothing* (1826) is founded on the dream of an intact world in which ultimately everything is good. "The good-for-nothing is a miller's boy who was given the nickname because he was not fit to do anything at home except stretch out in the sun and play the violin. His father, aggravated, sends him out on his wanderings to earn his bread elsewhere. 'So,' says the boy, 'if I am a good-for-nothing, that is fine, so I want to get out in the world and make my fortune.' And while right and left his acquaintances and comrades set off for work, just like yesterday and day before yesterday and always, digging and plowing, he sets forth through the village out into the free world, taking with him his fiddle and a perpetual-Sunday mood. With his brand new song, 'Whom God Wants To Show Real Favor,' he understandably attracts the attention of two ladies who overtake him on the highway in a "priceless traveling coach." They let him ride the running-board to Vienna, which he had spontaneously named as his destination, thus beginning the dreamed-of circle of his German-Italian adventure, the story of his love for 'the very beautiful gracious lady.' This planless story, in which the experiencing and narrating character reveals himself as utterly faithful and irresponsible, strays into becoming an operetta-type intrigue that is resolved in a childlike manner to everyone's satisfaction." (Thomas Mann)

(The good-for-nothing is able at a palace in Vienna to carry off the "gracious lady," an alleged duchess, as his bride. In reality she is the niece of the old gatekeeper with whom he had been friends.)

The sun had long since set behind the mountains. What remained was like a reddish haze over the warm evening with its dying noises, in which the murmur of the Danube became more audible as the stillness increased.

I fixed my gaze on the Countess who, flushed from running, stood so close to me that I could hear her heart beating. Because I was suddenly so alone with her, I had no idea what to say, for I was overcome with respect. Finally, summoning all my courage, I took her small white hand. She then impulsively drew me to her and threw her arms around my neck, and I embraced her tightly.

But she quickly freed herself and, greatly confused, reclined in a window in order to cool her burning cheeks in the evening air.

"Oh," I cried, "my heart is ready to burst, but I cannot fathom all of this. It all seems like a dream!"

"It does to me as well," said the lovely lady. "When I returned from Rome with the Countess last summer," she added after a pause, "and we had found Miss Flora and brought her back with us, but heard from you neither here nor there—I never thought that everything would end like this! Only today at noon the jockey, that good and speedy lad, came galloping breathlessly up to the castle yard and brought the news that you were arriving with the mailboat." Then quietly she laughed to herself. "Do you recall," she said, "how you saw me the last time on the balcony? It was exactly like today, such a quiet evening, and music in the garden."

"Then who has died?" I asked hurriedly.

"What do you mean?" said the beautiful woman and looked at me with surprise.

"The husband of your ladyship," I replied, "who stood there on the balcony."

She flushed quite red. "What strange notions you have in your head!" she cried out. "But that was the Countess's son who had just returned from his travels! It just happened to be my birthday, and he led me out onto the balcony, so that I too would be cheered. But is that the reason you ran away from here?"

"Oh God, of course!" I cried out and struck my forehead with my hand. She, however, shook her dainty head and laughed very merrily.

I felt so comfortable with her chatting happily and familiarly next to me that I could have listened to her until morning. I was pleased to the depths of my soul, and I fetched from my pocket a handful of shell-almonds that I had brought back from Italy. She took some, and we cracked and ate them and looked contentedly out over the quiet country-side. After a while she said, "Do you see the little white castle shining there in the moonlight? The Count has given it as well as the garden and the vineyards to us. That's where we'll live. He knew long ago that we loved one another and is very well-disposed toward you. Had you not been with him when he carried off the young lady from the boarding school, both of them would have been caught before they had had time to make peace with the old Countess, and everything would have turned out differently."

"Oh my God, dearest, most gracious Countess!" I cried out. "I do not know where my head is with all these unexpected bits of news; you mean to say that Mr. Leonhard . . . ?"

"Yes, indeed," she broke in. "That is what he called himself in Italy. He owns those estates over there, and he is now going to marry our Countess's daughter, the lovely Flora. But why do you keep calling me 'Countess?' " I looked at her wide-eyed. "I'm not a countess at all," she continued. "Our gracious Countess took me into the castle, because my uncle, the doorkeeper, brought me here when I was a small and orphaned child."

A weight had been lifted from my shoulders. "God bless the doorkeeper for being our uncle!" I responded with great delight. "I have always thought highly of him."

"He means well with you too," she replied. "If only he would be a bit more distinguished, he always says. You have to wear more elegant clothes now!"

"Oh," I cried happily, "English frock coat, straw hat and knickerbockers and spurs! And immediately after the wedding we're off to Italy, to Rome. They have beautiful fountains there. We'll take the students from Prague with us and the doorkeeper!"

She smiled quietly and looked at me contentedly and amiably. The music still echoed in the distance, and flares flew from the castle through the still night across the garden, and the murmuring of the Danube came up to us—and all was right with the world!

TRANSLATED BY CHRISTIAN-ALBRECHT GOLLUB

## (22) The fairest hopes of sweet fulfillment

WILHELM AND KAROLINE VON HUMBOLDT, Betrothal Letters

At a ball in Erfurt in 1789, the twenty-three-year-old Wilhelm von Humboldt became engaged to Karoline von Dacheröden, daughter of a wealthy Thuringian landowner. The letters of the betrothed created an earthly paradise of love. Their marriage, of course, was not a bower of ecstatic delight. "In the course of the marriage, the woman, who was frequently in poor health and suffered from pains in the chest, bore eight children. This marriage has often been idealized into an unproblematic family idyll, overlooking the fact that from the outset it was based on mutual freedom and that neither partner was spared painful tensions and periods of alienation. A task for psychologists (which need not be felt as a sacrilege) might be to penetrate more deeply into the secrets of this alliance and into the deviations of Humboldt's erotic temperament. Nonetheless it is clear that in this instance a great experiment was successful and that two unusual people flourished all their lives, each showing respect for the inner freedom of the other, enjoying the most intimate intellectual and spiritual exchange and achieving an extraordinary degree of maturity with each other." (Herbert Nette)

[Berlin] Thursday evening [February 17]

I am so terribly sad, my Li, my being is consumed by longing, and my spirit cannot find that peace that it so anxiously seeks. Oh! what is it that drives me so, me, so happy, so near to the fairest hopes of sweet fulfillment? A consciousness of the present drowns out the gentle voice of hope, I do not have her, my poor heart sighs, and no glimpse, oh!, though it may be of the very near future, can lessen its sadness. Sometimes I think, too, this is a voice that comes to me from you and then I weep, for Li is grieving. For there is certainly such a consciousness of one in the other, though the distance may be great, that often the thought lays hold of me with too great certainty, with a feeling of actuality: Now her spirit is wholly with me. How infinite are the joys of a loving heart! In the midst of the pain of separation, enduring the most desolate loss of all that to which my soul is so singly bound, I feel indescribable bliss. And you share the feeling with me. In you, too, exists this eternal, unceasing undulation from the most extreme pain to the most rapturous ecstasy; in you, too, the most dreadful melancholy is mixed with such lofty joy. When in other days I imagined such a feeling, how little did I understand it, what little notion did I have of its possibility, how I yearned without precisely visualizing that ideal toward which I strove! Then, for the first time I found everything, everything in you. Oh you, my Li, how you have consecrated your Bill to yourself, dedicated him eternally to you, how you have intermingled that most zealous, most fervent life of your soul with that of his, how you have lifted him to heights to which, reeling, he himself dared not look up. Li, I cannot thank you for what you have given me. But my life and my love shall be my thanks, in every moment you shall know that I am yours!

Karoline to Humboldt

[Erfurt] Friday evening [February 18]

Oh, my dear, dear creature, what a morning you have given me! My spirit had sunk into such a dull stupor, vainly I sought to extricate myself, vainly to compose a cheerful attitude toward life—I could not do it, could not write you and recite to you all the misery in my heart. There it lay like a heavy weight, oh, and within me it was so desolate, my whole being so torn asunder. Your poor child did not have the comfort of soothing tears. Thus three anxious days passed, oh, doubly anxious because I could not be alone, three nights—let me keep silence about their torment. Then today your letter came. How many tears I shed over it—what relief as they dissolved my spirit's dull ache. Now I can feel you again, feel the ever present company of your love, and a breath of new life drifts over me. Oh, let me cry, let these returning tears bless me and the sweet delight of inexpressible pensiveness that sustains my wavering life. So near the goal I failed to grasp it; the golden rays of hope were extinguished in dark night. Void of every courageous impulse, I perceived that I had fallen back and was deathly frail and my better life stolen away.

Beloved man, let me keep silent about these anxious days—let me thank you for the fresh life that you give back to me: a gift of your compassionate love, it will awaken the best forces of my nature to preserve myself for you. Oh, only life's most beautiful, most perfect blossoms are worthy to be presented to you; if in the brightest moments of my existence I nourished myself with the hope of bringing them to you, then it was an act of blissful inspiration to which the contemplation of your ineffable being lifted me. The pure breath of truth must needs eternally hover about my soul's sweet promises. Loved by you with this peerless love, my whole being surrendering unto you, as it does, whatever it is given human beings to attain must become mine. My soul soars up again. It is as if I heard your sweet voice say to me: "Be comforted and strong, my Li"; as if I saw your eyes, as I so often saw them, as you lay on my breast and, exalted above all earthly things, hearkened more deeply to the rule of beauty. Oh sweet love, how holy each memory is as it floats before me again!

When in these moments I felt the beating of your heart redouble, when I saw in your features the ineffable rapture of your soul and felt the profound and sacred ardor of your being and saw you as, through the veil of the sensual, you searched for and found the spiritual, translated it in your soul, and intermingled your being so fervently with the sacred patterns of beauty, then I sank down before you—ever, ever to lie thus before you, to look up to you as one looks up to higher portentous beings, that was my sole wish! Oh, let me say it, often you seemed to me too grand, too noble for me ever to be able to possess your love—the magnitude, the splendor of appearances alone filled me. In more peaceful hours how sweet it was to retrace the fragile filaments and so often find them joined to one of my favorite ideas, to a delicate sentiment of my spirit. A divine joy, a sweet presentiment of that which I could become through cultivation at your hand sent a thrill through my heart.

Thus eternally changing, eternally new and still emanating eternally from the same source, these are the infinite joys that your love gives to me. Oh, I cannot thank you, for there is no sufficient expression for a happiness like mine, only let my soul lose itself in the feeling of our peerless love. More blessed and more worthy of you, I will return each time to you, you grand, fine creature. I dare well call it unique, this love; for where else would there be this amazing harmony of inexpressible love that makes its whole nature conform to that of the beloved and to the most unrestrained freedom?

My Wilhelm, how often I sit for hours through lonely nights and re-flect upon this and perceive it more and more clearly—oh, with such sweet joy—how separate in themselves, how divorced from the fascination of romantic love our feelings are. So I perceive your heart and so my own, perceive that the surrender of our beings to one another will determine our existence. Oh, and not just this existence alone! Let it be granted to the soul glowing with love to lift the veil of the future. A glimpse into eternity will fill it with the anticipation of a higher existence, of a purer love, of a more ardent overflowing into the beloved and often.

Oh Wilhelm, is it not so with you too? Do you not often feel, when you think of a future existence, a sweet nameless desire, like upon return-ing to an old, familiar place? Could it be a delusion? Could something so deeply felt be illusory? Oh, no! The moments when, borne up by the holy glow of your being, I hovered surrounded by a purer prospect of things, these moments unbound my long-fettered soul. Then I perceived that all aspiration, all striving for ennoblement that fills the human breast was a desire to grasp again the first, simple, high archetype of our being! Oh, let me live by your side in freedom from all external circumstances so that nothing may disturb the harmony of our existence, so that I may see you live in the fullness of your most precious, most individual ideas, making use of all the spiritual aspects of your soul. My heart will glow with a new life, my being will be elevated to a higher beauty and give to you the purest delight of mankind!

Who has a heart like yours to comprehend the sweet emotion of being the author of a good creature's happiness? Who has, as you do, the power to bring about such happiness? Oh, it lies hidden within your nature, before which I will eternally bow in adoration—my Wilhelm, in this divine simplicity, in your gentle, tender spirit, its clear, broad outlook, in your respect for all that pertains to your own freedom and the freedom of others. Who has no respect for himself will never have respect for others. But to few is given this fine sense that never allows one to reach into the sphere of other people's interests. It is the possession of great spirits alone. Oh, how well you are endowed with it, in such fullness and beauty and blended with such strength of resignation!

Best creature, beloved, dearest man! Oh, what a future unfolds before me! Cherished on your breast; nourished, sustained by your love; your wife, your beloved—continuous witness to your beautiful life, confidante of your heart, its first and best possession—oh, let me desist, does earth have a happy fate that matches this? Let me reflect on you and my love; only through it can I draw near you, you grand, unattainable creature!

TRANSLATED BY JEANNE R. WILLSON

## (23) A stopping place

ADALBERT STIFTER, Indian Summer

Adalbert Stifter, the son of a poor weaver, was born in 1805 in the Bohemian Forest. Following a happy childhood in which he was especially influenced by his mother and grandparents (his father was killed by an overturning cart when Stifter was twelve), he was able to attend the *Gymnasium* at Kremsmünster, an old Benedictine abbey. He initially studied jurisprudence, then philosophy, history, mathematics, and natural sciences in Vienna. As a teacher and educator he lived a completely withdrawn life, dedicating himself to painting and writing. In 1848 he moved to Linz. In a revolutionary era that seemed to destroy all order he took over the position of a school inspector. Soon thereafter, in the yoke of a subordinate bureaucracy, he retired. He was subject to deep depression following the death of his mother and the suicide of his adoptive daughter, whom he had taken in since his own marriage was childless. He suffered tremendously from cancer of the liver and a nervous disorder and died in January 1868 following an attempted suicide.

In the novel *Indian Summer*, which was written in 1853 and published in 1857, the young Heinrich Drendorf, son of a rich Viennese businessman, happens upon the estate of Baron von Risach during his wanderings through the lower Alps. At Asperhof, the Risach estate, he finds a world that portrays the ideal picture of harmonious order in the middle of a turbulent era. Baron von Risach, renouncing marriage, is bound by love and affection to Mathilde, whom he had loved in his youth. Mathilde, now a widow, lives on a nearby estate.

One day I was walking from the high mountains down toward the hills. Having decided to emigrate from one mountain chain to another, I had chosen a road through part of the open country. Everyone knows the foothills that form a passage between the high mountains and the open land. Covered with deciduous or evergreen forests, they stretch out in pleasing colors. Here and there one can see the blue head of a high mountain above them, or a bright meadow in between. Through them all water that comes from the mountains runs down to the countryside. Displaying many a building and church, the foothills follow the mountain slopes out in all directions toward the more cultivated and settled parts.

Going down the slope of these mountains, I gained a freer view and saw, veiling the heavens in the west, the gentle clouds of a storm that was quietly beginning to form. I strode vigorously onward, observing the increase and growth of the clouds. Going farther, I found myself in a part of the land where gentle hills alternated with moderate plains; dairy farms were scattered; forests of fruit orchards spread throughout the land; church towers shimmered among the dark leaves; brooks rushed through the furrows of the valley; and everywhere I could see the jagged blue band of the high mountains. Finally I began thinking about going inside somewhere, for the village in which I had meant to rest could hardly be reached in time. The storm had progressed so far that it might break out in an hour, in favorable circumstances even sooner.

Before me lay the village of Rohrberg, whose church tower looked out over cherry and willow trees, sharply illuminated by the sun. It lay just a little apart from the road. Nearer by were two dairy farms, each resplendent among meadows and fields at a moderate distance from the road. There was also a house on a hill. It did not seem to be a farmhouse or farm building, but more like the country house of a city dweller. I had often looked at the house before when I came through this area, but I had never taken a serious interest in it. Now it attracted my attention all the more because it was the nearest shelter from my current position, and because it promised to provide more comfort than the dairy farms. To this was added a unique attraction. It was still brightly lit by the sun, while a large part of the country with the exception of the Rohrberg church tower already lay in shadows. It looked out over the gray and blue of the landscape with inviting, shimmering white.

I decided to seek shelter in this house and looked for a path that would lead from the road up to the hill. Being familiar with the area, I easily found the path, bordered by a fence and bushes. I strode up it and reached the house, still illuminated by the sun. But now that I came closer I saw something remarkable. The house was covered all over with roses. As usual in that fertile hilly country, when anything blooms, everything else blooms at the same time. The roses seemed to have promised each other to open all at once, in order to envelop the house in a mantle of the most enchanting color and in a cloud of the sweetest scents.

When I say the house was completely covered with roses, that should not be taken too literally. The house had two rather high stories. The wall of the ground floor was covered with roses that reached up to the windows of the second story. The rest of the house, free up to the roof, was the glowing white strip overlooking the landscape which had more or less enticed me up there. The roses, all little trees, were fastened to a trellis in front of the house wall. There were tiny ones whose leaves began at ground level, then taller ones whose trunks rose above the first, and so on to the last whose branches looked in the windows of the second story.

The roses were planted and tended in such a way that there was no gap, so that the house wall was completely covered by them as far as they reached.

I had never seen anything of this sort on such a large scale.

In addition, almost all the species of rose I knew were there and some I didn't know yet. The colors ranged from the pure white of the white roses through the yellowish-and-reddish-white of the half-toned roses to the subdued red and crimson and the bluish- and blackish-red of the red roses. The shapes and forms were just as varied. The roses were not separated by color; rather, the purpose of their planting seemed to be that there should be no interruption in the wall of roses. Thus the colors blossomed out in a random medley.

The green of the leaves also attracted my attention. It was very pure, and I saw no leaves in poor condition, none of the frequent diseases that appear in roses more often than in other plants. No withered leaf could be seen, none devoured by caterpillars or warped by their cocoons. Even the bugs that so like to nest among roses were missing. Completely unfolded, the leaves stood out in their various shades of green. Mixed with the colors of the blossoms, they made a remarkable cover for the house. The sun, which still seemed to be shining on this house alone, gave the roses and the green leaves the same golden and fiery colors.

After I had stood for a while before these flowers, forgetting my intention, I admonished myself to think of what was to come. I looked around for an entrance to the house, but saw none. Nowhere in the rather long wall was there a door or gate. Nor was the entrance to the house marked by any path, for the whole area in front of it was covered with clean, neatly raked sand. This was separated by a strip of grass and a hedge from the neighboring fields which lay behind me. On the long sides of the house were gardens, separated from the sand by a high, green-painted iron fence. So the entrance had to be in this fence.

And so it was.

In the fence closest to the path leading up the hill I discovered the gate, or actually two wings of a double gate, which were entered in the fence so that they could not be distinguished from it at first glance. In the wings were two brass handles, and on the side of one of the wings was a bellpull.

First I looked through the fence into the garden. The sand continued behind the fence, here bordered by flowering shrubs and interspersed with tall shady fruit trees. In the shadows stood tables and chairs, but no one was nearby. The garden stretched back around the house for quite a distance, it seemed to me.

Then I tried the brass handles, but they did not open the gate. Next I resorted to the bellpull and rang.

At the sound of the bell a man came out toward me from behind the shrubbery of the garden. When he stood before me on the other side of the fence I saw that he had snow-white hair, which he had not covered. He was simply dressed, wearing a kind of house jacket or whatever the thing is called, which fitted him closely all over and reached down almost to his knees. He looked at me for a moment and then said: "What do you want, sir"

"A storm is approaching," I said, "and soon it will reach this area. I am a traveler, as you see from my knapsack, and so I ask that you give me shelter in this house until the rain or at least the heavier part has passed."

"The storm will not break out," said the man.

"It won't be an hour before it's here," I replied. "I know these mountains very well, and I also understand something about clouds and storms."

"But in all probability I have been familiar with the place where we are standing much longer than you have with the mountains, since I am much older than you," the man answered. "I also know its clouds and storms, and know that no rain will fall today on this house, this garden, or this area."

"Let's not spend a long time discussing whether a storm is going to dampen this house or not," I said. "If you are reluctant to open this gate for me, please be good enough to call the master of the house."

"I am the master of the house."

Upon these words I looked at the man more closely. To be sure, his face indicated an advanced age; but it seemed younger to me than his hair. It was one of those friendly, well-tanned faces that has not been distorted by the fat of advanced years, so that one never knows how old they are. Hereupon I said, "Now I must ask pardon that I have been so insistent in counting on your observing the custom of this area. If your assertion that no storm is approaching is intended to turn me away, I will leave immediately. Don't think that I fear rain so much; after all, I'm a young man. To be sure, I prefer staying dry to being soaked, but being soaked is not so unpleasant that I would choose to place a burden on someone for that reason. I have often been rained on, and it doesn't matter if it happens again today."

"There are actually two separate questions," replied the man, "and I have a response for both. The first is that you have said something incorrect about natural matters, which perhaps is based on your knowing too little about the conditions in this part of the country or paying too little attention to natural phenomena. I had to correct this error, for in matters of nature the truth must be spoken. The second response is that if you want to come into this house, with or without a storm, and if you are of a mind to accept its hospitality, I will be very glad to accommodate you. This house has already had many a guest, and sheltered many gladly; and I can tell that it will gladly shelter you and care for you as long as you find necessary. So I ask you to enter."

TRANSLATED BY MARGARET WOODRUFF

## (24) Mass migration

JOHANN WOLFGANG VON GOETHE, Wilhelm Meister's Years of
   Wandering

The novel *Wilhelm Meister's Years of Wandering, or the Renouncers* by Johann Wolfgang von Goethe, was published in 1821 (in an expanded version in 1829). It is a large pedagogical novel, a continuation of *Wilhelm Meister's Apprenticeship.* The division into three books corresponds to the stages that lead to the improvement of Wilhelm Meister's personality. He experiences the archetypes of the humane conduct of life (as in his son, Felix's, education in the "pedagogical province"); he glimpses the standards that should be acceptable in a future society, and he experiences the world of actualization (Wilhelm abandons his goal of a well-rounded education, commits himself to the practice of a socially useful craft, and trains as a surgeon).

The courage and farsightedness of those who continue to develop is juxtaposed to the commitment to perseverance and to the structuring of the immediate environment. America and Europe become a synthesis, and as such become symbol of a social utopia.

The time is past when people rushed forth at random into the wide world. Through the labors of scientific travelers, describing wisely and copying like artists, we are well enough informed to have a general sense of what awaits us everywhere.

Yet the individual alone cannot achieve perfect lucidity. Our society is founded upon the principle that each person, in his degree and for his own purposes, be thoroughly informed. If a man has some country in mind towards which his wishes are tending, we try to clarify for him in detail what was hovering before his imagination as a whole. To piece together for one another a survey of the inhabited and inhabitable world is the most pleasant and rewarding of diversions.

In this sense we may consider ourselves members of a world alliance. Simple and grand is the thought, its realization easy with the aid of reason and strength. Unity is all-powerful; no division, therefore, no conflict among us! Insofar as we have founding principles, they are common to us all. Let man learn, we say, to conceive of himself without any constant external relation; let him seek logical consistency not in circumstances but in himself. If it is there he will find it, and there he must lovingly nurture it.

He will mold and equip himself to be everywhere at home. He who devotes himself to the most urgent matters will reach his goal with the greatest assurance; others, however, seeking something more sublime and delicate, must be more cautious even in their choice of a path. Yet whatever man may possess and wield, the individual will not be self-sufficient. Society remains the highest requirement of an upright man. All useful human beings should stand in a relation to one another, just as the builder looks after the architect, and he in turn after the masons and carpenters.

How and in what manner our alliance has been sealed and established is common knowledge. We see no one among us who cannot at any moment appropriately exercise his function; who is not assured that wherever chance, inclination, even passion may lead him, wherever he may find himself, he will be recommended, received, and assisted, and even, as far as possible, rescued from any misfortune.

Wherefore we have rigorously assumed two duties: to honor every form of religious worship, for they are all more or less comprehended in the Creed; and furthermore, to recognize equally all forms of government; and since all require and promote useful activity, we must strive within ourselves, however long it may take us, to obey their will and intention. Finally we hold it our duty to practice morality without pedantry or harshness, even as our self-respect demands, arising from the three points of honor which we all profess and this higher general wisdom into which we all have had the joy and good fortune to be initiated, some of us indeed from youth on. All this, in the solemn hour of parting, we have thought good to consider, to declare anew, to hear and to acknowledge, and also to seal with a confident farewell.

Quit your dark, constricting bowers,
Gaily venture, gaily roam!
Head and arm bear cheerful powers,
And they are everywhere at home.
While we revel in the sunlight
We live free of every care;
Space is ours, the world is wide
That we may travel everywhere.

TRANSLATED BY DAVID JACOBSON

# TITANISM

# SUSPENDING
# THE WORLD

*Kant mentions that there can only be* a *reason, hence only* one *("reasonable")* *philosophy, thereby prefiguring the vigorous and powerful claim to the absoluteness of the titanism of the German spirit of the nineteenth century.* Spirit, will, and idea *are considered to be the actual moving forces; reality is accordingly interpolated or negated. Karl Marx maintained, of course, that philosophers should not only interpret but change the world, but his thinking also remains cerebral.*

History is everything: *titanism professes to recognize purposeful development, or teleology, in all history, and to portray God's course through the world. Soon, however, there emerges a realistically oriented historiography based on facticity.*
*In Ranke's view, each epoch is immediate before God—that is, history conceived as the repetition of a static process means that the comprehensive imparting and interpretation of meaning recedes in favor of a method of observation focused on individual phenomena.*

The civil state *proves to be the goal of social and political reforms. It remains mired in reaction and restoration, however; democratic patriotism either takes refuge in utopia or, alternately sarcastically and elegiacally, despairs of reality. Industrialization, which is accompanied by social misery and is not initially beneficial to the civil state, nonetheless also contains great potential for emancipation—as expressed, for example, in social agitation.*

Suspending the world: *in the realm of philosophy, history, and sociopolitics, existing systems and interpretations of the world are "banished" ("destroyed"). That which is essential is simultaneously "preserved," acquired, and handed down. Ultimately, reality that does not "bend" to the system is not recognized as such and is transcended. The threefold root of the word "to suspend" [aufheben] is the basis of Hegel's philosophizing, so strongly characteristic of the nineteenth century.*

# SPIRIT, WILL, AND IDEA

In Johann Wolfgang von Goethe's *Faust* (1808) the character Faust would like to know "the inmost force / That bonds the very universe":

> I have pursued, alas, philosophy,
> Jurisprudence, and medicine,
> And, help me God, theology,
> With fervent zeal through thick and thin.
> And here, poor fool, I stand once more,
> No wiser than I was before.
> . . . . . . . . . . . . . . . . . . . .
> So I resorted to Magic's art,
> To see if by spirit mouth and might
> Many a secret may come to light;
> So I need toil no longer so,
> Propounding what I do not know;
> So I perceive the inmost force
> That bonds the very universe,
> View all enactment's seed and spring,
> And quit my verbiage-mongering.

The "magic" of the German nineteenth century to be used as an aid in interpreting the totality of phenomena and in deciphering the codes of being was called philosophy. Since reality was after all incomprehensible, the intellect created a systematically formed, powerful, artfully arranged structure. The world as will and idea: that is to say, in an era of extreme poverty and danger there was a wealth of intellect, of knowledge assisted by an all-penetrating reason. The reasonable nature, according to Immanuel Kant in *Foundations of the Metaphysics of Morals*, differentiates himself from others by himself positing a purpose. Law governs both the external and the inner event. Man is enjoined by the categorical imperative: "Act in such a manner that your maxims should simultaneously serve as universal law (of all reasonable beings) . . . Action that can exist concommitantly with the autonomy of the will is permitted; if it cannot, it is not permitted. The will whose maxims necessarily concur with the laws of autonomy is a sacred, absolutely good, will."

The powerful and even vigorous attempt to make duty and inclination identical (duty as inclination, inclination as cheerfully fulfilled duty) was supported by the Enlightenment's conviction that each conception of the world could only be a reasonable one; where theodicy seemed misguided, it was compelled back onto the path of reasonableness by the strength of the philosophical will. This exertion of the will, which sought under all circumstances to make the irrationality of the world rationally comprehensible, and which aspired to bridge all dangers and abysses by the power of the ultimately reasonable world spirit, emerges even in the works of Johann Joachim Winckelmann.

Winckelmann's aesthetics, oriented toward a model from antiquity, anticipated the aesthetics of the classic writers. Using the example of Greek art, he lauded ideal nature, which reflected less the "possession" of harmony than the longing for the beautiful human being. "The universal, primary characteristic of the Greek masterpieces is ultimately a noble simplicity and a quiet greatness both in attitude and expression. Just as the depths of the ocean remain at all times quiet, regardless of how turbulent the surface, similarly the expression in the creations of the Greeks even in the extremes of passions displays a great and composed soul."

In Goethe's opinion of Winckelmann, the ultimate product of a nature that is constantly exceeding itself is the beautiful human being. To be sure, nature can only rarely produce the beautiful human being; even for nature's omnipotence it is impossible to tarry long in completeness and to give duration to the beauty produced. Strictly speaking, one could say the beautiful human being is beautiful only for a moment. "In contrast, art now enters: insofar as he is placed at the apex of nature, man again regards his entire nature, which within itself must again produce a peak. Man responds to the challenge by permeating himself with all perfections and virtues, summoning choice, order, harmony, and meaning—finally rising to the production of the work of art that assumes a brilliant place beside his other deeds and creations."

The world as will and idea was a world beyond all actuality. The strength to wrest such ideality from reality can in a twofold sense be called "titanic": on the one hand, for the purpose of characterizing both the excess of spirituality contending with law and order, the self-presumption of reason; and on the other hand, for characterizing a reality that behaves titanically (barbarically) and should be brought to reason.

> To the Apollonian Greek "titanic" and "barbaric" seemed also to be the effect created by the Dionysian—without, however, his being able to deny that he himself was simultaneously related inwardly to those fallen titans and heroes. Indeed, he had to feel still more: that his entire being, in all its beauty and proportion was based on a concealed substratum of suffering and knowledge again disclosed to him by that Dionysian element. And, lo! Apollo was unable to live without Dionysus! 'Titanic' and 'barbaric' were ultimately simply a necessity like the Apollonian! (Friedrich Nietzsche)

As a titanic world, the world as will and idea is also a tragic world. The structure rising high above the basis of reality and seeking to leave it behind is nonetheless established in this reality: a massive structure on a slight foundation. Its strength is fragile, the pathos of its construction often enough can only arduously resist the shocks of a vacillating substratum. Nowhere is this clearer than in the titanism of music, in the "heroic" compositions of Beethoven in which the melodies of sublimity, of a hermetic metaworld, and of an impalpable, uncanny existence that is both unmastered and unmasterable are equally sounded. Due to the phenomenon of the numinous, the optimism of will and idea is always close to pessimism. The transcending of a titanic philosophy is connected with the suffering from immanence characterized by "panic." Primarily, though, "will and idea" means a revolution of civilization: Prometheus, the bearer of human civilization, was a titan. The realm of the spirit is opened by protest, by storming Olympus.

Carl Friedrich von Weizsäcker considered German titanism a modern development. Western civilization, international capitalism, the scientific-technological world are titanic; they were made possible by thinking, by technological reason, businesslike planning, and political organization. The intellectual conquest of the world by theory discloses the philosophical query behind the objectively titanic accomplishments of practical reason; physics, economics, political philosophy, and metaphysics as the common conceptual basis of all these. Seafarers, business people, engineers, government officials, parliamentarians, rulers were not usually also theoreticians, of course. The daily demands of practice sooner robbed them of consciousness of their own titanism. Nevertheless, in the realm of theory, where the German spirit of the nineteenth century was expressed with particular forcefulness, there was definitely an awareness and feeling of modern titanism.

Among the powerful nations of modern Europe, the Germans had the most tangential access to real power, the historical reasons for which date back to the Middle Ages. The early medieval conquest of the Roman imperial legacy by the German kings and the central powers' obsolescence in the struggle to preserve this legacy were probably the main factors. In the early and middle periods of the modern era, the Germans are too close to the modern power process in the transformation of the world to perceive it as their own doing, yet too distant to accomplish it themselves. They nonetheless think it through more thoroughly than their Western neighbors.

Titanism as a form of experiencing, Weizsäcker proceeds in his argumentation, is a German phenomenon, especially since the middle of the eighteenth century. The thinker who conceives the whole has an experience of power that can be more concentrated and also admittedly more ambiguous than that of the real ruler whose awareness of the pure system is constantly distracted by genuine responsibility. Precisely for this reason, the tension between theory and practice is a typical topic of German theory. Weizsäcker argues:

> The core of German titanism is the titanism of philosophy. Philosophy, the thinking of the whole, is an invention of the Greeks, an intellectual possibility that is not self-evident. A Frenchman, René Descartes, marks the beginning of the titanism of modern philosophy. He is titanic through radicalism: radical doubt, the unassailability of the *ego cogito,* the claim of complete lucidity, the mathematical founding of the scientific a priori. . . . Kant understands philosophy's claim of thinking the whole as the requirement for a reasonable system, and he radically pursues this demand. In the *Preface to the Metaphysics of Morals* he states, looking back on critical philosophy, i.e., on his philosophy: "It sounds arrogant, egoistic and, for those who have not yet renounced their old system, disparaging to assert that prior to the creation of critical philosophy, there was none at all. . . . But since, objectively considered, there can only be *one* human reason, there can also not be many philosophies—i.e., only *one* true system of philosophy consisting of principles is possible. . . . If, therefore, someone announced a system of philosophy as his own invention, it is simply as much as to say: prior to this philosophy there can have been no other. . . ." The truly titanic philosophy is the philosophy of German idealism. Its conceptual radicalism derives from Kant, its human abundance from Goethe, the pathos of its outbreak from the French Revolution. The most profound influence

came from Kant, who awakened in Fichte and Schelling the consciousness of what philosophy is. This consciousness led them to the critical philosophy of the one, which in their langugage is the philosophy of the absolute, of the anhypotheton, of that which requires no presupposition. The absolute is explained to the philosophical layperson as a philosophical designation of God; to the philosopher of idealism, the God of religion is a manifestation of the absolute.

The titanic thinkers of the titanic spirit felt themselves to be the administrators of God's secret, or to be God's thinkers. The singular striking feature of the Hegelian philosophy of self-reliance is the "ultimate titanism by being simultaneously the ultimate humility." (Karl Barth) Entrance into the realm of God is borne by a piety that comprehends the all, the one, nature, world, and mankind. Science is perceived as the true fabric of divine life, as the system of the living logos, as the disclosed and realized system of the true being of God.

The first version of the poem "To the Germans" by Hölderlin, who studied at the same time as Hegel and Schelling at the seminary in Tübingen (a particular source of titanic thinking), shows the discrepancy between thought and deed as follows:

> Oh do not mock the child, when with whip and spur
> on the wooden horse he swells with pride,
> for you Germans, you too are
> poor in deeds and great in thoughts.
>
> Or, as the sunbeam comes forth from the cloud
> will the deed come forth from thoughts? Will books soon live?
> O dear ones, take me then,
> that I may expiate this blasphemy.

A decade later, in 1834, Heinrich Heine uses the storm simile in an altered sense in his work entitled *Religion and Philosophy in Germany:*

> Don't laugh at my advice, the advice of a dreamer who warns you against Kantians, Fichteans, and natural philosophers. Don't laugh about the fantasts who await the same revolution in the realm of appearances that took place in the realm of the spirit. The thought precedes the deed as lightning precedes the thunder. The German thunder, though, is also a German, is not very tractable and rolls along somewhat slowly; but it will come, and when you once hear it roaring as it never before roared in the history of the world, just know: the German thunder has finally reached its goal. . . . A work will be performed in comparison with which the French Revolution may seem but a harmless idyll.

Here the warning is sounded that the world will tremble if the Germans were to start to do what they thought. This should be understood to mean in effect that German titanic idealism bore within itself the perversion of action, the baseness of the act. At that moment, however, when proceeding from Schelling and Hegel to Siemens and Halske, from the tenacity of speculation to the manifoldness of existence, from the irreality of thinking to the reality of practice, when reality was to be interpreted and legitimated according to the criteria of an all-embracing system—i.e., at that moment when the titanism of a theoretical, cerebral world turned into the hybris of practical unquestionableness, when the basic contradiction between theory and practice was displaced by *Weltanschauung,* "the extirpation of the German spirit in favor of the German Reich began," (Nietzsche) and the titanic achievement of the German spirit—of simply being pure spirit—is perverted. Thinking of the whole (of being) does not at all contradict the necessity of realizing and thus accepting existence in its infinite, "plural" manifoldness. Hence the texts ordered under the heading "Suspending the World" are in dialectical contrast to those (as Part III shows) which justify the world, which seek reason in a world that is often so full of horror.

In 1818, when Georg Wilhelm Friedrich Hegel, in a speech delivered for the inauguration of his lectures in Berlin, postulated that the spiritual life must comprise the basic element of existence of this (Prussian) state as well as of the state altogether, he committed himself to the moral power of the spirit at a moment that forms the line of demarcation between two epochs (25). The national exultation caused by the Wars of Liberation in reaction against the Napoleonic claim to totality remained mired in restoration and reaction, which attempted to impede the participation and/or codetermination of the people and instead to reestablish feudal structures. The Congress of Vienna in 1814 had accordingly rearranged the map without consideration of the wishes of the people—that is, rearranged it by restoring old conditions. The Carlsbad Decrees of 1819, which were directed against political and intellectual freedom, remained in effect until 1848. In addition, there were signs that the national uprising that had reached a particular climax in the German student fraternities' commemoration of the Wartburg in 1817, was losing its republican-democratic intentions. The longing for national unity became more important than the longing for inner freedom, and finally

German life started to register the first harbingers of the economic and social complex of problems caused by the Industrial Revolution.

In 1818 Hegel asserted that science had taken refuge among, and endured only among, the Germans. Moreover, that the Germans, whose mission it was to cultivate and nourish the sacred light entrusted to them and to see that the highest that man can possess, self-consciousness of his being, should not die out and perish. In this same year, Karl Marx, the founder of historical materialism, was born.

Like Hegel, Marx was also a titan, ready and capable of thinking of the world as a whole. With Marx, this whole was supported by the base [infrastructure], the economic-political-social data that determine the cultural superstructure. Still more predominant, though, was the intellectual concept to which reality had to be "obedient." Of middle-class origin himself, Marx proclaimed to the middle classes their decline as the bourgeoisie. A comprehensive critique of capitalism provided instructions for the action needed to achieve the revolutionary reordering of society. Class struggle as a dialectical principle was laid over world history.

> The history of all previous society is the history of class wars. The free person and the slave, patrician and plebeian, master and serf, guild member and apprentice—in short, oppressed and oppressor stood in constant opposition to one another, waged an uninterrupted struggle at times concealed, at times open—a struggle that each time ended with a revolutionary reordering of the whole society or with the mutual decline of the struggling classes.

Marx wanted to compel conditions to dance; it was necessary merely to play them their own melody—i.e., the melody of his thinking (26). In a titanic act of cerebration, reality was reconstructed into the system; what stood on its feet was cerebrally "bent aright." Marx's political successors no longer performed this feat cerebrally; rather, they used violence and power in actual practice. The titanism of speculation turned into totalitarian oppression.

Titanism—suspending the world: in the presence of widespread contempt and disdain for phenomena opposing the system, for phenomena refuting or exacerbating the system, the cosmos of the system was to be induced to shine through the chaos of appearances. Suspending: that meant negation of the world of appearance to the extent that it contradicted the system. Or, alternatively, suspension meant reinterpretation.

If the reasonable was declared to be what was actually real, the unreasonable had to be understood as that which was actually unreal. If reality contradicted the system, then all the worse for reality! Reality then had to be suspended—destroyed; or, from the standpoint of being uplifted, reality had to be demoted as unimportant. Within the system, mainly phenomena that could be drawn on for verification were suspended—but suspended in the sense of preserving.

To be sure, it was shown that there is no ultimate synthesis; rather, each synthesis is in turn only a thesis and is destined to turn into its opposite. Hegel gave rise to a school that referred to itself as Hegelian, but this was what he himself had called "imitation in the reversal." The generation that became predominant in the late 1820s

> . . . completed the antithesis with an energy that exploded all the more violently because of having been long pent up. It turned against all Romanticism and everything that was reactionary in the state, in belief, in art, in life-style; against the world of "unreal kisses" and unreal kings; against the whole theater of unreal characters whose ghostly existence endured in the shadow of the Holy Alliance. It turned against German Romanticism's unreal concepts whose last and most sovereign master had been Hegel. He was overthrown—overthrown, in fact, in the name of Hegel. (Egon Fridell)

Arthur Schophenhauer emphatically referred to himself as a Kantian, even as the only genuine and worthy successor of Kant. He disdainfully rejected the Fichtean-Hegelian systems. Subjectivity comes to the fore (27). The world—the world of things, of perception, of nature (about which natural science speaks)—is appearance, idea, and object for the perceiving and thinking subject. The categories of space, time, and causality, inseparably connected with the subject, hence "subjective," are the only possible forms for experiencing the world of objects (28). In experiencing the will, the limits of individuality are subjected to a breakthrough (the experience of the drive toward self-survival and the survival of one's genus); the ego transcends the bounds of its subjectivity. The ego, the organized entity of the individual, is itself, the "appearance" of this drive; it is the portrayal of the drive in the material, temporal-spatial form of the object. "Strength" in itself is "will";

> . . . a unified will is concealed behind the world of physical phenomena and also behind the diversity of physiological and psychological appearances. The science of physics, biology, and psychology observes the diversity of objectively comprehensible contents in order to relate them lawfully as cause

and effect; "metaphysics" divines the one subject behind this objective diversity: the will of the world. Like Fichte, Schelling, and Hegel, Schopenhauer does not remain within the limits posited by Kant. And, like them, Schopenhauer seeks the point at which our route via "appearance" to "in itself" is opened up to us: "in the ego." (Ernst von Aster)

Schopenhauer's "will of the world" is thus altogether related to the Fichtean "absolute" and to Hegel's "absolute spirit."

To Schopenhauer, however, this absolute is not a systematically comprehensible "spiritual something" that develops itself purposefully; rather, it is a blind will that lacks an object; it is an organ or a means of the life of instinct. The basis of the world is opposed to reason, or irrational; Schopenhauer's titanism, like Beethoven's (29,30), means liberation from the Apollonian; it borders on panic, which must be endured but cannot be overcome.

Schopenhauer's pessimism strives for redemption not only *of* the world but *from* the world. On the one hand, this makes possible detached contemplation that is without interest and desire and free of any purpose or goal; on the other hand, it makes possible the enduring and final triumph over egoism, over the clinging to the goods of the world, by means of sympathy or by means of that "suspension of the world" exemplified by the Christian and Buddhist saints.


## (25) Everything is of a spiritual nature

GEORG WILHELM FRIEDRICH HEGEL, Opening Address at His Lectures in Berlin, October 22, 1818

Georg Wilhelm Friedrich Hegel, the son of a ducal treasury official, was born in Stuttgart on August 27, 1770. After graduating from the local *Gymnasium*, he attended the University of Tübingen, where he became a friend of Hölderlin and Schelling. He subsequently worked as a tutor in Frankfurt and then taught in Jena, where he took his degree and wrote *The Phenomenology of the Spirit*. In 1806 he moved to Bamberg to come editor of the *Bamberger Zeitung*.

In 1808 he became the headmaster of the Aegidien Gymnasium in Nüremberg. While there he married twenty-year-old Marie von Tucher, a daughter of one of the oldest and most respected patrician families. After teaching for a short time in Heidelberg, he was invited to Berlin in 1817 to hold the chair in philosophy vacated by the death of Fichte. Hegel died of cholera on November 14, 1831.

"Large, wide-open eyes—the eyes of a grown-up, brilliant child. As frequently in Biedermeier portraits, Hegel's features in the well-known engraving combine childlike traits with those of an elderly person. Hard lines surrounding the broad, voluptuous mouth (he thoroughly enjoyed eating and drinking) reveal traces of the profound sorrow of which he was always aware but rarely showed. At age thirteen, he was shattered by the death of his mother, and just a few weeks before his own death he recalls that his first child, his only daughter, died shortly after birth. His wife reported after Hegel's death that he often sighed, 'Oh, to be condemned by God to be a philosopher!'

"Those eyes, those large, wide-open eyes that often look strained, even overstrained, disclose the archaic trust that characterizes this last great thinker of old Europe. It is the self-confidence of the thinking, believing person; it is trust in being, a knowledge and faith that all is well in the abyss of being and creation, where 'good' and 'evil,' bitter and sweet, joy and pain, life and death are still intact as a unity." (Friedrich Heer)

. . . However, not only is it spiritual life in general that forms a fundamental element in the existence of this state, but, more particularly, the people's great struggle along with their prince for independence, for the annihilation of foreign and heartless tyranny, and for freedom of mind—this struggle has really begun. The ethical power of the spirit has felt its energy, raised its banner, and asserted its feeling that it has the authority and power of reality. We must recognize as an invaluable fact that our generation has lived and effectively acted in this feeling, a feeling in which all aspects of right, morality, and religion are concentrated. In this kind of profound and all-encompassing activity the spirit raises itself to its true worth; the flatness of everyday life and the shallowness of particular interests have perished, and the superficiality of individual insights and opinions has been exposed and has evaporated. This more profound seriousness, which has entered all our minds, is also the true foundation of philosophy. What stands opposed to philosophy is, on the one hand, submersion in the interests and needs of the day and, on the other hand, the conceit of individual opinion. A mind prejudiced with such conceit allows no room for reason, which as such does not pursue what is peculiar to the individual. The emptiness of such conceit must vanish once it has become necessary for man to concern himself with his substance, and once things have come far enough that only such a man can assert himself. But precisely in such substance have we seen this age, have we seen the core emerge, whose further development in all directions—politics, ethics, religion, science—has been entrusted to our time.

Our calling and task is to foster the philosophical development of that substantial basis which recently has been rejuvenated and strengthened. This rejuvenation, which showed its immediate effect and expression in political reality, has its further manifestation in the greater ethical and religious seriousness, in the demand for thoroughness and solidity in general, which have befallen all relations in life. The most solid seriousness is in and for itself the serious pursuit of truth. This need, whereby our spiritual nature distinguishes itself from mere sensation and enjoyment, is thus the deepest need of the spirit. It is in itself a universal need. Partly it is the seriousness of these times that has more profoundly aroused it; partly it is a peculiar possession of the German spirit. As far as this exceptional position of the German spirit in philosophical culture is concerned, the nature of this study and the meaning of the word "philosophy" in other nations shows that, while they have retained the word, they have changed its meaning: its subject matter has decayed and disappeared, and indeed to such an extent that scarcely any memory or idea of it has remained. This science has fled to the Germans and continues to live only among them. To us has been entrusted the preservation of this sacred light, and it is our calling to foster and nourish it, and to ensure that the highest thing that man can possess, the self-consciousness of his essence, will not be extinguished and perish.

However, even in Germany, before its rebirth, the shallowness of earlier times had gone so far that people claimed to have discovered and proved that there *is* no knowledge of truth. It was said that God, the essence of the world and of the spirit, is incomprehensible and unintelligible; that the spirit had to stand by religion, and religion itself by believing, feeling, and intimations, without any knowledge based on reason. It was said that knowledge was concerned not with the nature of the absolute, of God, and of what is true and absolute in nature and in the spirit, but rather partly with either the negative principle that nothing true is known (only what is untrue, temporal, and ephemeral enjoys the privilege of being known); or—and this actually should be subsumed under the negative—that knowledge is concerned with externalities, i.e., merely historical and contingent circumstances under which the ostensible knowledge itself belonged. Such knowledge was to be taken merely as an historical fact and investigated critically and learnedly from all those external perspectives—its content could yield nothing serious. These people went as far as Pilate, the Roman proconsul. When Pilate heard Christ use the word "truth," he replied with the question "What is truth?" like one who was through with the word and knew that there is no knowledge of truth. Thus what always had been considered the most disgraceful and unworthy thing, to renounce knowledge of truth, was exalted by our age as the highest triumph of the spirit.

This despair in reason, as it emerged, was still connected with pain and sorrow. But soon religious and ethical mindlessness, and then the insipidity and shallowness of the knowledge that called itself Enlightenment, frankly and freely confessed its impotence and expressed its arrogance by thoroughly forgetting all higher interests. And finally, so-called Critical Philosophy gave a good conscience to this ignorance of what is eternal and divine, by assuring that it had proven that nothing could be known about the eternal and the divine. This purported knowledge even arrogated to itself the name "philosophy," and nothing was more welcome to the shallowness of knowledge and character, nothing was snapped up so eagerly by it as this doctrine of ignorance, whereby precisely this vapidity and shallowness were given out as excellence, as the goal and result of all intellectual striving.

Not to know what is true but to recognize only temporal and contingent appearances—only vanities—it was this conceit which spread in philosophy and is still spreading in our time and loudly proclaiming itself. It can indeed be said that, since philosophy began to come into prominence in Germany, prospects have never looked so bad for this science. That such a view, such a renunciation of knowledge and reason, should achieve such presumption and such circulation—a view that dragged itself over from the preceding period and which stands in such sharp contradiction to the more solid feeling and substantial spirit of recent times. I welcome and appeal to this dawn of a more solid spirit. Only with it am I concerned when claiming that philosophy must have content and elaborating this content before you.

But above all I appeal to the spirit of youth. For youth is the beautiful time of life, not yet caught up in the system of limited ends and needs and, in itself, capable of the freedom that lies in scientific work unaffected by particular interests. It is equally not yet caught up in the negative spirit of vanity, of the lack of content associated with merely critical endeavors. A yet sound heart still has the courage to pursue truth. And it is in the realm of truth that philosophy is at home; this is the realm that it constructs and in which, through the study of philosophy, we will participate. Whatever in life is true, great, and divine is so through the Idea. The goal of philosophy is to grasp it in its true form and universality. Nature is bound by the requirement of consummating reason only with necessity. But the realm of the spirit is the realm of freedom. Everything that holds human life together and that has value is of a spiritual nature. And this realm of the spirit exists only through the consciousness of truth and right, through the grasping of Ideas.

TRANSLATED BY CHARLES LARMORE

## (26) Forcing conditions to dance

KARL MARX, A Contribution to the Critique of Hegel's
Philosophy of Right

Karl Marx was born on May 5, 1818, in Trier. "The details about the person, each comprising a fact of world history, are as follows: he is a Jew, a German, a Prussian, a
Rhinelander; he is a renegade Jew, a renegade Prussian, a renegade German without ever
ceasing to be a Jew, a Prussian, a German, and without ever ceasing to suffer from his
Jewishness, his Prussianness, his Germanness. These details concerning the person also
apply to the historical forces from which 'Marxism' grew." (Michael Freund)
    Marx starts his studies in Bonn in 1835, continuing them the following year in Berlin,
where he is strongly influenced by Hegel's philosophy. He completes his degree in democratic and Epicurean natural philosophy in Jena in 1841 and works as a journalist on the
*Rheinische Zeitung,* a bastion of the Young Hegelians.
    Ludwig Feuerbach's *The Essence of Christianity* was of particular importance to Marx's
thinking, which was also decisively influenced by his friend Friedrich Engels. Engels, who
came from a Wuppertal business family, selflessly "persevered in servile commerce" to
enable Marx to exist as an unemployed writer committed to social revolution.
    Marx studied capitalism and its effects in England, where he lived with his family in
extreme poverty. He died in 1883, soon after his wife's death (four children had already
died). At his death he was considered, as the author of the *Communist Manifesto* and *Das
Kapital,* to be one of the most respected and feared world conspirators of the socialist
movement. Marx's scientific socialism constituted an attempt, using scientific means, to
restore "a new, historic-dialectic derivation of the ancient expectations of paradise that had
been discredited by modern science. The Marxist Utopia hence proves to be a particularly
extreme instance of the modern scientific utopia, revealing an immediate faith that science
and technology can create a paradise on earth." (Franz Borkenau)

The foundation of irreligious criticism is this: man makes religion; religion does not make man. Religion is, in fact, the self-consciousness and
self-esteem of man who has either not yet gained himself or has lost himself again. But man is no abstract being squatting outside the world. Man
is the world of man, the state, society. This state, this society, produce
religion, which is an inverted world-consciousness, because they are an
inverted world. Religion is the general theory of this world, its encyclopedic compendium, its logic in popular form, its spiritualistic *point
d'honneur,* its enthusiasm, its moral sanction, its solemn complement, its
universal basis of consolation and justification. It is the fantastic realization of the human being because the human being has attained no true
reality. Thus, the struggle against religion is indirectly the struggle
against that world of which religion is the spiritual aroma.

    The wretchedness of religion is at once an expression of and a protest
against real wretchedness. Religion is the sigh of the oppressed creature,

the heart of a heartless world and the soul of soulless conditions. It is the opiate of the people.

The abolition of religion as the illusory happiness of the people is a demand for their true happiness. The call to abandon illusions about their condition is the call to abandon a condition which requires illusions. Thus, the critique of religion is the critique in embryo of the vale of tears of which religion is the halo.

Criticism has plucked the imaginary flowers from the chain, not so that man shall bear the chain without fantasy or consolation, but so that he shall cast off the chain and gather the living flower. The critique of religion disillusions man so that he will think, act, and fashion his reality as a man who has lost his illusions and regained his reason, so that he will revolve about himself as his own true sun. Religion is only the illusory sun about which man revolves so long as he does not revolve about himself.

It is the task of history, therefore, once the other-world of truth has vanished, to establish the truth of this world. It is above all the task of philosphy, which is in the service of history, to unmask human self-alienation in its secular forms, once its sacred form has been unmasked. Thus, the critique of heaven is transformed into the critique of the earth, the critique of religion into the critique of law, the critique of theology into the critique of politics.

The following exposition—which is a contribution to this task—does not deal directly with the original, but with a copy, i.e., with the German philosophy of the state and of right, simply because it deals with Germany.

If we were to begin with the German status quo itself, even in the only appropriate way, which is negatively, the result would still be an anachronism. For even the negation of our political present is already a dusty fact in the historical junkroom of modern nations. If I negate powdered wigs, I still have unpowdered wigs. If I negate the German conditions of 1843, I am according to French chronology barely in the year 1789, and still less at the center of the present day.

Indeed, German history prides itself on a development which no other nation has previously achieved or will ever imitate in the historical firmament. We have shared in the restorations of modern nations without ever having shared in their revolutions. We have been restored, first because other nations ventured a revolution, and second because other nations endured a counterrevolution; in the first case because our leaders were afraid, and in the second case because they were not. Led by our shepherds, we have only once been in the company of liberty, and that was on the day of its interment.

One school of thought, which justifies the infamy of today by the infamy of yesterday, a school which interprets every cry of the serf under the knout as a cry of rebellion once the knout is time-honored, ancestral, and historical, a school to which history shows only its *a posteriori* as did the God of Israel to his servant Moses—the Historical School of Law— might well have invented German history were it not itself an invention of German history. A Shylock, but a servile Shylock, it swears by its bond, its historical bond, its Christian–Germanic bond, for every pound of flesh cut from the heart of the people.

On the other hand, good-natured enthusiasts, German nationalists by sentiment and enlightened radicals by reflection, seek our history of freedom beyond our history in the primeval Teutonic forests. But then how does our history of freedom differ from that of the wild boar, if it is only to be found in the forests? Besides, as the saying goes: what is shouted into the forests echoes back from the forest. So peace to the primeval Teutonic forests!

But war upon the conditions in Germany! By all means! They are beneath the level of history, beneath all criticism; yet they remain an object of criticism just as the criminal who is beneath the level of humanity remains an object of the executioner. In its struggle against them criticism is no passion of the brain, but is rather the brain of passion. It is not a scalpel but a weapon. Its object is its enemy, which it wishes not to refute but to destroy. For the spirit of these conditions is already refuted. They are not, in themselves, objects worthy of thought, but rather existences equally despicable and despised. Criticism itself needs no further self-clarification regarding this object, for criticism already understands it. Criticism is no longer an end in itself, but now simply a means. Indignation is its essential pathos, denunciation its principal task.

It is a matter of describing the stifling pressure of all the social spheres on one another, the universal, passive ill-feeling, the recognized yet misunderstood narrow-mindedness, all framed in a system of government which, living by the conservation of all this wretchedness, is itself wretchedness in government.

What a spectacle! The infinite division of society into the most diverse races confronting one another with their petty antipathies, bad conscience and crude mediocrity, and which, precisely because of their mutual ambiguous and suspicious disposition, are treated by their masters without distinction, though with differing formalities, as merely tolerated existences. And they are to recognize and acknowledge the very fact that they are dominated, ruled and possessed as a concession from Heaven! On the other hand there are the masters themselves, whose greatness is in inverse proportion to their number!

Criticism dealing with this situation is criticism in hand-to-hand combat; and in this kind of combat one does not bother about whether the opponent is noble, or of equal rank, or interesting; all that matters is to strike him. It is a question of permitting the Germans not a single moment of illusion or resignation. The burden must be made still more oppressive by adding to it a consciousness of it, and the shame made still more shameful by making it public. Every sphere of German society must be described as the *partie honteuse* of German society, and these petrified conditions must be made to dance by singing to them their own melody. The nation must be taught to be terrified of itself in order to give it courage. In this way an imperative need of the German nation will be fulfilled, and the needs of nations are themselves the final causes of their satisfaction.

TRANSLATED BY J. O'MALLEY


## (27) The subject as supporter of the world

ARTHUR SCHOPENHAUER, The World as Will and Representation

"But inherited wealth attains its greatest value if the recipient is equipped with mental powers of a higher order and is in pursuit of goals not easily compatible with earning, for he is then doubly endowed by fate and can now live for his genius, but he will repay his debt to mankind a hundredfold by accomplishing what no one else could and by creating something that will benefit and even do honor to the whole of mankind." This is Schopenhauer speaking of himself. A sophisticated, enlightened and natural talent, Schopenhauer was born in Danzig in 1788, the son of a businessman. He inherited a fortune that provided him with modest financial independence and enabled him to work as an independent scholar (he lived most of his life in furnished rooms, took his meals out, and only at age fifty bought any furniture for himself). Schopenhauer's relationship with his mother, Johanna, a talented novelist and travel writer, was unhappy. After the death of her husband, her life-style was that of a merry widow in Weimar. She was "a real horror for the melancholy, gloomy son, the born hermit, the misanthrope who was aware of his own value." (Heinrich Zimmer)

Schopenhauer, the egoistic loner who called Fichte and Schelling braggarts and Hegel a fat and useless charlatan, died in 1860. In his last will, of June 1852, he named as his sole heir "the fund established in Berlin for the support of Prussian soldiers disabled in the uprisings of 1848 and 1849 while fighting for the maintenance and creation of legal order in Germany."

That which knows all things and is known by none is the *subject*. It is accordingly the supporter of the world, the universal condition of all that appears, of all objects, and it is always presupposed; for whatever exists, exists only for the subject. Everyone finds himself as this subject, yet only in so far as he knows, not in so far as he is object of knowledge. But his 'body is already object, and therefore from this point of view we call it representation. For the body is object among objects and is subordinated to the laws of objects, although it is immediate object. Like all objects of perception, it lies within the forms of all knowledge, in time and space through which there is plurality. But the subject, the knower never the known, does not lie within these forms; on the contrary, it is always presupposed by those forms themselves, and hence neither plurality nor its opposite, namely unity, belongs to it. We never know it, but it is precisely that which knows wherever there is knowledge.

Therefore the world as representation, in which aspect alone we are here considering it, has two essential, necessary, and inseparable halves. The one half is the *object,* whose forms are space and time, and through these plurality. But the other half, the subject, does not lie in space and time, for it is whole and undivided in every representing being. Hence a single one of these beings with the object completes the world as representation just as fully as do the millions that exist. And if that single one were to disappear, then the world as representation would no longer exist. Therefore these halves are inseparable even in thought, for each of the two has meaning and existence only through and for the other; each exists with the other and vanishes with it. They limit each other immediately; where the object begins, the subject ceases. The common or reciprocal nature of this limitation is seen in the very fact that the essential, and hence universal, forms of every object, namely space, time, and causality, can be found and fully known, starting from the subject, even without the knowledge of the object itself, that is to day, in Kant's language, they reside *a priori* in our consciousness.

TRANSLATED BY E. F. J. PAYNE

## (28) The world as idea

ARTHUR SCHOPENHAUER, Parerga and Paralipomena

Arthur Schopenhauer's *Parerga and Paralipomena,* published in 1851 are, according to the author, "aphorisms written from a popular viewpoint . . . dealing with the art of the conduct of life in the most agreeable and happy manner possible." They are instructions for a happy existence, which "upon cool and sober reflection is decidedly preferable to non-existence." "Half of all worldly wisdom consists in 'neither hating nor loving,' 'saying nothing and believing nothing' is the other half. Surely people will gladly turn their backs on a world that makes such rules necessary."

The fundamental character of all things is their fleeting nature and transitoriness. In nature we see everything, from metal to organism, corroded and consumed partly by its own existence, partly through conflict with something else. Now how could Nature throughout endless time endure the maintenance of forms and the renewal of individuals, the countless repetition of the life process, without becoming weary, unless her own innermost kernel were something timeless and thus wholly indestructible, a thing in itself quite different from its phenomena, something metaphysical that is distinct from everything physical? This is the *will* in ourselves and in everything.

The entire *center of the world* is in every living being, and therefore its own existence is to it all in all. On this rests also *egoism*. To imagine that death annihilates it is absolutely absurd as all existence proceeds from it alone.

We complain of the obscurity in which we pass our lives without understanding the connection of existence as a whole, but in particular that between ourselves and the whole. Thus not only is our life short, but our knowledge is also entirely limited thereto; for we cannot look back to the time before our birth or forward to the time after our death. Consequently, our consciousness is, so to speak, only a flash that momentarily lights up the night. Accordingly, it really looks as if a demon had mischievously obstructed from us all further knowledge in order to gloat over our embarrassment.

But this complaint is not really justified, for its springs from an illusion, the result of the false fundmental view that the totality of things came from an *intellect* and consequently existed as mere *mental picture or representation* before it became actual, and that accordingly as it had sprung from knowledge, it was bound to be wholly accessible thereto and thus capable of being fathomed and exhaustively treated. But in truth the case might rather be that all we complain of not knowing is not known by anyone, indeed is in itself not even knowable at all, in other words, is not capable of being represented in anyone's head. For the *representation,* in whose domain all knowing is to be found and to which all knowledge therefore refers, is only the external side of existence, something secondary and additional, hence something that was not necessary for the maintenance of things generally and thus of the world as a whole, but merely for the maintenance of individual animal beings. Therefore the existence of things in general and as a whole enters knowledge only *per accidens* and consequently to a very limited extent. It forms only the background of the picture in animal consciousness where the objects of the will are the essential thing and occupy first place. Now it is true that, by means of this accident, the entire world arises in space and time, that is, the world as representation which has no such existence at all outside knowledge. On the other hand, the innermost essence of this world, that which exists in itself, is quite independent of such an existence. Now since, as I have said, knowledge exists only for the purpose of maintaining each animal individual, its whole nature, all its forms, such as time, space and so on, are adapted merely to the aims of such an individual. Now these aims require only the knowledge of relations between individual phenomena and certainly not that of the inner essence of things and of the world as a whole.

TRANSLATED BY E. F. J. PAYNE

## (29) Beethoven: In the progress of human culture, he forges far ahead

BETTINA VON ARNIM, Goethe's Correspondence with a Child

Bettina von Arnim (1785–1859), wife of Achim von Arnim, and sister of Clemens Brentano, lived in Berlin. There she attracted a circle of important persons. "Goethe, the celebrated 'prince of poetry,' maintained a safe distance from 'the extraordinary creature.' " *Goethe's Correspondence with a Child* was published in 1835.

Vienna, May 28, 1810

When I saw this man, about whom I now want to tell you, I forgot the rest of the world, just as the world also fades away when memory seizes me—yes, it fades away. My horizon begins at my feet, arches over me, and I stand in a sea of light that emanates from you, and in silence I soar on tranquil wings over hill and dale to you. Ah, forget all else, close your dear eyes, live in me for a moment, forget what lies between us, the many miles and the long hours too. Look upon me from the point where I saw you for the last time; if only I stood before you now! If only I could make it clear to you! The deep chill that shakes me whenever I have observed the world for a time and then look into the loneliness behind me and feel how truly foreign everything is to me! How does it happen that I nonetheless thrive and flourish in this wasteland? From what source do I receive dew, nourishment, warmth, blessing? From this love between us, in which even I feel myself to be worthy of love. If I were with you, I would want to give you recompense for everything. It is *Beethoven,* about whom I now want to tell you and in whose presence I forget you and all the world besides; although I am not yet of age, I know I am not in error when I claim (what perhaps no one else now understands and believes) that he forges far ahead in the progress of human culture. Shall we ever overtake him?—I doubt it. If he may only live until the mighty and awesome riddle that lies hidden in his spirit has ripened to complete fruition, yes, if he may only reach his highest goal, then he will certainly leave in our hands the key to a heavenly knowledge that will bring us one step nearer a truly blessed state.

I can safely confess to you that I believe in a divine magic that is the natural element of the spirit. This is the magic that Beethoven practices in his art; everything he can teach you is pure magic, every arrangement is the organization of a higher existence, and therefore Beethoven feels himself to be the founder of a new, sensual basis of spiritual life. I know you will understand what I mean to say, and what is true. Who could replace this spirit for us? From whom could we expect its like? To him all human activity is like a clockwork mechanism; he alone creates entirely out of his own self that which has never before been made or dreamed of. How then should any traffic with the world be of importance to him, who is already about his holy work before the sun rises, and after the sun sets scarcely looks about himself, forgets the nourishment of his body, and is swept on the stream of inspiration swiftly past the banks of our insipid everyday life? He himself said, "When I lift my eyes, I am forced to sigh, for what I see is against my religion, and I must despise the world, because it does not see that music is a higher revelation than all wisdom and philosophy. Music is the wine that inspires new creations, and I am the Bacchus who supplies man with this glorious wine and

makes him drunk in spirit. When he returns then to the dry shore of
sobriety, he finds he has brought with him a strange and wonderful catch.
I have no friends, I must live with myself alone; but I well know that
God is nearer to me than to the others in my art, I converse fearlessly
with him, I have always known and understood him; nor do I fear for my
music, it can have no evil destiny. When my music makes itself understood to someone, that person becomes free of all the misery that burdens
the rest of mankind." Beethoven told me all this when I first saw him; a
feeling of awe overcame me, that he should express himself to me with
such friendly candor, since of course I must have been entirely insignificant for him. I was also astonished, for I had been told that he is very
shy and never enters into conversation with anyone. Everyone was afraid
to lead me to him; I had to seek him out alone. He has three lodgings,
in which he hides himself alternately; one in the country, one in the city,
and the third on the city walls, which is where I found him on the fourth
floor. I entered without announcing myself; he sat at the piano, I told
him my name. He was very amiable and asked if I wanted to hear a song
he had just composed. Then he sang in a sharp and piercing voice, so
that his melancholy affected his listener, *"Kennst du das Land?"* "It is
lovely, isn't it?" he said with enthusiasm, "marvelously lovely! I want to
sing it again." He was pleased by my hearty applause. "Most people are
moved to tears by something good, but they are not artistic natures;
artists are fiery, they do not weep," he said. Then he sang another of your
poems, which he had also recently set to music, *"Trocknet nicht, Tränen
der ewigen Liebe.'* He escorted me home and on the way he said much that
was very beautiful about art; and he spoke so loudly, coming to a complete halt to do so, that it required courage to stand and listen to him.
He spoke with great passion and so unexpectedly that I also perforce must
forget the life on the street around us. The people were very surprised to
see him enter with me the large company that had assembled at our house
for dinner. After dinner he did not wait to be asked, but seated himself
at the instrument and played for a long time and wonderfully. His pride
was as much in ferment as his genius; in such a state of excitement, his
spirit creates the inconceivable and his fingers perform the impossible.
Since that time he visits every day, or I go to him, missing for his sake
invitations, galleries, theaters, and even the tower of St. Stephen's.

TRANSLATED BY SHARON JACKIW

## (30) Do not forget me wholly in death

LUDWIG VAN BEETHOVEN, The Heiligenstadt Testament

Beethoven's physical condition deteriorated rapidly after the autumn of 1826, when the disease that had long plagued him entered its final stages. Even on his deathbed he longed for the pleasures of wine, champagne, and punch, which constituted the few joys of his life.

Beethoven, born in 1770 in Bonn, was the son of a tenor. Even as a boy he performed his compositions in public. He completed his musical studies in Vienna, working briefly with Haydn. A hearing disorder gradually led to deafness. Despairing of life, he wrote his will in 1802 at age thirty-two in Heiligenstadt near Vienna. One of his students (Ferdinand Ries) reports from that period: "He lived in the country. Occasionally at eight o'clock after having had breakfast, he would say, 'Let's go for a short walk.' On one of these outings Beethoven gave me the first striking indication of his loss of hearing . . . I called his attention to a shepherd playing a flute quite nicely in the forest, and for a good half-hour Beethoven was unable to hear anything and became extremely quiet and sad, although I assured him that I, too, no longer heard anything."

Karl van Beethoven, who is mentioned in the will, could not carry out his brother's last testament, as he died eleven years before the composer. Karl was survived by his wife and a ten-year-old son whose guardian Ludwig van Beethoven became. Although they never developed a close relationship, Beethoven touchingly saw to the education and training of his nephew.

E. T. A. Hoffmann wrote that Beethoven's music opens up the realm of the incredible and boundless. "Luminous rays permeate the deep night of this realm, and we notice gigantic shadows welling up back and forth, enclosing us ever more tightly and destroying us. But we do not notice the pain of endless longing in which every desire has rapidly ascended in jubilant tones before sinking and vanishing. Only in this pain, devouring but not destroying love, hope, joy, this pain that makes our breast want to burst with a fully orchestrated harmony of all passions,——only in this do we go on living as enchanted visionaries." Beethoven's music triggers fear, awe, horror, and pain, and awakens the endless longing that is the essence of Romanticism. Beethoven himself, though, was a lonely person all his life who arduously had to earn his meager means of support. A titan of music, at home nowhere.

Heiligenstadt, October 6, 1802

For my brothers Karl and – – – – Beethoven

Oh, you people who consider me antagonistic, peevish, or misanthropic, how unjust you are to me! You do not know the secret reason why I appear to you to be so. Ever since childhood my heart and mind were imbued with the tender feeling of goodwill, and I wanted to accomplish even great deeds. But just think that I was befallen six years ago by an incurable complaint that was aggravated by incompetent doctors. Deceived from year to year in the hope of improvement, I have finally been compelled to accept the prospect of a lasting misfortune (whose cure would perhaps take years or even be impossible). Born with a fiery, lively temperament and receptive to the distractions of society, I soon had to withdraw and spend my life in solitude. If at times I wanted to ignore all these considerations, alas! how cruelly was I then driven back by the intensified, sad experience of my poor hearing. Yet it was not possible for me to say to people, "Speak louder, scream, for I am deaf!" Oh, how would it have been possible for me to mention the impairment of a sense which in me should be more perfectly developed than in other people, a sense which I possessed in the greatest perfection, even to a degree of perfection that few in my field have or have had—Oh, I cannot do it, so forgive me when you see me withdraw where I should like to have mingled with you. My misfortune pains me doubly, inasmuch as it leads to my being misjudged. For me there can be no relaxation in human company; subtle discussions and mutual exchanges of confidence cannot take place. I must live almost completely alone and expose myself to society only as much as required by extreme necessity. I must live like an outcast. If I approach company, I am overcome by a burning anxiety, fearing being placed in the danger of having my condition be noticed. Thus it was, too, during these last six months that I spent in the country. Commanded by my reasonable doctor to protect my hearing as much as possible, it almost suited my present natural inclination although, sometimes drawn by the urge for company, I let myself be tempted. But what humiliation when someone stood beside me and heard a flute from afar and I heard nothing, or someone heard the shepherd singing and I again heard nothing. Such incidents brought me close to despair, and but for a little I would have ended my life. Only art restrained me. It seemed to me impossible to leave the world before I had produced all the works I felt an urge to compose. And thus I have dragged on this miserable life—a truly miserable existence, having such a sensitive body that any somewhat sudden change can turn my best condition into the worst. I must choose patience as my guide, it is said. I have patience. I constantly hope it should be my resolve to persevere until it pleases the implacable Parcae to break the thread. Perhaps my condition will improve, perhaps not; at any rate, I am now resigned. Compelled even at age twenty-eight to become a philosopher, it is not easy—more difficult for the artist than for anyone. Almighty God, you look down into my innermost soul. You see into my heart and know that it is filled with love for humanity and a desire to do good. Oh, my fellowmen, when some day you read this statement, remember that you were unjust toward me, and let some unfortunate person find comfort in the thought of having found another, equally unfortunate, who, despite all the obstacles imposed by nature, nonetheless did everything in his power to be taken into the legions of worthy artists and human beings. And you, my brothers Karl and —— —, when I am dead, request on my behalf that Professor Schmidt, if he is still living, describe my disease, and attach this written document to his record, so that, at any rate, after my death the world and I may be reconciled as far as possible. At the same time, I name you both the heirs to my small fortune (if it may be called thus). Divide it justly, live in harmony and help one another. You know that you have long ago been forgiven for the harm you did me. I again thank you, brother Karl, in particular for the affection you have shown me in recent years. My wish is that both of you should have a better and more carefree existence than I have had. Commend virtue to your children. Only virtue, not money, can make them happy. I speak from experience. Only virtue sustained me in my misery. It was thanks to virtue and also to my art that I did not put an end to my life by suicide. Farewell, and love each other—I thank all friends, particularly Prince Lichnowsky and Professor Schmidt. I would like Prince Lichnowsky's instruments to be preserved by one of you, but they should not be the cause of strife between you. As soon as they can serve a more useful purpose, just sell them. How glad I shall be if in my grave I can still be of use to you. Well, that is all. Joyfully I go to meet death. Should it come before I have had an opportunity to develop all my artistic capacities, then in spite of my hard fate it will still come too soon, and no doubt I would like it to postpone its coming. Yet even so I should be content. Does it not, after all, free me from a condition of continual suffering? Come then, Death, whenever you like. I approach you courageously. Farewell; and when I am dead, do not wholly forget me. I deserve to be remembered by you, having thought of you often during my lifetime and tried to make you happy—Be happy—

TRANSLATED BY MARTHA HUMPHREYS

# HISTORY IS EVERYTHING

The Enlightenment had freed itself from history, in which it saw a
mere collection of senseless events beyond all reason. History in Hegel's conception is the general embodiment both of the world spirit and
of the principle of reason (31). In an utterly Hegelian spirit, Goethe
writes: "All will/ is merely wanting just because we ought to. When will
confronts, discretion keeps quite still." In Hegel's dialectic, the Enlightenment was suspended before becoming the dialectic of the Enlightenment by being turned into its opposite. The opposite is also a part of the
whole; the opposite is a part of a self-realizing "good totality." History
proves to be God's course through the world.

Schiller had already disclosed consciousness of such historical theodicy:
History is the manifestation of a moral-ethical idea (32).

In the dispute with the conception of history, Goethe's text from the
*Campaign in France* indicates a position that relies entirely on the observation and registration of facticity for the purpose of making intuitive
conclusions (33). The science of history also increasingly removed itself
from reliance on the idea of a system of thought and was regarded as
phenomenology. The epigones (34) were unable to discover meaning in
the unfolding of history; Jacob Burckhardt, for example (35), renounced
any interpretation of the hereafter. In Ranke's writing, historical realism
is of course related to the Hegelian readiness to see in the flight of all
appearances the effect of progress (36). The clearly apparent rejection both
of the metaphysical and the fatalistic concepts of history in the writings
of Marx and Engels reveals the emancipatory idea in the historical realization of the human being. If man makes his history himself (37), this
is a renewed confirmation of the influence of the dynamics of the super-
structure-infrastructure that supplants the determinist juxtaposition of
infrastructure-superstructure. But man's resultant freedom as a thinking
and acting subject is nonetheless bound into the objectivity of the event

and is the expression of a wish that is simultaneously a responsibility (38). The course of history "perforce" brings man's liberation from the enslavement of work from which he is alienated. But the route into paradise cannot be found without the individual's revolutionary action. Marx's historical idealism has a realistic foundation; his realism is admittedly retracted "into the head," and as a cerebral act leads to a secularized eschatology.

The historicism that came into being around the middle of the nineteenth century, especially as influenced by Ludwig Feuerbach, interprets being not as something without presupposition, unchanging, and suspended from time but as something created by action. The idea is not as such present a priori; rather, it "becomes," it constitutes itself in the process of becoming. The changeability of all circumstance is shown as the regulative principle of historical knowledge. Burckhardt stresses the reversibility of any- and everything, which is why order "fluidified" into transitory, hence changeable, precepts. Burckhardt considered the permanence of change to be the great, consistent, main phenomenon.

The popular conversion of the concept of development was admittedly far removed from such relativism. People believed in the consistent historical realization of liberal freedom and national unity. To an increasing extent, however, unity was emphasized at the expense of freedom.

Historicism determined the national celebrations of the nineteenth century, as expressed in numerous festivities focused on singing, gymnastics, etc. During the first phase there was a longing for power, strength, and security; traditional festivities (such as those celebrating ethnic groups and various customs) increasingly stressed the desire for national greatness. Their politicization was expressed by references to the Middle Ages and to great rulers and heroes of the battlefield. Democratic ideals lauded by the people as a progressive force, such as had typified the 1832 Hambach Festival, receded.

The second phase of nineteenth-century celebrations—i.e., after 1871, was no longer characterized by patriotic longing but by national certainty. The prevailing slogan was "It is achieved!" Unification of the state was lauded as a national identity. The festivity in quest of power had become a festivity protected by power, confirming (affirming) what formerly had been merely a festive "intimation."

The inclusion of the Germanic and medieval legacy in national celebrations and festivities (in addition to the early Germanic era, great emphasis was placed on the Hohenstaufer era as an epoch of religious commitment, confessional unity, strength of belief even including readiness for sacrifice, as the period of the emergence of the Christian-Germanic spirit, the golden era of German art and poetry, and it was idealized as the high-point of the splendor of the German Kaiser and empire) is reflected in the historical processionals that played such an important role either as independent festivities or as part of the celebrations during the nineteenth century. Here, too, as in celebrations altogether, it is possible to recognize the previously mentioned two phases:

–Prior to 1817, these parades are the expression of longing: various inventive costumes expressive of a national consciousness, of the creation of a unity among all Germans, sometimes of the democratic-republican spirit transcending cultural consciousness;

–After 1871, these parades become more one-dimensional; the dream is absent from the positivistic belief in progress; there was a belief that what had been longed for had finally been attained; the historical processional, no longer transcendent, was for the purpose of demonstration.

In Gottfried Keller's novel *Green Henry* (1855), the course of the 17 February 1840 Munich Carnival celebrating the artist, with the special theme of Kaiser Maximilian and Albrecht Dürer in Nüremberg, is described. Vast numbers of artists, "glittering in hundreds of colors," surge about and intermingle. Each participant expresses a theme and content; each one looks happily at his neighbor who, similarly, appears to advantage in a beautiful ethnic costume. Diverse crafts and guilds are formed; living sculptures prepare for their appearance. Doors are opened, trumpets and drums greet the procession. The historical longing for the unity of people and ruler, of craftsman and artist, of middle class and farmer is brilliantly staged. One group after the other moves forward.

Preceded by what builds and decorates a city, it might be said that the city itself appeared. Accompanied by two bearded halberds, the big banner was presented to the city. The waving flag was held high by the bold standard bearer dressed in a garment with many slits, his left fist proudly braced against his side. Then came the town major, magnificently attired in martial red and black, wearing his shield, his head covered with a broad beret sporting feathers. He was followed by the mayor, the syndic, the city councillors, including many a respected and salutary man, and finally the festive rows of noble families. Silk, gold, and jewels shone in conspicuous excess. The mercantile patricians whose wealth floated on all seas, who simultaneously defended the city in warlike posture with weapons they had forged themselves, and who participated in the wars of the realm, exceeded the lesser nobility in magnificence and wealth as well as in communal sympathy and ethical dignity. Their wives and daughters rustled like large living flowers, some with golden veils and caps and beautifully braided hair, others with hats adorned with feathers; the latter dressed in the finest linen, the former surrounding their bare shoulders with clouds of expensive perfumery. In the middle of these splendid rows of people there were some Venetian gentlemen and painters, conceived to be guests, who were poetically wrapped in their foreign purple or black coats.

The narrator is profoundly fascinated by such historical show and abandons himself entirely to "all manner of nationalistic self-satisfaction." Admittedly he does not consider "how tirelessly the vessels of fate ascend and fall."

National self-satisfaction was generally symptomatic of historicism: its intention of producing a new popular national identity by magnificent reference to the past constricted the concept of history until it was reduced to nationalism and chauvinism. The arrogance of pride disregarded the shifts of fate; people felt confident of the future. Consequently the route from the past led to national assertiveness in the world. It proved, however, to be a route that led first to confusion, then to decline. Not only was history not everything: it ended in nothingness. The vision of historicism (brilliantly staged once more as a total work of art in Richard Wagner's *Meistersinger of Nüremberg*) was replaced by the "dark vision" that Burckhardt's insight into the reversibility of all and everything made clear in expressive images. Order disintegrated. Errors, confusions, and then the course of war that ran amok.

## (31) The aim of world history

GEORG FRIEDRICH WILHELM HEGEL, Lectures on the Philosophy of World History

For Hegel, history was "progress in the consciousness of freedom"; he was convinced that world history proceeds reasonably, that history is a product of eternal reason, a product of the "reasonable, necessary course of the world spirit." The posthumous work published in 1837 is based on manuscripts of the lectures on the philosophy of history delivered by Hegel in Berlin starting in 1822.

The question at issue is therefore the ultimate end of mankind, the end which the spirit sets itself in the world, and which it is driven to realize incessantly and with irresistible power. The more specific implications of this ultimate end follow on from what has already been said with regard to the national spirit. We have seen that the spirit cannot be concerned with anything other than itself. Nothing is higher than the spirit, and nothing is more worthy of being its object. It cannot rest or occupy itself with anything else until it knows its own nature. This thought, which we have specified as the highest and only interest of the spirit, is, of course, of a general and abstract nature, and there is a wide gulf between it and that which constitutes the interests of nations and individuals as we observe them in history. On the empirical level, we see specific ends and particular interests with which nations have been occupied for centuries. We need only think, for example, of the antagonism between Rome and Carthage. And knowing these empirical phenomena is a far cry from recognizing in them that process of thought which, as already said, constitutes their essential interest. We shall not discuss until later the opposition between the immediately obvious interests of the spirit and its absolute interest as specified above. At least it is not difficult to grasp the general significance of the idea that the relationship of the free spirit to itself is a necessary one, precisely because it is a free spirit; otherwise it would not be free at all but dependent. We have defined the goal of history as consisting in the spirit's development toward self-consciousness, or in its making the world conform to itself (for the two are identical). It might equally be said that the spirit produces its concept out of itself, objectivizes it, and thus becomes the being of its own concept; it becomes conscious of itself in the objective world so that it may attain its salvation: for as soon as the objective world conforms to its internal requirements, it has realized its freedom. When it has determined its own end in this way, its progress takes on a more definite character in that it no longer consists of a mere increase in quantity. It may also be added that, even on the evidence of our own ordinary consciousness, we must acknowledge that the consciousness must undergo various stages of development before it becomes aware of its own essential nature.

The aim of world history, therefore, is that the spirit should attain knowledge of its own true nature, that it should objectivize this knowledge and transform it into a real world, and give itself an objective existence. The essential point to note is that this aim is itself a product of the spirit. The spirit is not a natural entity like an animal, for the animal is no more than its immediate existence. The spirit is such that it produces itself and makes itself what it is. Thus the first form it assumes in its real existence is the outcome of its own activity. Its essential being is actuosity, not static existence, for it has produced itself, it has come to exist for itself, and made itself what it is by its own agency. It can only be said to have a true existence if it has produced itself, and its essential being is process in the absolute sense. This process, in which it mediates itself with itself by its own unaided efforts, has various distinct moments; it is full of movement and change, and is determined in different ways at different times. It consists essentially of a series of separate stages, and world history is the expression of the divine process which is a graduated progression in which the spirit comes to know and realize itself and its own truth. Its various stages are stages in the self-recognition of the spirit; and the essence of the spirit, its supreme imperative, is that it should recognize, know, and realize itself for what it is. It accomplishes this end in the history of the world; it produces itself in a series of determinate forms, and these forms are the nations of world history. Each of them represents a particular stage of development, so that they correspond to epochs in the history of the world. Or on a more fundamental level, they are the principles in which the spirit has discovered itself, and which it is impelled to realize. There is therefore an essential connection between them in which the nature of the spirit alone is expressed.

World history is the expression of the divine and absolute process of the spirit in its highest forms, of the progression whereby it discovers its true nature and becomes conscious of itself. The specific forms it assumes at each of these stages are the national spirits of world history, with all the determinate characteristics of their ethical life, their constitutions, their art, their religion, and their knowledge. The world spirit has an infinite urge and an irresistible impulse to realize these stages of its development; for this sequence and its realization are its true concept. World history merely shows how the spirit gradually attains consciousness and the will to truth; it progresses from its early glimmerings to major discoveries and finally to a state of complete consciousness. We have already discussed the ultimate end of this process. The principles of the national spirits in their necessary progression are themselves only moments of the one universal spirit, which ascends through them in the course of history to its consummation in an all-embracing totality.

This vision of a process whereby the spirit realizes its aim in history clashes with a widespread attitude concerning the nature of ideals and their relationship to reality. For no opinion is more widely held or more frequently voiced than the lament that ideals cannot be translated into reality—be they ideals of the imagination or ideals of reason, so long as they claim to be ideals. In particular, we are told that the ideals of youth dissolve into dreams in the cold light of reality. Whatever ideals of this kind do founder on the rocks of harsh reality in the course of the voyage of life must be primarily subjective; they can belong only to individuals who consider themselves superior to and wiser than others. As such, they have no place in the present discussion. For the fancies of isolated individuals cannot become binding upon reality at large, just as the laws of the universe are not framed solely for the benefit of single individuals, who may in fact be most unfavourably affected by them. It may certainly happen that the ideals of individuals are not realized. Individuals often have their own peculiar opinions of themselves, of their lofty intentions, of the splendid deeds they hope to perform, and of their own supposed importance from which the world, as they think, must assuredly benefit. Be that as it may, such ideas merit no further attention here. The dreams of the individual are often no more than exaggerated estimates of his own personal significance. Furthermore, the individual may well be treated unjustly; but this is a matter of indifference to world history, which uses individuals only as instruments to further its own progress.

But these are not the only kind of ideals. There are also the ideals of reason, those ideas of the good, the true, and all that is best in the world; and these have a genuine claim to be satisfied, for their nonfulfillment is generally recognized to be an objective injustice. Poets such as Schiller have expressed their grief over unfulfilled ideals with great pathos and emotion. But if we say that universal reason is fulfilled, this has of course nothing to do with individual empirical instances; the latter may fare either well or badly, as the case may be, for the concept has authorized the forces of contingency and particularity to exercise their vast influence in the empirical sphere. When we consider particular instances, we may well conclude that there is much injustice in the world, and there is certainly much to find fault with among individual phenomena. But we are not concerned here with empirical details; they are at the mercy of chance, which has no place in the present discussion. It is only too easy to indulge in criticism, and it helps to confirm men's estimates of their own superior knowledge and good intentions. Subjective criticism of this kind, directed solely at particular matters and their shortcomings—regardless of the universal reason behind them—is extremely facile; and inasmuch as it conveys an impression of good intentions toward the welfare of the whole, and lends itself an air of sincere benevolence, it can become extremely self-important and full of conceit. It is easier to perceive the shortcomings of individuals, states, and the course of world affairs than to understand their true import. For in passing negative judgments, one looks down on the matter in hand with a superior and supercilious air, without having gone into it thoroughly enough to understand its true nature, i.e. its positive significance. The criticism may well be justified, except that it is far easier to detect shortcomings than the true substance (as in works of art, for example). People often think they have done their job when they have found something which can be justly criticized; they are right, of course, in one respect; but they are also wrong in so far as they fail to recognize the positive factor. To see only the bad side in everything and to overlook all the positive and valuable qualities is a sign of extreme superficiality. Age, in general, takes a milder view, whereas youth is always dissatisfied; this is because age brings with it maturity of judgment, which does not simply tolerate the bad along with the rest out of sheer lack of interest, but has learned from the seriousness of life to look for the substance and enduring value of things. And this is not so much equity as justice.

But to return to the true ideal, the Idea of reason itself, philosophy should help us to understand that the actual world is as it ought to be. It shows us that the rational will, the concrete good is indeed all-powerful, and that this absolute power translates itself into reality. The true good, the universal and divine reason, also has the power to fulfill its own purpose, and the most concrete representation of this goodness and reason is God. For goodness, not just as a general idea but also as an effective force, is what we call God. Philosophy teaches us that no force can surpass the power of goodness or of God or prevent God's purposes from being realized; it shows us that God's will must always prevail in the end, and that world history is nothing more than the plan of providence. The world is governed by God; and world history is the content of his government and the execution of his plan. To comprehend this is the task of the philosophy of world history, and its initial assumption is that the ideal is fulfilled and that only that which corresponds to the Idea possesses true reality. The pure light of this divine Idea, which is no mere ideal, dispels the illusion that the world is a collection of senseless and foolish occurrences. The aim of philosophy is to recognize the content and reality of the divine Idea, and to defend reality against its detractors. For it is through reason that we apprehend the work of God.

What is usually called reality is seen by philosophy as no more than an idle semblance which has no reality in and for itself. If we have the impression that the events of the past are totally calamitous and devoid of sense, we can find consolation, so to speak, in this awareness. But consolation is merely something received in compensation for a misfortune which ought never to have happened in the first place, and it belongs to the world of finite things. Philosophy, therefore, is not really a means of consolation. It is more than that, for it transfigures reality with all its apparent injustices and reconciles it with the rational; it shows that it is based upon the Idea itself, and that reason is fulfilled in it. For in reason, the divinity is present. The basic content of reason is the divine Idea, and its essence is the plan of God. In the context of world history, the Idea is not equivalent to reason as encountered in the subjective will, but to the activity of God alone. We conceive of reason as a means of perceiving the Idea, and even its etymology* suggests that it is a perception of something expressed, in other words, of the Logos—the true. The true acquires its truth in the created world. God expresses himself, and himself alone; he is that power whose nature is self-expression and whose expression can be perceived by reason. And what reason perceives is the truth and image of God. Thus philosophy concludes that nothing which is empty of significance can be an ideal, but only that which possesses reality, and that the Idea reveals itself to perception.

TRANSLATED BY H. B. NISBET

## (32) From every merit a path to infinity lies open

FRIEDRICH SCHILLER, What Is, and for What Purpose Does One Study Universal History?

Schiller's inaugural lecture as professor of history in Jena (1789) was characterized by belief that the fragments of historical knowledge could be ordered into a reasonable, structural whole. The previous generation, without knowing or aiming for it, had tried to "bring about our human century."

And treated in such a way, the study of world history will afford you a pursuit as attractive as it is useful. It will ignite light in your reason and a beneficial enthusiasm in your heart. It will draw your mind away

---

* Hegel is alluding to the etymological relationship between *Vernunft* (reason) and *vernehmen* (to perceive).

from a common and small view of moral matters, and by unfolding the great panorama of epochs and people before your eyes, it will improve the precipitous decisions of the instant and the narrow judgments of selfishness. By accustoming man to encounter the past in its entirety and to hasten forward into the future with his conclusions, it thus conceals those boundaries between birth and death that enclose the life of man so tightly and oppressively; in optical illusion it thus expands and leads the individual, unperceiving, into his species.

Man is transformed and flees from the stage; his opinions flee and are transformed with him. History alone remains constantly on the scene, an immortal citizen of all nations and times. Like Homeric Zeus, it looks with an equally tranquil gaze upon the bloody toil of war and upon the peaceful peoples who nourish themselves innocently on the milk of their flocks. However arbitrarily man's freedom seems to tamper with the course of the world, it watches the confused game calmly, for its far-reaching gaze discovers even at a distance where this arbitrarily roaming freedom is led by the leash of necessity. What it keeps secret from the punishing consciences of a Gregor and a Cromwell, it hurries to reveal to humanity: "that a selfish man, though he can pursue lowly aims, will unknowingly further excellent ones."

No false gleam will blind it, no current prejudice will sweep it away, for it experiences the ultimate destiny of all things. To it, everything that *ceases* has endured with equal brevity; it holds the olive wreath it has earned and shatters the obelisk erected by vanity. By opening out the fine network through which the quiet hand of Nature has been developing its plan for the strengths of man since the beginning of the world, and by indicating exactly what has been won for Nature's great plan in each epoch, it thus restores the true measure of happiness and merit that the ruling delusions in every century falsified anew. It cures us of the exaggerated admiration of antiquity and of the childish yearning for times gone by; and by calling our attention to our own possessions, it keeps us from longing for the extolled golden ages of Alexander and Augustus.

All earlier ages—without knowing or intending it—have exerted themselves to bring about our *human* century. Ours are all the treasures that diligence and genius, reason and experience ultimately brought home in the long ages of the world. Only from the history of the world will *you* learn to place value on the goods that habit and undisputed possession so willingly rob of our gratitude. Precious and dear goods, to which clings the blood of the noblest and best, the goods that have had to be won by the hard toil of so many generations! And who among you, where a clear spirit is joined with a feeling heart, could be mindful of this high obligation without a quiet wish stirring within him to discharge the debt to the coming generation that he can no longer repay to the preceding one? A noble desire must be kindled within us to contribute from *our* own means to the rich heritage of truth, nobility, and freedom that we have inherited from our forebears and must pass on, richly enhanced, to posterity and to anchor our fleeting existence to this immutable chain that winds through all generations of mankind. However varied the lot be that awaits you in bourgeois society—all of you can contribute something! From every merit a pathway to immortality lies open, to true immortality, I mean, where deeds live and hurry onward, even if the name of their originator should remain behind.

TRANSLATED BY RALPH R. READ

## (33) A new epoch in world history dawns

JOHANN WOLFGANG VON GOETHE, Campaign in France

In 1792 Goethe was part of the entourage of Duke Carl August of Sachsen-Weimar in the campaign against revolutionary France. Approximately thirty years later the poet describes his impressions (his work was published in 1822). The sufferings caused by war are objectively seized; to the removed observer, the political event seems more chaotic than meaningful. Goethe proves to be a historical realist.

I had heard so much about battle fever, and wanted to know what it was really all about. Boredom and a spirit that is aroused to boldness, indeed recklessness, by every danger tempted me to ride, quite composedly, up to the outworks La Lune. It had been retaken by our side, but afforded a wild sight: the shattered roofs, the scattered bundles of wheat, the mortally wounded stretched out here and there, and now and then cannon shot that, still straying over, clattered into the remnants of tile roofs.

All alone, left to myself, I rode off left onto the heights and could clearly oversee the favorable position of the French; they were situated in an amphitheater, quite calm and secure, yet Kellermann on the left wing might be more possible to reach.

I encountered good company: they were acquaintances, officers from the general staff and from the regiment, thoroughly puzzled to find me here. They wanted to take me back with them, but I spoke of a special undertaking, and without further ado they left me to my well-known, peculiar obstinacy.

I had now gone well into the region where the bullets were whizzing by; the sound is strange enough, as if it were compounded of the humming of a top, the hissing of water, and the whistling of a bird. They were less dangerous due to the damp ground; wherever they hit, they would stick, and so my foolish foray was at least spared the danger of a ricochet.

Under these circumstances, however, I soon noticed that something unusual was taking place inside me; I observed it precisely, and yet the sensation could only be communicated metaphorically. It seemed as if I were in a very hot place and simultaneously completely saturated with the same heat, so that I felt completely identical with the same element in which I found myself. The eyes lose nothing of their strength nor clarity, but it is as if the world had a certain reddish-brown tinge that makes one's condition as well as objects even more appreciable. I was unable to notice any agitation of the blood; rather, everything seemed to be consumed in that glow. This illuminates in what sense the condition could be called a fever. It remains noteworthy, however, that this feeling of hideous dread is brought to us only through our ears; for the thunder of cannon, the howling, whistling, crashing of the balls through the air is, after all, the real cause of these sensations.

When I had ridden back and was in perfect safety, I found it curious that all the glow had immediately vanished and not the slightest trace of feverish agitation was left. This condition, by the way, is one of the least desirable; as I, then, among my dear and noble comrades of war found scarcely a one who would voice a truly passionate appetite for it.

Thus the day had passed; the French stood unmoving. Kellermann too had taken up a more comfortable position; our men were pulled back from the gunfire, and it was as if nothing had happened. Great consternation spread among the army. This very morning they had thought of nothing but forking the French up and swallowing them down, to the last man. Indeed, such an absolute confidence in such an army, in the Duke of Brunswick, had lured even me to take part in this dangerous expedition; but now the men kept to themselves, not looking at each other, or if they did, it was only to damn or to swear. Just as night was about to fall we formed a circle, in the middle of which not even the usual fire could be lighted; most were silent, a few spoke, and yet each of them was devoid of perspective and proportion. Finally they called upon me—what did I think of it all? for I had often amused and refreshed the group with little sayings; this time I said: "Here and today a new epoch of world history commences, and you can say that you were there."

At this moment, as no one had anything to eat, I requisitioned a little bread from that procured this morning, and the contents of a small brandy bottle left over from the wine so generously dispensed yesterday; and therefore I had to resign completely the role of the welcome miracle worker I had played so boldly at the fire yesterday.

The bombardment had scarcely ceased when rain and storm descended again and made for the most miserable conditions under the open sky and on sticky clay ground. And yet, after waking so long, after such agitation of mind and body, sleep announced its presence as murky night descended. We had settled in as best we could behind a rise that cut off the wind when it occurred to someone that we should dig in for the night and cover ourselves with our coats. We prepared to do so right away, and a number of graves were shoveled out, for which the horse artillery lent us the tools. The Duke of Weimar himself did not disdain such a premature interment.

So for the payment of eight *groschen* I received the cover in question, wrapped myself in the coat and spread it over myself as well, hardly feeling its dampness. Ulysses, in the mantle he acquired in similar fashion, cannot have rested with greater comfort and self-content.

All these preparations had taken place against the will of the colonel, who made us take notice that the French had a battery placed behind a thicket on a hill opposite us, with which they could bury us in earnest. But we did not wish to give up this tranquil place and our sagely devised comforts, and this was not the last time I noticed that, in order to elude discomfort, people do not shun danger.

TRANSLATED BY RALPH R. READ

## (34) The misery of later generations

KARL LEBERECHT IMMERMANN, The Epigones

Immermann (1796–1840) became director of the higher district court in Düsseldorf after completing his study of jurisprudence, philosophy, and history. Under his influence as director of the city theater there, it became one of the exemplary stages in Germany. His period novel, *The Epigones* (1836), reflects the widespread feeling of oppression by the powerful Classical and Romantic legacy. Despite utter sobriety and lack of illusion, people feel helplessly consigned to dissolution and skepticism, powerless against the newness of a future heralded by profound signs of crisis. The human being, "a feather on the ocean," is overcome by moral seasickness.

We cannot deny that a dangerous epoch of the world has been ushered in. At all times mankind has had misfortune enough; the curse of the present race, however, is to feel unfortunate without any particular grief. A desolate irresolution and perturbation, a ridiculous quest for security, a distractedness, a chasing after one knows not what, a fear of terrors that are the more uncanny for having no form! It is as if mankind, cast about in its boat on an overpowering sea, is suffering from a moral seasickness whose end can hardly be conceived.

It is necessary to have belonged at least partially to a different period to be entirely able to feel the contrast of both eras, the more recent of which began with the revolution. Our blatherers of the day look with great contempt on that condition of Germany which developed toward the last quarter of the previous century, producing an effect that lasted for a number of years. To them it seems vapid and sorry, but they are mistaken. People at that time admittedly did not know and do as many things as now; the circles in which they moved were smaller, but they were more at home in their own circles. Activities were pursued for their own sakes, hence in my speech I argue for limitation by referring to quite a modest old saying: the shoemaker should stick to his craft. Nowadays every shoemaker's skills are inadequate, and no shoe seems any longer to fit comfortably, regardless of how it is positioned.

To express the whole misery in *one* word, we are epigones and bear the burden with which each successor and later generation is usually stuck. The great endeavor in the realm of the spirit undertaken by our fathers from their huts and cottages supplied us with numerous treasures that are now spread out on all market tables. Without any particular exertion, even a slight talent is capable of acquiring the small change of every art and science. But with borrowed ideas it is as with borrowed grain: anyone who traffics foolishly with foreign goods always becomes poorer. The heavenly goddess's obligingness toward every simpleton has given rise to a quite peculiar ruin of the word. This palladium of mankind, this birth certificate of our divine origin has been turned into a lie, its virginity dishonored. With slight effort, the most clever, the richest, and most forceful figures of speech are everywhere to be found for the most vain appearance, for the shallowest opinions, for the emptiest heart. Old, straightforward *conviction* has therefore gone out of fashion, and people think it proper to speak of views. But with this, too, an untruth is mostly stated, for as a rule people have not even looked at the things about which they speak and pretend to be concerned.

TRANSLATED BY MARTHA HUMPHREYS

## (35) Concerning the state

JACOB BURCKHARDT, Reflections on World History

Burckhardt's *Reflections on World History* date back to lectures he delivered in 1870–1871. As a historian, he was characterized by a deep aversion toward the Hegelian philosophy of history (as shown, for example, in *The Era of Constantine the Great* and *The Civilization of the Renaissance in Italy*). Burckhardt did not want to construct but to observe; his observations detected repetition rather than development in history. A philosophy of history, proceeding chronologically, places greater emphasis on contrasts between successive eras and peoples; it observes the past as the opposite of the present and as a preparatory stage to the development that we represent. Burckhardt, in contrast, wanted to point out identities, relationships, and similarities—i.e., the constants, repetitions, that which was typical.

Burckhardt was born in 1818 in Basel and died there in 1897. From an early age he was "most profoundly imbued with the value and dignity of the individual person. The least possible amount of coercion should be exerted by the state on the thinking and actions of the valuable individual person. Strictly in the humanistic tradition, too, is his idea that true civilization and genuine cultivation of the individual are attained only through an individual, inherently lawful development that is nourished solely by the most elevated values and content. It is not astonishing, however, that for the skeptical Burckhardt, whose lyrical ego attachment was from an early age the source of his involvement in observing the world of things and of historical achievements, the mere individual does not represent an ultimate value. Rather, Burckhardt's love is reserved only for the individual who freely and independently posits his own tasks, with the added stipulation that this individual be both a creator and bearer of civilization." (Rudolf Marx)

Regardless of its origin, a state (a people forming a political entity) will prove its viability only if its force is transformed into strength.

Of course, as long as external growth continues, every power strives toward utter completion and perfection, both internally and externally, and does not recognize as valid any law of weaker peoples.

In this respect, peoples and dynasties act exactly the same, the only difference being that, among peoples, the desires of the masses is decisive, while among dynasties reason of state is decisive. It is not merely lust for conquest but so-called necessity, as perhaps exemplified by the Carolingian dynasty.

Apart from its internal acts, such as abrogation of all inherited special rights and the extension of the concept of power to absolutely everything, ostensibly in the interest of the common good, even to the ultimate consequence of *l'état c'est moi,* its conduct is shown externally in its most naïve form by the ancient world empires. They conquered, enslaved, plundered, and pillaged far and wide. Followed by their booty and their slaves, their kings marched into Thebes or Nineveh and were considered by the people to be the beloved of God until a stronger, new world empire came into being. In modern Europe, however, periods of extended tranquility alternate with periods of territorial crises, because at some point the so-called balance of power (which never existed) has been disturbed.

And it now turns out—if one thinks of Louis XIV, Napoleon, and revolutionary popular governments—that power in itself is evil (Schlosser). That is, if religion is given no consideration, the right of egoism is denied the individual and permitted the state. Weaker neighbors are subjected and annexed or otherwise made dependent, not to deter their enmity, for that is the least concern. On the contrary, they are subjected to impede another from seizing and using them politically. That is, the potential political ally of an enemy is enslaved and, having gotten on this track, there is no stopping. Everything becomes excusable, for "nothing would have been achieved by mere contemplation. On the contrary, we would soon have been devoured by other scoundrels" and "the others do it, too."

The next step is that such measures take place as a precaution without any particular cause, in accordance with the principle of "if we take it soon enough, we will avert a dangerous war in the future." A permanent desire for territorial rounding-off finally develops; anything that is convenient and can be seized—such as "vital" stretches of coastline—is taken, using in doing so all the weaknesses, internal disorders, and enemies of the victim. The degree of desirability of accumulating smaller territories, the prospect of quadrupling the value by merely doubling the territory, etc., becomes irresistible. Perhaps even the peoples affected, especially those in small states lacking freedom, desire a reunion because it offers them the prospect of an enlargement of customs and industrial zones, quite apart from the artificial lament of recent times.

Wherever possible, misdeeds must occur naïvely, for the aesthetic effect of legal justifications and recriminations by both sides is horrible. Power, craved and attained by all manner of crime, is registered as shame, since law still has a numinous sound that is considered indispensable. The result is such sophistry as that indulged in by Friedrich II during the first Silesian war, the tidy doctrine of "unjustified existences."

The subsequent successful, real amalgamation of what was stolen is not an ethical exoneration of the robber, just as altogether no resultant good can exculpate an evil past.

Mankind must even come to terms with the worst, once it has happened, summon what is left of its intact strength, and continue to build.

Even the state established against strong protest is compelled in time to develop a kind of law and civilization, a result of its gradual usurpation by its just and civilized citizens.

Ultimately the colossal, indirect excuse is made that, without the perpetrator's previous cognizance, remote aims of significance for world history have been promoted.

Later generations especially, who know that their temporal advantage is based on what subsequently occurred, reason in this manner. But the counter-questions arise: What do we know of aims? And, if such existed, could they not have been attained by other means? And does the destruction of universal morality by successful crime not count at all?

One thing is nonetheless conceded by most: culture's royal prerogative to the conquest and enslavement of barbarism, which must now abandon internecine warfare and heinous customs and adjust to the general moral norms of the civilized state. Above all, it is permissible to divest barbarism of its dangerousness, its potential power of aggression. It remains questionable, however, whether it is really possible to civilize barbarians more than superficially. What good can come from the descendants of rulers and conquered barbarians, especially of different races? It must be asked whether their retreat and demise (as in America) is not more desirable and whether the civilized person flourishes everywhere on alien soil. In any case, the means of subjugation and containment used by the previous barbarism should not be surpassed.

What affects the state internally did not come about by abdication of individual egoism. Rather, the state *is* that abdication, it *is* the compensation to these individuals, so that the greatest possible number of interests and egoisms thereby permanently get their due and ultimately completely merge their existence with it.

The highest value attained by the state is then to engender a sense of duty, or patriotism, among the better citizens. On the levels both of the primitive and of the derivative cultures, patriotism is more directly manifested as the high virtue of race. Partially fostered by hatred of the other, patriotism among the educated is expressed as the need for consecration to a universal; the need for rising above the selfishness of the individual and of the family to the extent that this need is not met by religion and by society.

For the state to wish directly to realize moral purposes, which can and may only be done by society, is degenerate and constitutes philosophical and bureaucratic arrogance.

The state is truly the "standard-bearer of law and of the good" that must be established somewhere, but it is no more than that. The "realization of morality on earth" by the state would have to fail a thousand times from the inner inadequacy of human nature in general, even from the inadequacy of the best of humanity in particular. The forum of morality is essentially different from that of the state; it is indeed a lot that the state even upholds conventional law. With the greatest likelihood, it will remain sound if it remains aware of its nature (perhaps even of its basic origin) as the institution of necessity.

The benefit conferred by the state consists in its being the guardian of law. The separate individuals are subject to laws and judges equipped with the right of coercion that protects both private obligations entered into between individuals as well as the general necessities. It does so far less by the real exertion of force than by the beneficial fear of force. The security necessary to life consists in the confidence that this will also occur in the future—i.e., that within the state, as long as it exists at all, it will no longer be necessary to bear arms against one another. Everyone knows that force can increase neither wealth nor power. On the contrary, the use of force can only hasten its user's ruin.

The state must also impede contention about the various interpretations of the "civic life." The state should be above parties; admittedly each party will seek to gain power over the state and to pass itself off as the universal standard.

Finally: in late, mixed configurations of the state, which harbors classes having various, even antagonistic religions and religious concepts (and in the latter sense, there is religious toleration in all civilized states), the state at least tries to assure that not only egoisms but differing metaphysical concepts avoid bloody strife (which, without the state, would happen

unavoidably even today, for the fanatics would start and would be imi-
tated by others).

TRANSLATED BY MARTHA HUMPHREYS

## (36) All generations of mankind appear before God with equal rights

LEOPOLD VON RANKE, How the Concept of Progress Is to Be
Understood in History

Leopold von Ranke was born in a small Thuringian village in 1795, the year of the Basel
Peace. He later interpreted the date to be the time when the idea of toppling the revolution was abandoned and the system of Prussian neutrality created.

Ranke's attitude toward the world was conservative. His sympathies lay where the
movement of the world took place without upheaval. He studied theology in Leipzig and
turned to historiography from religion rather than from politics. Under the maxim that
each epoch was immediate before God, Ranke was the exemplary representative of a science of history that sought to free itself from the idealistic, Romantic, subjective method
of observation in a thrust toward objectivity and facticity. "I should wish both to extinguish my own self and to let the things speak, to let the powerful forces appear."

His principal works were *The Roman Popes, German History in the Era of the Reformation,
Nine Books of Prussian History, French History,* and *English History.* Ranke died in 1886.

If, like many philosophers, one wanted to assume that all of mankind
progressed from a given primitive state to a positive goal, one could conceive it in two ways: either that a universally guiding will promoted the
development of the human race from one point to the next, or that mankind has, so to speak, an aspect of spiritual nature that of necessity drives
things toward a definite goal. I should not like to consider either of these
views philosophically tenable or historically provable. The point of view
cannot be declared philosphically acceptable, because in the first case it
absolutely suspends human freedom and brands people as tools lacking
will, and because in the other instance people would absolutely have to
be God or nothing.

Historically these views are also not provable, because first of all the
largest part of mankind is still in the primordial condition even at the
outset. Then, too, there is the question of what is progress? Where can
the progress of mankind be noticed? There are aspects of great historical
development that are established in the Roman and Germanic nation,
where there is certainly a spiritual power developing by degrees. Indeed

in all of history a certain historical power of the human spirit cannot be denied. It is a movement established in primordial time that continues with a certain constancy. However, within mankind altogether there is only one order of peoples that participates in this universally historical movement, while others are excluded from it. In general, however, we also cannot consider the nationalities comprehended in the historical movement as being in constant progress [. . .]

Secondly, though, another error must be avoided—namely, the error of imagining that the progressive development of centuries simultaneously comprehended all aspects of human nature and ability. History shows us—to stress one instance, for example—that in recent times art flourished most in the fifteenth century and in the first half of the sixteenth century; in contrast, it declined most at the end of the seventeenth century and in the first three-quarters of the eighteenth century. With poetry it is precisely the same. Here, too, there are only moments where art is really prominent. It is not shown, however, that it increases in the course of centuries to a higher potency.

If we thereby exclude a geographical law of development and if, on the other hand, we must assume, as history teaches us, that peoples among whom the development has begun, although neither constant nor continuous, can perish, we will better recognize in what the continuous movement of mankind really consistes. It is based on the fact that the great spiritual tendencies dominating mankind are at times conspicuous, at times sequential. These tendencies, however, always have a definite, particular direction which predominates, causing the other to recede. Thus, for example, in the second half of the sixteenth century the religious element was so predominant that the literary element receded in its favor. In contrast, in the eighteenth century the drive toward utilization gained such ground that art and related activities had to yield to it. In each epoch of mankind, therefore, a certain great tendency is expressed, and progress is based on the fact that a certain movement of the human spirit is expressed in each epoch, accentuating first one tendency and then another, characteristically manifesting itself in it.

In contrast to what is expressed here, if one wanted to assume that progress consists in the fact that in each epoch the life of mankind gains in potency, that each generation utterly surpasses the preceding, the last generation consequently being of course the most privileged and the preceding generation merely the transmitter of the subsequent generation, it would be an injustice toward the deity. In and for itself, such an evenly mediated generation would have no meaning; it would be meaningful only to the extent that it was a stage toward the subsequent generation and would not stand in immediate reference to the deity. I, however, maintain: each epoch is immediate to God, and its value is not at all based on what emanates from it. On the contrary, its value emanates from its own existence and its own identity. The reflection on history, particularly on the individual life in history, is thereby given quite a singular stimulus, necessitating the consideration of each epoch as something valid in itself and extremely worthy of scrutiny.

The historian therefore must first direct special attention to how people thought and lived in a particular period. The historian will then find that, apart from certain immutable, eternal, central ideas such as the moral idea, for example, each epoch has its special tendency and its own ideal. If, however, each epoch in and for itself has its justification and value, what emanates from it cannot be overlooked. The historian must therefore next give attention also to the difference between the separate epochs in order to observe the inner necessity of the sequence. A certain progress is hereby undeniable; but I should not like to assert that it moves in a straight line. Rather, it moves more like a stream that wends its own way. If I may be permitted the observations, I conceive the deity in such a manner that, since no time lies ahead of it, it surveys the entire history of mankind in its totality and finds equal value everywhere. The idea of the education of the human race admittedly has something true in itself; but all generations of mankind appear before God with equal rights, which is also how the historian must regard the matter.

TRANSLATED BY MARTHA HUMPHREYS

## (37) We make our history ourselves

FRIEDRICH ENGELS, Letter to J. Bloch

Friedrich Engels (1820–1895) was the son of a Wuppertal textile manufacturer who remained committed to Marx in unselfish friendship following their initial meeting in 1842. While on a business trip in 1842–1843, Engels became familiar with "the conditions of the working classes in England" (which is also the title of a work published in 1845) that prompted his transition from bourgeois-democratic sympathies to a socialist viewpoint.

Toward the end of his life, Engels repeatedly warned against a schematic and one-sided application of the categories of a materialistic interpretation of history, demanding a more differentiated method of observation. Despite his extensive participation in the events of the time, the by now elderly Engels, who by the time of his death had lived for nearly a half-century in England, had become somewhat detached critically. He did not mince matters, but he never "attempted to be patronizing toward his political friends or to use his authority as 'Marx's successor' to silence them. . . . The revolutionary Friedrich Engels lived at peace with nature, because he believed to the end that the dialectical development in nature and society will lead to the realization of socialist ideals. This does not mean that Engels underrated the role of the active revolutionary deed or of conscious organization, but it seems certain to me that he had a less tortured relationship to reality than did Karl Marx. Despite his utter commitment, Friedrich Engels retained something of the gentleman's generous composure." (Iring Fetscher)

London, Sept. 21–22, 1890

According to the materialistic view of history, the production and reproduction of real life is the *ultimately* decisive factor in history. Neither Marx nor I have ever asserted more. If now someone distorts this to say that the economic factor is the *sole* determining factor, then he transforms that statement into a meaningless, abstract, absurd phrase. The economic situation is the base, but various factors of the superstructure exert their influence on the course of historical struggles and in many cases predominantly determine their *form*. These factors include political forms of the class struggle and its results, constitutions established by the victorious class after winning a battle, and so forth; forms of law and perhaps even the reflexes of all these real-life struggles in the brains of the participants; political, juridical, philosophical theories; religious views and their further development into dogmatic systems. It is a reciprocal effect of all these factors, in which the economic movement, over and above the countless number of random events (i.e., of things and occurrences whose internal cohesion is so remote or unprovable that we can consider it to be nonexistent and therefore disregard it) finally prevails as something necessary. Otherwise the application of theory to any given period of history would indeed be easier than the solution to a simple equation of the first degree.

We make our history ourselves, primarily under very specific presuppositions and conditions. Among these the economic ones are ultimately decisive; but also political ones and others, even tradition, haunting the heads of men, all play a role, even if not the decisive one. The Prussian state, too, ultimately came into being and developed due to historical, ultimately economic causes. It can hardly be asserted however that, of all the many small states of North Germany, it was precisely Brandenburg that was destined by economic necessity alone—and not by any other factors—to become the major power that has epitomized the economic, linguistic, and, ever since the Reformation, the religious difference as well between the North and the South. (And above all, its involvement with Poland through the possession of Prussia, and thereby with international political relationships which, after all, are decisive in shaping the landed aristocracy of Austria.) One cannot tolerate an economic explanation of every small German state past and present, or the origin of the High German sound shift that expanded the geographical partition formed by the mountains from the Sudeten to the Taunus into a veritable split through Germany, without making oneself ridiculous.

In the second place, history is constituted in such a way that the end result always emerges from the conflicts of many individual wills, each conflict in turn made what it is by a large number of particular circumstantial imperatives. Thus there are countless forces crisscrossing, an endless group of vector-parallelograms from which one resultant emerges—the historical result that, in turn, can itself be considered the product of a power functioning unconsciously and completely without volition. What each individual wants is impeded by all the others, and what results is something that no one wanted. Thus history up to now has proceeded like a sort of natural process and is also subject to essentially the same laws of motion. But just because the individual wills—each desiring what its physical constitution and external, ultimately economic, circumstances (either its own personal or generally social ones) compel it to—do not attain what they want, but rather fuse into an overall average, a common resultant, it must not be concluded that they cancel each other out and become zero. On the contrary, each contributes to the resultant, and to that extent is included in it.

From here on I would ask you to study this theory in its original texts and not at secondhand; it is really much easier. Marx wrote little in which it does not play a role. Particularly, "The 18th of Brumaire of Louis Bonaparte" is a quite excellent example of its application. There are likewise many references in *Kapital*. I also refer you to my own writings: "Eugen Düring's Revolutionary Science" and "Ludwig Feuerbach and the End of Classical German Philosophy," where I have given the most extensive account of historical materialism that, to my knowledge, exists.

That more weight than it deserves is occasionally placed on the economic side by younger dialecticians is partly the fault of Marx and myself. Facing our opponents, we needed to emphasize the principle denied by them, and there was not always the time, place or opportunity to do justice to the other factors active in the reciprocal effect. But when it came to a depiction of a historical period, and thus to practical application, things changed, and there no error was possible. Unfortunately, people too frequently believe they have completely understood a new theory and operate on it without further ado as soon as they have assimilated the main theses, and even then perhaps incorrectly. And I cannot spare many a new "Marxist" this reproach, and what wondrous stuff have they fabricated . . .

TRANSLATED BY RALPH R. READ

## (38) Emancipation into man

KARL MARX/FRIEDRICH ENGELS, Feuerbach

The 1845–1846 subtitle of *The German Ideology* was "Critique of the Most Recent German Philosophers as Represented by Feuerbach, B. Bauer, and Stirner, and a Critique of German Socialism in its Various Prophets." There was to be an accounting of the "former German conscience." "The intention was carried out in the form of criticism of post-Hegelian philosophy." The first part, which dealt with "Feuerbach, the contrast between materialistic and idealistic viewpoints," clarifies and develops in historic detail for the first time the concrete historical thinking of Marx and his collaborator Engels in contrast to Feuerbach's abstraction and in particular to the thinking of the other philosophical contemporaries. The concepts of superstructure and base, the relations of production (commercial relations, etc.) which were subsequently trivialized into all too comfortable interpretive cliches, can be comprehended and experienced here in their origin." (Iring Fetscher)

History is nothing but the succession of individual generations, each exploiting the materials, capital, and forces of production bequeathed to it by all preceding generations. On the one hand, history is the continuing transmittal of activity under entirely different circumstances, and on the other hand, it is the modification of old circumstances with an entirely different activity. Past activities now can be speculatively twisted so that later history is made out to be the goal of earlier history. For instance, the discovery of America is attributed to the goal of helping the French Revolution to its breakthrough, whereby history receives its special purposes and becomes a "person next to other persons" (such as "self-consciousness, critique, individual," etc.), whereas that which one characterized with the words "destiny," "purpose," "seed," "idea," of earlier history is no longer anything but an abstraction from later history—an abstraction of the active influence that past history exercises on later history.

In the course of this development, the farther that the individual, reciprocally influential circles expand, and the more the original seclusion of the individual nationalities is destroyed by improved means of production, transport, and the naturally produced division of labor between various nations, all the more does history become world history. So, for example, when in England a machine is invented that deprives countless workers of bread in India and China and disrupts the entire mode of existence of these countries, the invention becomes a world-historical fact. So, for another example, sugar and coffee proved their world-historical significance in the nineteenth century in that the shortage of these products—generated by the Napoleonic Continental System—induced the Germans to revolt against Napoleon and thus became the real basis of the glorious Wars of Liberation of 1813. It follows from this that the transformation of history into world history is not just an abstract deed of the "self-consciousness," "World Spirit," or some such metaphysical spook, but rather a quite material, empirically provable deed: a deed for which every individual, as he lives and breathes, eats, drinks, and dresses, supplies the proof.

The thoughts of the ruling class are the ruling thoughts in every epoch; that is, the class that is the ruling *material* power of the society, is at the same time its ruling intellectual power. The class that has the means to material production at its disposal also dispenses the means to intellectual production so that those who lack the means of intellectual production are subordinate to it. The prevailing ideas are nothing more than the idealistic expression of prevailing material relationships, the prevailing material relationships expressed as thoughts; thus the relationships that make that one class the ruling one, thus the thoughts of its hegemony. Among other things, the individuals who comprise the ruling class have consciousness, too, and therefore they think. Thus to the extent that they rule as a class, and determine the entire expanse of a historical epoch, it is only natural that they do so to their entire potential, and therefore, among other things, rule as thinkers, as producers of thoughts, who regulate the production and distribution of the thoughts of their time. At a time, for instance, and in a country where royal power, aristocracy, and bourgeoisie compete for supremacy, where rulership is thus divided, the ruling thought proves to be the doctrine of separation of power, which is then expressed as an "eternal law."

TRANSLATED BY RALPH R. READ

# THE CIVIL STATE

At age seventy-one, Immanuel Kant reflected on the possibilities of an "everlasting peace." In his treatise *On Everlasting Peace* (1795) he states:

> Nevertheless this is the desire of every state. . . . thus to achieve a permanent state of peace in order to rule the whole world if possible. But nature will have it otherwise and uses two means, the difference in languages and in religions, to deter people from interbreeding and to keep them apart. To be sure, inherent in these two means is a tendency toward mutual hate and a pretext for war; nonetheless, with increasing civilization and the gradual approach of people toward greater accord in principles, they lead toward accord in peace which, unlike that of despotism (based on the cemetery of freedom), which is achieved by the weakening of all forces, is produced and assured by a balance of powers in the keenest competition with each other.

The background of Kant's appeal for the peaceful coexistence of people was the spirit of the Enlightenment and a new bourgeois consciousness. Accordingly, he states in the first "Definitive Article on Everlasting Peace" that the civil constitution in every state must be republican:

> Firstly, the constitution must be founded on principles of freedom of the members of a society (as human beings); secondly it must be in accordance with tenets of the dependence of all upon a single, shared legislation (as subjects); and, thirdly, in accordance with the law of equality of these (as citizens of the state), the only constitution that derives from the idea of the original contract on which all legal legislation of a people must be founded is the republican.

According to Kant, everlasting peace is not only supported by "theoretical reason," which is reflected in the republican constitution; mutual self-interest also assures against violence and war:

156

It is the spirit of commerce, which sooner or later overcomes every people, that cannot exist together with war. Since of all powers (means) subordinated to the power of the state the power of money may well be the most reliable, states thus see themselves compelled (to be sure, not exactly by the motives of morality) to promote noble peace and to resist war, wherever it threatens to break out in the world, by negotiations, just as if they were in steadfast alliance for that purpose.

The civil state of the nineteenth century was based on the third estate's longing for freedom and striving for ownership. The market exerted a rationalizing function by breaking through the old class, religious, and traditional barriers, by awakening interests and bringing them into play in a disciplined, ordered manner through factual calculation, methodical organization of work, and the restriction of irrational elements. According to Bedrich Loewenstein, the person who either owns or hopes to acquire property is accustomed to long-term planning and contracts and knows the importance of adherence to established rules of the game. The market tends toward the use of means of coercion and of arguments; emphasis is placed on means of convincing, a kind of "wrestling match with intellectual weapons." (W. Sombart)

A liberal movement also developed in Germany in the wake of the Enlightenment and the French Revolution. The demand for basic freedoms based on natural law is the focus of their program. Great value is placed on the separation of powers as protection against the misuse of the power of the state; the constitutional monarchy is considered the most desirable form of state. Liberal individualism directs its attacks against the state administration's dictatorial policy toward its subjects as well as against the continued existence of class barriers; liberal rationalism battles the influence of churches; economic liberalism sounds the call for free competition. Liberalism allied itself with the idea of the nation, an alliance which in Germany supported the development of a middle class that was less an ownership class than an educated class, hence committed to ideas to an extraordinary extent.

The suppression of liberal and national strivings increased after the Congress of Vienna. Governments were particularly alarmed in 1817 at the Wartburg Festival by the prominence of the General German Fraternity (*Allgemeine Deutsche Burschenschaft*) that had been founded in 1815. The assassination of Kotzebue (a German writer in the service of the Russians) by a student named Sand was used by Metternich as a pretext to hold a conference in Karlsbad in 1819. In response to pressure exerted by

Austria and Prussia, the results of the conference (Carlsbad Decrees) were elevated by the German Confederation, a federation of states comprised of thirty-five princes and four free cities that had been founded in 1815, to a resolution stipulating: strict supervision of the universities, dissolution of the fraternity, increased censorship, and use of a central investigative commission against "demagogues."

The reforms of the "era of awakening," especially those that had been submitted by Baron von Stein (39), starting in 1807, had nonetheless so strengthened the democratic-republican consciousness that the wheel of history could no longer be completely turned back. Resignation admittedly also increased as a result of the discrepancy between a fanatically longed-for national freedom and prevailing repression.

The suffering caused by Germany was expressed with particular forcefulness in Friedrich Hölderlin's poetry, which is characterized by both euphoric and disappointed patriotism (40, 41).

Adam Müller, one of the Romantic theoreticians who specialized in state issues, was strongly influenced by English parliamentarianism. He formulated the question of how a people, fragmented among themselves, might find their way from the petty provinciality of everyday life to inner and outer sovereignty.

> Removed from all their greater thinkers scattered over the vast area of knowledge, more familiar with antiquity than with the present, having more friendly exchange with the most distant Orient than with their neighbors, preferably extending a hand to the dead rather than to the living, preferring to speak with those who can no longer listen and answer and who, if they could hear, would frighten us back into our century to do here what they did, which was to be excellent in their century.

The prospects for a civil state seemed sad.

"To think of Germany at night keeps me awake till morning light." Heinrich Heine, the author of these lines (42) and of "Germany, A Winter's Tale," a satirical-ironic elegy on republicanism's missed opportunities, was close to the Young Germany movement and to such associated authors as Karl Gutzkow and Heinrich Laube. In 1835 the works of Young Germany were forbidden by the German Confederation. Two years later, the appearance of the "Göttingen Seven," professors at the university in Göttingen, made a mark that could not be overlooked by the civil state: they turned against the king of Hanover's breach of the constitution. Their protest was punished with dismissal (44).

Altogether the consciousness of the necessity of a civil state was characterized during the first third of the nineteenth century by:

- high-flown ideas derived from general philosophical and constitutional systems;
- experiences with reforms that were implemented evolutionarily and came to a standstill after a while;
- resigned disappointment in response to the success of feudal and conservative counterforces that suppressed liberalism, democracy, and republicanism.

Revolutionary protest ultimately carried the day: in response to the July Revolution in Paris in 1830, several medium-sized and smaller German states were given constitutions; at the Hambach Festival, in 1832 and 1833, South German democrats attacked the Frankfurt police headquarters. The February Revolution of 1848 in France caused uprisings in Austria and Prussia. Following street fighting in Berlin, representatives of the liberal middle class were summoned to the South German state governments, where, without severe disruptions, freedom of the press, jury trials, and general mobilization were granted. The Frankfurt National Assembly, the parliament resulting from the vote for a national assembly to produce a constitution, met for the first time on May 18, 1848, in Frankfurt's Paulskirche. The civil state thereby constituted was almost exclusively made up of the middle class: peasants, craftsmen, and workers were to a large extent missing. Besides a few business people and industrialists, there were numerous journalists, lawyers, judges, civil service officials, and teachers from universities and other institutions of higher learning.

In a speech given by the poet Ludwig Uhland on January 22, 1849, in support of the all-German solution (the inclusion of Austria in the new state) and in opposition to hereditary monarchy, he states at the end:

We want the construction of a dome. When our ancient masters built their monumental Münster, uncertain of the completion of the audacious work, they constructed one tower and laid the base for the other. The tower of Prussia soars high into the air; let us keep a place for Austria's tower. We do, to be sure, have a great number of spires. Let me express myself differently, though. In the midst of the disunion of this assembly it was an elevating feeling that, as much as we often struggle against one another, we are nonetheless forged together as with iron bands by the established commandment of Germany unity, which is in the consciousness of the people and which can no longer be broken. If you exclude Austria, the bond is broken. In conclusion, gentlemen, reject heritability, do not create a single dominating state, do not reject Austria. Save the right to vote, this valuable right of the people, this last enduring token of the new authority's popular origin. Do believe that no light will beam forth over Germany unless its head of state has been anointed with an ample drop of democratic oil!

The prognosis proved disappointing: the ruling heads soon thereafter placed no particular value on "democratic oil." The counterrevolution triumphed both in the Habsburg and in the Hohenzollern monarchies. When the imperial troops had put down the democratic revolution in Vienna, the Prussian king in Berlin also dared the counterattack (45). The new constitution did not derive from the sovereignty of the people but was instead bestowed ("imposed from above") from the absoluteness of imperial power, and voting rights established on the basis of three classes assured the predominance of the ownership class. The middle class adjusted. As formulated by Karl Marx, it entered into an alliance with the feudal kingship against the people. The Frankfurt National Assembly dissolved itself; the attempt of the radical democrats to mobilize the people remained unsuccessful; the Prussian army conquered one nest of opposition after the other. In 1849 quiet was again restored in all quarters. Emigration, execution, or the dungeon were the lot of the revolutionaries. The remainder of the National Assembly, mostly representatives of the Left, had convened in Stuttgart since June 6, but had to yield as early as June 26 to the Württemberg government's command to dissolve.

The attempt of the liberal and national movement to establish a German civil state—a civil national state in the form of a constitutional monarchy—had failed.

The advance of industrialization could not be stopped. The spirit of commerce of course freed itself from republican consciousness. The state made up of the emancipated third estate became the state of the bourgeoisie. Industrialization, however, also caused the social movements that gradually—in Germany of the nineteenth century and with only partial success until 1918—converted the bourgeois state "back" or, as the case may be, "forward" into a civil state.

The most essential condition for the existence and dominance of the bourgeois class is the accumulation of wealth in the hands of private persons, the formation and increase of capital; the condition of capital is hired labor. Hired labor is based exclusively on competition among workers. The progress of industry, whose representative is a bourgeoisie lacking opposition and will, replaces by means of competition worker isolation with the revolutionary unification of the workers through association. With the development of large industry, therefore, the very basis on which it produces and acquires products is pulled out from under the feet of the bourgeoisie. It mainly produces its own gravediggers. Its decline and the victory of the proletariat are equally unavoidable.

The dialectic of history thus described in the *Communist Manifesto* of 1848 did not, however, take a revolutionary but an evolutionary course in Germany; in addition, the aspect of class conflict in the dogma obscured the focus on the antifeudal, democratic forces contained in or caused by industrialization itself. This is illustrated with particular clarity by the railroad system.

When the Danish poet Hans Christian Andersen came to Nüremberg in 1840, he was profoundly impressed by the first railroad, which was built in Germany. "Old Nüremberg was the first city to respond to the new era's monumental idea of connecting cities with one another by steam and iron ties." The rails seemed to Andersen magical threads drawn by human acuteness. In a triumphant feeling beyond compare, the poet enjoys the intoxication of speed; the trip seems to him like a flight on a cloud.

Oh, what a splendid work of the mind this invention is! One feels powerful like a magician of olden times! We harness our magic horse in front of the car, and space vanishes; we are flying like clouds in a storm. Mephistopheles was not able to fly faster with Faust on his skullcap! We are by natural means as strong in our era as was possible in the Middle Ages only through the devil's help! Rarely in my life have my feelings been so stirred as by this train trip.

Friedrich List recognized the uses of the railroad more concretely but by no means less enthusiastically (46). A Tübingen professor of government policy whose liberal views necessitated his emigration to America, he perceived the railroad as an important factor in the realization of democratic conditions in the nation. Even to the point of obsessiveness, he recognized that the railroad represented the dream of forming an extremely valuable network for the creation and "promotion" of a modern, democratic state. The revolution in the conditions of production, technological innovation, and new methods of production resulting from industrialization were accompanied by a

. . . change in social structures, forms of domination, changes in social benefits and group formations, of sociocultural standards of behavior and orders of value, all of which caused the gradual transition from the feudal-absolutist agrarian state to the civil-liberal industrial state. In Bavaria and throughout Germany the railroad was the advance guard of a comprehensive change in the economic and social structure; it was also the counterforce against the social, governmental, and economic system of the feudal, prein-dustrial era. The construction of the railroad transformed the infrastructure in all countries, and hence challenged the state economic policy that had long vacillated between mercantilist and liberalistic concepts and measures. The state, uncertain whether it should build railroads at all, initially partic-ipated in each separate construction venture. The absence of a policy led to a disruptive question concerning constitutional policy, since the capital-in-tensive requirements of railroad construction could not be met without a steady supply of state funds. This in turn was possible only by means of state loans requiring the approval of the people's representation. Many gov-ernments avoided the approval of such loans as a means of avoiding an admission of dependence on the parliaments. Since Prussia, in 1847, did not yet have constitutional representation of the people, the demand for a state railroad loan triggered the constitutional question, and in this manner railroad construction became the impetus toward political revolution. (Karl Bosl)

The civil state as the expression of a rational spirit in the era found new support in the rationality of industrialization. If profit maximization of a democratic society was not initially beneficial, since it exploited peo-ple and strengthened both social and economic contrasts, then industrial-ization nonetheless functioned as a dynamic force in combatting the rig-idity of social relations. In addition, it led an increasing number of people to the social product. Greater mobility led to a spiritual flexibility that corresponded in many respects to the peace-serving blend of the spirit of commerce and republicanism asserted by Immanuel Kant.

## (39) The will of free peoples is established

BARON CARL VON STEIN, Statement of November 24, 1808, Upon His Dismissal

Carl Freiherr von und zum Stein was born in Nassau. He entered the service of Prussia in 1780 in the Bureau of Mines, and subsequently worked in the Westphalian provincial administration. He was appointed Minister in 1804. Stein championed demands for re-form with such vehemence that he made himself unpopular among the nobility and at

court. King Friedrich Wilhelm III dismissed him in 1807 but recalled him shortly thereafter and appointed him to head the government in the terrible situation following the
Peace of Tilsit.

From the outset, Stein had a pan-German goal in mind in his assault on extensive
reform. In one of his letters he states, "I have only one Fatherland, and that is Germany,
and since in accordance with the old constitution I belong only to it and to no one part
of it, so, too, am I committed with all my soul only to it and to no part of it."

The main trouble was that it was no longer considered an honor to be a citizen in the
predominant state. In the hands of a centralizing bureaucracy addicted to administration,
the economic-technological system was devouring itself; the officials were dehumanized
by ink and petty details, the spirit of those who were governed was being destroyed, and
everything had disintegrated into sterile mechanisms.

The "Edict on the Liberation of the Serfs" was to release serfs from the condition of
being subject to the manorial authority, and to entitle them to independent authority
over their possessions and freedom of choice in occupation. The urban property-owning
middle class became entitled through municipal ordinances of 1808 to the administration
of their own community through self-elected institutions. The ordinances also restricted
influence by the state to general supervision.

Reform of the army (realized by August Graf von Gneisenau and Gerhard von Scharn-
horst) was designed to have the citizen share public responsibility through the introduction of general conscription.

School reform (upon recommendation of Stein, Wilhelm von Humboldt had become
head of the Prussian educational system in 1809) was directed toward restructuring the
Gymnasium and the university. Income and proof of education rather than class privileges
were to be decisive for obtaining leading positions in state and society.

Stein, whose immediate goal was to bring about the end of Napoleonic domination,
failed in his attempt. This was due to opposition from the court and the nobility, who
forced his dismissal in 1808. The "Jacobin's" reform projects were interrupted and remained incomplete.

No description is needed of the circumstances that necessitated my re-
tirement from the service of the state for which I live and will continue
to live.

Necessity rules so strongly and powerfully in external conditions that
the voice of an individual can accomplish little. I set my goal in the
administration of domestic matters. The main task was to alleviate discord among the people, to destroy the grievous contention between the
classes, to establish legally the possibility that each person can develop
his strengths freely in the moral sphere; and in this manner to engender
such love of king and Fatherland in the people that they are gladly willing
to make the sacrifice of wealth and life to them.

Gentlemen, with your support much has already been accomplished.
The last remains of slavery, of serfdom, is destroyed, and the unassailable
support of every throne, the will of free peoples, is established. The people have been restored the right to provide themselves their primary needs

of life. The cities are declared of age, and other less important bands that served only individuals, thereby crippling the love of Fatherland, have been severed. If what has been achieved until now is maintained with consistency, only a few principal measures still remain . . .

1. Government can emanate only from the highest power . . . Only the king is master, to the extent that this designation indicates police power, and his justice may be carried out only by the person on whom it is conferred in each instance by him . . .

2. The person who should make judgment is dependent only upon the highest power . . .

3. Serfdom is abolished. In some regions, however, there still exist regulations governing rights and duties of servants that cripple the freedom of the people. Attempts have also been made to restore certain features of serfdom by new regulations governing rights and duties of servants. This will be the source of the most vigorous attack on the first basic law of our state, our *habeas corpus* act. In my view, what is required is not new regulations, but rather the suspension of existing regulations governing the rights and duties of servants. What establishes the universal jurisdiction over servants seems to me entirely adequate. The freedom of servants, their rights and fidelity to the king, are established in these three tenets. All regulations based on them can achieve only good. The next instrument of progress would seem to be . . .

4. A general national representation. The law and the authority of our king were sacred to me and remain sacred. But in order for this law and this unrestricted authority to accomplish their inherent good, it seems to me necessary to provide the highest power with the means of learning the wishes of the people for giving life to their decisions. If all participation in the operations of the state is withheld from the people, the administration of their communal concerns is denied them; the result is that the state soon is partly regarded indifferently, partly in specific instances, in opposition to the people. Where representation of the people occurred among us until now, it was set up in an extremely imperfect manner. My plan, therefore, was that each active citizen of the state who owns 100 hides (of land), who is engaged in agriculture, manufacture, trade, or a civil profession, or who is bound by a spiritual tie to the state, should

have a right to representation. Several plans submitted to me were implemented by me. The weal and woe of our state depends upon the execution or elimination of a plan, for only in this manner can the national spirit be positively awakened and animated.

5. There is no contact whatever between our two main classes, the nobility and the bourgeoisie. Anyone who moves from the one class into the other entirely renounces his previous class, perforce creating the existing tension between them. The nobility is too numerous—and is constantly becoming more numerous—to assert the value that can be ascribed to them. For the preservation of the whole, competition had to be permitted, both in the professions and in the service of the state, that was previously reserved only for the nobility. The nobility will therefore have to enter businesses and professions that are in contradiction to the distinction to which they laid claim on the basis of birth. The nobleman thereby becomes the object of mockery and as a consequence soon loses the esteem due him even as a citizen of the state . . .

This attitude partly gave rise to the opinion of the necessity to reform the nobility. Through the connection of the nobility with other classes, the nation will be made into a whole, making possible to a higher degree the preservation and the remembrance of noble actions worthy of eternity. This connection will simultaneously . . .

6. Actively establish the universal duty toward defense of the Fatherland, and this universality must, of necessity also create equal enthusiasm for the government within each class. Only the peasant will consequently still require some positive support toward enhancing his personal value because of having been so long held back by serfdom. I include among these . . .

7. The creation of legal means for the elimination of villenage . . .

8. In order that all these provisions completely fulfill their purpose of, in fact, promoting the inner development of the people, and of promoting fidelity to, the belief in, and love of king and Fatherland, the religious sense of the people must be reawakened. Precepts and regulations alone cannot achieve this. The government is nonetheless obligated earnestly to encourage this important matter.

9. Concerning this point, and concerning the whole as well, the most can be expected from the training and education of youth. If every spiritual force is developed from within, by a method based on the inner nature of the person, and if each noble principle of life is stimulated and nourished, all one-sided education avoided, and if the drives, hitherto often neglected with stupid indifference, on which the strength and dignity of the human being are based, are scrupulously cultivated along with a love of God, king, and Fatherland, then we can hope to rear a physically and morally strong race and see a better future open up . . .

TRANSLATED BY MARTHA HUMPHREYS

## (40) Greetings to you, my Fatherland!

FRIEDRICH HÖLDERLIN, "Song of the Germans"

Hölderlin was strongly moved by the agitations of the time. The French Revolution was particularly decisive in determining his hope for the realization of the "ideals of mankind." "Longing for Greece" was coupled with a longing for a new Germany in which harmony and a noble form of life having genuine content would be realized.

O holy heart of peoples, O fatherland!
All-patient, like the taciturn Mother Earth,
And undervalued, even though from
Your depths the foreigners derive their best!

They harvest their thought, their intellect from you,
Gladly they pluck the grape, and yet they scoff at
You, amorphous grape tendril! that you
Vaguely and wildly trail over the ground.

You land of lofty and sober genius!
You land of love! Surely I am one of yours,
Often I wept grimly, that always
You disavow timidly your own soul.

Yet some beauty you cannot conceal from me;
Often I stood, gazing on your noble green,
The sweeping garden, high within your
Skies atop the bright mountain and saw you.

On your rivers I traveled and thought of you,
While the nightingale shyly uttered its call
Upon the springy heath and softly
'Gainst the darkling ground the wave did linger.

And upon the banks I saw cities blossom,
Noble ones, where the toil in the workshop rests,
The sciences, and where your sunlight
Mildly lights the artist's inspiration.

Do you know Minerva's children? They embraced
The olive tree most dearly; do you know them?
It lives still, reigns still the soul of the
Athenians, the thinkers, among men.

Though Plato's pious garden no longer blooms
Near the ancient stream and the needy ploughman
Turns the heroes' ashes and shyly
The bird of night grieves upon the pillar.

O holy wood! O Attica! Were you struck
Also, not spared his terrible ray, so soon,
And did they flee, your inhabitants,
Released by the flames into the ether?

And yet, like the springtime, genius wanders
From land to land. And we? Is there even one
Of our young men, who does not conceal
A resentment, a puzzle in his breast?

Thanks to the German women! They have preserved
The friendly spirit of the divine image,
And daily the clear and gracious peace
Atones once more for the evil tangle.

Where now are the poets, selected by God,
As our ancients, to be cheerful and pious,
Where the wise men, such as our own? the
Cold and daring, the incorruptible?

Well! Greetings to you, my noble fatherland,
With a new name, the ripest fruit of the times!
You ultimate and first among all
Muses, Urania, greetings to you!

Still you wait in silence, plan a joyous work,
Which will prove your worth, plan a new creation,
The only one which, as you, is born
Of love and goodness, as you yourself are—

Where is your Delos, where your Olympia,
That we may find each other at the high feast?—
Yet how is the son to guess what you,
Immortal one, have long prepared for yours?

TRANSLATED BY ADRIAN DEL CARO

## (41) On the unnaturalness of the Germans

FRIEDRICH HÖLDERLIN, Hyperion, or The Hermit

The focus of the two-volume novel *Hyperion* (1797–1799) is the appeal to prophetic, poetic creativity. The hero tells of childhood, youth, years of studying and travel, and maturity. In letters resembling a lyrical monologue, contemporary German *misère* is projected onto the novel's setting of modern Greece around the year 1770 (Hyperion reports to his friend Bellarmin of the failure of the attempt to liberate Greece from Turkish domination).

Hyperion's happy childhood, reflecting Hölderlin's recollection of his own early youth, proves to be the symbol of mankind's youth altogether. But naiveté is destroyed by reason: "Oh, if only I had never attended your schools. The science I pursued so thoroughly and from which I, foolish youth that I was, awaited confirmation of my pure joy, spoiled everything for me. . . . Oh, man is a god when he dreams, a beggar when he reflects, and when the enthusiasm is past he stands there like a misguided son thrown out of the house by his father, staring at the miserable pennies given him along the way by compassion."

Hyperion finds the true teacher in the form of Adama and enthusiastically consecrates himself to the service of beauty, truth, and devotion to mankind.

The struggle with everyday affairs occurs during the years of wandering. The person born to and reared for greatness finds no place among the many, each of whom is only out for himself and can enjoy only himself. Love of mankind is crushed.

Maturity is a release, through love, from alienation from the world and from contempt of man. Diotima (modeled on Susette Gontard in whose house Hölderlin had worked as a tutor from 1796–1798 and whom he loved) signifies the bliss that follows pain. Hyperion, who has robbed her of her self-sufficiency, must nonetheless experience her languishing and death.

He takes leave of the "dear Greeks" and returns to the Germans to experience their reality.

Thus I came among the Germans. I did not demand much, and was prepared to find even less. I came humbly, like homeless, blind Oedipus to the gate of Athens, where the grove of the gods received him, and beautiful souls met him.

How differently I did fare!

Barbarians from time immemorial, grown more barbarian through diligence and science and even through religion, wholly incapable of any divine feeling, corrupt in every fiber for the bliss of the sacred Graces, insulting in every degree of excess and impoverishment to every well-fashioned soul, hollow and without harmony, like the shards of a discarded vessel—those, my Bellarmin! were my comforters.

These are harsh words, and yet I say them because it is the truth: I can imagine no people more torn than the Germans. You see artisans, but no humans; thinkers, but no humans; priests, but no humans; masters and slaves, young and mature people, but no humans—is that not like a battlefield, where hands and arms and all other limbs hacked to pieces lie in confusion, while the spilled blood of life trickles into the sand?

Each does his own, you will say, and I say that too. Only he must do it with his entire soul, must not smother any strength within him that happens not to fit his style neatly, must not in his paltry fear hypocritically be only that which he is called, with seriousness; with love he must be that which he is, then a spirit would live in his actions, and if he is pressed into an employ where the spirit cannot live at all, he should thrust it away with disdain and return to nature! Your Germans, though, like to stay with what is most basic and for that reason so much muddled work is among them and so little that is free and gladdening. Yet that could be tolerated if such men were not so unfeeling toward everything beautiful in life, if only the curse of godforsaken unnaturalness did not lie everywhere upon this people.

The virtues of the ancients were only radiant faults, some spiteful tongue, I know not whose, once said. But their very faults are virtues, for there a childlike, a beautiful spirit lives on, and of all they did nothing lacked in soul. The virtues of the Germans, though, are a radiant evil, and nothing more; for they are but patchwork, of craven fear, wrung from barren hearts with slaving toil, and leave disconsolate every pure soul that finds refreshment in beauty, oh! that spoiled by the sacred harmony in nobler natures cannot bear the discord screaming in all the dead order of these people.

I tell you: there is nothing holy that is not desecrated, not debased to a feeble prop by these people, and what even among savages is usually upheld as divinely pure, this the all-calculating barbarians work at as if it were a trade, and cannot help themselves. For when a human creature has once been trained, it serves its purpose there, it seeks its profit there, it no longer rhapsodizes, God forbid! It remains steady and when it celebrates, and when it loves, and when it prays, and even when the precious rite of spring, when the world's time of conciliation eases the cares of all and conjures innocence into a guilty heart, when, drunken by the sun's warm rays, the gladdened slave forgets his chains, and soothed by the god-inspired air, the enemies of man are peaceful as children—even while the grub takes wing and the bee swarms, the German sticks to his employ and but little heeds the weather.

TRANSLATED BY RALPH R. READ

## (42) Since I have left that country

HEINRICH HEINE, "Night Thoughts"

"Heine's position in and toward Germany is unique in the era prior to the inception of the workers movement. Of the leading intellects during the era of the rise of the German middle class, he is the one who can least be accused of that infamous German philistine pedantry ascribed by Friedrich Engels even to such extraordinary figures as Goethe and Hegel. Heine early turned away from German bourgeois narrowness and the deeply ingrained expression of Germany's social and political backwardness . . .

"For him there were two Germanies, 'the old official Germany,' 'the mouldy land of philistines,' the ruling political and social order that historically was long outdated and which he bitterly opposed; and the 'real Germany,' the 'great, uncanny, so-to-speak anonymous Germany of the German people' to which he felt bound, to which he lent his voice, and for which he wanted to prepare a happy future. And he protested—but in vain for more than a hundred years—that his fury and mockery about the land of the philistines was interpreted as enmity toward the German people." (Hans Kaufmann)

> To think of Germany at night
> Keeps me awake till morning light,
> I cannot close my eyes to sleep
> For all the burning tears I weep.

The years have come and they have passed!
Since I have seen my mother last,
Twelve years so far that I have counted;
The longing and the need have mounted.

My longing and my need still grow.
She has me in her thoughts I know,
I'm thinking always of my mother,
May God preserve her like no other!

That the old woman's fond of me
Shows in the letters I receive,
Her script is shaky from emotion,
A mother's heart in real devotion.

My mother never leaves my mind.
These dozen years have been unkind,
These dozen years have left their traces
Since last we traded fond embraces.

But Germany will ever stand,
It is a hale and hearty land;
And I could journey hither knowing
That oak and linden would be growing.

I'd bear my yearning patiently
If she were not in Germany;
The fatherland will perish never,
But mothers cannot live forever.

Since I have come to France to stay
So many people passed away,
The ones I loved—to count them only
Bleeds my soul and makes me lonely.

And count I must—though as I do
My tortures rise in number, too;
Their corpses seem to reach for me—
Praise God! the specters turn and flee.

Praise God! for through my window slants
The cheerful morning light of France;
My wife comes in, a new tomorrow,
And smiles away my German sorrow.

TRANSLATED BY ADRIAN DEL CARO


(43) Homecoming

HEINRICH HEINE, Germany, A Winter's Tale

This work, which was critical of the era, was published in 1844 and relates impressions of Heine's trip through Germany in the fall of 1843. In twenty-seven chapters the poet attacks primarily militant nationalism, fraternities, hatred of the French, separatism, and the ecstasy over the Middle Ages. In the preface Heine castigates those who would reproach him for soiling his own nest: "I can already hear their beery voices: 'You even slander our colors, you despiser of the Fatherland, friend of the French, to whom you would cede the Rhine!' Calm yourselves. I will respect and honor your colors when they deserve it, when they are no longer an idle and slavish frivolity. Plant the black-red-gold flag on the heights of German thought, make it the standardbearer of free mankind, and I will sacrifice my best life's blood for it. Calm yourselves—I love the Fatherland just as much as you. Because of this love, I have spent thirteen years of my life in exile, perhaps forever, in any case without whining and without making a long-suffering sour face. I am a friend of the French just as I am friend of all human beings if they are reasonable and good, and because I myself am not so stupid and bad as to wish that my Germans and the French, both the chosen peoples of humanity, should break their necks for the benefit of England and Russia and for the malicious delight of all Junkers and priests of this planet. Be tranquil—I shall never cede the Rhine to the French for the simple reason that the Rhine belongs to me. Yes, it belongs to me through inalienable right of birth, I am the free Rhine's far-freer son, my cradle stood on its banks, and I do not at all see why the Rhine should belong to anyone else but its own countrymen."


T'was the doleful month of November,
The days passed gloomily,
The trees were losing their leaves to the wind
When I journeyed into Germany.


And as I arrived at the border
I was feeling quite shaken inside,
My heart palpitated so strongly
I believe that I even cried.

And when I heard German being spoken,
I was seized by a curious feeling;
My heart took wings and soared away,
But my senses remained and were reeling.

A little girl sat playing the harp.
Oh, she sang in ecstasy,
Truly I was touched by her song
Though she sang it out of key.

She sang of love and its travails,
Of parting and meeting again
Up there in the better than possible world
Where all suffering has its end.

She sang of the earthly vale of tears,
Of joys that pass so suddenly,
Of heaven, where the blessed souls
Engage in blissful gluttony.

She sang the song of resignation,
The song of the sweet resurrection,
With which the masses are lulled to sleep
At the hint of an insurrection.

I've heard it before and I've studied the text,
I know who has written each line;
In public they preach on the virtues of water
In secret they're guzzlers of wine.

It's time we wrote a better song,
My friends, and I will give it birth!
We want to be the founders of
The reign of heaven here on earth.

We want our earthly happiness
And we will starve no longer;
The fat shall cease to squander wealth
Secured by the toil of the stronger.

There is bread enough on earth
For all the children of the race,
And roses, myrtle, beauty and joy,
With sweet green peas in every place.

Yes, sweet green peas for everyone,
Just bursting from their pods!
We'll leave the dream of heaven for
The angels and the gods.

If after death we should sprout wings
Then surely we will fly
Up there to spend the day with you
And share the blessed pie.

Another song, a better song!
The strains of violin and flute!
The miserere is no more,
The funeral bells are mute.

The maiden Europe is engaged
To wed the spirit of liberty,
They're lying in each other's arms,
And kisses seal their destiny.

Without the blessing of the Church
Still valid will their marriage be—
Long live the groom, long live the bride,
Long live their future family!

A nuptial blessing is my song,
A better new creation!
Within my soul are rising stars
Of higher consecration—

Inspired stars, and glowing bright,
Exploding into flaming brands—
I feel the wondrous strength in me
To crush an oak tree with my hands!

Since I have trod on German soil
I feel the flow of magic power—
A giant finds his home again,
His strength increases by the hour.

While the little one trilled and played
About the heavenly graces,
The Prussian customs officers
Inspected my suitcases.

Snuffled through everything, rummaged about,
They unbuttoned my shirts to make sure;
They rummaged for lace, they hunted for jewels
And forbidden literature.

You fools who rummage in my bags!
You should be looking elsewhere instead!
The contraband which I have brought
Is locked up safely in my head.

Here is my lace, and finer yet
Than that of Mechlin or any place,
When I've unpacked it you will see
The people jeering to your face.

The future's crown jewels are in my head,
It is filled with precious stones,
The temple gems of a different god,
Of the powerful God Unknown.

My head contains a stack of books!
I hope that you are heeding;
My head is a twittering robin's nest
Of confiscatory reading.

Believe me, books which are more evil still
Than the ones which old Satan might loan;
The books of Hoffmann von Fallersleben
Are child's play compared to my own!—

A passenger who stood next to me
Began to proudly explain,
That here was the Prussian Customs Union,
One link in the great customs chain.

"The customs union"—so he observed—
"Will help us found the nation,
It will weld the splintered fatherland
To a whole of interrelation.

It gives us exterior unity,
As fruit is encased in a peel;
The censor provides the spiritual form,
The one which is truly ideal—

It gives us interior unity,
So our thoughts won't flutter about;
We need a united Germany,
United within and without."

TRANSLATED BY ADRIAN DEL CARO

### (44) No one can be released from his oath
### on the constitution

JAKOB GRIMM, My Dismissal

The brothers Grimm—Jakob (1785–1863) and Wilhelm (1786–1859) were strongly influenced by the simplicity, piety, and love of people, Fatherland, and homeland imbued
in them by their parents from early childhood. While studying in Marburg, both decided
to succumb to the appeal of the Romantic movement. They collected and edited children's
fairytales (1812 ff.) and German sagas (1816 ff.). "All genuine poetry is preserved in
them—poetry can never be without reference to life, for it has its origin in life and returns
to it." Their studies made accessible courtly poetry, epics from the first great golden age
of German poets, and the history of the German language. Philology was introduced into
Germany by their *German Dictionary.*

No one could abrogate the oath on the constitution except the king
together with the estates convened according to the law of 1833, or a
legal pronouncement of the diet. A third way did not exist. We would

have submitted to either decision with respectful obedience but without complete conviction, no release could occur, and any doubt would have brought with it an intolerable state of the soul. I can see the cold smile of those who call themselves clever and see nothing here but evasiveness. For I have heard myself that an oath in politics does not count for much or that a compulsory one is not binding, that one lives up to it or not, as one pleases. It's a good thing, some say, that there is an opportunity to overthrow a liberal constitution; if it succeeds, the end will have justified the means. We have a higher right which need not respect the rights of a contrivance. And others think, what do I care about politics if it interferes with my comfort or my learned pursuits? But religious sentiment has not disappeared so utterly that there would not be many who know something higher than worldly cleverness and who deeply feel the true seriousness of what is at stake. There are still those who have a conscience even when they deal with power.

Later, another interpretation was looked for: the king, people said, is the sole master, it is to him and to no one else that the oath was sworn, and it is within his power to release the servant from that oath. Certainly, the king is the sole master; certainly, the oath was sworn before his authorized representative, but it is not within the king's power to abrogate an oath sworn before God. The oath was taken to preserve the basic law and as long as this law has not been validly rescinded, it must be inviolate. I made no political theory and have none to advocate. I must hold to what was given me from above but given the basis on which the law rests, one can say with perfect assurance that the oath was also sworn to the country. Need one look for analogous circumstances? Does an appellate court have a master other than the king? And does he have the power to absolve its members of the oath they have sworn to uphold the legal order? Would anyone have dared advance such an interpretation a year ago? And does anyone believe that sophistries of this sort will persuade an honest man of simple good sense?

As I now turn to speak of the attitudes and actions which became manifest in Göttingen after the two decrees had been set forth, I recall first the tragic mischance which caused this interruption of the public order to occur at a time when the greatest festivities since its founding were to be held at the university. All were profoundly expectant and the eyes of all of Germany were turned toward Göttingen. Fate had already added to the unprecedented splendor of the academy an ingredient of disquiet and pain which was still muted during the solemn days because the publication of the first decree had produced a merely questioning, not yet desperate, anguish. The still clear, festive sky was lightly edged with threatening clouds. The streets of the town, filled as never before by throngs of visitors and spectators, had again become deserted and a short holiday had begun. Then, directly with the start of the new term, the feared catastrophe occurred and immediately revealed itself as far more seious than had been anticipated. The unexpected but quickly confirmed report that the old ministers had yielded made the general dismay complete.

It was natural that no other part of the entire kingdom would be as keenly and profoundly affected by this event as the university. Not only because of the influx and departure of large numbers of young men but because of their teachers who are precisely attuned to this; the proven and excellent German institutions will always be extremely sensitive to whatever good or evil occurs in the country. If it were otherwise, they would no longer fulfil their purpose as they have in the past. The open, uncorrupted intelligence of the young demands that, on every occasion, its teachers trace every question concerning important matters in life and the state to its purest and most critical core and that they answer it honestly. Hypocrisy is inadmissible, and the authority of the law and of virtue over the unprejudiced minds of the listeners is so strong that they turn to what is right without prompting and abhor all distortion.

And there cannot be any beating about the bush when it comes to teaching the nature, conditions and consequences of a government that brings happiness to its people; such teaching has to be free and subject only to inner conviction. Professors of public law and politics are obliged to draw the principles of public life from the purest source of their insights and investigations. Professors of history must never fail to state what influences constitution and government have on the weal and woe of nations. Professors of philology forever come upon moving passages in the classics which deal with the governments of antiquity, or they have to show the lively influence of a free or inhibited national development on the growth of poetry and even the inner life of language.

All these results impinge on and support each other. It need hardly be mentioned that by endeavoring to reveal the mysteries of religion and nature, all of theology and even medicine must contribute to adjust and strengthen the sense and the need of youth for the sacred, the simple and the true. How pervasively must the university therefore be affected when it is learned that the constitution of the country is in danger of being overturned. A great many young men feel the results of the changed situation of their parents, brothers, friends and teachers; the change in their own. All have a general sense of impending violence. It is superfluous to state on which side they stand.

TRANSLATED BY MICHAEL SHAW

## (45) Truer the worth that true deeds lend

FANNY LEWALD, Recollections of the Year 1848

Fanny Lewald (1811–1889), the daughter of a Jewish businessman, was born in Königsberg, East Prussia. She was a keen participant in the French Revolution of 1830 and the Polish uprising of 1830–1831. She began writing at age thirty, concentrating on novels dealing with the emancipation of women and Jews. Travels took her to Italy, France, England, and Scotland. She settled in Berlin and married the liberal publicist Adolph Stahr. The *Recollections of the Year 1848* were published in 1850.

Berlin, March 8, 1849

Yesterday, Good Friday, when the church services had ended and memorial rites had once again been held for the man who, eighteen hundred years ago, delivered the world from the shackles of bondage into love's freedom, we made our way, amid the sound of the church bells, toward Königsstadt, to pay a visit to the Friedrichshain, the royal grove where the victims of Berlin's struggle for freedom are buried. It was about two or three years ago that the grove was planted, to provide future residents of the town built beyond the Spree with a promenade, just as Friedrichsstadt in Berlin has one within its zoo. The project was a very commendable one, for Berlin is surrounded by sandy desert, without trees or shrubbery, as far as the eye can see.

Beyond Alexanderplatz, on which the Königsstadt Theater stands, and to which Italian opera draws the wealthy and aristocratic, Berlin proper ends for these classes of society. What begins is a *terra incognita,* of whose existence and of whose inhabitants the *beau monde* of linden trees and Behrenstrasse sees and knows about as much as it does of Tierra del Fuego. This is the case even though it is in Königsstadt and all the quarters beyond the Spree that the productive, laboring population of Berlin resides; the very population that makes the city rich and important.

We walked along Landsbergerstrasse: there was a Sunday calm in the air. Young girls and women were sitting at their windows, their knitting and their reading alike fallen from their hands, relaxing after a six-day work week and wholly enjoying their rest. Leaning her head on her arm, a blondhaired girl dreamily peered out at the street. A pair of children lolled about at a window sill, under the supervision of their father and mother. Servants stood chatting in front of houses, boys were playing marbles, and husbands and wives of the artisan classes strolled about with their children. We eventually reached the Landsberger Gate. The ground here rises several feet, and this elevation affords a view of the entire flat surrounding area. At the foot of the hill several carriages and hack cars had stopped; a crowd of people began to ascend with us, and all at once we found ourselves standing at the resting place of those slain last March.

They are buried in a circle. Evidently it had been thought at the time that they would be the first and last sacrifices on the altar of Prussian freedom, for it was a closed circle, leaving no room for future casualties. The graves encircled the lawn in double rows; there may have been more than two hundred of them. The center of the lawn is adorned by a young tree, which is supposed to be replaced by a memorial as soon as possible. Close by the graves there is a windmill whose sails turn with every slight stir of air.

Silent and yet so eloquent, the graves faced us, a distinct, self-contained piece of reality. At our feet lay Berlin—grand, opulent Berlin, crowned by its church steeples, and by the proud, newly constructed dome of the royal palace. This dome, intended as the keystone of the building, had been completed by Friedrich Wilhelm IV at the very moment when the revolution was dealing its first hammer blows to the foundations of this royal house. Nature and world history obey the same basic principles, the same irrefutable laws. The flower goes to seed, for the fruit must evolve and mature. Thousands of young, still leafless, trees stretched forth their naked branches around this death mound, raising themselves out of the pale yellow marshland, imploring the heavens for the warmth and nourishment that this barren soil could provide only feebly. But the sky was cold and overcast; no light for these young trees to find. One might be led to despair of their ever flourishing if one could not count upon their inner impulse to survive and reproduce.

Some months ago a bronze bust of old Fritz, the namesake of these grounds, was installed in this nursery on a marble column. A citizen of Berlin had donated it in honor both of the grove itself and of the dead, as though the historical instinct had led him to set a memorial for one of the most brilliant absolute monarchs next to a memorial for those fallen in the struggle against absolutism. Revolution and absolutism, despotism and revolt meet here as forever paired extremes.

Our eyes soon turned from a survey of the landscape to the graves themselves. What a difference between the truthfulness of the funeral rites here and the merely customary forms of gravestone decoration and inscription elsewhere. Great upheavals restore men to themselves, help them to recognize their own true worth, in contrast to the received opinion held of them by the privileged. Because the people had to learn to regard themselves as a power over against other powers, they found the courage to speak their own language. Here each person feels justified in giving himself over wholly to his grief, and to each is given the sympathy and respect he justly deserves.

Near the marble headstone of the student Gustav von Lenski, erected by his classmates, a servant girl lies buried. The Committee for the Slain has set a wreath there for her. "She was shot in her room," it reads, after giving her name and age. We walked from grave to grave, and I want to share with you the inscriptions I copied down. "Here in God's grace rests my unforgettable son Karl August Theodor Deichmann, foreman-carpenter, born the 24th of September, 1823, died the 18th of March, 1848, in the struggle for freedom, from two shots in his body. He follows his mother to the grave by six weeks. My third son was wounded at the same place, the corner of Friedrich- and Dorothee-Strasse, with five head-wounds, but he is well again. Dedicated by their grieving father." A laborer standing near us was saying to his companion, "Those are the two Deichmann brothers, the ones they picked up defenseless in their father's house. The younger said to the lieutenant who was present, 'Lieutenant, you see I've got no weapons, please protect me!' But he was the first to beat him on the head with his sword hilt, and then all the others went at him too. And we're supposed to keep peace with soldiers who shoot and hack at their defenseless countrymen as if they were enemies instead of brothers!"

They drifted away from the spot, still talking. We walked up to one of the other graves. "Here lies the locksmith Julius Frankenberg, 29 years old. To die struggling for the freedom of the people—so reads the will and testament of which we are heirs." Another inscription reads: "Here in the grace of God sleeps my dearly beloved husband, the baker Gustav Ripprecht. Shot while in my company, quietly sitting at my side, March 18. Dedicated by his wife." "Here rests the body of Wilhelm Brüggemann, upholsterer, died the 18th of March in the struggle for freedom.

This monument set for him by the intended bride he left behind." The people's language, mistakes and all, is transfigured here and appears stirring and sacred.

Where the means for erecting even the smallest wooden cross was lacking, love found a way to create new gravemarkers in the form of little wooden boxes with glass lids, that would protect yet leave visible a handwritten slip of paper. The following poem was in one of these boxes, clearly bearing the stamp of folk poetry:

> A holy, shuddering awe o'ertakes me
> Whenever I come near this place,
> For here the bones of good men rest,
> Among the noblest of their race.
>
> A rapture flames up in my heart
> For the deaths these brave souls did not shun.
> The light that heaven gave their virtue
> Will shine again in battles won.
>
> This hill on which so many slumber
> Will be hallowed until time's end;
> And though the monuments are humble,
> Truer the worth that *true deeds* lend!

"These verses written for the apprentice locksmith Karl Lamprecht by a loving friend." On March 18, 1849, a second piece of paper was also laid upon this grave, trimmed at the edges with the German colors, and bearing the inscription: "In life you fought to defend these colors, in death you shall wear them!"

TRANSLATED BY DAVID JACOBSON

## (46) Perfecting the German national situation

FRIEDRICH LIST, On the Use of the Railway

Friedrich List, born in 1789 in Reutlingen, considered railroad construction and the customs union he championed to be the basis for Germany's brilliant ascent. He had gained such expansive perspectives as an emigrant in North America. Liberal sentiments had compelled him as a young professor of political theory in Tübingen to leave the country. (As founder of the German business and trade association, he had been sentenced to confinement in a fortress.) One year after his return from America, he published his treatise *On a Saxonian Railroad System as the Basis of a General German Railroad System* (1833). Like his work entitled *The National System of Political Economy* (published in 1841), it was to a large extent not understood. List was crushed by political controversies and futile efforts, causing his suicide in 1846 in Kufstein.

The railway system and the customs union are Siamese twins; born at the same time, physically attached to one another, *of one* mind and purpose. They mutually support one another, strive for one and the same great goal, for the unification of the German peoples into one great and cultured, one wealthy, powerful and inviolable nation. Without the customs union a German railway system would never have come up for discussion, let alone have been completed. Only with the help of the German railway system is the coöperative economy of the Germans able to soar to national greatness, and only as a result of this prosperity can the railway system attain its full importance.

Meanwhile the German railway system functions not merely by promoting material national interests, but also by strengthening all of the intellectual and political forces toward the perfection of German national affairs:

—as *an instrument for the national defense;* for it facilitates the mustering, dispersion and directing of national armed forces;

—as *a means for the promotion of culture;* for it expedites the distribution of all literary products and all products of the arts and sciences; it brings talent, knowledge and skills into reciprocal contact; it enhances the cultural and educational means of all individuals, from every class and age group;

—as *an insurance institution* against inflation and famine and against exaggerated fluctuations in the prices of life's basic necessities;

—as *a health institution;* for it nullifies the distance between the ailing and the remedy;

—as *an agent of friendly traffic;* for it unites friend with friend and relative with relative;

—as *a tonic for the national spirit;* for it eradicates the evils of provincialism and of provincial self-conceit and prejudice;

—as *a tight belt about the loins of the German nation,* which unifies the limbs into a *single* martial and powerful body;

—as *the nervous system* of community spirit as well as legislative order; for it imparts strength to public opinion in the same measure as to the state.

In all these respects, for no other nation is the railway system of such great importance as for the *German.*

Exposed to foreign attacks from all sides, due to its geographical location, and meagerly endowed by nature with means of communication, no nation has such need of artificial means in order to concentrate its defense forces and to hurl them from one border point to the other with speed.

Nowhere is culture more essential than in Germany, lacking a central location for science, art, literature and education, for facilitated and swifter means of communication, and nowhere are the latter of such great use in this sense.

Robbed of almost all attributes of nationality by earlier divisiveness, no nation so desperately needs internal unification of its limbs.

With this means of unification Germany assumes possession of those immeasurable advantages which in other nations grow out of their national capitols, without the great disadvantages connected with them; Germany thereby gains the advantages of the centralization system, without losing the blessings of the federative system.

If one takes into consideration the effects of the railway system enumerated here, and if one also takes into account how powerfully all the intellectual and political perfections will effect the promotion of material prosperity, then one cannot but agree with us when we maintain that the production of a German railway system would be sufficiently justified by this alone, even in the event that one could not promise oneself any financial gain at all. Culture, existence, independence, inviolability of the nation are goods of immeasurable value, and a nation which would not be able to expend a negligible part of its national wealth for the acquisition and security of these goods would not deserve to exist; it would be comparable to the miser who would abandon his treasures and his life to foreign greed in order to save the cost of lock and key. The French calculate the cost of their two invasions at 6 billion francs, if we do not err, and a German invasion could hardly be mounted more cheaply. Hence if the railway system prevents *one* invasion in a century, it already repays its construction costs tenfold.

If we return to the material interests and the customs union, then the railway system seems to be a principal means for effecting the division of labor and the confederation of productive forces on a national scale, and balancing industrial production with agricultural, export with import. Therefore we must, first of all, illuminate the value of this balance in order to make visible the entire importance of the railway system in this regard.

TRANSLATED BY ADRIAN DEL CARO

# OF HORROR
# AND
# FLOURISHING

# JUSTIFYING
# THE
# WORLD

*The idyllic is Panic; that which is Panic is idyllic: the Biedermeier epoch is characterized by a cheerfulness based on melancholy. Political-economic constrictions and reactionary intellectual repression cause a flight to that which is within. Widespread agnosticism proves to be "belief in immanence." A philosophy comes into being that affirms and praises "presentness." Enjoying oneself becomes the slogan for forgetting "injury." The Panic attitude is expressed both in melancholy and cheerful, in resigned and defiant forms. The humor that casts light on nocturnal gloom is often bitter but is a laughter founded on sympathy for nature and people.*

*The idyll is embedded in the chthonic. People are entirely earth-bound; they have their short time in the sun and then go to the grave. Nature remains untouched by human suffering. Hölderlin calls nature's remorselessness aorgic and suffers from the cleavage. At the highpoint of realism, nature's domination is considered a consolation. Grass grows over everything and flourishes.*

*The "green ethos" senses "the gentle law": Whatever is small, enduring, permanent, constant is large. Only a small interval remains for hope, which one should nonetheless thoroughly savor before forgetting and being forgotten.*

*Horror and flourishing form a unity: uneasiness before the numinous and comfort in the immanent are entwined together. Justify what is without justification, find a grounding in acceptance of the incomprehensible. Though we are thrown into the world, it is not possible to fall out of it. The Acherontic chill knows a chthonic composure. With both longing and uneasiness we face evening. Becoming. Change. Decay. Disintegration.*

# THE PANIC ASPECT

Jean Paul notes in his diary that November 15, 1790 is

the most important evening of my life, for I had the thought of death and that there is absolutely no difference whether I die tomorrow or in thirty years. On that evening I projected myself thirty years ahead to my death-bed, saw myself in the draped shroud, saw myself with a face sunken from disease, glassy eyes, and heard my fantasies battling during my final night. You are coming—you, the final night of my dream! Since it is so certain that one day that is past and thirty years that are past are one and the same, I am now taking leave of the earth and its heaven, the wings are dropping away from my wishes and plans . . . But I no longer pay any heed to all that, and I want to love you more, fellowmen, and give you more pleasure! Oh, how I would like to torment life into you in your two December days you fading pictures of earth colors; a trembling reflection of life?—I will never forget the fifteenth of November.

The more profound dimension of the idyll becomes clear through such a quotation: the consciousness of death evokes the pleasure of life; the idyll is a moment of joy in existence, characterized by the certainty that the eyes will soon close and that pleasure may rapidly yield to pain. The idyll is the Panic hour; the god Pan is asleep, but soon horror will reawaken him and suppress flourishing hope. From the confrontation between security and insecurity, between life and death there emerges in the idyll an equally defiant and sad commitment to existence. When *The Life of the Merry Schoolmaster Maria Wutz in Auenthal* (which Jean Paul in the story of the same name calls a "kind of idyll") is over, the narrator says, "Your life and death were as gentle and as quiet as the ocean, you merry school-master Wutz!" The narrator once again looks back at the house of mourning and the burial plot where the grave is just in the process of being dug. The sentence succeeds, in a particularly shattering manner, in cir-cumscribing human existence under the rubric of the Panic element

. . . "I felt us all to be nothing and swore to disdain, to deserve and to enjoy such an insignificant life."

Jean Paul's apocalyptic nightmares reflect the anxieties of the dawning nineteenth century in the face of nothingness and the dark depths of emptiness. The pillars of faith were shattered. At the end of the century Nietzsche proclaims in triumph that God is dead. Ludwig Feuerbach's principal work, *The Essence of Christianity*, was published in 1841. Feuerbach maintained that man had created God in his image rather than the reverse. Gottfried Keller states in *Green Henry* that Feuerbach was a wondrous bird who, sitting alone in the shrubbery, "sang God away from the breasts of thousands." Heinrich Heine contended that sacraments are administered to a dying God at the sound of a bell.

Although the titanism of German philosophy conveyed the idea of a world structure utterly permeated by God, realism's emergence from and replacement of the Biedermeier era proves to be oriented toward agnosticism and atheism. It is doubted that the world has its reason in the sacred. There is an attempt to justify the world anew and in fact to find support in the here and now, in immanence. Poised between the not-yet and the no-longer, people turn to the in-between, to the moment of the idyll. The idyllic aspect of what is characterized as Panic, the Panic aspect of what is characterized as idyllic, means cheerfulness on the basis of melancholy, but it also means resignation, sadness, discontent.

Melancholy is not only a quality of individual poets but is seen more or less in every face. Immermann observes at the time that many showed the wrinkles of displeasure on their foreheads even before the wrinkles of age. The feeling of crisis, according to Friedrich Sengle, was ineluctable for most people of the Biedermeier generation even when the conviction was held that the old order could only be temporarily disturbed. The restlessness, the conflict, the provinciality of the restoration were produced by national disappointment, lack of inner freedom, widespread poverty, increased collectivism, and the loss of religious certainty. Rescue had its origin in the same experiences: tenacity, courage, a wish to exist and to survive. Jean Paul indicated three possibilities for becoming "happier" (not happy) in *Note to my Friends* (47). They are routes along which the Biedermeier civilization moved, an epoch that in the midst of the severest distress found stability and support in the small, in the gentle law. Cholera was raging; the restoration impeded free intellectual life (48); petty states impeded the emergence of a successfully organized economic system. The idyll becomes the refuge from the growing powers of endangerment, both inner and outer, religious and political. To be modest, to limit oneself, to turn away from external life and to direct one's energies toward one's inner development, to be inwardly happy despite dark powers of fate—such introvertedness became the goal: "Lord, send what You will, / Happiness or grief; / I am content that both / Flow from Your hands. / Neither with joys / nor with suffering / will You overwhelm me at all! / But in the middle / is gentle modesty." (Eduard Mörike)

A struggle for quiet happiness, an effort to escape the gravity of existence for a time, an often despairing attempt to master one's own demonic forces; to be able to control the dark impulses within one's own ego—all this typified the emotional life of the epoch. Summer, as one half of life, is balanced out by the dread that accompanies winter; the momentary fiction of permanence merges into the lament of transitoriness (49). Before the coming of dark night there blooms in the fantasy of the evening a longing for security (50). In its genesis Hölderlin's spiritual landscape is heroic, but the surge of angry protest from the depths discernible in his early writing is resolved into serenity: it is admittedly the harmony of a withdrawal due to insanity: "The round of earth adorned with rock / is not like the cloud that drifts away at eve, / it is revealed in one golden day, / and its perfection has no fault."

The world, here utterly tranquil, withdrawn from the sea of chaos like an island, is viewed from the perspective of displacement, a capacity that the poet lost in the end. His "imbecility" prevented him from grasping anything. In lucid moments he was still only able to lament the loss: "I have enjoyed what's pleasant in this world, / how long it is, how long, since my hours of youth have flowed away, / April and May and July are far, / I am nothing now, I am not glad to live!"

For me this poem is among the most shattering produced by German literature. It renounces all poetic decor and directly names Hölderlin's situation in his tower on the Neckar without circumlocution: "I no longer enjoy living!" Both exclamation marks in the second line ("How long! How long!") have the effect of desperate cries for help. The verses are as different as night and day from Hölderlin's youthful poetic creations—one need only think of his famous poem "Half of Life," in which similar themes and motifs are sounded. (Hans Christoph Buch)

The world in all its sensuality that people want to grasp and praise, the world which passes away and survives only in the elegy, this "landscape" of expectation and renunciation characterizes the art of Philipp

Otto Runge (51) and Caspar David Friedrich. Their paintings create variations on "waiting for the idyll"; Runge achieves this in a manner that is both cheerful and self-conscious, humanly open, versatile and creative; Friedrich does so in a melancholy, introverted, asocial, one-sided manner. Runge wrote in 1802 that "with us something is going to ruin, we are on the fringes of all the religions that arose from the Catholic faith, abstractions are going to ruin, everything is more airy and lighter than what preceded." The painter sees himself at a nadir of history, at a transition in the world of art; from this point on, he creates paintings full of longing for nature (whose primordiality had been lost), longing for the historical past (from which people were cut off), for a social future (that seems unattainable), for "unity" altogether. Jörg Träger asserts that Runge expresses the fundamental experience of the Romantic individual, which is best described existentially and in its various aspects by the concept of "separatedness." The psychological posture of longing results from this sense of life. According to Carl Gustav Carus, a student of Friedrich,

> If the modern artist, jammed between the wheels of an era bent upon violent and strange transition, must feel his wounds all the more deeply due to the poetic mind's irritability, the artist feels the need to give voice to this pain in his art. Hence the expression of longing that is actually predominant in these works. Gravestones and sunsets, ruins of abbeys, moonlight, paintings of fog and winter as well as dark forests with meager light breaking through are such mournful laments of a discontented existence.

In Runge's work the soul of the individual subject is scrutinized, in Friedrich's work, the infinite distance of a landscape without human beings. Heinrich von Kleist writes in his cordial review of Friedrich's painting, *Monk at the Sea:* "Nothing can be sadder and more uncomfortable than this position in the world; the only spark of life in the vast realm of death, the lonely central figure in the lonely circle." Abandoned to a protruding dune of the sea's endless breadth and to the enormous emptiness of a sky without bounds,

> . . . the tiny figure embodies detachment from everything—from culture and civilization, from any more closely discernible historical context, from human community, indeed from any kind of organic life. Its only environment is a piece of earth consisting of sand from which grows an occasional reed, air in which a few gulls are flying, and water. The fourth of the ancient elements of existence, life-giving light, is concealed in a murky firmament. Wrapped in a cape, the garment of flight from the world, is a figure—to quote a Rückert poem—"lost for the world." (Jörg Träger)

The idyll has here been divested of the charm characteristic of the genre; its expression remains blankly Panic, an aspect which one confronts as if it were an outpost, indeed an outpost that is already a lost position; one is abandoned but nonetheless composed.

Of horror and flourishing: at times anxiety is greater, at other times hope is predominant. In the Panic state both hope and anxiety are compressed; they are, so to speak, mutually balanced out in the immanence of the moment. "Master! Send whatever you please" . . . even death. According to Hegel, the *ars moriendi,* the art of being well and properly prepared to die, belongs, like the art of eating and drinking well, to the accomplishments of life that a real man must be capable of if he wishes to survive in the communication and communion of the living and the dead. For Hegel such an ability to die is "self-understood" in the sense of the complete incorporation of death into thinking; for Hegel, dying is the first and last topic of philosophizing; it is treated without sentimentality, tragicality, self-reflection, or self-pity. His understanding of death as reconciliation is based on transcendence. Through death God reconciled the world and reconciles himself with himself. Death means identity of the divine and the human. At the same time, the Panic aspect of the idyll is addressed. In the preface to the *Phenomenology of the Spirit* it is stated: "The life of the spirit is not the life that shies away from death and preserves itself purely from decay; rather, it is the life that endures it and achieves itself in it. It gains its truth only by finding itself in the conflict. It is this power only by looking the negative in the face and by staying with it. This tarrying is the magical force that reverses it into being." The Panic feeling of life does not shy away from death and does not keep itself pure of destruction; on the contrary, it endures death and achieves its spirituality in it. The Panic element finds its truth in itself in an absolute conflict between death and life. The negative is looked at squarely, is tarried with, but in this tarrying a magical force is released that chisels out a piece of being from nonbeing.

The idyll is not the way to be happy; it is merely the way to become happier. The world with its pitfalls and charnel houses and lightning rods is adjacent—just one step and one is at the abyss. The satiated hour of peace contains in itself the state of being lost. Utter happiness runs aground on transitoriness. "Oh, we poor people, is all of life not such a corridor to the place of judgment? And yet we are happy and ecstatic about the flowers along the way and see heaven and earth in each dewdrop along the route. Poor, happy heart of man!" (Wilhelm Raabe). The *vita activa* is the expression of preidyllic existence. In the idyll, on the other hand, the desire for power, brilliance, and world status is laid to rest, greatness is perceived as danger, fame as an empty game; action casts "empty shadows" (52).

In the moment of the idyll, time holds its breath before running out. In Mörike's novella, *Mozart's Journey from Vienna to Prague,* the composer comes into the garden of an old palace. He tarries in front of an orange tree that stands alone outside the row, quite to the side, full of the most beautiful fruit. This "look at the South" evokes "loving recollection" of boyhood. The hand holding the "magnificent roundness" and the "juicy refreshment" in the fruit experiences a feeling of timelessness. In looking at the abundance of oranges, Mozart experiences the "utter happiness of limitation." With his small knife he divides the spherical orange mass from top to bottom. "In doing so, he may have in some remote way have gotten a dark feeling of thirst; in any case, the stimulated senses were content with inhaling the priceless smell. He stared for several minutes at both of the inner surfaces, put them together again, carefully separated them again, then once more closed them." The experience of utter harmony is disturbed by the sound of steps nearby. The gardener catches the "intruder," but the owner of the palace receives the composer cordially. Conversations, sympathy, and festivity then follow. Hours pass, Mozart leaves; the piano on which he had played is closed, the volumes of songs returned to their place; an old page falls out. The "most natural coincidence" proves oracular: "A pine sapling is growing somewhere, who knows where, in the forest, a rosebush in who can tell what garden. They are already pre-ordained—Oh, soul, remember this—to strike root and grow in your grave."

Withdrawn from everyday affairs, the soul has responded to the unusual: exorbitance, which is registered in scrutinizing the orange, is a stepping-out of the world. But hardly has one turned back before it is lost. The small pine tree from which the casket is to be made has already grown. The seed of death is contained in all things.

Johan Peter Hebel anecdotally pointed out death's omnipresence and omnipotence (53). In a metaphorical sense, *Kannietverstaan* means that life cannot be understood; it is nonetheless necessary to find a reason in life. According to Arthur Schopenhauer, in infinite space and infinite time the humane individual recognizes himself as mortal, consequently as an entity hurled into it against that receding magnitude and, because of time's boundlessness, one which has only a relative but never an absolute when and where of existence, for his place and duration are finite parts of what is infinite and boundless. His actual existence is only in the present whose unimpeded flight into the past represents a constant transition into death. In his hands the present constantly becomes past; the future is uncertain and always brief. Existence: a constant hurling of the present into the dead past, a constant dying. The idyll is the moment when the fall comes to an apparent standstill. Life means the present (54). "Why does the sight of the full moon have the effect of being so beneficial, quieting, elevating? Because the moon is an object of observation but never of desire. 'The stars—people do not want to own them, people enjoy their magnificence.' " The sphere (the roundness of the earth, the round fruit of the orange tree, the round slice of the moon) is symbol of the momentary. The external world, also the cosmos of Goethe's house through which the poet Karl Immermann wanders (55), is the exterior of the inner world: concretized present seen from the perspective of once upon a time. Goethe reigned here; now he is dead. The force of his personality was able to form life into an idyll, to look the negative in the face, and, staying with it, to turn back to existence, to being there. The poet has died; his life has fallen into the past; what is real has survived, however, and documents the possibility of the momentary.

"Dwelling is the manner in which human beings on earth and under the sky complete the wandering from cradle to grave." (Martin Heidegger) The idyllic character of Biedermeier culture is particularly expressed in its style of cultivating the act of dwelling. It makes clear to what a great extent people's environment reflects the individual, how much the ritual of relationship to objects is also capable of achieving human dialogue.

The Biedermeier period is a culture of the "dwelling community" (56). Ludwig Richter delineated it (57). The Biedermeier person finds in the living room protectedness: a refuge of family life. Introvertedness has its dwelling here; melancholy finds support from objects; ideas of order are concretized. The longing for peace assumes form; mental energies become coziness. The frame of domesticity is simple and modest; empty walls without wallpaper, bounded at best by molding or painted architectural ornaments. Windows and doors are brightly painted, a rosette on the ceiling; the pictures on the walls are mostly silhouettes, lithographs, etchings; the sofa scene, which determines the symmetry of the arrangement, is particularly important. Usually only the upper part of the window is covered by a thin gathered white curtain. The furniture is characterized by utility, reflected in straight lines and in simplicity of construction.

The aesthetic value of furniture consists less in the decoration and detail (with the exception of the secretary) than in the manner in which the attractiveness of the material is stressed, uniting practicability and charm. Furniture is mostly made of light woods such as cherry, pear, birch, and maple, the chairs lightly upholstered in cotton, velvet, or with embroidered silk. Anyone unable to afford a sofa makes do with a settee, the angular cushioned bench. Many charming items are kept in the drawers of the small chests and commodes: clasps, notebooks, watches, trinkets, tie pins, lace handkerchiefs, caps, flowers, feathers, bows, braids. The *servante* is a showpiece of the living room, a place for keeping mementos. The mirrored wardrobe contains porcelain, crystal, wedding and baptism presents, mementoes of friendship and love, teapots and cups, wood carvings, and things to be sipped. Particular favorites are painted cups, medallions, charming souvenirs that cannot be seen without being touched. The sewing table, the housewife's headquarters, stands at the window; a bird flutters in the brass cage. A simple repast is usually brought to the birch table; the bourgeois luncheon table is still without excess and luxury. "At noon only one course; in the evening we children rarely were given a piece of meat, frequently a watery soup that our mother had made appealing by the addition of roots or milk . . . Wine was brought out when a dear visitor came." (Gustav Freytag)

The secretary is of particular importance. The lower half is divided into drawers; the upper part has a writing surface that can be lowered and closed. When closed, it conceals drawers; the upper half is frequently constructed in a special manner. A magnificent example of this kind of secretary is described by Stifter in *Indian Summer:*

> Four dolphins which brace the underside of their heads on the ground; their bodies stretch up in a curved position, supporting the body of the cupboard. At first I thought the dolphins were made of metal, but my companion told me they were carved from linden wood and given a yellowish-green metallic finish, a medieval technique of finishing that has been lost. The body of the cupboard has rounded work on all sides with six drawers. Above it was the middle piece that folded back smoothly, containing the surface that could be opened and used for writing. The upper part, with twelve curved drawers and a door in the center, was atop the middle piece. At the edges of the upper part and on both sides of the middle door gilded figures served as columns. The two largest figures at the sides of the door were strong men who carried the main decoration. From each of their chests hung a tag that could be opened to reveal the keyholes. The two figures on the front side edges were mermaids, each of which, in harmony with the supporting dolphins, ended with a fish tail. The remaining two figures on the rear side

corners were girls in pleated garb. All the fish as well as the columns seemed to me very natural. The drawers had gilded knobs by which they could be pulled. On the eight-cornered surface of these knobs were embedded half-length portraits of men in armor or festively attired women. The entire cabinet was of inlaid wood. Maple foliage in dark nutwood settings surrounded by intertwined bands and flaming alder. The bands were like rumpled silk, a consequence of their being made of finely ornate multicolored rosewood that had been vertically inlaid on the axis. The inlaid work was not merely, as is often the case with such objects, on the front but also on the sides and on the friezes of the columns.

Regardless of whether it is summer or winter, it is possible to rest up near the stove. Mörike describes it as a secure refuge in the idyll "The Old Weathervane": "An old stove stood in the corner on the left. It stretched like a tower, almost reached the ceiling. With columns, floral ornament, curly and pointed, o charming quiet place to sit! On the very top on the little wreath, the smith plants me on a little post. Let's look at the work closely. I see a whole cathedral, well decorated with scenes and trimmed with Christian verses. I learned many a word there, as the stove was a good refuge for bag and baggage and old people to chat when it stormed and snowed."

In the Biedermeier era, dwelling is the symbol for protectedness, and for finding a place for the moment before everything collapses into nonbeing. Dwelling makes it possible not to be anxious about time; the sentimental and cozy apartness is a stepping out of the passage of time (58). "Here and now" it is possible to enjoy a little piece of the world and oneself (59); here the table is set (60), here it is comfortable (61). But then—"one-two-three: time races, and we, too, race." The "apartness" has no beyond, life in this world remains without forward motion, existence finds no basis. The hut of Philemon and Baucis is swept away; when the Fates have snipped Mr. Knopp's threads of life, he collapses like an empty wrap.

The great spiritual achievement of the idyll admittedly also has its petit bourgeois side. The narrowness is then not overcome by a spiritual element; people settle down in a rut and surrender to the force of gravity, and the thought of flight into the spheres is forgotten. No notice is taken of pitfalls and charnel houses. People come to terms with the familiar, with the finite, and enjoy being satiated.

The transitions from the true to the false idyll are frequently very fluid. In the second half of the nineteenth century an inoffensive emptiness predominates. Romantic and Biedermeier epigones usurp newspapers, pocket books, calendars, readers, and the "official" publicity that affects the masses. Insulation led to mustiness; the world of the village and small town was idealized apathy; the nightwatchman proved to be a costumed reactionary, the model of the boorish philistine who does not stick his nose beyond his four walls, who is content with God and the world, and who above all "keeps quiet," come what may. "The hand that still cherishes and tends the little garden . . . is already the one that denies asylum to the political fugitive." (Theodor W. Adorno)

The limited and frequently very malicious "Biederman morality," the facade-like character of the middle-class cultural idyll, was revealed especially by Gottfried Keller in his novellas about *The People of Seldwyla* (62), by Wilhelm Busch, and by Heinrich Heine. The petit bourgeois sitting in front of his house on a sultry summer evening, his "white nightcap on his head, a meerschaum pipe in his mouth, quite comfortably believing that it would be nice if, without having his pipe go out and without having his life's breath expire, he could vegetate into dear infinity"—this image threw Heine into an anxious fury (63).

Ernst Keil's absolutely brilliant sense of publicity recognized around the middle of the nineteenth century that the time had come to satisfy the middle-class German's need for "inwardness" by a journal that could "safely be entrusted to one's daughters and that would promote 'good morals,' 'propriety,' 'honor,' and the 'happiness of society.' " A liberal of the year 1848 and a prisoner of the restoration, Keil initially kept his journal *Die Gartenlaube* clear of conservative and socially regressive thinking. The conception and style of the journal were nonetheless the essence of what was petit bourgeois and reactionary. Idyll and inwardness became a cultural facade; it was only a question of time until the paper assumed a nationalist-chauvinist content, and in fact Germania was soon one of the journal's patron saints. She was frequently depicted as an enormous woman wrapped in an Oriental carpet with the decorations of the *Reich,* wearing health sandals and all manner of weapons, holding up a wrought-iron laurel wreath and crown which she was about to place on her flowing hair.

The first issue of the *Gartenlaube* proclaims

> Greetings to you dear people, to all friends and readers in the land of Germany. When you are sitting around the familiar stove in the circle of your dear ones during the long winter evenings or with a few friends under a shady arbor in the spring when the white and red petals fall from the apple

tree, read our publication, which is intended for home and family, for young and old, for everyone whose warm heart beats against her ribs and who still craves the good and noble. . . . But may there be a breath of poetry floating over everything like the aroma of the flower in bloom. May it be at home in the arbor, where good German coziness that speaks to the heart is to be found. Try out one of our issues, and God be with you.

With its mixture "of peasant girls and a lavish spread of counts, defiant hearts and sensitive nymphs from cultural history and Germanic myth, cloying sweetness and mild stupidity," (J. Wachte) it caught the popular taste of the time, especially the "official" spirit of Wilhelminism. The idyll had lost its ethical-moral justification; now it was no longer retreat from a deeply-felt danger but was glossed-over contentment. The dream was not longing for the "unchangeable," was no longer striving upward; it was simply "reverie" and a plunge into the pleasures of trivial aesthetic delights. Sentimentality and elation could be immediately coupled with any- and everything—with nature, the Fatherland, war, God, religion, even with crime, for they ultimately did not touch people's core. They were detached sentiments that one could accept or reject according to the time of day.

In Friedrich Schiller's comments about the idyll in *Naïve and Sentimental Poetry* he states that the effects of the "false idyllic idealism were horrible." Whereas the true idealist abandons nature and experience and withdraws into other realms because he does not find the "unchangeable, which is unconditionally necessary and which reason dictates should be striven for," the fantast abandons nature out of mere arbitrariness "to be able all the more unimpededly to pursue self-willed desire and the moods of his imagination." "He bases his freedom not on independence from psychic needs but in being absolved of moral necessity. The fantast hence denies not only the human; he denies all character, he is completely lawless and therefore nothing and good for nothing." This led to an "endless fall into a bottomless depth" that had to "end in complete destruction," since an estimable human propensity could not be fulfilled but was instead perverted.

A development was thereby anticipated that even politically was to have dire consequences. From the sentimental derived the sentimental idyll. The age was dawning when the comfy Germans would turn out to be the uncanny Germans, when coziness and emotionality became the facade behind which the forces of barbarism were organizing. As early as 1857 Wilhelm Raabe mourned in his first work, *Chronicle of Sparrow Lane,* for a Germany that could still be found only in remote alleys and attic rooms; the Germany of the soul, full of faith, goodness, modesty, and patience (64).

The existential sense of "being hurled" that led to the search for a humane basis in immanence was no longer registered in horror (65). Scare tactics would now be used to intimidate others and catch up on what had been withheld (and sublimated) during the Biedermeier era with its political, economic, and governmental deprivation. Imperialistic pretentions were directed toward curing the world with the German essence. The green hope of the idyll was thus destroyed. The banality of an emptied pathos pushed Biedermeier inwardness aside and spread out on the cushion of platitude. The debris of an ostentatious petit bourgeois ideology soon collected over the true idyll, one of the greatest and most beautiful achievements of the German spirit of the nineteenth century.

## (47) Three ways to become happier

JEAN PAUL, A Note to My Friends Instead of a Foreword. The Life of Quintus Fixlein

Jean Paul defined the idyll in his *Primer of Aesthetics* as "utter happiness within limitations." Idylls of the eighteenth century as typified by the Zurich author Salomon Gessner described peaceful rural scenes and customs, and gentle, undisturbed happiness. They portrayed "the complete existence of the shepherd," "where at most a sheep or goat emerges from the watercolors while human figures appear blurred." It was from this form of the idyll that Jean Paul wished to set himself apart, as indeed did Goethe ("Hermann and Dorothea" 1796) and Johann Heinrich Voss (author of the idyll "Luise" 1795). In Jean Paul's work the bourgeois world is not intact. The only thing that is idyllic is the hero's method of asserting himself in catastrophic situations. The *Note to My Friends* was subjected to many misunderstandings. "The sentence, 'The most necessary sermon one can preach to our century is to remain at home,' is quoted as an example of utter philistinism, while the irony of the remark is overlooked. Or the irony is referred to, mentioning such words as Brutus, republican, and revolution that are used in a positive sense, explaining the whole as a satire of German conditions by a Jacobin. The truth, however, lies somewhere in between—in the author's attempt to pawn off his own conflict as harmony." (Günter de Bruyn)

In Jean Paul's life and work the first two routes indicated in the *Note* are never united; on the contrary, they run parallel in polar tension. As for the third route, Jean Paul offers himself as an example, insofar as he was in fact "still capable in the midst of the creation of this note to keep in mind that when it is finished the baked roses and elderberries being simmered in butter for the author will also be finished." "The many poor people, though, who are unable to become heroes or artists—the slaves, the 'bound people' who despite having good fins are not permitted to swim because their prison, the 'fishbox of the state . . . swims in the name of fish,' the standing army of the state's slaves and writers, the crabs in the crab basket that for refreshment are covered over with a few nettles, are of course only capable of the second route, guidance for which is provided by idylls. But precisely in the description of this route it is impossible not to notice the irony in the heroic gesture of a sentence like, 'If I succeed in that, then my book will serve in posterity to train men who are refreshed by everything—by the warmth of their parlors and their sleeping caps . . .' Hence the preface to the story of the jolly little schoolmaster Fixlein serves as a warning against the lifestyle it recommends. Along with love, sympathy, and knowing better, resignation is always present in the melancholy merriment of these stories; i.e., if I am unable to free myself from this microbial world, how should you be able to!" (G. de Bruyn)

I was never able to discover more than three ways to become, not happy, but happier. The first, which ascends into the heights, is this: to rise so far above the clouds of life that the entire external world and all its wolf's dens, charnel houses, lightning rods, lies far beneath one's feet, looking like the shrunken garden of a child. The second is this: to drop straight down into that tiny garden and there to build a homey nest inside a furrow, so that when one peers out of this warm lark's nest, one does not see the wolf's dens, charnel houses and lightning rods at all, but rather only the single ears of grain, each of which is a tree and a shelter from sun and rain for the nestling. The third, which I take to be the most difficult and the wisest, is this: to alternate between the other two.

Now I want to make that very clearly understood.

The hero—the reformer—Brutus—Howard—the republican tossed by civil storms—the genius similarly moved by artistic tempests—in short, every human being with a grand resolve or merely with an enduring passion (even if it were only a passion for writing the thickest folio-volume ever), all of these people enclose themselves and their inner worlds within walls against the cold and heat of the outer world, just as the madman does in a bad sense. Every *idée fixe,* which governs at least periodically every genius and every enthusiast, divorces man nobly from the bed and board of this earth, from its dog holes and stinging thorns and dungeon walls—like the bird of paradise, he sleeps in flight, and on widespread wings he slumbers in the heights, blind to the earthquakes and conflagrations below him, in a long and lovely dream of his ideal homeland. . . . Oh! few are granted this dream, and these few are awakened so often by the hounds that patrol the heavens!

This ascendant flight, however, is only for the winged portion of the human race, the smallest portion. It can be of no concern to the poor kinsmen of the chancery, whose spirits often have no wing cases, much less anything beneath—or to those subjected souls with the very finest pectoral, ventral and dorsal fins who are expected to stay quite still inside the fish box of the state and not to swim, because the box of state, long chained to the shore, is already swimming in the fishes' behalf. What way can I show the standing and writing army of burdened servants of the state, scriveners, notaries, clerks of every department, and all the little crayfish piled one on top the other in the crayfish pot of the state's counting house, covered for their refreshment with a layer of stinging nettles? What can I point out to such as these as the way to find bliss in this world?

Only my second way, which is this: to take a compound microscope and with its aid to see that their drop of burgundy is actually a red sea, the dust on butterfly wings a peacock's plumage, the mold on a crust of bread a field in bloom, and a handful of sand a house of jewels. These microscopic pleasures are more enduring than all the costly pleasures of the world's watering-places. . . . But I must explain these metaphors with new ones. The purpose I had in sending Fixlein's *Life* to the printers in Lübeck is just this: to reveal to all the world in this life—for which reason I have little need of it in this letter—that small sensual pleasures are to be esteemed more highly than great ones: the dressing gown more than the cutaway coat, that Pluto's *Quinterne* must rank below his *Extracts,* a piece of gold below the bit put by for a rainy day, and that it is not the great stroke of good luck that makes us happy, but rather the small one. If I succeed in my purpose, I shall be educating for posterity men who find pleasure in everything: in the warmth of their parlors and their nightcaps; in their bed pillows; in the three holy feast days; in mere saints' days; in the moral tales told by their wives in the evening after they have spent the afternoon as ambassadresses visiting some widow's seat, having been unable to move their husbands to join them in this good work; in the day on which these lady novelists of theirs undertake a thorough spring cleaning; in the day on which the butchering, preserving and pickling for the harsh winter is begun, and so on. It can be seen that I urge the human race to take the tailor bird as its model, not among the beating branches of the vast, storm-tossed tree of life, but rather on just one of its leaves to stitch itself a nest and make it warm inside. The most needful sermon one can preach for our century is this: Stay at home.

The third way to happiness is the alternation of the first and second. The aforementioned second way is not good for man, who needs to take up not only the fruit hook, but also the plowshare. The first way is too good for him. He does not always have the strength of a Rugendas, who in the midst of raging battles painted his battle scenes, or of a Bakhuizen, who in shipwreck seized no other board than his drawing board, in order to capture the scene on paper. And then his *pain* sometimes endures as long as his *feebleness*. Even more often his strength lacks elbow room in which to exert itself; only the smallest part of life gives a working man the Alps—revolutions—the Rhine falls—the Diet of Worms—and wars with Xerxes, and that is on the whole as it should be: the greater part of life is a greensward beaten flat as a threshing floor and without any lofty Mount Gotthards, often also a tedious ice field without a single glacier glowing in the rising sun.

However, it is by walking that man gains the strength for climbing, and by the experience of small joys and duties the preparation for great ones. The conquering tyrant must know how to turn the battlefield into a field of flax and turnips, and the theater of war into a household stage on which his children can perform a few good pieces from *The Children's Friend.* If he can do that, if he can turn so adroitly from the glorious path of genius into the path of domestic bliss, then he is very like me, who now—though modesty should forbid my calling attention to it—who now, I say, in the midst of composing this letter am still quite capable of remembering that, when it is finished, the elderberry and the rose-petal fritters will also be finished, which now are being fried in butter for the author of these lines.

Since I wish to add to this billet a postscript, I intend to save a few things I have to say about the third, half-satirical, half-philosophical part of the book for that epilogue.

Here the author, respecting the rights of a personal letter, drops his quasi anonymity and signs for the first time his true full name.

Hof in Voigtland, June 29, 1795.
Jean Paul Friedrich Richter

TRANSLATED BY SHARON JACKIW

## (48) Cholera in Berlin

KARL GUTZKOW, Memoirs

Gutzkow (born in Berlin in 1811, died in 1878) considered himself the leader of the Young Germany group. Along with Heinrich Laube, he fought against the obscurantist forces and powers of the restoration, especially those in the German Confederation. His élan as a publicist and journalist drew on the milieu of the emerging metropolis whose urbanity was admittedly menaced by cholera and by constant persecutions by demagogues. Gutzkow was banished from his Prussian homeland, went first to Württemberg which did not like him and which he did not like, and subsequently to Frankfurt and Hamburg. "The loss of the homeland and the orientation toward the abstract conception of freedom also led to a disdain of the 'province,' a cherished value of the Biedermeier era. His aloofness toward Swabians is a result of this attitude. Gutzkow very disdainfully criticizes pointless Swabian poetry: 'This form of poetry is so restricted to its valleys, so local, quiet, and happy.' Heine's mockery deals even more severely with the idyllic Swabians, and he disdains the pious, stupid province as a matter of principle: 'I conceive France to be Paris, not the province; for what the provinces think is as much a matter of indifference as what our legs think. The head is where thinking occurs.' This statement illustrates the literary-geographical consequences of liberalist abstraction with particular clarity. The main thing is to live in some large city." (Friedrich Sengle)

Somber autumn days had come to Berlin in the year 1831. A deathly silence reigned in the streets. The "Asian guest"—cholera—had reached Europe for the first time. Nothing could have restrained it, not even the closing of the Russian and Polish borders. No "cholera cordon" in Posen province which, since it also would have to serve as a cordon against the plague of revolution, a revolution recently put down in Poland by Paskievich after the murderous battles of Ostrolenka and Prague, a revolution which was reckoned as if it had been one year of war for the military personnel employed there. No use. The scourge of God, as it was called on the pulpit, had arrived, and even in Berlin, the capital of the intelligentsia, a city where Schinkel and Rauch and Humboldt lived and taught abstract thought to forget material substance—even there, it had come. Schleiermacher found the contrast between spirit and substance so horrifying that it made him sick, and Hegel succumbed to it directly.

Full of somber thoughts, I stood in one of the streets of Berlin where the noise of wagons was unbearable for those with sensitive auditory apparatus. At that time grass grew as undisturbed on Kochstrasse as in the country. Berlin's population was just over 200,000. Nevertheless, the number of those who were taken from us daily by cholera had climbed to 200. There were cholera hospitals in every quarter. Patients were brought in on long oilcloth-covered stretchers. Burials took place at night. People acted as they may have during the Middle Ages when the Black Death struck. The pallbearers and all others who served in the business of transporting the dead and dying wore green oilcloth smocks. Everything one touched smelled of chlorine.

Whoever could leave Berlin did so. I, too, took my leave of the deathly quiet corner of Friedrichsstrasse and Kochstrasse. There dwelt the object of my love; there also lived the friend who accompanied me a few steps from Number 70. The sails were to be trimmed, the high seas of daring and tests of youthful strength to be traveled. The blossoms of student days had long since wilted, now even more completely since everyone was preaching "moderation." Lectures were deserted, professors monosyllabic. Professor Hecker, who had written a history of medicine and monographs on the "English sweat" and on the whipping fever, was the talk of the town. What similar kind of ecstasy would be next! There had already been an uproar over the wells. The rich were supposed to have poisoned them in order to do away with the poor. The way in which people called down the wrath of heaven, the public assumption of the power of prayer, grew unbearable.

Bürger and I, a circle of fellow students, friends since school days, had formed a "fraternity sewing circle" that met together every Saturday in a quiet secluded square in Splittgerbergasse, near the Free Masons' lodge "At the Three Globes." A hidden garden, separated from the cult of the Eleusinian mysteries by a picket fence, and the large dining hall of an inn had offered us the opportunity to make use of the oft-mentioned "excess of youthful good spirits." This excess, which totally contradicts the Delphic pronouncement (and one hopes that of freemasonry also) *Ne quid nimis!*—nothing to excess!—ruled our youthful souls. What were we to do with our flaming passion, our need to love, to admire, even to mourn and weep? In old age it is inconceivable whence might have come the exaggerated ceremoniousness with which we sang, in powerful voices, "The Father of the Land" (we used to substitute "Fatherland"), the "King of Fools," the rounds "My Life is Love and Desire," "Brother, What is Your Beauty's Name?" and the like. Whence came the pedantic earnestness which could see a drinking bout through to the very end? The custom of drinking before and after, then a few duels, which to be sure arose not from our own circle, so permeated with friendship and love, but from other fields which extended into ours and affected one or the other of us as First, or Second, or Neutral—these were all highly important things, like the opening speech of the Congresses of Vienna and Verona. Particular characters, like a certain amiable and intelligent North Albigensian Meyer from Ratzeburg (later Professor in Riga and Hamburg), contributed to these formalities a fantastically solemn dedication capable of connecting them with Schelling, Hegel, Barbarossa, Mar von Schenkendorf, and the treasure of the Nibelungs.

Our song book was the well-known one by Serig of Leipzig. The "excess of high spirits"—or should I say self-instigation to emotion—attained, in certain verses of the song "We Had Built a Stately House," the kind of vibrating tones that might be heard for example among the American Shakers when they believe they see heaven opening. Fortunately, the heavy floor could absorb the furor of our stomping on our glasses. By the time we got to the words "And trust in God, mind not rain and storm and fright," our voices rose to an Anabaptist tremolo for the fate of the fraternity and of all Germany. "All form has crumbled, the spirit lives on in us"—the sluices of the soul were opened and Jean Paul's ideal world, the starry vision of his rainbow-clad heroes, seemed to have come over us. No one glanced at the door, to see if possibly the university warden had arrived to demand identification cards from all of us. As long as the German can sing a chorale ("Dear Fatherland, be calm") and be overcome by emotions and thoughts of his mother, then he is capable of the greatest things.

In later years I met the Holsteiner August von Binzer, composer of the above-mentioned song, in Augsburg. My astonishment at the contrast between my youthful, overflowing spirits in singing his song and the poet's changed attitude, perhaps also that of the *Zeitgeist,* was something I could not reveal to him. The sphere which surrounded the erstwhile demagogue from Kiel saw itself as the most authoritative in every respect. His wife, a witty lady whose talents were evidenced by several things she had written, at first under the name Beer and later as Ernst Ritter, had become a special friend of the Austrian poet Christian von Zedlitz. A confidante of Count Metternich's, von Zedlitz had taken the Binzer family and all the connections of the old fraternity and Wartburg heroes and set them up in the highest expectations of Viennese aristocratic society.

The farewell in Kochstrasse did not occur because of the cholera epidemic but would have taken place even under less cheerless circumstances. The pressure of opposition against the absolutist bureaucracy had ruined for me any positive impression that Berlin might still have to offer. The writer had hatched from the egg and was wielding his pen against anything at all that could still be attacked at that time—one year after the July Revolution—in an age of jailings, dismissals, banishments. The strictest censors watched every printed letter; every advertisement in the *Intelligencer* was checked for hidden political meanings. Unaccountably, and only to be explained by the fact that I stood in the favor of the generally feared Minister von Kamptz, I was granted permission, upon application to the Ministry, to publish a journal in which I was even allowed to write about religion and politics. Special Attorney Bardua was employed as censor for the students.

The costs of first breaking the ice in this way came out of my own pocket. Under the lindens, in the rear courtyard of what was at that time the best restaurant in Berlin, the "Traiteur Jagor," I entered a printshop as a customer for the first time. As a boy I was familiar with this black magic, for I had first become acquainted with the peculiar smell of a printshop at the home of a relative who had done well by producing a newly invented roller to ink the type. And here at Konrad Feister's—this was my printer's name—the misprints would be my own!

And the censorship was so mild! The Special Attorney didn't scratch out a single thing. For I scorned the freedom to write about the governments of Petersburg and Vienna. It seemed to me as if the freedom offered me was like blackberries surrounded by too many stinging nettles.

With the pride of the true philologist I had the paper printed in Latin letters so that the English and the French would find it easier to read. Essentially it was my task to protect the man of my heart, Wolfgang Menzel, against the attacks of his enemies. There were outpourings of the truest devotion to an interpretation of literature that seemed destined to dominate the critical field. Of course I was only a Romantic. The newly adopted diabolic twists that Heinrich Heine was putting at the ends of his poems—these I couldn't bear—much less the literature of word play and the Saphirists. To get involved in Berlin's journalistic gossip and in the feuds of Saphir with his opponents seemed to me far beneath the dignity of a writer who had been suckled "on the milk of classical antiquity"; this is why I still cannot understand how the young scholars Wilhelm Wackernagel and Karl Simrock, in trifling coffee-and-tea papers like the *Estafette* and the *Courier,* could get so excited over "Jews breaking into literature."

To be sure, the word literature did not mean to me the cultivation of ballads and romances or of novellas and pieces for the theater. The spirit from which everything must be born anew, it seemed to me, simply could not be found in the rustling autumn leaves of Unter den Linden in Berlin. The journal reached a high of seventy subscribers. It died. I wanted to continue my literary apprenticeship with Wolfgang Menzel in Stuttgart. My style at that time owed much to Jean Paul.

TRANSLATED BY NINA MORRIS-FARBER AND FREDERICK D. BOGIN

## (49) Woe is me

FRIEDRICH HÖLDERLIN, "Half of Life"

This poem appeared for the first time in the *Notebook Dedicated to Love and Friendship* (1805). In 1802 Hölderlin was suddenly in a terrible state of agitation, "with confused expressions and raging gestures, in a state of the most desperate madness," having returned home from Bordeaux where he had accepted the position of tutor with a consul from Hamburg. At that time Diotima (Susette Gontard) died following an illness of ten days, and the poet showed the first signs of mental illness. From 1807 on, he lived peacefully for 36 years, his mind shrouded over, in Tübingen in the house of a carpenter who cared for him. Pierre Bertaux, however, does not consider Hölderlin mentally ill. He considers him to be a split personality and an eccentric. He views Hölderlin as a peculiar person characterized by a profoundly disturbed relationship to his mother, who had contributed significantly to his becoming a broken person considered a "mental cripple," a poet who vacillated between the sublime heights of idealism exalted by nineteenth century literary historians and concrete sensuality. (The "holy love" for Diotima was surely not so untainted by "flesh.") The conflict that led him to spend decades as a lonely hermit who sought to keep people at a distance is also reflected in the poem "Half of Life," which coincided with Hölderlin's "midlife."

> Emburdened with yellow pears
> And swollen with wild roses
> The land meets the lake,
> You most gracious swans,
> And drunken with kisses
> You dip your head
> Into sacred sober water.
>
> Woe is me, where shall I
> When it is winter, find the flowers,
> And the sunshine
> And shadows of earth?
> The walls persist
> Speechless and cold, in the wind
> The vanes are rattling.

TRANSLATED BY ADRIAN DEL CARO

## (50) Longing for the idyll

FRIEDRICH HÖLDERLIN, "Evening Fantasy"

The poem was written in 1799 and published in 1800 in the *British Ladies' Calendar*. Individual nervousness is juxtaposed to the visionary image of peace. Where should I go?

The peacefulness of the idyll does not always prove to be a lie, but it is a lie in the false idyll. Nonetheless, it is without duration. In the midst of fateful entanglements there emerges the hope of becoming old and of being exempt from the obligation toward activity. In the first two stanzas in particular the poet turns his dream entirely toward the "common" life, a reflection of Hölderlin's social and revolutionary attitude.

Before his hut quietly in the shadow
Sits the plowman, his stove smokes for the humble.
Hospitably the evening bell tolls
In the peaceful town for the wanderer.

And the sailors now return to the harbor,
In distant cities, cheerfully subsided
The market's busy noise; in peaceful
Gardens a festive meal is shared by friends.

Whither then shall I go? We mortals must survive
On wages and work; turning from toil to rest
All are happy; why then does the thorn
Slumber no longer only in my breast?

A spring is blossoming on the evening sky;
Numberless bloom the roses and quiet seems
The golden world; O take me hither,
Purple clouds! And may it be that up there

My love and sorrow will turn to light and air!
Yet, as though banished by foolish wishing, the
Magic flees; it grows dark, and lonely
Beneath the heaven, as always, am I—

Come now, gentle slumber! Too much does the heart
Demand; but finally, youth! you will burn down,
You restless, you visionary one!
Peaceful and cheerful then will be old age.

TRANSLATED BY ADRIAN DEL CARO

## (51) The connection of the whole universe

PHILIPP OTTO RUNGE, Letter to His Brother Daniel

Runge was born in Wolgast in 1777 and died in Hamburg in 1810. He was trained at the Academy in Copenhagen and was the originator of Romantic paintings of symbolic figures and landscapes. The poetry of fulfilled proximity to nature is united with symbol-laden stylization in his works. There are many sketches and fragments of his painting *The Four Periods of the Day* but he only completed *Morning*. Goethe, both repelled and fascinated by Romanticism, commented to Sulpiz Boisserée concerning *Morning:* "Here you see what kind of a thing this is! It is enough to drive one crazy! Both beautiful and fantastic. To be sure, it attempts to comprehend everything; consequently it repeatedly strays off into the elementary, although with infinite beauty in the details. But just look at it! What a devilish thing! And then, too, what charm and magnificence the fellow produced! But the poor devil did not sustain it—he is already dead. It is not possible any other way: anything that is so much on the edge has to die or go insane. There is no mercy."

Runge's writings on the theory of art, most of which were published by his oldest brother after the painter's early death, were of great importance for nineteenth century painting.

Dresden, March 9, 1802

When the heavens above me teem with innumerable stars, when the wind rushes through the wide reaches of the universe, when the waves break with a roar in the breadth of night, when the ether grows rosy above the forest and the sun illumines the world, when the mists of the valley rise and I throw myself down in the grass among sparkling drops of dew; and each leaf and each blade of grass throngs with life, the earth lives and moves beneath me, everything sounds in a single harmony— then my soul exults and flies about in the infinite spaces around me, below and above no longer exist, time exists no longer, there is no beginning and no end, I hear and feel the living breath of God who bears and cherishes the world, in whose breath everything lives and acts. This is the highest thing that we can imagine—God! This deepest sensing in our soul that God is above us; that we see how everything has come into being, been, and passed away; how everything around us comes into being and is present and passes away; and how everything will come into being, will live, and again will pass away; how there is no peace and no cessation within us; this living soul in us, which came from him and will return to him, which will exist when heaven and earth have passed away—this is the most clear and certain consciousness of our self and of our own eternity.

We feel that something relentlessly stern and frighteningly eternal and a sweet, eternal and boundless love firmly oppose each other in a fierce struggle, like hard and soft, like rock and water; we see these two everywhere, in the smallest as in the greatest thing, in the whole as in the part: these two aspects are the basic essence of the world and are founded in the world . . . —

—When emotion seizes us so that all our senses tremble in their foundations, then we seek the hard, significant signs that others outside us have discovered, and we unite these with our own feeling; in one most beautiful moment we can convey this to others, but if we try to stretch this moment, it becomes strained to excess; that is, the spirit flees from the outward signs and we cannot attain the connection again within ourselves until we have either returned to the original intensity of our inner feelings or else become children again. This circle, in which one repeatedly suffers death, is experienced by everyone, and the more often one experiences it, the deeper and more inward becomes the emotion. And it is thus that art is born and dies, and nothing remains but the lifeless signs when the spirit has returned to God. This sensation of the connection of the whole universe with ourselves; this exultant rapture of the deepest and most vital spirit of our soul; this single harmony, which in one sweep touches every string of our heart—love, which cherishes and bears us through life, this sweet creature at our side, which lives in us and in whose love our soul catches fire: it is this that impels and urges at our hearts, to impart to us; we cling to the highest peaks of these sensations, and thus certain ideas arise within us.

TRANSLATED BY NINA MORRIS-FARBER

## (52) Quiet concord of the soul

FRANZ GRILLPARZER, The Dream, A Life

A characteristic of bourgeois Biedermeier creativity is that inner conflicts remain concealed and that the titanic element of the ego is suppressed, repressed, or silenced. Grillparzer remarked of himself, "One of my main faults is that I do not have the courage to assert my individuality." Compelled to unconditional loyalty as an Austrian civil servant, oriented as a writer for the theater to the norms and judgment of bourgeois or aristocratic society, it was difficult for him to find his own identity, especially as he still felt burdened by his mother's suicide (from religious insanity). "Not understood as a person, overlooked as an official, at best tolerated as a poet, I drag my monotonous existence along."

In the Oriental-Romantic fairytale play, *The Dream, A Life* (1834), the hunter Rustan, no longer content with a quiet life with Massud and his daughter Mirza, is incited to the *vita activa* by the black slave Zanga. A dream that anticipates this life cures him of the desire for power, brilliance, and worldly success. "Faced with broad prospects," Rustan shouts for joy on the eve of his proposed departure shortly before his dream and ensuing sobriety. "Every one of his fibers quivers," his hands are clenched, "fiery glances shoot from beneath deeply drawn brows." In the morning, however, he wants only to find his happiness at the side of his beloved in the peaceful hut.

Such withdrawal into the idyll as is "performed" on the stage is in contrapuntal contrast to what the theater was striving for in the eighteenth century. The historical situation was similar—there was no nation. But while Grillparzer resignedly lauds "quiet inner peace" as the sole happiness, the poets of the era of the Enlightenment, especially Lessing, had championed a national theater as the locus of collective self-discovery. Implicit in the "principle of a national theater" was "a class, the bourgeoisie, which in the wake of the Enlightenment slowly became socially emancipated and was to use the stage as a tool to articulate its own scale of values, its own ideals of virtue, its own conceptions of happiness, humanity, and justice. And this was not to take place in a provisional framework but in established theaters that had permanent ensembles; it was to occur without regard for narrow national and class divisions on stages that should go beyond arbitrary territories in an appeal to the nation." (Walter Jens)

With the triumph of the characteristically bureaucratic bourgeois over the *citoyen*, the "kind-hearted idea of providing the Germans with a national theater, since we Germans are not a nation" (Lessing) was laid *ad acta*. Grillparzer's drama *The Dream, A Life* signalizes not only personal retreat from history; it is also symptomatic of the direction taken by the German spirit away from social responsibility into private inwardness.

*Rustan [rising up suddenly and touching his arms].*
Am I living? Am I captured?
Then the stream did not devour me?
Zanga! Zanga! Woe is me!
*Zanga [in livery as in the first act, enters with a lamp, which he sets down].*
Finally awake! It's dawning,

And the horses have been readied.
*Rustan.* Monster! Snake! Assassin! Devil!
Did you come here to deride me?
Though your hair resembles vipers
And your pupils are like flames
And you hold a bolt of lightning,
Still, a mortal led astray,
I shall moderate my vengeance
And the dagger here shall test
If your body the same metal
As your forehead, fury, breast!

*[He has seized the dagger that hangs beside the bed and is about to throw it.]*
*Zanga.* Help! Alas, he is a madman!
Mirza! Massud! Someone, hear! *[He flees.]*
*Rustan.* He has fled! I am not powerless,
Not invincible his might!
I'll away now from these chambers
Circumscribed with deadly fright!

First the light must be extinguished
That reveals me to my foes.
*[He blows out the lamp. Though the broad arched window that encompasses over*
*half the background one sees the horizon bordered by the first signs of daybreak.]*
Where's the door? Is there no exit
From this place of fears and woes?
Am I to be forced to die here?—
Listen, someone nears apace.
I will dearly sell my life then;
First shall kill, then death shall face.
*[He grasps the saber that is standing beside his bed. Massud and Mirza enter.*
*The latter is carrying a brightly burning light.]*
Ha, the king comes, and Gülnare?
Not the king!—How can this be?
Massud, is it you?—And Mirza!
Are you dead, and am I also?
How did I come here among you?
Do I see this hut once more?

Do not squander so your gazes.
Do not cast your loving glances
On the dark one at your feet!
For what love to me has given
I'll repay with bloody hate.—
Yet, I find I do not hate you!
No, I hate not you—nor you.
Hate? What are these warming showers
Through my inner self suffused?
Do not hate you! Hate nobody,
Would forgive the world entire
As with tears long unfamiliar

I can feel my eyes renewed.
*Mirza.* Rustan!
*Rustan.* No, do not come near me!
If you knew all that has passed
Since we last saw one another.
*Mirza.* You say "saw each other last"?
*Rustan.* Days, weeks—
*Mirza.* Weeks, days?
*Rustan.* How should I know? How should I know?
Time has power that is dreadful.
*Mirza.* Was it more than just one night?
*Zanga* [*appearing in the doorway*].
Master, did you call for horses?
*Mirza.* Try to bring it back to mind.
Just last evening, father, tell him;
I am finding it too hard.
*Massud.* Don't you know about last evening?
You were then about to leave us,
Ordered horses for today.
*Rustan.* Just last evening—?
*Massud.* Why, when else then?
*Rustan.* Just last evening?—And the sum of
What I saw, what I experienced,
All the grandeur, all the horror,
Blood and triumph, death and war—?
*Massud.* May have been mysterious warning
Given by an unknown might
That perceives of hours as years,
Of a year as like one night;
Wanting that be manifested
All the thoughts that you concealed;
And would threaten and forewarn you
And the truth has now revealed;
Takes away the threat with darkness.
Use the gift, the gods' advice.
They will scarcely help you twice.
*Rustan.* Just one night, and was a lifetime!
*Massud.* Just one night. It was a dream.
See, the sun, the very same one

Only older by a day.
That, as your defiance parted,
Saw your hardness, firmness stay.
See, in its eternal orbit
How it climbs the mountain there,
Seems astonished, pointing to you,
Who so slowly change your course;
And my son, if you would travel,
It is time; to horse! to horse!
[*The region visible through the window, that has already shown all stages of the
    approaching day, now beams forth in the full brilliance of sunrise.*]
*Rustan* [*falling to his knees*].
Sun eternal, bless'd present,
Greetings to you, holy dawn!
As your beaming exiles darkness
And the mist and fog are gone,
So it penetrates my vitals
Conquering my darkest night.
What was secret, is no longer;
What perverted, now grows right.
All the light is turned to warmth now,
And the warmth, it is the light.

Thanks be, thank you, that those terrors
That my hand with blood have hemmed,
Were a warning, not the truth,
Did not happen, just were dreamt;
That your beams in their translucence—
You, the world's illuminer—
Find me not a bloody wanton,
Fall on me, now pure again!

Oh, dispense it with your beaming!
Plant it deep in every breast:
One joy only, one joy whole—
Quiet concord of the soul,
Heart by absolution blessed.
For in greatness there is danger,
And renown's an empty game

Bringing with it idle shadows.
Far too high the price of fame.

TRANSLATED BY MINETTA ALTGELT GOYNE

## (53) A spacious house and a narrow grave

JOHANN PETER HEBEL, Kannietverstaan

Johann Peter Hebel was born in Basel in 1760 and died in 1826 in Schwetzingen. His dialect poems provided an important model for the Biedermeier era. "Despite the predominance of parochial art around 1900, it is perhaps possible to assert that dialect poetry reached its zenith in the Biedermeier civilization simply because it was closely connected with the emergence of German studies and also because it was somewhat conditionally substantial, not a despairing counter-image in opposition to modern civilization. The separate territories were still considered to be the 'Fatherland.' Dialects that had developed in the various regions were only dissipated around 1850 by industrialization. It may be said that a tradition which is not endangered is hardly cherished the way dialect is in the Biedermeier era, and one may be reminded of the parallel appearance of the cult of the peasant in village tales of the period. But the relationship to dialect poetry is at that time too sober to be considered a swan song." (Friedrich Sengle)

Hebel was able in his "folk stories" to speak with folksy simplicity and anecdotal complacency to the hearts of simple peasants and the bourgeoisie.

*The Treasure Chest of the Rhineland Friend of the Family* (1811) was a selection of a hundred short pieces selected by Hebel from the *Baden Calendar* published by him. Between 1804 and 1819 he wrote three hundred such pieces, including stories, riddles, arithmetic examples, short speeches and biographies, reports about curiosities (warm winters, miracles of the sea, comets, fantasies). "Just as Grimm's fairytales guided our feelings and provided images of childhood from which we learned shuddering and feeling secure, hope and fidelity, change and liberation, Hebel's stories confronted us with the pleasure of understanding, with the amusement and intelligence of morality, with artisanry and with humaneness." (Hartmut von Hentig)

One has almost daily opportunities, in Emmendingen and Gundelfingen just as well as in Amsterdam, to make observations concerning the impermanence of all earthly things, if one wishes, and to grow content with one's own destiny, even though one may not chance upon a pot of gold at the end of every rainbow. But one young German journeyman in Amsterdam came through error to insight into such truths by way of the strangest detour. For when he had come to this great and prosperous commercial center with its magnificent buildings, rolling ships and busy people, his attention was immediately caught by a grand and beautiful house, the likes of which he had not yet seen on his entire journey from

Tuttlingen to Amsterdam. For a long time he gazed in admiration at this costly edifice, the six chimneys on the roof, the lovely mouldings and the tall windows, taller than the door of his father's house at home. Finally he could no longer restrain himself from accosting a passerby.

"Dear friend," he said, "could you not tell me the name of the gentleman who owns this wonderful house with its windows full of tulips, anemones and gillyflowers?"

The man however, who presumably had something more important to do, and who unfortunately understood just as much of the German language as his interrogator understood of Dutch, namely nothing at all, responded curtly and rudely, *"Kannietverstaan,"* and hurried on. This is a Dutch word, or rather three, if one considers it properly, and means loosely "I cannot understand you." But the good traveler believed it to be the name of the man about whom he had inquired. He must be a very wealthy man, this Mr. Kannietverstaan, he thought and went on. He wandered up one street and down another and finally came to the harbor that is called Het Ey, that is to say, The Y. And there stood ship after ship and mast after mast, so that at first he did not know how he should be able to see enough of all these remarkable sights with only his own two eyes, until finally his attention was drawn to a large ship that had arrived from East India a short time before and was just now being unloaded. Long rows of crates and bales already stood beside and atop one another on the dock, and still more and more were added to them, as well as barrels full of sugar and coffee, rice and pepper, not to mention mouse droppings. After observing these goings-on for a long while, he asked someone carrying a crate out of the hold on his shoulder for the name of the happy man to whose port the sea had borne all these wares.

*"Kannietverstaan,"* was the answer. And then he thought: Aha, so that's how it goes? No wonder. Anyone for whom the sea washes up such riches can well afford to put such houses into the world and such tulips in gilded pots in front of the windows.

Now he retraced his steps and gave himself over to sad thoughts about himself, what a poor man he was among so many rich people in the world. But just as he was thinking, "If I just once should have things as good as this Mr. Kannietverstaan has," he came around a corner and beheld a long funeral procession. Four horses draped in black drew a hearse similarly covered in black cloth as slowly and as sadly as if they knew that they were conducting a dead man to his final rest. A long train of friends and acquaintances of the deceased followed after the hearse, pair after pair, all silent and dressed in black coats. In the distance a lone bell tolled. And now our traveler was seized by the melancholy feeling that no good person escapes at the sight of a funeral procession, and he remained standing with his hat reverently in his hand until it had passed by. Then he approached the last member of the procession, a man who was calculating in peace and quiet the profits he would reap on his cotton if the price should rise by ten guilders per hundredweight. Our traveler took him gently by the sleeve and innocently begged his pardon.

"That must have been a dear friend of yours," he said, "for whom the bell is tolling, that you should walk here so sunk in grief and thought."

"*Kannietverstaan!*" was the answer.

And then our good Tuttlinger shed a few big tears, and felt at once both heavy and light at heart. "Poor Kannietverstaan," he cried, "what have you now of all your wealth? Just as much as I one day will have of my poverty, a funeral suit and a shroud, and of all your pretty flowers perhaps on your cold breast a sprig of rosemary or of rue."

With these thoughts he accompanied the corpse, as if he belonged to the funeral party, all the way to the grave; watched the man he took to be Mr. Kannietverstaan lowered into his resting place, and was moved more profoundly by the Dutch funeral sermon, of which he understood not a word, than by many German ones of his past experience to which he had never paid attention. Finally he departed with the others. Light at heart, he consumed with good appetite a piece of Limburger cheese in an inn where German was understood. And whenever thereafter it again seemed hard to bear that so many people in the world were so rich and he so poor, he thought of Mr. Kannietverstaan in Amsterdam—of his spacious house, his rich ship and his narrow grave.

TRANSLATED BY SHARON JACKIW

## (54) Life is the present

ARTHUR SCHOPENHAUER, The World as Will and Representation

The fourth book of Schopenhauer's principal philosophical work (published in 1819), from which this text is excerpted, deals with the "affirmation and negation of the will to life." The will of the world rules blindly, there is no reason for hope of a change in the bad condition of the world, sufferings will continue, and even pleasures have only a negative meaning—i.e., as the temporary end of a misfortune. Despite or precisely because of such pessimism, both existence and present are "defiantly" affirmed: "Above all we must clearly recognize that the form of appearance of the will, hence the form of life or of reality, is actually only the present, not the future nor the past: these are present only in the concept and only in the context of knowledge to the extent that they follow the precept of cause. No person has ever lived in the past or ever will live in the future; on the contrary, only the present is the form of all life; it is also its certain possession that can never be lost. The present including its content is ever present. Like the rainbow on the waterfall, both stand firm without moving. For life is certain of will; the present is certain of life. To be sure if we think back on past millennia and on the millions of people who lived in former times, we then ask: What were they? What happened to them? But on the other hand we may recall the past in our own lives and vividly revive scenes of the past in our fantasy and now ask again: What was all that? What happened to it? As with it, so it is with the lives of millions. Or should we believe that the past obtained a new existence from being sealed by death? Our own past, even the most recent past and yesterday, is still merely an idle dream of fantasy, and the same applies to the past of all those millions of people."

But just as on the globe everywhere is above, so the form of all life is the *present;* and to fear death because it robs us of the present is no wiser than to fear that we can slip down from the round globe on the top of which we are now fortunately standing. The form of the present is essential to the objectification of the will. As an extensionless point, it cuts time which extends infinitely in both directions, and stands firm and immovable, like an everlasting midday without a cool evening, just as the actual sun burns without intermission, while only apparently does it sink into the bosom of the night. If, therefore, a person fears death as his annihilation, it is just as if he were to think that the sun can lament in the evening and say: "Woe is me! I am going down into eternal night." Conversely, whoever is oppressed by the burdens of life, whoever loves life and affirms it, but abhors its torments, and in particular can no longer endure the hard lot that has fallen to just him, cannot hope for deliverance from death, and cannot save himself through suicide. Only by a false illusion does the cool shade of Orcus allure him as a haven of rest. The earth rolls on from day into night; the individual dies; but the sun itself burns without intermission, an eternal noon. Life is certain to the will-to-live; the form of life is the endless present; it matters not how individuals, the phenomena of the Idea, arise and pass away in time, like fleeting dreams. Therefore suicide already appears to us to be a vain and therefore foolish action; when we have gone farther in our discussion, it will appear to us in an even less favourable light.

Dogmas change and our knowledge is deceptive, but nature does not err; her action is sure and certain, and she does not conceal it. Everything is entirely in nature, and she is entirely in everything. She has her center in every animal; the animal has certainly found its way into existence just as it will certainly find its way out of it. Meanwhile, it lives fearlessly and heedlessly in the presence of annihilation, supported by the consciousness that it is nature herself and is as imperishable as she. Man alone carries about with him in abstract concepts the certainty of his own death, yet this can frighten him only very rarely and at particular moments, when some occasion calls it up to the imagination. Against the mighty voice of nature reflection can do little. In man, as in the animal that does not think, there prevails as a lasting state of mind the certainty, springing from innermost consciousness, that he is nature, the world itself. By virtue of this, no one is noticeably disturbed by the thought of certain and never-distant death, but everyone lives on as though he is bound to live for ever. Indeed, this is true to the extent that it might be said that no one has a really lively conviction of the certainty of his death, as otherwise there could not be a very great difference between his frame of mind and that of the condemned criminal. Everyone recognizes that certainty in the abstract and theoretically, but lays it on one side, like other theoretical truths that are not applicable in practice, without taking it into his vivid consciousness. Whoever carefully considers this peculiarity of the human way of thinking, will see that the psychological methods of explaining it from habit and acquiescence in the inevitable are by no means sufficient, but that the reason for it is the deeper one that we state. The same thing can also explain why at all times and among all peoples dogmas of some kind, dealing with the individual's continued existence after death, exist and are highly esteemed, although the proofs in support of them must always be extremely inadequate, whereas those which support the contrary are bound to be powerful and numerous. This is really in no need of any proof, but is recognized by the healthy understanding as a fact; it is confirmed as such by the confidence that nature no more lies than errs, but openly exhibits her action and her essence, and even expresses these naïvely. It is only we ourselves who obscure these by erroneous views, in order to explain from them what is agreeable to our limited view.

TRANSLATED BY E. F. J. PAYNE

## (55) The outer world of the inner world

KARL IMMERMANN, Goethe's House on the Frauenplan in Weimar

When Johann Wolfgang von Goethe arrived in Weimar on November 7, 1775, in response to the invitation by Duke Karl August, the town, a rural community surrounded by a wall, had approximately six thousand inhabitants. Nonetheless, Goethe joyfully wrote to his friend Merck: "I am completely involved in all court and political matters and will hardly ever be able to get away. The duchies of Weimar and Eisenach are after all a showplace, and my situation is advantageous enough to try out a role in the world."

Approximately two decades later the duke presented Goethe with the house on the Frauenplan where he lived until his death. The rooms were preserved as he left them as a kind of museum. In the fall of 1837, the poet Karl Immermann interrupted a journey from Düsseldorf to Franconia and Thuringia to spend two days in Jena and three in Weimar. He visited the tomb in which Schiller and Goethe were buried and Goethe's house in Weimar. His impressions are described in his diary.

On an open square enlivened by a fountain stands a house of two stories, washed in reddish-gray color, its windows set in black frames, spacious in appearance, but in no way exceeding the measure of a well-to-do bourgeois house. We step over the threshold and find ourselves in an entrance hall made bright and cheerful by its pale yellow stone. We climb stairs constructed with massive stone bridgeboards, whose broad steps curve upward in the gentlest of inclines. The size of these stairs takes one by surprise; they bear no relation to the other dimensions of the house and occupy most of the lower level of the building. It is interesting to hear how this came about. During Goethe's stay in Rome, the house was built for him by the Duke; even a appropriate staircase had already been finished, when Goethe saw in Rome one whose construction delighted him. He immediately had a drawing made of it and sent this drawing to Germany with orders to build such a staircase in his house. All objections dispatched over the Alps were in vain, and the orders had to be carried out. When he returned, he looked thoughtfully at the stairs that rose from the lower floor, climbed them in silence, shaking his head, and even afterward never spoke of the matter.

In the upper vestibule the figures of sleep and of death and the colossal head of Juno look at us from niches in the wall. Views of Rome hanging above the stairs also remind us of the land; after leaving which, Goethe was accustomed to say, he never again became truly happy.

A small drawing room, rather long and yellow, opens from the vestibule. There he dined with his guests. Meyer's drawings of objects from antiquity or á la Poussin adorn the walls; behind a green curtain he preserved the watercolor copy by Meyer of the *Aldobrandini Wedding,* which he considered his most precious treasure. The side rooms to right and left also contain objects that belong to this genre and to this period of art. Everywhere there is the past and memory; for one well acquainted with Goethe's works the warp and woof of many of his fabrics come alive here. A historical feeling seizes us, the feeling that always makes me happy from the bottom of my heart. For there is nothing here that was not a part of his nourishment during his formative years, and he severely denied admittance to anything that came later. We are moved to look at the poor and trifling things by means of which the great man was able to achieve such self-cultivation.

To the right of this drawing room we see the so-called "ceiling room." Why Goethe decided to give it this name is not known, since all the rooms have similar ceilings of decorated stucco. To the left is his blue reception room and behind it the so-called Urbino room, christened for the portrait of a Duke of Urbino that he brought back from Italy. At the threshold of the reception room its friendly *"Salve!"* greets us. When Goethe received guests, he never came by way of the stairs, as we have done, into the blue room; instead he went from his workroom through a communicating corridor into the Urbino room, and from this room then, collected and readied, he approached his guests. He did not love it when

> . . . the moment in its mad,
> Tyrannical dominion would command him.

These then are the rooms that were accessible to visitors during Goethe's lifetime. He permitted no one in his workroom except his most intimate friends: Coudray, Riemer, Müller, Eckermann. When the king of Bavaria paid his famous birthday call in 1827, he asked Goethe to grant him also a view of the workshop of his spirit. Goethe looked embarrassed and said that his workroom was not furnished in a manner worthy of the eyes of royalty. The king did not press his petition, but after a little time he simulated a nosebleed, forbade anyone to follow him from the room, and told Goethe's servant, who stood outside the room, to lead him to a washbasin. Surprised, indeed confounded, the servant led him into Goethe's bedroom, which lies behind the workroom, and left the king at royal command alone there. The king was absent for a long while. Finally Goethe himself went to look for him and found him in his workroom, sunk in contemplation of the things he saw there.

The descriptions of these rooms found in memoirs and travel diaries had all given me an inaccurate image of them. I expected a certain luxury, such as may be found in the houses of those who have the talent and the means to adorn their surroundings. I had been misled in this assumption by the glittering words of previous visitors. They saw Zeus here, and therefore they expanded the walls around him to temple halls, glowing in the light he shed. It very probably would have been the same for me. But now when one walks through the deserted rooms, the illusion disappears, giving way to a modest truth. It is a comfortable dwelling, decent, cheerful, but entirely simple, furnished in an earlier fashion, here and there even somewhat shabby with use. It is the house of a patriarch whose fondest memories attach to pieces of furniture, to mouldings and colors from the distant past, which he therefore takes care to preserve around him, even when they have begun to grow worn and faded.

Death lifted the master's ban: we walked freely through small communicating rooms across the upper floor to the study and workroom. In one of the little rooms we paused for a moment; it is the one in which he dined when he was alone with his children. A canopy of foliage outside the window casts a green light into the room; with one step one is in the garden, in which Goethe was accustomed to enjoying every sunny moment in his leisure hours. In the corner stands a little summerhouse, in which he kept his laboratory apparatus.

In the anteroom of the museum I saw in cabinets and under glass, ranged along the walls, samples of ore, rocks, shells, fossils, in fact everything that had become the object of his scientific investigations. I found it all maintained in excellent condition and arranged with a certain elegance. A door opening on my right permitted a view of the library. It could well seem small for such means as had been at his disposal. Goethe intentionally limited his collection of books, because the libraries of Weimar and Jena stood open to him; indeed, in order to prevent the accumulation of such possessions, which may have seemed to him unnecessary, he gave away most of the books sent to him from near and far as soon as he had read them.

Now the secretary of the library, Kräuter, at one time Goethe's copy clerk (before John had been engaged in that position) and now the loyal guardian of this holy of holies, opened the door of the workroom, and I was touched by what I saw within. I remembered from Eckermann's conversations occasional remarks of Goethe's that led me to expect here an extreme simplicity, but once again the reality was otherwise. This small unadorned green room—with its low ceiling, roller blinds of dark serge, flaking windowsills, partially rotted window frames—was the place from which such an abundance of the most glorious light had poured forth! I felt deeply moved and had to take care not to fall into a state of emotion that would have deprived me of the power to see.

Nothing has been moved from its spot. Kräuter insists with pious severity on keeping every scrap of paper, every shaving of quill exactly where it was when the master passed away. The clock still shows the hour of his death, half past eleven; it stopped at that time, coincidence creating something like a miracle. Next to the clock, at a window on the right, stands the little writing table that Goethe had had made for his grand-children, and which he again took into his own keeping and his own nearest environment after the death of their father. Little Wolf was his favorite. Walther was less so: he frequently and with some annoyance called the pretty lad, whom the ladies somewhat dandified, "our little dancing master." Alma had to sit at the writing table next to her brothers and, in order to learn to sit still, unravel small scraps of silk. They lie there still, in an envelope.

Here every smallest spot is holy ground, and a thousand objects that fill the little room speak of the nature and of the activity of the spirit.

TRANSLATED BY SHARON JACKIW

## (56) A visit with Mörike

THEODOR STORM, Letter to Hartmuth Brinkmann

Eduard Mörike's writing was of great importance in Theodor Storm's development. He acquired Mörike's first books (*Poems,* 1838, and *Maler Nolten,* 1832) while studying in Kiel. Storm describes his impressions from that time in his first letter to Mörike on November 20, 1850: "Our small group has scattered since then, but among all the things with which I have maintained some contact, the most unchanged devotion to your muse's deep and 'powerful autumnal' character has endured, only that each of my former school-mates has acquired new friends for your work in his present circle of friends. Three years ago I was able to present your *Lake Constance Idyll* to my young wife at Christmas. That evening we sat together alone, and I began to read, 'Close by the lake's edge—in Klee-feld'. And when old Merten starts to play the clarinet until laughter cuts off his wind, both of us were also overcome by heartwarming laughter. And I now must convey my wife's thanks in addition to my own. She is in every respect worthy of savoring the drink from your golden vessel."

Mörike's answer was received only in 1853. "The reliability of this flattering judgment naturally amused me not a little." They subsequently wrote to each other only occasion-ally. In 1855 Storm visited Mörike in Stuttgart and reports about it in a letter dated September 28 of the same year to his friend and classmate Hartmuth Brinckmann.

September 28, 1855

At the Stuttgart railroad station it wasn't Mörike who met me—he was teaching his only class (a literature course) at the *Katharineum* just then—

rather, it was his friend Wilhelm Hartlaub, known to you from the poems. Hartlaub, who is a clergyman in the vicinity and who often visits Mörike, had with him a message from Mörike in Latin: *Salve Theodore! Negotio publico distentus amicum, ut meo loco te excipiat, mitto carissimum.* Hartlaub is a lanky, shabby-looking kind of clergyman, but he has an inherently serious nature; and, among the admirers of his friend, he is foremost. On the way to Mörike's, he told me something I had not known: four months ago a baby girl, Fanny, had arrived and Eduard was very happy. "You're coming at a good time," he said. "Eduard just finished something, something of overpowering beauty."

When we arrived, Mörike still wasn't there. Hartlaub went to get the lady of the house. I looked around the apartment. They live three flights up, are simply but comfortably furnished. As it is everywhere in the South, the furniture was made of walnut, a wood that I liked very much. A few good pictures and curios on the walls. From the windows, you can see between the houses across the way through to the vineyards that surround the city.

Soon Mörike's wife Gretchen came in—a slender woman of thirty-five, with noble features and particularly beautiful, gentle, and, at the same time, mischievous eyes, but with a very tanned complexion. . . . She greeted me in the heaviest Swabian accent and served me a meal of hot rolls, unsalted butter and cheese, along with homemade wine, which, of course, we drank like water, out of beer glasses. Then Eduard Mörike arrived. He looks more relaxed, not as stuffy as in the picture that you're familiar with, although they say that he can be very formal when he wants to. Even a local acquaintance who didn't quite get along with him remarked about this: "That's damned right!" His fine features have somewhat deteriorated; he's sickly, a hypochondriac, so that he's able to work only a few hours a day. He's fifty years old now.

He took hold of both my hands, looked into my eyes and, turning to his wife, said, "Isn't this just how we thought he'd look, dear?" A picture of Constanz and me has been hanging above his sofa for the past year. He is exactly the same in person as he is in his writings. I have never met anyone else who expresses himself with such objectivity. "Just now, as I was coming in, I had to look up at the stairs to see whether Storm might've climbed them." Then he led me to the bedroom and showed me two robins. I had written him about my father's starlings. "They come out with sounds of pure gold and silver; they sing so softly you'd think they didn't want to wake the baby."

Living with them are Mörike's sister Clara and his mother-in-law. After we had eaten and drunk our coffee (with Swabian pastries), Mörike, Hartlaub and I went walking for a couple of hours. The city, with its old-fashioned simplicity, gave me a comfortable feeling; even the people's dress seems much less pretentious than in the North. Add to that the friendly vineyards that you see all around, and to top it off I was in such good company. After returning home we withdrew to the back room. Although it was still light out, Mörike shut the blinds tightly, had a lamp brought in, and asked his wife if she had something warm to sip. So then we had tea, with more Swabian pastries. Mörike dragged his big cordovan leather armchair over to me from his small study. I began drinking my tea; and he read, quite well too and not in dialect, *Mozart on his Journey to Prague.* It's a small masterpiece in which everything is completely fabricated. During a break in the reading, Hartlaub, very excited, turned around to me and said, "Tell me, isn't this just overwhelming?" It was indeed beautiful. Mörike is extremely knowledgeable about music but, in his appreciation, doesn't go beyond Haydn and Mozart. He and Hartlaub call them "the Saints," like Schiller and Goethe. The next day (I spent the night at Mörike's and slept like a prince under the most beautiful crimson satin quilt) my parents arrived, and we took another walk with Mörike and his sister. You should have seen Mörike and my father, arm in arm, taking in the city sights, both of them with their hats tipped back and in the best of spirits. Now and then Mörike would let go and grab me by the arm, "But, *en passant,* you have very nice parents!" Then, when we were standing in front of the statue of Schiller, he turned to me and declared, "Your father looks just like a Swiss." But my father declined the compliment, saying, "What 'ya talkin' 'bout? I'm just a country boy from Westermöhlen." They didn't understand each other half the time because of their different dialects, but in spite of that they got along splendidly.

After we had walked but a short hour, Mörike said again, "There's something about your mother that's so bright, glowing and charming. I can't get over my joy and surprise. You've really got great parents. . . ."

That same evening we went to Heilbronn. At Mörike's urgent request—"You'll be seeing him for the last time!"—I still wanted to visit Kerner at a vineyard a half-hour away; but we arrived there too late. The next morning, we traveled down the Neckar . . .

TRANSLATED BY JOHANNES W. VAZULIK

## (57) Heavenly beauty, sensuous beauty

LUDWIG RICHTER, Annuals and Letters to His Son

Ludwig Richter's pictures are little dreams of cozy happiness: child with lamb chasing a butterfly; a lark singing above a silvery brook; a small girl, followed by a dog, bringing food and drink to harvesters; red cherries shining against dark green; stars shining above the tender dew, rainbow landscape; the first snow; a chapel high in the mountains, a hermit in the valley; grandfather reading from the old primer; a boy daring his first reticent kiss; a nightwatchman tolling the hour at midnight. But everyone is already fast asleep except for a cat walking on an old wall in the moonlight.

The painter believed that without people the cornerstone was lacking in nature and that a landscape without a human figure was a riddle without a solution. Nature is portrayed as an organism awakened to life by people; the human being and nature are like partners. "The one needs and loves the other, takes care of it. The mutuality is truly astonishing— nature is like a friendly domestic animal to people. It never shows its claws, its danger, its bad aspects. It does not profiteer; it prefers to flatter, lends itself to being woven into protective fences, forms an umbrella and shield, and bends its tendrils and branches into any desired form, places ornaments around the human being, frames everything it touches. 'Wild' animals do not occur in it, hence it is all the more the domesticated companion of man." (Gottfried Knapp)

Richter's conservative utopia is green and is repeatedly oriented toward a distant, child-like paradise. Its idyllic aspect, however, is by no means free of vulnerability and anxiety. Richter is aware of the menace and of the Panic element. He was deeply shattered by the painful death of his beloved daughter: "For several years after we moved into this house in the country the pale figure of our dear Marie, who had contracted an incurable disease of the chest from a cold, wandered in the flourishing garden. What contrasts meet and blend at times in life! At a time of abundant, rich creativity, our hearts were nonetheless overcome by a deep and silent sadness. The doctor had told my wife and me that there was no hope of saving our dear Marie. Even now the picture is vividly before me of how I was sitting in the arbor, watching her thin pale figure walking slowly back and forth, her glance occasionally focusing on me as if questioning 'whether Father probably knows that I will soon die?' while her lips remained silent. At her feet, however, was cradled a laughing bed of tulips, and the red and white roses shone in abundance along the green garden wall."

Richter was born in 1803 in Dresden. For several years he lived in Rome where he had close contact with the Nazarenes. After 1826, he again worked in Dresden. He died in Loschwitz in 1884.

1851:

If, out of love, one chooses the best from the small treasure in one's heart and passes it on, an unbelievably rich blessing falls back on our head and into our lap. The person who has money and wealth can do much to help and to dry tears; and he who has nothing like that has or can have good thoughts, insights of all kinds, or can be like an angel through his words, his love or his prayer. Isn't art also called to such angelic service? Surely that is its most splendid, indeed its heavenly task. One should faithfully make this known, search for and seek to imitate this spirit and not rest until it has been found. Of course, there are those who think art is nothing but soap bubbles, and for others it is the devil's filth, prettily gilded. For the upper crust, it is like a cream they have for dessert, and finally even the donkey will take the rose for a thistle and enjoy it.

If one can bring joy to others through art, one should do it with all one's heart, for that is art's best reward. Earning money is only the necessary evil, and honor or so-called immortality are not worth turning around for. If it comes of its own accord, well and good, one lets it follow one.

The older I become and the more I understand about the nature of all art, the more pleasure it brings me. More and more, it becomes a marvelously beautiful angel who accompanies those who are well intentioned and often leads them from their altogether too shady paths to sunny, flowery spots where they can rest; where joy grows and the longing for that great, splendid sun- and flowerland that is reserved for those who follow the ringing of its wonderful, powerful bell. There is a distant echo of that sound in art, occasionally in the sciences, in Nature. All Sunday children hear the bell and to become a Sunday child, one need only be pure in heart.

May 15, 1854, Loschwitz:

O God, how splendid from my spot here on the mountain the spacious terrain, what heavenly, what sensuous beauty! The deep blue sky, the immense, green world, the beautiful bright May landscape with its thousand voices. How strongly I feel in all that appears to our senses and through them the beauty of our dear father above.

Everything around me is of this earth. What poverty it would be if I saw, loved and worshiped God only in the black letters and in my immaterial thoughts. A flowering tree, fragrant, with bees buzzing about it—such a vision has often been dearer to me than the most brilliant theological or philosophical treatise on the nature of God. All things are sacred, are transfigured, stand in the most intimate relation to their Creator. Only the ruining of such good things is sin. If love is there on all its levels, physical, psychological, spiritual, divine, is it not so pure, so powerful in its innermost being that there is nothing more beautiful and powerful than this flower of life, this power which is sacred in God's hands? Is it not a reflection of and a prelude to God's and the human soul's community? An intimation of that bliss which we cannot now wholly feel and understand because of our corruption, or which only the best and the purest can feel in moments of bliss?

August 28, 1872, Loschwitz:

During the night I walked back and forth in front of the house. The low little building looked black as it lay before me; the door was open and the light from the kitchen fell on it. Above me, the Big Dipper was sparkling over the roof. I felt sad about all the misery on earth. Could it be that there is even more distress and wretchedness on all those stars? But perhaps they are worlds full of jubilation or of silent, blissful happiness. I thought perhaps our planet is the lost son who is in misery among the animals, and whose longing will drive home into the arms of his compassionate father. Our Father who art in heaven, yes, and we, your children, are away from home, far away from the father, in profound misery.

New Year's Eve 1873:

Since the fall, I have been unable to work; my eyes are too weak, I feel my age, and my physical and spiritual powers are ebbing. What grieves me most now is that life is over and I did not use that beautiful time as I could and should have. In all my relations, in art, in teaching, everywhere, there were tasks where my belief should have tried and proven itself much more. But often I was more concerned with giving greater strength to my religious feelings, or striving for a better understanding of the content of the faith than with daily and hourly practice of the faith (the recognized truth). To practice mildness and patience in this way, to deny and overcome oneself in matters large and small, to reject all mean-spirited thoughts and everything ignoble in one's conception of life, of art, etc. And how often do the trivial ties of everyday life and activity rule us! In order to retain, after the example of Christ, our Lord, the magnanimity the Christian faith should always demonstrate and which the life of our Lord teaches, I should always have been more keenly conscious of practicing my faith in the most profound humility.

May things change and improve, may the time God still grants me bear fruit that is pleasing to Him.

TRANSLATED BY MICHAEL SHAW

## (58) Be not afraid

Detlev Baron von Liliencron (1844–1909) was an officer in the wars of 1866 and 1870/71. "Because of debts and wounds" he was forced to leave the service. His poetry is of arresting forthrightness (*Adjutant Rides and Other Poems*)—sensuous, direct, impressionistic, couched in slovenly turns of phrase and everyday expressions. The intimation of death is superimposed on the joy of life and a preoccupation with things of this world. The magnificence of summer is short, and only through sleep can we be reconciled to the difficult hours that threaten all of us.

Theodor Storm was born in 1817 in Husum, Schleswig, which technically belonged to Denmark at that time. He died in 1888. He came from an established patrician family. "I never heard any talk of religion or Christianity. Once in a while my mother or grandmother must have gone to church, but not often. There was not a close relationship between parents and me in my youth. I cannot remember ever being embraced or even kissed by them. In the North there is not usually anything more than a handshake . . . I cannot think of anyone who exerted any special influence on me up to age eighteen. On the other hand, I received strong impressions from the locale—from the heath, which at that time was situated between Husum and a village to which I went almost every two weeks, from my great-grandmother's lonely garden, from the knight's hall of Husum castle whose walls were covered with paintings; also from the swamp that was just outside of town, and the ocean, especially the North Sea beach that was so splendidly barren at low tide. I never learned anything practical, and work as such I learned only as a poet."
   Storm's poems and novels are characterized by a strong feeling for transitoriness, even to the point of sentimentality. They frequently end in resigned pessimism. Faith no longer provides hope and comfort; what remains is fear that ultimately nothing endures, the intimation that in the end one is alone and abandoned—anxiety before the night of forgetting. The optimism of materialism is lacking, and intermittent longing for the idyll recurs. The poet experiences a "dream of harvesting honey" while closing his eyes; the contrast to an agitated era is not provided by eternity but by withdrawal. The gloomy feeling of a great loss, the general atmosphere in which the feeling of political disappointment and knowledge of economic need merge with religious agnosticism permeates Storm's writing as a melancholy "once-upon-a-time."

DETLEV VON LILIENCRON

## *Village Church in Summer*

Sleepy is the sexton's drone,
Parish voices rising thinner.
On his pulpit all alone
Pastor prays for saint and sinner.

Then the sermon, great success!
Matchless in its domination.
Weeping is the baroness
In her lofty segregation.

Amen, blessing, open doors,
Organ tone and final singing.
Downward summer sunlight pours,
Butterflies and swallows winging.


THEODOR STORM

## *Elsewhere*

It is so still; the heather lies
Beneath the warming noonday sunshine,
A rosy reddish shimmer flies
Among the heather's ancient headstones;
The herbs in bloom; the heather scent
Trails off into the firmament.

Encased within their golden shells
Ground beetles scurry through the bushes,
The bees which cling to flowers' bells
Explore the noble heather's blossoms;
The birds dart from their herbal lair
While lark song fills the summer air.

Here stands a house in ill repair,
The bleaching sunshine pouring over;
The keeper in his doorway stares
Indulgently upon the clover;
His son is squatting in the weeds
And cutting pipes from hollow reeds.

Scarce heard upon the quiet skies,
A distant village bell is quaking;
The old man now has closed his eyes,
He dreams of harvests he'll be taking.
—No rumor of society
Invades this lonely piety.

DETLEV VON LILIENCRON

## *A Prayer for Sleep, After the Hardest Hours*

But still before the whip-crack of the new day
Calls me once again into the desert,
Summon your brother to my bedside.
Kindly the old gentleman lays his hand
Upon my eyes, which want to open,
And speaks a lullaby, slowly the words,
So slowly speaking:

        So, so, so . . .
        Be not afraid . . .
        So, so . . . so . . .

TRANSLATED BY ADRIAN DEL CARO

## (59) Enjoying oneself

ARTHUR SCHOPENHAUER, Parerga and Paralipomena

Schopenhauer states in the *Aphorisms Concerning the Wisdom of Life,* from which the text below is excerpted, that the concept of the wisdom of life is entirely in the immanent sense—i.e., in the sense of the art of conducting life in the most agreeable and happy manner possible. The basis of the difference in the lot of the mortal can be traced to three basic determinations. These are:

"1. What one is: i.e., the personality in the broadest sense. Accordingly this includes health, strength, beauty, temperament, moral character, intelligence, and training.

2. What one has: i.e., possession and property in the usual sense.

3. What one conceives: this expression is usually understood to mean what one is in the conception of another—hence actually how the person is conceived by others. Accordingly it consists in their opinion of the person and is divided into honor, rank, and fame."

"It always depends on what a man is and accordingly has in himself; for his individuality always and everywhere accompanies him and everything experienced by him is tinged thereby. In everything and with everything, he first of all enjoys only himself; this already applies to physical pleasure and how much truer it is of those of the mind. Therefore the English words 'to enjoy oneself,' are a very apt expression; for example, we do not say 'he enjoys Paris,' but 'he enjoys *himself* in Paris.' "

### *What a Man Is*

We have in general recognized that this contributes much more to a man's happiness than what he *has* or *represents*. It always depends on what a man is and accordingly has in himself; for his individuality always and everywhere accompanies him and everything experienced by him is tinged thereby. In everything and with everything he first of all enjoys only himself; this already applies to physical pleasures and how much truer is it of those of the mind! Therefore the English words "to enjoy oneself" are a very apt expression; for example, we do not say "he enjoys Paris," but "he enjoys *himself* in Paris." Now if the individuality is ill-conditioned, all pleasures are like choice wines in a mouth that is made bitter with gall. Accordingly, if we leave out of account cases of grave misfortune, less depends, in the good things as well as in the bad, on what befalls and happens to us in life than on the way in which we feel it, and thus on the nature and degree of our susceptibility in every respect.

What a man is and has in himself, that is to say, personality and its worth, is the sole immediate factor in his happiness and well-being. Everything else is mediate and indirect and so the effect thereof can be neutralized and frustrated; that of personality never. For this reason, the envy excited by personal qualities is the most implacable, as it is also the most carefully concealed. Further, the constitution of consciousness is that which is permanent and enduring and individuality is at work constantly and incessantly more or less at every moment.

Everything else, on the other hand, acts only at times, occasionally, temporarily, and in addition is subject to variation and change. Therefore Aristotle says: "For we can depend on nature, not on money." (*Eudemian Ethics,* VII. 2.). This is due to the fact that we can bear with more composure a misfortune that has befallen us entirely from without than one that we have brought upon ourselves; fate can change, but our own nature never. Therefore subjective blessings, such as noble character, a gifted mind, a happy temperament, cheerful spirits, and a well-conditioned thoroughly sound body, and so generally "a healthy mind in a healthy body" (Juvenal, *Satires,* X. 356), are primarily and most importantly for our happiness. We should, therefore, be much more concerned with promoting and preserving such qualities than with possessing external wealth and external honor.

Now of all those qualities, the one that most immediately makes us happy is cheerfulness of disposition; for this good quality is its own instantaneous reward. Whoever is merry and cheerful always has a good reason for so being, namely the very fact that he is so. Nothing can so completely take the place of every other blessing as can this quality, whilst it itself cannot be replaced by anything. A man may be young, handsome, wealthy, and esteemed; if we wish to judge of his happiness, we ask whether he is cheerful. On the other hand, if he is cheerful, it matters not whether he is young or old, straight or humpbacked, rich or poor; he is happy.

In my youth, I once opened an old book in which it said: "Whoever laughs a lot is happy, and whoever weeps a lot is unhappy," a very simple remark, but because of its plain truth I have been unable to forget it, however much it may be the superlative of a truism.

For this reason, we should open wide the doors to cheerfulness whenever it appears, for it never comes inopportunely. Instead of doing this, we often hesitate to let it enter, for we first want to know whether we have every reason to be contented; or because we are afraid of being disturbed by cheerfulness when we are involved in serious deliberations and heavy cares. But what we improve through these is very uncertain, whereas cheerfulness is an immediate gain. It alone is, so to speak, the very coin of happiness and not, like everything else, merely a check on a bank; for only it makes us immediately happy in the present moment. And so it is the greatest blessing for beings whose reality takes the form of an indivisible present moment between an infinite past and an infinite future. Accordingly, we should make the acquisition and encouragement of this blessing our first endeavor.

Now it is certain that nothing contributes less to cheerfulness than wealth and nothing contributes more than health. The lower classes of workers, especially those in the country, have more cheerful and contented faces; peevishness and ill-humor are more at home among the wealthy upper classes. Consequently, we should endeavor above all to maintain a high degree of health, the very bloom of which appears as cheerfulness. The means to this end are, as we know, avoidance of all excesses and irregularities, of all violent and disagreeable emotions, and also of all mental strain that is too great and too prolonged. Two hours' brisk exercise every day in the open air, many cold baths, and similar dietetic measures encourage good health. Without proper daily exercise no one can remain healthy; all the vital processes demand exercise for their proper performance; exercise not only of the parts wherein they occur, but also of the whole. Aristotle rightly says: "Life consists in movement and has its very essence therein."

Ceaseless and rapid motion occurs in every part of the organism; the heart in its complicated double systole and diastole beats strongly and untiringly; with its twenty-eight beats it drives the whole of the blood through all the arteries, veins, and capillaries; the lungs pump incessantly like a steam engine; the intestines are always turning in peristaltic motion; all the glands are constantly absorbing and secreting; even the brain has a double motion with every heart beat and every breath. Now when there is an almost total lack of external movement, as is the case with numberless people who lead an entirely sedentary life, there arises a glaring and injurious disproportion between external inactivity and internal tumult. For the constant internal motion must be supported by something external. That want of proportion is analogous to the case where, in consequence of some emotion, something boils up within us which we are obliged to suppress. In order to thrive even trees require movement through wind. Here the following rule applies: The more rapid a movement is, the more it is movement.

How much our happiness depends on cheerfulness of disposition, and this on the state of our health, is seen when we compare the impression, made on us by external circumstances or events when we are hale and hearty, with that produced by them when ill-health has made us depressed and anxious. It is not what things are objectively and actually, but what they are for us and in our way of looking at them, that makes us happy or unhappy. This is just what Epictetus says: "It is not things that disturb men, but opinions about things."

In general however, nine-tenths of our happiness depends on health alone. With it everything becomes a source of pleasure, whereas without it nothing, whatever it may be, can be enjoyed, and even the other subjective blessings, such as mental qualities, disposition, and temperament, are depressed and dwarfed by ill-health. Accordingly, it is not without reason that, when two people meet, they first ask about the state of each other's health and hope that it is good; for this really is for human happiness by far the most important thing. But from this it follows that the greatest of all follies is to sacrifice our health for whatever it may be, for gain, profit, promotion, learning, or fame, not to mention sensual and other fleeting pleasures; rather, should we give first place to health.

TRANSLATED BY E. F. J. PAYNE

## (60) Lay the table for us, hurry

JOHANN WOLFGANG VON GOETHE, Faust. Part Two

After the Helena experience Faust presses on to great new deeds. With the help of the demonic creatures—Raufebold, Habebald, and Haltefest—summoned by Mephistofeles, he achieves the victory of the hereditary ruler over the usurper. He is rewarded with a stretch of coastline where he wishes to realize his plan for gaining fertile land by damming off the ocean. The hut of the peaceful elderly couple Philemon and Baucis is in the way. It is burned down, and the couple dies. The doer is without scruple. The titanic element of thought, characterized by the expansive urge toward effect and reality, turns into culpable activity.

What Goethe presents as an anomaly, however, is subjected by later historians of literature to a reinterpretation into one-dimensionality—the active person becomes an idol, and the guilt is banished by ideology. Faust emerged, especially after 1870, from the realm of poetry into the realm of a national code. "In a typically Romantic process, the esthetic component turned into an issue of *Weltanschauung* that also attracted pseudoreligious emotions. The 'Faustian' spirit became a propaganda word, a 'mythical' code word for a certain *Weltanschauung* that soon came to stand for a desired political attitude. It became a national 'self-misunderstanding.' " (Hans Barth)

" 'Faustian' became one of the (Romantic) oppositional indicators against the other so-called 'Western' world. In this self-identification the groundlessness of such emotional ciphers went unrecognized, and for a long time it was no longer examined on the basis of the text of the tragedy from which its phonetic construction came.

"The 'Faustian' slogan as an ultimately exemplary type of German national action, is exalted in a mythical-religious sense and brought from the literary realm into a context of qualities 'indigenous to the folk.' It then in turn falsifies political reality, constituting the second falsification in this process. A belief that 'this-is-how it shall and must become,' based on the authority of Faust, forced itself upon the real 'this is how it is.' A 'substitute world,' a 'second reality' (Heimito von Doderer), this 'Faustian reality' covered over the 'primary' reality. Perspectives of infinity were soon regally adorned and disguised what was appropriate to the nation. What was 'Faustian,' allegedly carrying the weight of a spiritual directive, usurped any reasonable consideration of the possible.

This distortion of real national behavior and real political action by the slogan and the self-posited, apparently poetic guiding image of the 'Faustian' is what I call the 'Faustian ideology.' It too is, like numerous analogous events in the nineteenth century, the expression of the 'specifically German distance between spirit and power.' In the absence of a genuinely 'normative idea,' an attempt was made to bridge this distance with a 'German ideology,' with a 'mission to mankind altogether' as had been proclaimed in the realm of the spirit by Fichte and Hegel at the beginning of the century." (Hans Schwerte)

## Open Country

*Wayfarer*. Aye, the same dark linden swaying,
  Now matured to aged strength,
  Welcome, after years of straying,
  They salute me back at length!
  Aye—the selfsame humble acres!
  To that hut of refuge fair
  I repaired when storm-lashed breakers
  Cast me on the sand-dunes there.
  Who received me when I foundered,

I would bless the honest pair,
Hardly to be still encountered,
Old as even then they were.
Those were folk of pious living!
Should I knock, call out? All hail!
If you know the bliss of giving
As of old, and never fail.

*Baucis.* [*a little granny, very old*] Hush! Keep quiet, dear arrival,
Let him rest, my frail old man!
Lengthy slumber grants revival
For brief vigil's active span.

*Wayfarer.* Is it you, then, Mother, living
To receive my second thanks,
For the life-gift jointly given
To the youth cast on your banks?
Are you Baucis who devoutly
Quickened once this faltering lip?
    [*The husband enters.*]
You Philemon, who so stoutly
Snatched my hoard from water's grip?
Silvery pealing from your arbor,
From your hearth the nimble flame—
You in gruesome plight were harbor
Whence relief and comfort came.

Let me scan the boundless ocean,
Kneel upon the sandy crest,
Pour in prayerful devotion
What would burst my crowded breast.
    [*He strides forward upon the dune.*]

*Philemon.* [*to Baucis*] Lay the table for us, hurry,
In our little garden bright.
He will start aback and scurry,
See and not believe his sight.
[*standing beside the wayfarer*] What so fiercely overbore you,
Rolling breakers, foam-bespewed,
See as garden-land before you,
Glimpse of paradise renewed.
Older, slower to be aiding

Ready-handed as of yore,
I beheld, my powers fading,
Surf already far offshore.
Clever masters' daring minions
Drained and walled the ocean bed,
Shrank the sea's entrenched dominions,
To be masters in her stead.
Gaze on hamlets, common, stable,
Luscious meadows, grove and eave,—
But enough—let us to table,
For the sun would take his leave.
See the sails from farthest westing
Safe to anchorage repair!
Well the seabirds know their nesting,
For the harbor now is there.
Outward pressed to distant spaces
See the ocean's azure sheen,
Breadth of densely settled places
Right and left and all between.

> [*The three at table in the little garden.*]

*Baucis.* Silent? And, it seems, unable
   To relieve your hunger, too?
*Philemon.* He would hear the wondrous fable;
   Tell him, as you like to do.
*Baucis.* Well! A wonder, do not doubt it!
   Still it makes my reason fret;
   Something wrong was all about it
   That I cannot fathom yet.
*Philemon.* On the Emperor dare one blame it,
   Who conferred on him the shore?
   Did a herald not proclaim it,
   Trumpets flourishing before?
   Here a footing first was grounded,
   Not far distant from our bluff,
   Tents and huts—but green-surrounded,
   Rose a palace soon enough.
*Baucis.* Vainly in the daytime labored
   Pick and shovel, clink and strike,
   Where at night the elf-lights wavered,

By the dawn there stood a dike.
Human victims bled and fevered,
Anguish on the night-air borne,
Fiery torrents pouring seaward
Scored a channel by the morn.
Godless is he, he would savor
This our grove and cabin here;
Now the newly strutting neighbor
As his subjects we should fear.
*Philemon.* Yet he pledged, you have forgotten,
Homestead fair on new-won land!
*Baucis.* Do not trust the ocean bottom,
Steadfast on your hill-brow stand!
*Philemon.* To the chapel let us wander,
Greet the parting sun once more;
Ring and kneel in worship yonder,
Trusting God as heretofore.

TRANSLATED BY WALTER ARNDT

## (61) The old boy is comfortably settled

WILHELM BUSCH, Mr. and Mrs. Knopp

Wilhelm Busch (1832–1908), who was from Lower Saxony, used humor and caricature as weapons against the era's busy, acquisitive drives, castigating weaknesses, errors, and the absurdity and evil of the petit bourgeois world. His pessimistic philosophy detracted from the mockery; the skepticism that motivated him was tempered by sympathy. The people he criticized are more victims than perpetrators. As he said of himself in 1886, "Thus my position is low down on the shaded side of the mountain, but I have not become morose; on the contrary, cheerful, somewhat amused and touched, I hear the merry laughter coming from the sunny side where youth has moved on, striving upward in confident joy."

His breakfast time our Knopp does please,
For that is when he's most at ease.
After Lizzie brings the tray,
His Doris pours *café au lait*.
Today is made especially pleasant
By Doris' unexpected present:
A morning cap of her creation

With lavish, sequined decoration.
An appliqué of ribbon shapes
Around the crown a wreath of grapes.
Indeed, our Knopp could not be vainer
Of his becoming head container,
Which also serves to mitigate
The chill of winter on his pate.
He sits so proudly in his chair—
His cap makes him quite debonair.
Tobacco gives him pleasure still,
While Doris holds the lighted spill.
The morning hours are fleeing fast,
And soon will come his noon repast.
In this regard, one cannot claim
That Knopp has reason to complain.
He might in vain look far and wide
For better pancakes than his bride
Will serve him at the midday hour.
She mixes milk, a spoon of flour,
Three eggs—or even four, I fear,
Whenever they are not too dear—
And bakes this tasty golden batter
And serves it on Knopp's luncheon platter.
And every time Knopp says with pleasure,
"My dear, you really are a treasure!"
Oh, how easy is his rest,
Reclining on her faithful breast,
Where he is very much attached
To having his bald noggin scratched.
His thinking ends where it began:
"How nice to be a married man!"
. . . . . . . . . . . . . .

Wedding vows exchange, omitting
Nothing proper and befitting.
Under Klingebiel's direction
Bridal song achieves perfection,
While he wipes his tears away,
Sadness being his métier.
In the meantime his old cronies

Miss the wedding ceremonies,
Sealing with a flask of wine
Friendship lasting and benign.
In this world Knopp's life is through:
He has nothing more to do.
He's fulfilled his only purpose.
His appearance quite disturbs us:
Though he once was always spruce,
Coat and trousers now hang loose;
Pipe and cap, once exquisite,
Now no longer seem to fit.
Then the Parca in the sky—
She whom none can mollify—
Takes her scissors, cuts snip! snop!
And that is the end of Knopp.

TRANSLATED BY SHARON JACKIW

### (62) A strange and merry town

GOTTFRIED KELLER, The People of Seldwyla

The setting of the novellas in the collection entitled *The People of Seldwyla* (1856 and 1873–74) is an imaginary, somewhat odd and depraved Swiss city. In their youth the people of Seldwyla are enterprising and daring, in maturity they become whimsical philistines who withdraw in favor of cloistered security. The author is aware of the cleavage in middle-class existence and of the resistance among the petit bourgeois to participating in the spirit of the time. "In so far as the people of Gottfried Keller's Seldwyla represent an economic type and are presented as a community, the stories are a great monument, a literary farewell symphony to the preindustrial and preliberal concept of work and lifestyle. The individual heroes of the story are all atypical for the collectivity . . . The Seldwylans refuse to conceive of work as a process of upward mobility. They refuse to subject separate stages of the work process to the law of 'value according to speed.' Therein lies the reason for Keller's odd and evidently obscure comment that the Seldwylans are all 'conspicuous for their understanding of how to eat fish skillfully.' To be sure, there is no activity in which there is a greater discrepancy between product and expenditure of time than in eating fish. With the greatest composure the Seldwylans take note of their own insolvency, their economic bankruptcy. After all, they are sustained by the justified conviction that in the end nothing can happen to them, and economic collapse is never in any way an existential failure (the real reason for it is their communal ownership of the forest). And above all they have the capacity of deriving huge pleasure from any trifle. They still fully exploit the ancient forms of pleasure which have now become invalidated by the total addiction to speed and replaced by sensible leisure activity." (Peter von Matt)

In earlier times Seldwyla meant "a blissful and sunny place"; and that does indeed apply to the small town of that name located somewhere in Switzerland. It still has the same old city walls and towers of three hundred years ago, and thus is still the same old place. The purpose of the original settlement is obscure; when we consider that the founders located the town a good half hour from a navigable river, it was a clear sign that nothing should become of it. But the location is beautiful— amidst green mountains that are open toward the south, so that the sun but no rough breezes can indeed get in. Thus a rather good variety of grape thrives around the old town wall, while higher in the mountains immense forests stretch out, constituting the wealth of the town.

For here is the characteristic and strange destiny of Seldwyla: the community is rich and the citizens poor, to the extent that no one in the town has anything and no one knows what they have actually been subsisting on for centuries. They live quite merrily and in high spirits and see comfortable living as their special art. Whenever they go where other wood is burnt, they begin by criticizing the comfort there and claiming that no one can surpass them in this line of work.

The essence and the glory of the Seldwylans consists of the young people around twenty to thirty-five or thirty-six years old. They set the fashions, maintain the standards, and constitute the splendor of Seldwyla, for at this age they practice the business, trade, or whatever it is they have learned. That is, as much as possible they let strangers work for them and take advantage of their profession to carry on a first-rate traffic in debts. Precisely this is the basis of the power, splendor and comfort of the gentlemen of Seldwyla and is observed with remarkable reciprocity and deep understanding.

But, to be sure, that happens only in this aristocracy of youth. For as soon as one reaches the limit of the aforesaid flourishing years, at which time the men of other towns are just beginning to take stock of themselves and gain strength, in Seldwyla he is finished. He must abandon his previous way of life. If he is an ordinary Seldwylan, he continues living in the town, now impotent, expelled from the paradise of credit. If anything remains in him that has not yet been expended, he joins foreign armies and learns there to do for a foreign tyrant what he was too arrogant to do for himself: to button up and stand up straight. These Seldwylans, returning after a number of years as able men of war, belong among the best drill sergeants in Switzerland. They know how to train the young enlisted men so that training is a pleasure. Others depart for adventures in foreign parts around their fortieth year, and in the most obscure corners of the world one can meet Seldwylans. They are all distinguished by their great skill in eating fish—in Australia, California or Texas as well as in Paris or Constantinople.

But whoever stays back and grows old in the town learns late in life to work. It is a matter of hustling for a daily penny, doing a thousand trifling things that one is not really trained to do. And the aging, impoverished Seldwylans with their wives and children are the busiest little people of the world, after they have given up their learned trade. It is moving to see how actively they busy themselves in trying to earn the means for a good piece of meat such as they used to. All citizens have plenty of wood, and the community sells a large amount yearly, which supports and nourishes them in their great poverty. And so the old town continues to this very day in that same invariable cycle. But on the whole the Seldwylans are always contented and cheerful.

And whenever any shadow darkens their souls, whenever some all-too-stubborn financial crisis lingers in the town, they pass the time and cheer each other up through their great political mobility, which is a further characteristic of the Seldwylans. That is, they are passionate party members, constitutional revisors and petitioners. When they have thought up a really crazy motion and submitted it through their elected representative, or when a call for constitutional revision goes out from Seldwyla, it is known throughout the land that at the moment no money is circulating there. But at the same time they love alternating opinions and principles and are always found among the opposition to a government the day after it has been elected. If it is a radical government they flock together around the conservative, pious town pastor, whom they were teasing only the day before, in order to annoy the regime. They court him by crowding into his church with feigned enthusiasm, praising his sermons, and ostentatiously passing around his little printed tracts and reports from the Basel Missionary Society—naturally without contributing a penny. But if the regime at the wheel looks even halfway conservative, they immediately gather around the town schoolteacher, and the pastor must start paying the glazier for broken windowpanes. If, on the other hand, the government consists of hypocritical financiers and liberal lawyers who care a lot about form, the Seldwylans rush at once to the nearest socialist and annoy the government by voting him in with the battle cry: Enough of political formalism! It is the financial interests alone that are causing problems for the people!

One day they want a veto and even the most direct self-government possible, with a permanent national assembly. (For this, to be sure, Seldwylans would have more time than anyone else.) The next day they act tired out and blasé about public matters and leave the elections to a half dozen old reactionaries who declared themselves bankrupt thirty years ago and have been silently rehabilitating themselves ever since. Then they watch cozily from the windows of the taverns as the reactionaries creep into the church; and laugh behind their fists like the boy who said, "It serves my father right if my hands freeze off. Why doesn't he buy me any gloves?" Yesterday they had nothing but praise for life in the Swiss Confederation and were highly indignant that complete unity had not been achieved in the year '48; today they are quite obsessed with cantonal sovereignty and will no longer elect representatives to the national assembly.

But if any of their motions or agitations become troublesome and inconvenient for the majority in the country, to quiet them down the government usually sends a fact-finding committee which is supposed to regulate the administration of the Seldwyla community property. Then they turn their concerns to themselves exclusively, and the danger has been averted.

All this furnishes them with great enjoyment, surpassed only every fall when they drink their new wine, the fermented cider that they call *Sauser* ("evening of carousing"). If it is good, one's life is not safe among them, and they make an infernal noise. The whole town smells like new wine, and the Seldwylans are absolutely worthless. But strangely enough, the less a Seldwylan is worth at home, the better he behaves when he moves away. And whether they set out singly or together, as for example when they used to march off to war, they always behave well. As speculators or businessmen many Seldwylans have become quite energetic and active, once they were out of the warm sunny valley in which they were not thriving.

In such a strange and merry town there can be no lack of all kinds of strange tales and life stories, since idleness is the root of all evil. But in this little book I will not tell stories that suit the already described character of Seldwyla, but rather some strange aberrations that have occurred now and then, as exceptions in a sense, and yet could only have happened in Seldwyla.

TRANSLATED BY MARGARET WOODRUFF

## (63) To vegetate on into blessed eternity

HEINRICH HEINE, Travel Images

Heinrich Heine's first prose work, *Journey Through the Harz Mountains,* was heavily censored when it was first published in 1826. Heine had studied in Göttingen and was expelled for dueling; *Journey Through the Harz Mountains* describes his experiences while hiking from Göttingen through the Harz Mountains. Additional travelogues followed: *The North Sea, Ideas: The Book of Le Grand, A Trip from Munich to Genoa, The Baths of Lucca, English Fragments.* Heine states in the preface to the 1834 French edition of *Travel Images* that the work was written before the July Revolution at a time when political pressure in Germany silenced everything and minds had sunk into a lethargy of despair. At that time the more the person who dared speak up despaired about the triumph of freedom, and the more vigorously he was opposed by the party of the clergy and the aristocracy, the more passionately he had to express himself.

Heine's journalism admittedly tones down the sharpness of his text. "This book is a sideshow. Come right in. Don't be afraid. I am not as evil as I look. I've only painted my face in such wild colors to frighten my enemies still more in battle. Actually I am gentle as a lamb, so don't get excited, and shake hands with me. You can touch my weapons, even the quivers and arrows, because I have, as is the custom among us wild people when approaching a sacred place, dulled their points. Just between us, though, these arrows were not only pointed but very poisonous. Today they are not dangerous all. They are completely harmless, and for the fun of it you can also look at the colorful feathers on them. In fact, your children could even use them as a kind of toy."

The name Goslar has such a pleasant ring to it and so many ancient remembrances of emperors are connected with it that I expected an imposing, stately city. But so it goes when one views celebrities at close range! I found a decayed and moldy nest with mostly narrow, labyrinthine, crooked streets, through the middle of which flows a small bit of water, probably the Gose, and a pavement as bumpy as Berlin hexameters. Only the old parts of the setting, such as the remains of walls, towers, and battlements, give the city a somewhat piquant appearance. One of these towers, called the Zwinger, has walls so thick that entire rooms are hewn from them. The area in front of the city, where the far-renowned shooting contest is held, is a large beautiful meadow with high mountains all around. The market place is small; in the center stands a fountain, its waters pouring over into a large metal basin. When there is a fire, the basin is struck several times and produces a far-reaching tone. Nothing is known about the origin of this basin. Some say that one night the devil put it there in the market place. In those days people were still stupid, and the devil was also stupid, and they gave each other presents.

The town hall of Goslar is a guardroom painted white. The guildhall next to it has a somewhat better appearance. At about an equal distance from the earth and the roof stand statues of German emperors, smokily black and partly gilded, a scepter in one hand, a globe in the other; they look like roasted university proctors. One of the emperors is holding a sword instead of a scepter. I could not guess what this difference was supposed to mean, and it surely has a meaning, because Germans have the curious habit of thinking about everything they do.

In Gottschalk's *Handbook* I had read quite a bit about the ancient cathedral and about the famous emperor's throne at Goslar. But when I wanted to see them both, I was told that the cathedral had been torn down and the emperor's throne had been brought to Berlin. We live in a time filled with meaning; thousand-year-old cathedrals are razed and emperors' thrones are tossed into the lumber room.

Some of the curiosities of the holy cathedral are now set up in the Church of St. Stephen. Paintings on glass, which are quite beautiful; a few bad paintings, among which is said to be a Lukas Cranach. In addition there is a wooden Christ on the Cross and a pagan sacrificial altar of unknown metal; it has the shape of a longish, four-cornered chest and is borne by four caryatids who, in a stooped position, hold their hands supportingly above their heads and make unpleasant, ugly faces. Even more unpleasant, however, is the already-mentioned large wooden crucifix standing near it. This head of Christ with natural hair and thorns and a blood-smeared face shows, of course, most masterfully the dying of a man, but not of a divine Savior. Only material suffering is whittled into this face, not the poetry of pain. Such an image belongs in an anatomy lecture room rather than in a house of God.

I stayed at an inn near the marketplace where the dinner would have tasted even better had the innkeeper, with his long, superfluous face and his boring questions, not sat down beside me. Fortunately, I was soon released by the arrival of another traveler who had to endure the same questions in the same order: *quis? quid? ubi? quibus auxiliis? cur? quomodo? quando?* This stranger was an old, tired, worn-out man who, to judge from his talk, had journeyed through the whole world, had lived especially long in Batavia, had made quite a bit of money and had lost it all again and now, after a thirty-year absence, was returning to Quedlinburg, his native city. "Because," he said, "our family has its burial ground there." The innkeeper made the very enlightened remark that it was really a matter of indifference to the soul where one's body is buried. "Do you have it in writing?" answered the stranger, while terribly cunning rings formed about his pitiful lips and faded little eyes. "But," he added with an anxious effort to please, "it was not my intention to say anything bad about the graves of strangers. The Turks bury their dead far better than we, their cemeteries are orderly gardens, and they sit there on their white, beturbaned gravestones, in the shade of a cypress, and stroke their serious beards and calmly smoke their Turkish tobacco in their long Turkish pipes. And as for the Chinese, it is a real pleasure to observe how they politely hop about the resting places of their dead and pray and drink tea and play the violin; and see how well they know how to adorn the beloved graves quite prettily with all sorts of gilded latticework, porcelain figurines, scraps of bright silk material, artificial flowers and colorful lanterns—all very pretty. How far do I have to Quedlinburg?"

The churchyard in Goslar did not really appeal to me very much. All the more, however, did that wonderful little curlyhead who smilingly looked out of a somewhat higher ground-floor window when I arrived in town. After eating, I looked for the dear window again; but now only a glass of water containing bluebells stood there. I clambered up, took the pretty little flowers from the glass, placed them calmly in my cap, and concerned myself very little with the wide-opened mouths, petrified noses, and goggle eyes with which the people on the street, particularly the old women, observed this qualified theft. When I passed the same house an hour later, the lovely one was standing at the window and, when she perceived the bluebells on my cap, turned a deep red and started back. I had now seen the beautiful face even more clearly; it was a sweet, transparent embodiment of the breath of a summer evening, moonlight, the song of nightingales, and the fragrance of roses. Later, when it had become completely dark, she stepped out in front of the door. I came—I approached—she draws back slowly into the dark hallway—I take her by the hand and say: "I am an admirer of beautiful flowers and kisses, and what I am not given voluntarily I steal." And I kissed her quickly—and as she is about to flee, I whisper soothingly: "Tomorrow I am going away and may never be coming back"—and I feel the secret return pressure of her lovely lips and tiny hands—and I rush away laughing. Yes, I have to laugh when I consider that I unconsciously uttered that magic formula by which, more often than by their mustachioed kindness, our redcoats and bluecoats conquer the hearts of ladies: "Tomorrow I am going away and may never be coming back!"

My lodgings offered a wonderful view of the Rammelsberg. It was a beautiful evening. The night raced by on its black steed, its long manes fluttering in the wind. I stood at the window and observed the moon. Is there really a man in the moon? The Slavs say his name is Chlotar and that he causes the waxing of the moon by watering it. When I was still young, I had heard that the moon was a fruit which, after it had ripened, was plucked by God and laid together with the other full moons in a big cupboard standing at the end of the world that is nailed up with boards. When I grew older, I noticed that the world is not so narrowly limited and that the human spirit had broken through the wooden barriers and had opened all seven heavens with a gigantic St. Peter's key, with the idea of immortality. Immortality! Beautiful thought! Who thought of you first! Was it a common citizen of Nuremberg who, with white night-cap on his head and white clay pipe in his mouth, sat before his house door on a warm summer evening and quite comfortably reflected that it would surely be nice if he could vegetate on into blessed eternity, just like now, without his pipe and his breath of life going out! Or was it a young lover who thought those thoughts of immortality in the arms of his sweetheart, and thought it because he felt it and because he could feel and think nothing else! Love! Immortality! My breast was suddenly so hot that I believed the geographers had moved the equator to another place so that it was now running right through my heart. And from my heart poured the feelings of love, poured forth longingly into the wide night. The flowers in the garden beneath my window had a stronger scent. Scents are the feelings of flowers and, much like the human heart which feels stronger in the night when it believes itself to be alone and unwatched, so too the flowers, pensively shamed, seem to await the covering darkness in order to give themselves fully to their feelings and to breathe them out in sweet scents. Pour forth, you scents of my heart! Look for the beloved of my dreams behind those mountains! She is lying now asleep; at her feet angels kneel, and when she smiles in her sleep, it is a prayer which the angels repeat; in her breast heaven lies with all its happiness, and when she breathes, my heart trembles in the distance; behind the silken lashes of her eyes the sun has set, and when she opens her eyes again, it is day, and the birds sing; and the little herd bells sound, and the mountains shimmer in their emerald garments, and I bind up my knapsack and wander.

TRANSLATED BY CHRISTIAN-ALBRECHT GOLLUB

## (64) Alone, yet not alone

WILHELM RAABE, Sparrow Lane Chronicle

Wilhelm Raabe (1831–1910), the son of a petty justice official, was first apprenticed as a book dealer and then became a freelance writer. "I have literally experienced nothing that could interest people." In his writing Raabe was in quest of that "other Germany" which he considered to be the embodiment of faith, goodness, modesty, and patience. It pained him that the middle class was inwardly impoverished while outwardly becoming wealthy and gaining control of the world with technological inventions and achievements. "His heroes are off-beat characters, odd fellows, cranks, the people who have tripped in their scramble upwards and who, although not directly expelled by society, live at its fringes, trying to preserve a spark of humanity for themselves though forced to renounce all external recognition." (Herbert Roch)

*The Chronicle of Sparrow Lane* (1856) describes from the perspective of a lonely, elderly person the various events in an old Berlin lane. Homesickness for the idyll of the small city has been captured here in images uniting all the elements of longing and recollection, devotion and sentimentality, happiness and resignation, love and mild criticism that comprise the Biedermeier lifestyle.

November 20th

I love these older sections of big cities with their narrow, dark, crooked lanes where the sunshine dares only to peek in; I love them with their gabled houses and wonderful rain gutters, with their old cast-iron cannons and gun barrels placed at the corners of buildings as guardstones. I love this center of a time past where the streets and squares of a new way of life have been added on, laid out as if lined up for a parade. I can never turn the corner into my Sparrow Lane without tenderly touching the old gun barrel dated 1589 that leans there. Even the people who live in the older section of the city seem to be a more eccentric, peculiar lot than those who live in the modern areas. Here in these twisted lanes, the frivolous ones live right alongside the sober, working people; and the close contact between the two throws them together in wilder, more amusing scenes than one would ever see in the more fashionable but, at the same time, drabber streets. Here the old patrician houses still stand— most of the families, of course, are long gone—houses that live on, many popularly known by some unusual name given them because of a unique architectural design or some other distinguishing feature. Here are the dark, smoke-blackened offices of the important old commercial firms. Here is the true realm of the cellar and attic apartments. Twilight and night produce more wonderful lighting effects here by lamp- and moon-light, and more unusual sounds, than anywhere else. Rusted weather vanes clatter and groan; the wind rattles the roof tiles; children cry, cats meow, women scold. Where does it all sound more fitting—one might say, more suited to the place, than here in these narrow lanes, between these tall houses, where every angle, every corner, every projection catches the sound, breaks it up, and casts it back different!

Listen! At the very moment that I am writing this, there below in that archway the hurdy-gurdy is starting up; its lamenting sound waves are truly melodic as they roll out over the dull murmur and rumble of human labor! To be sure, the voice of God speaks clearly enough in the rushing wind, the roaring waves, and the thunder, but not more clearly than in these undefinable sounds of the hustle and bustle of humanity. I maintain that an aspiring poet or painter—a musician, of course, is another thing—should not be allowed to live anywhere but here! And if you ask where the freshest, most original works of art were created, the answer will usually be: in a *garret*! It was in a garret in Wine Office Court that Oliver Goldsmith, locked up by his landlady for overdue rent, searched out for Dr. Johnson from among his old papers, worn-out jackets, empty Madeira bottles, and trash of all kinds a soiled manuscript with the title, *The Vicar of Wakefield*.

It was in a garret that Jean Jacques Rousseau wrote his most passionate, inspiring books. And in a garret Jean Paul learned how to sketch Siebenkäs, legal counselor of the poor, and the little schoolmaster Wuz, and the life of Fibel!

Sparrow Lane is a short, narrow passage that connects Crown Street with a bank of the river that wends its way through the big city in many branches and canals. It is so crowded and lively that someone suffering with a tension headache could be driven mad by it and end up in an insane asylum; but for me it has for many years been an invaluable stage depicting life in the world, where war and peace, fortune and misery, hunger and plenty, all the antinomies of existence are reflected.

In Nature everything lies scattered into infinity; in consciousness the universe is focused on a single point. That's the way my old professor of logic once lectured. Although I diligently copied it into my notebook at the time, I wasn't too concerned about the truth of this sentence. I was young then, and Marie, the pretty little milliner, was living across from me and would usually be sewing at the window, while I, holding Kant's *Critique of Pure Reason* in front of my nose, had my eyes—only on her. Very nearsighted and too poor to get spectacles, binoculars, or opera glasses for these studies at the window, I was in despair. I comprehended the meaning of the statement: Everything lies scattered into infinity.

Then, one beautiful afternoon, I was standing at the window as usual, my nose pressed against the pane; and over there, among the flowers, in a happy, bright sunbeam, my *ombra adorata* was, in fact, sitting. What wouldn't I have given to know whether she was smiling across to me!

Suddenly, I noticed one of those tiny little bubbles that glass panes often have. By chance, I looked through it at my little milliner, and—I comprehended that the universe could be focused on a single point.

That's just how it is in this dream-and-picture book of Sparrow Lane. The stage is small; those who appear on it are few; and yet they can comprise a world of interest for the writer and a world of boredom for the stranger; one who doesn't have the calling and in whose hands these pages will someday end up.

TRANSLATED BY JOHANNES W. VAZULIK

## (65) The big, black, cold ditch

WILHELM RAABE, The Skidderump

Looking back on the events since the first publication of his novel in 1869, the writer states in the preface to the second edition of 1894, "Within this period of time much that is good, noble, and dear, and much that had the pretense of being important or which was considered important, epoch-making, indestructible has landed on a rickety cart that continues to roll on through the world. Gentlemen, nothing can be changed about that. These wheels cannot be stopped."

Raabe's most important novel is named for a hearse from the time of the great plague, symbolizing the power of death and of the passions, which he considers evil. The frightening thing in the world is that the scoundrel is boss and remains boss. Such reality must be confronted and firmly resisted. Life then loses its horror of death, and death loses its terror in the face of evil life. We should be able to laugh about life and death. Laughter is the only lesson learned by the heroine of the novel from her dreadful experiences. The horror of life and death hold each other in check. Humor consists in being able to laugh despite everything.

I had arrived by mail coach at a bright, cheerful little North German town that shall remain nameless in order not to arouse the envy and jealousy of others of the sort. After eating my midday meal I had two or three completely free hours before the new coachman would take the fresh horses out of the stable for the continuation of our journey. In such a case, everybody who is not on a business trip dedicates himself to a comfortable inner contemplation that, however, tends to change to a peculiar restlessness. One stretches, yawns for a while on a bench under the arbor in front of the inn; one gets up and strolls down the nearest little alley as far as the next corner. There one gazes dreamily at the dusty dead flies behind a shopkeeper's windows, and returns to one's table and one's bench before the inn and resumes a lively battle with the flies of the place. Most travelers then succumb to a somewhat apathetic stupor and only liven up again when the horses are being harnessed. I, on the other hand, who make use of much that other people scorn, always inquired about the closest things of interest in the municipality, *reservatis reservandis* naturally. That is to say, I reserved the rights that a knowledgeable man does reserve for himself, namely, whether or not to view the curiosities. So I made my inquiries this time and must say that it didn't matter much when the innkeeper, a pleasant man, scratched behind his ear and couldn't think of anything remarkable in the environs to recommend to me, either natural or man-made.

So with an involuntary sigh of satisfaction I leaned back into the shadow of a linden tree. Suddenly a dusky little man who was sitting on the bench by the other side of the door spoke to me. (He was smoking a black pot, so he was being avoided with great revulsion by the flies.) He had a melancholy look and his voice was timid as he said, "We still have a skidderump. If the gentleman would like to see it, he is welcome to do so. There is enough time too, and, if I may be permitted, I will lead the gentleman there."

"A skidderump? What is a skidderump?" I asked, unusually attracted to the word.

"Just come with me, sir," the little man said even more dejectedly than before. "It won't cost any more than you choose to give. I am the gravedigger of the town, and since the grave of the forestry clerk is ready and prepared, and the forestry clerk won't be coming to me until four o'clock, there is sufficient time, as I have said, before the mailcoach will depart and, be it added, for the funeral of the forestry clerk."

I felt a little spasm move me there on the bench. The dusky little fellow, who combined these two methods of going and traveling indifferently and with such solemn wisdom, was beginning to make me quite uncomfortable. On just that account the basic substance of our conversation became all the more interesting. What connection did the skidderump have with the forestry clerk? Did the forestry clerk have any sort of connection with the skidderump? I put an end to a whole list of similar questions by jumping up, grabbing my hat, and saying that I was ready and prepared for the skidderump. But then the melancholy little man gave me a dubious sidelong glance, shook his head, and whispered, as he started to light his pipe, that he hoped I was, for he was ready for me. With that we went toward the church, crossing diagonally through a part of the town.

Located behind the church was the cemetery, and nearby was the official residence of my companion. Close beside this was an ancient stone vault, barred by a door of rusty black iron grating. This door the sad little man unlocked, pointing into the dark space and saying in a weirdly hollow voice:

"There it stands!"

And with an uncanny satisfaction he added:

"And everybody must admit that it is a great marvel and would be a great honor for any mausoleum!"

There it really did stand—a high black cart on two wheels, with a half-erased white cross on its front and the date 1615 on its back. My companion tenderly laid his hand on it and spoke:

"Just come closer, sir. People say, and it has also been written, that it is the only one in the entire world. It was last used in the year 1665— you see, sir—in this way!"

And with this the cheerful fellow pulled the cart around, pushed aside a bar, and at that the dreadful machine leaped and tilted and shook out an imaginary load of plague corpses into the pit.

"Heh, heh," the little man tittered. "What do you say to that, sir? That was convenient and spared the likes of me lots of work—eh? Yes truly, two years ago during the time of the cholera we almost brought it out again and gave it a position of honor; but the honorary magistrate and the consistory and, above all, the most worthy citizenry were far too afraid of it, and so things remained as they were, and yours truly had the drudgery of it. It would have saved a lot of effort. Would you like to try the machinery yourself, sir? I assure you, sir, it is comfortable for both parties."

I thanked him heartily for the offer, but with an undisguised shudder; and gave him a generous tip in order to cut off all further expectations. Only it did please me that from now on I would know what a skidderump was, and I did, in fact, consider it something very remarkable. Then once more I looked down into the grave of the forestry clerk where it had been dug next to the grave mound of his deceased wife. At that moment the coachman blew his horn; I rushed back, climbed into the coach, and rode on through the green and grassy plain in the sunshine toward the Golden

Meadow. But I kept the skidderump in my memory forever. Yes, forever, and that despite the fact that I have thought of, seen, and heard many other things that should have surpassed the ancient ghost with living terrors and pains.

I saw its shadow cast into all sorts of splendor and light; in all manner of melodies played by flutes and violins I detected its hollow thumping; and I rid my soul of many a refreshing good wish and much else when, like that dusky little man, I unhooked the chain, tilted the cart, and let the load slide down into the big, black, cold ditch in which the differences between people or things no longer count for anything. So the skidderump gradually became the pivotal point of an entire philosophical system that I developed in depth and in breadth, and I should be really pleased if, in the course of this book, I should accumulate some adherents, disciples, and apostles for my system.

TRANSLATED BY MINETTA ALTGELT GOYNE

# THE CHTHONIC

Gottfried Keller states in *Lost Laughter*, "If the eternal and infinite always remain so motionless and concealed, why should not we, too, just for once be able to be pleasantly and peacefully quiet? . . . But the quiet and peace thus gained is not death; on the contrary, it is life that continues to flourish and shine like this Sunday morning, and with a good conscience we wander through it, awaiting the things that will then come or not come."

The idyll is embedded in the chthonic: in the consciousness that it is possible, belonging to the earth and resting in it entirely, to live in it happily and peacefully for a period of time. The consciousness of immanence, the restriction to what remains within "borders" without overstepping them is a tragic consciousness to the extent that knowledge about the "border situations" remains present. The eternal and the infinite remain quiet for only a moment and are not long concealed; the numinous proves to be an urgent, inconceivable power that awakens both trust and horror.

Adolf Muschg summarized Gottfried Keller's life and work under the rubric *Concerning Horror and Flourishing* [*Vom Grauen und Grünen*]. The impression made by Feuerbach's anthropology on the poet had led him to deny personal immortality and also to renounce its guarantees in the hereafter. Keller's atheism was characterized by joy in life and by turning to people, an attitude "that admittedly did not deny its origin in wintry renunciation and is indebted to this modification for its true feeling. There must be this one life that cannot be lost, they seem to say, for the sake of this life's dignity and beauty. And more softly it can be heard that it is not my life; I am lost for it. The renunciation of God also has its political aspect: neither in heaven nor on earth can absolute monarchs any longer be tolerated."

Once such humanity has been reached, God is no longer needed as a heuristic principle. Death is utterly included in life and even becomes an aid in exorcizing anxiety about death. In the name of death, people give themselves over entirely to life; by recognizing life's mortality, the joy of life is taken seriously. *Memento mori—carpe diem.* Realism's brave disdain of death is not characterized by dialectical tension or Baroque conflict but rather by agnostic resoluteness and composure: "Now we have turned the leaf/ and looked death straight in the eye;/ no uncertain aim any longer blinds us/ yet bush and grass seem greener!/ And it's become greener in our heart,/ as our jolly words bear witness;/ yet our songs and our jokes/ are based on a noble seriousness."

To live on the basis of limited time means: enjoy this limited time. Courage of life means: to speak the truth, to become conscious that people derive from what is uncertain and go into uncertainty; to stand bravely in the nonetheless and to form one's own life. In God's name name but not in the name of God. The color that "bears" such admission is green, which is the color of chthonic embeddedness. Grass grows over everything. Keller's green, according to Adolf Muschg, is a symbol for development in general, for the continuation of life and creativity; it is a limited command, and within its limitation an eminently sensible command not to let the form of life on this planet die out, to tend "the green" as if our soul and our survival depended upon it:

> Keller's green is the vegetative color containing all colors of life. It can stand for life against death's colors of black and white; it can stand for day against night, for summer against winter. And yet it itself needs the dark earth in the twofold sense of growth and contrast, of origin and background; this earth, to which green shall again return, not to vanish but to renew itself. The basic semantics are addressed in *Green Henry* at the beginning of the story of his youth and in the second version of the novel at the very beginning: here the beginning is developed from the end of human things— i.e., Keller does not start with the birth of the hero but with his village's cemetery: ". . . it is impossible that there should be a single grain within a depth of ten feet that has not made its pilgrimage through a human organism and once helped the rest of the soil to be turned over." That is the black layer of growth on which the green life of the hero is implanted: "Even the greenest grass grows on it, and the roses next to the jasmine flourish in heavenly disarray and excess so that single shoots are not placed on a fresh grave, but rather the grave must be carved into the forest of flowers."

A foretaste of a universe is conveyed in which the green life is destined to substitute abundance for frailty. That which has no locus in time appropriates all the more space for the luxuriant green. It is reined in by the author to a standstill in the moment; to that life in the midst of living whose soul is in brotherhood with everything that is transitory, whose spirit is the awareness of death. Here "development" does not occur by having the individual become what he is step by step but by having the individual give transitoriness its due by recognition and by his learning to offset the ineluctible through strength of character. The educational goal is to grow toward ever-present death without canceling out life and to be mindful of life's brevity. To become mature without blooming if necessary, to become mature by the strength of the green that is capable of nourishing other life after its own fading.

Such a "green ethos" characterizes not only Gottfried Keller's work; it belongs to the "basic melody" of realism altogether. It has its origin in the knowledge of the "aorgic" from which Hölderlin suffered; it ends in the "acherontic chill" of impressionism. According to Friedrich Hölderlin (in "Ground of Empedocles"), nature in its effects on the reflecting person is transformed "into the extreme of the aorgic, into the extreme of the inconceivable." Resembling the manner in which Goethe registered the demonic, Hölderlin experiences the aorgic in the forces of reality as something that is ungraspably alien for the human being, because everything human is confronted by something that is completely indifferent. In feeling, hence in art, too (as understood by Hölderlin) the human being is "together," connected to being, and feels secure. Reflection, however, makes it clear that he is "lost," that he is "outside"; he now sees himself confronted with the aorgic. "In the middle is the struggle and death of the individual." The organic, which has become aorgic, seeks to find itself again and to return to itself by reconciling itself with the aorgic—i.e., with what confronts it antagonistically. In "Death of Empedocles" such reconciliation is portrayed by the leap into Aetna, the plunge into the earth, pantheistic unification, the disintegration of individuality.

Along the way to realism, chthonic belief in the world and chthonic trust in reality lose the sting of the aorgic; mourning about the repellent severity of nature is transformed into mild composure: let it be as it is is! As expressed by Karl Leberecht Immermann (1832) in one of the *Chiliastic Sonnets:* "Words must sound to you like madness,/ For the primordially powerful splendor of things/ has never entered your quite impoverished senses,/ you pluck what's withered from the greenest meadows." The poet advises conceiving life as immanent transcendence, completely recognizing the "primordially powerful splendor" of things, grasping the truth as such in the greening of the meadow. Wish nothing further than to be there. The most beautiful thing under the sun is to be under the sun. Ask nothing further than can be answered by the here and now. To not be unhappy, since one cannot in any case be happy. To be pious by persevering in a reverential attitude toward things.

The three periods of realism—early, middle, and late—differ from each other in chthonic experiences. At times the horror in the face of the abyss at the basis of life predominates, at times support is found in the basis of life; at times the world eludes us, at other times it is grasped; at times gray predominates, at other times green predominates; at times people are overpowered by terror (horror); at other times the here and now (green) conveys comfort and hope.

"The essence" emerges from all things both menacingly and comfortingly in the works of Eduard Mörike and Georg Büchner. Ultimately, though, it confronts us as a power of sublime quiet, chill, indifference. We are lost and at the same time secure. We are delivered up to the sacred horror of the world but cannot fall out of its reality. Lenz, in the story of the same name by Büchner, attempts to grasp everything in himself; he burrows into the universe and wants to fathom the world which in its infinity is a pleasure that pains him. The peripeteia of the story and of his existence is the scene when he falls asleep in his room in the pastor's house (near Oberlin): "His head sank to his chest, he fell asleep, the full moon was out, tears hung from his lashes and dried on his cheeks. And that is how he lay there alone, and everything was quiet and still and cold, and the moon shone the whole night and was above the mountains" (66).

While nature persists here in aorgic mercilessness, Adalbert Stifter discovers in it the rule of a friendly, gentle law. The basis of the world lies beyond immensity and greatness; what is great is the small—the whir of air, the burbling of water, the growth of grain, the undulation of the sea, the verdure of the meadows, the brightness of the heavens, the glow of the stars (67). "Do you know why the beetles and buttercups make you so happy?/ Because you don't know people and don't see the stars! . . ./ But it had to be thus; so that you would excellently/ Portray the small, Nature cleverly removed the great from your grasp."

This is how Friedrich Hebbel attacks Stifter. To be sure, the attack was based on a misunderstanding, for Stifter's "green ethos" is not philistine pettiness. It emerges against the background of horror. It testifies to a tragic, brave desire to exist within a world in which chaos repeatedly intrudes. In Stifter's most famous novella, *The High Forest* (1841), the forest is not merely

> background or even stage setting, but the actual hero, the enduring and eternal, regardless of how human destinies may change. Consequently Stifter uses for his description not so much the human being's perspective of the forest and its objects as the perspective of these objects on people. Instead of having the riders glimpse the flowers on a forest meadow, it is the forest flowers that see the riders approaching. Two girls have found refuge from the confusions of the Thirty Years War at a forest lake. From the mountain they are able to discern through binoculars that the paternal castle has burned down. "It was an uncanny thought that at this moment perhaps tumultuous chaos of war and heart-breaking deeds were taking place, but in the vastness of the world and of the forest the tower itself was only a point. It was impossible to register anything of the chaos of war, and smiling, peaceful beauty was in the sky and above the whole wilderness."
>
> The whole world, represented particularly by the forest in Stifter's novella—the whole of life on earth is the great power before whose sublime smiling indifference everything human becomes insignificant. To behold this power has something oppressive but something comforting, too, and what is comforting begins gradually to predominate in the world of Stifter, Carus, and Immermann's Münchhausen. Büchner repeatedly expanded to the utmost the cleavage between the human and the powers in the inhuman. Hence the laughter upon Camille's remark to Danton corresponds to the smile of those other powers in Stifter: "Is then the ether with its eyes of gold a bowl containing golden carp on the table of the blessed gods, and the blessed gods are eternally laughing and the fish are eternally dying, and the gods eternally delight in the colorful play of the death struggle?" After Stifter's girls have returned home, the hunter Gregor, who is, incidentally, clearly modeled on Cooper's Leatherstocking, sets the forest house afire, scattering seeds on the site so "the deep virginal wilderness came into being the way it once was and as it still is today. An old man like an apparition was seen frequently walking through the forest, but no person can specify a time when he still walked or a time when he no longer walked." Even historical time has become insignificant: the shudder of the forest's eternity and reality touches us. (H. O. Bürger)

Johann Jacob Bachofen states in his autobiography (1854) that as a scientist he set forth on "the route to the mothers." His work *The Law of the Mothers: A Study of the Gynecocracy of the Ancient World According to Its Religious and Legal Nature,* appeared in 1861. Concerning the cult of the altar among the most ancient peoples, he states: "The destruction produced by the luxuriant proliferation of vegetation on the facades of graves

is not in the slightest disturbing. One does not scold the roots that have
. . . dislodged the roof or separated a piece of the gate, causing it to fall
down. . . . When the person has been completely deserted, the earth
still lovingly embraces this last stone house with its growth. In the context of antiquity, this is not merely an image but a truth." It was the
truth of the chthonic, to which Detlev von Liliencron's response was to
feel chilled (68). Arthur Schopenhauer gained comfort from the unity of
life and death (69). The "green ethos" is directed toward the "planet
earth." In addition to the fascinating exotic distance where the horizon
rests on the grass-covered ground (70), there is the homey cosmos of a
village dwarfed by the snowy desert of the mountain range (71). Everything has its place. Topography of immanence.

Just as there is a "belief in immanence," the mechanical conception of
life is capable of astonishment; respect for the lawfulness of the events of
life corresponds to the "green ethos." In the works of Rudolf Virchow
this astonishment is directed toward the cell, which "represents a cluster
of the inmost effects, a cluster of the most manifold combinations of
substance." However special, unique, and inward life is, it is to the same
extent only slightly exempt from the domination of chemical and physical
laws. "The miracle is the law"(72).

"In the microscopic knowledge of the smallest as well as in the tele-
scopic exploration of the largest we have now gained inestimable insights
that seemed unthinkable a hundred years ago," wrote Ernst Haeckel in
his remarkably influential book, *The Riddle of the World* (1899). Improved
methods of microscopic and biological research would not only have revealed to us everywhere in the realm of the one-celled Protista an invisible
world of life full of an infinite wealth of forms but would also, in the tiny
small cell, have made us acquainted with the "elementary organism"
whose social cell aggregates, the tissues, comprise the body of all multi-
celled plants and animals, including man.

> This anatomical knowledge is of the greatest significance; it is supplemented
> by the embryological proof that every higher, multicelled organism develops
> from a single simple cell, from the "fertilized egg cell." The important
> theory of cells based on this knowledge has only now opened up for us the
> true understanding of the physical, chemical, and even physiological pro-
> cesses of life for which explanations formerly assumed a supernatural "life
> force" or "immortal soul." Also, the actual nature of disease has only now
> become comprehensible to the doctor by cellular pathology, which is related
> to the aforementioned discovery.

It seemed to Haeckel, who considered the human being to be a "transitory aggregation of matter and energy," that in terms of a monistic philosophy the riddle of the world had been solved. Since the "basic cosmological law" proves the eternal preservation of force and of matter, the universal constancy of energy and of matter in the entire universe, "it has become the dependable guiding light that is leading our monistic philosophy through the enormous labyrinth of the riddle of the world to its solution."

No energy without matter, no matter without energy, was Ludwig Büchner's article of faith (in *Energy and Matter,* 1855). Energy in itself is as little conceivable as matter in itself; separated, both disintegrate into empty abstractions.

> Think of a substance without force, the smallest particles of which comprise a body, without that system of mutual attraction and repulsion which holds them together and imparts form and shape to the body; conceive of the absence of the so-called molecular forces of cohesion and affinity: what would be and what would have to be the consequence? Matter would immediately have to turn into formless nothing. In the sensual world we know no example of any particle of substance that would not be endowed with forces. By means of these forces it plays it given role, at times in one form, at times in another form, at other times in connection with similar particles of matter, and at still other times in connection with dissimilar particles of matter. But ideally we also are in no way able to form a conception of matter without energy. Let us think of a primordial substance however we wish; a system of mutual attraction and repulsion between its smallest particles would always have to take place. Without it, it would have to suspend itself and vanish without a trace in the universe.

The chthonic feeling of life brings about a rhapsodic natural science that was absolutely intoxicated by materialism and able to get along without God. "Even into our time the storm continues. Everything is in a whirl; every simplest question is being questioned. *Weltanschauungen* are collapsing, an incredible dust fills the era." (Wilhelm Bölsche) The natural scientist now thought he knew what held the world together at its innermost. The concept of development united with cell theory and the "green ethos."

> Look at that beautiful swallowtail and see how majestically it sinks down to the thyme. You, man—you, man of modern knowledge, developed from animals lower than this floating butterfly. Your tribe came from the primordial being that was still less developed than this mute thyme bathing

itself motionlessly in the glowing sun. Grotesque creatures without a trace of form is what you were—creatures that crawled along the sea's edge when this beach was still soft slime; this beach which today forms those knife-edged rocks against which the blue wave on the cape below beats itself into foam. And you are bound to all these creatures that were you and yet not you eons of time ago; bound by the incredible universal force of love, of creation, of eternal birth and becoming. Thousands and thousands of times, millions and millions of times you loved, suffered, and bled down there, were crucified and died, and nonetheless rose again on the third day. There in the past, in the immeasurable chain of this foreself of your own self that is living its peaceful Good Friday in the beauty of nature on Cape Verde lie the solutions to all your riddles, to all your deep secrets that weave through you like a dark net of fate, like a black spiderweb on which your tears shine like dewdrops.

Bölsche's *Lovelife in Nature: A Developmental History of Love* (1898) is a rhapsody to a nature "mendelizing" upward in which the ego ascends from the seething primordial slime to materialistic awareness. It ends in an acknowledgment of technological progress to which all forces and powers of time should pay homage as to a new god:

Look at that small white church over there between the raven-black cypresses. That is time which has faded away and still extends into our day. In the little yellowish tower with the small cupola there hangs a bell, green with age. It sounds of love that is not of this world. But look more closely: the cross that reaches from the cupola into the boundless miraculous blue ends at the top in a long, suspicious point. A lightning rod. The double insurance of the modern era: above the cross of mysticism the metal shaft that controls heaven's ray with the knowledge of physics, of scientific knowledge. . . . May the old green bell call when the black storm cloud throws itself like a bird of prey upon these open heights and claws with glowing talons . . . The lightning rod is stronger; it is the cross of our era.

Belief in immanence turned into hybris; the composure of the "green ethos" transformed itself into the field marshal's attitude toward natural science, which considered all battles won, all questions answered, all riddles solved.

The poetically articulated consciousness of decay formed the antithesis to such an optimistic scientism. Georg Büchner, Ludwig Büchner's brother, created in *Woyzeck* a character of dull instinct who carries the idea of belief in man as the highest of all creatures as much to the point of absurdity as the conviction that the structure of cells is the image of a clearly recognized lawfulness (73). Chaos rages in nature and in creatures; the person, having become *homo faber* from a single cell, is in the end nonetheless only a conglomeration of pure coincidences, and is moreover incalculable in his reactions. The human being: an abyss that makes one dizzy to look down into.

*Ignoramus et ignorabimus.* We do not know and also will not know. The chthonic composure of realism to which the natural scientific hybris of materialism was opposed, turned into desperate fatigue. "What is it about brains?" as it appears in Gottfried Benn's prose piece, *Brains.* This text marks the end of certainty in a materialistic interpretation of the world. Rönne, the young doctor employed in an institute for pathology, who has had two thousand corpses go through his hands without thinking about it, ends up exhausted and insane. "Pulverized foreheads—temples drifting." Nothing left but errors and confusions.

## (66) He bored his way into the universe

GEORG BÜCHNER, Lenz

Karl Georg Büchner, the son of a doctor employed in the Grand Duchy of Hesse, was born in 1813. His mother was an enthusiastic German patriot influenced by Romantic ideals of freedom. "Thus the otherwise happy marriage expressed the symptomatic extremes of the contradictions of the era—the conservatism of the father, who was justly called 'reactionary' by Karl Emil Franzos and whose adherence to the old monarchist structure compelled him to reject any liberal trend, versus the liberalism of the artistically and literarily talented mother who, influenced by German Romanticism, surely hoped for a united and possibly democratic Germany." (Gerhard P. Knapp)

After attending the *Gymnasium* Büchner studied medicine in Strassburg. In 1833 he moved to Giessen. In a letter written from Giessen he states: "The political conditions could drive me crazy. The people patiently drag the carriages on which the princes and liberals play their farce. Every night I pray to rope and lanterns."

Impressed by the 1934 uprising in France and shattered about conditions in Hesse, which were among the most extreme in the entire German Confederation, he was introduced by the pastor Friedrich Ludwig Weidig to revolutionary circles. He then wrote *The Hessian Messenger.* The work surely did more to frighten than to enlighten the peasants to whom it was addressed. Friends of the conspirator were arrested and Büchner fled into exile, first to Strassburg and then to Zurich, where he worked as a university lecturer.

Büchner died in Zurich in 1837. His drama about the French Revolution, *Danton's Death* (1834–35), was followed by an incompleted novella, *Lenz,* which focuses on the insanity and death of a person who remains untouched by any human suffering. In 1835 Büchner wrote to his family from Strassburg, "I have collected all kinds of interesting memos about one of Goethe's friends, an unhappy poet by the name of Lenz who stayed here for a while with Goethe and became halfway insane."

The 20th of January Lenz walked through the mountains. The peaks and high slopes in snow, the valleys below gray rock, green surfaces, cliffs and pines. It was cold and wet; the water trickled down the cliffs and sprang across the path. The branches of the pines dipped heavily in the moist air. Gray clouds drifted in the sky, but all so dense, and then the fog steamed upward and curled through the underbrush, heavy and damp, so sluggish, so shapeless. He walked on indifferently, unconcerned about the way, now up, now down. He felt no fatigue, only it bothered him sometimes that he could not walk on his head. At first it choked him when the rocks fell away, the gray wood shivered beneath him, and the fog now swallowed the shapes, now revealed prodigious outlines; there was an urgency in him, he was looking for something as if for lost dreams, but he found nothing. Everything appeared so small, so near, so wet; he would have liked to place the earth near the stove. He couldn't comprehend that it took so much time to climb down one slope, to reach a distant point. He thought he should be able to measure the whole distance in a couple of strides. At times the storm hurled clouds into the valley, and they steamed upward along the wood, and the voices on the cliffs awakened, now like distant resounding thunder and now rushing at him violently in tones, as if singing of the earth in wild jubilation, and the clouds burst upward like madly neighing chargers, and the sunshine came and went in between and drew its glittering sword across the peaks and into the valley. Or when the storm drove the clouds downward and tore into a lake of pale blue, and then the wind died down and far below, from the gorges, from the crowns of the pines it hummed upward like a lullaby and chiming of bells, and a soft red climbed into deep blue, and little clouds threaded their way along on silver wings, and all the mountain peaks sharp and firm sparkled and flashed far across the land. Then it tore at his lungs; he stood panting, bent forward, eyes and mouth wide open; he thought he should pull the storm into himself, pull everything inside. He stretched out and lay across the earth, he bored his way into the universe, it was a thrill that pained him. Or he lay still and rested his head upon the moss and half closed his eyes, and then it moved far away from him, the earth shrank beneath him, it became as small as a wandering star and submerged itself into a blustering storm which trailed its limpid flood beneath him. But these were only moments, and then he stood up sober, firm, as quiet as if a shadow-play had passed him by; he knew of nothing anymore. Toward evening he came to the summit of the mountains, to the snowfield from which one climbed down again and westward into the plain, and he sat down at the top. It had grown quieter toward evening; as far as the eye could see, the clouds lay firm and unmoving in the sky, nothing but peaks from which broad fields sloped downward, and everything so silent, gray, darkling; he became horribly lonely, he was alone, all alone. He wanted to talk to himself but could not; he scarcely dared to breathe; the bending of his ankle cracked like thunder beneath him and he had to sit down again. In this nothingness he was seized by a nameless fear, he was in the void, he sprang to his feet and bolted down the slope. Dusk had fallen, sky and earth merged into one. It was as if something were chasing him, as if something horrible would catch him, something that mortals cannot bear, as if madness were chasing him mounted on chargers. Finally he heard voices, he saw lights, he was relieved; they told him he had another half hour to Waldbach. He walked through the village; lights shone through the windows; he looked inside as he walked past. Children at table, old women, girls; everyone quiet; peaceful faces. It was as if the light were radiating from them. He was relieved. Soon he was in Waldbach at the parsonage. They were sitting at table when he entered; blond curls clung to his pale face, his eyes and mouth twitched, his clothes were torn. Oberlin welcomed him, thinking he was a craftsman.

"Welcome, though I do not know you."

"I am a friend of Kaufmann, and bring you his regards."

"Your name, if you please?"

"Lenz."

"Ah, well now—isn't it in print? Haven't I read some plays attributed to a gentleman by this name?"

"Yes, but be so kind as not to judge me on that basis."

They spoke further; he searched for words and talked rapidly, but it was tortuous; after a time he grew calm. The cozy room and the peaceful faces which looked out from the shadows, the bright face of the child upon which all the light seemed to focus; it looked up inquisitively and trustingly to its mother, who sat angelically silent in the darkness. He began to talk about his home; he drew all kinds of costumes, they gathered around him sympathetically, soon he felt at home. His pale childish face, which now wore a smile, his lively speech; he grew calm, it was as if old figures and forgotten faces stepped out of the darkness, old songs woke up in him. He was gone, far away. Finally it was time to go, they guided him across the street; the parsonage was too small, they gave him a room in the schoolhouse. He went upstairs, it was cold, a spacious room, empty, a tall bed in the background. He set the lamp on the table and began to pace up and down, he contemplated the day again, how he got here, where he was, the room in the parsonage with its lights and dear faces, it was like a shadow to him, a dream, and he became empty again, as upon the mountain, but he could no longer fill it with anything. A nameless fear seized him, he jumped to his feet, he ran through the room, down the stairs, before the house; it was no use, everything dark, nothing, he was a dream to himself, various thoughts occurred to him, he held on to them, it was as if he had to say "Our Father" again and again. He could no longer find himself, an obscure instinct drove him to save himself, he slammed himself against the stones, he gouged himself with his nails, the pain began to restore consciousness, he plunged into the fountain but the water was not deep. He splashed about. People came, they had heard him, they called to him. Oberlin came running; Lenz had revived, a total awareness of his situation dawned on him, again he was relieved. Now he was embarrassed and sorry that he had frightened these good people. He told them he was used to bathing in cold water and went back upstairs; finally his exhaustion let him fall asleep.

TRANSLATED BY ADRIAN DEL CARO

## (67) The gentle law

ADALBERT STIFTER, Preface to Colored Stones

The collection of stories entitled *Colored Stones* (1853) was intended as a "gift commemorating youth." The publisher had engaged Ludwig Richter to be the illustrator, but Stifter protested: "What a horror! Then all is for naught . . . . If I were the publisher, I would throw the vignettes away." The poet feared they would trivialize his intentions. The 1848 Revolution had failed, and the education of the new order of mankind was to start with the child.

The preface to *Colored Stones* is to be understood as an ethical and aesthetic profession of faith that juxtaposes to revolution a belief in evolution.

The blowing of the breezes, the trickling of water, the growing of grain, the surging of the sea, the greening of the earth, the shining of the heavens, and the shimmering of the stars are what I find great. I do not find the magnificently approaching thunderstorm, the lightning that splits houses, the strong wind that drives the surf, the volcano, the earthquake that covers countries with rubble, greater than the above phenomena; I actually find them less significant, because they are only effects of much higher laws. They occur in individual places and are the results of one-sided causes. The power that makes milk rise and boil over in the little pot of a poor woman is the same power that drives up the lava in the volcano and causes it to slide down the mountain. These manifestations are merely more conspicuous and tend to attract the attention of the ignorant and inattentive. The scientist tends to see primarily the whole and the general. In that alone he finds greatness, because it alone preserves the world. Details pass, and their effects are hardly recognizable after a short time.

We will explain this with an example. Say that each day for many years a man has observed a compass needle at certain set hours. He has seen that one tip always points north, and he makes note of the fact that variations occur whereby the needle points sometimes more directly, sometimes less directly, to the north. An unenlightened person would surely see this as a small and dilettantish beginning. But how awesome is this small matter, and how inspiring this dilettantism, when we discover that these observations are actually made all over the world and that from the tables summarizing their results one learns that many small deviations of the compass needle often occur in all parts of the earth simultaneously and to an equal extent. Thus an electrical storm affects the entire earth. The reaction is something like a magnetic shudder everywhere at once. If we had a sense organ to perceive electricity and its magnetism, just as our eyes perceive light, what a great world, what a wealth of immeasurable phenomena, would be revealed to us. But although we have no such physical eye for electricity, we do have the intellectual eye of science. This teaches us that electrical and magnetic power affects a tremendous area; that it is spread throughout the entire earth and heavens; and that it surrounds everything and shows itself to be gently and inexorably transforming, forming, and creating. Lightning is merely a very small characteristic of this power, which itself is a great power in nature.

Science only obtains grain after grain of truth, only makes observation after observation, only gleans the general from the particular. The number of phenomena and the domain of that which is given are infinitely great. God has thus made the joy and bliss of scientific discovery inexhaustible, just as in our laboratories we can only produce the individual, never the general, for that would be creation. Therefore the history of that which is great in nature consists of constantly changing views of this greatness. When men were in their childhood, and their intellectual vision had not yet been touched by science, they were struck with that which was immediate and obvious, and overcome by fear and admiration. But as their intellect awakened, when their attention began to be directed at connections, the individual phenomena sank deeper and deeper, and the law rose higher and higher. Wonders ceased; the wondrous increased.

Internal nature, that of the human race, works like external nature. What I find great is justice, simplicity, self-discipline, rationality, effective action in one's own sphere; admiration of the beautiful, combined with serene, patient endeavor. Powerful agitation of the heart, terribly thundering anger, lust for revenge, an inflamed spirit that seeks activity, tears apart, changes, destroys and in its excitement often casts down its own life—all this I do not find greater, but rather less significant. These things are hardly more than products of individual, one-sided forces, like storms, volcanoes and earthquakes.

Let us examine the gentle law that guides the human race. There are forces that aim at the survival of the individual, taking and employing everything needed for his development. They secure the stability of one and thus of all. But whenever someone insists on snatching up everything that he thinks he needs, even though he destroys thereby conditions necessary for the existence of another, then something higher in us becomes furiously angry. We help the weak and the oppressed, restoring the condition in which they can exist and go their way, human beings like any others. And when we have done this, we feel satisfied, even more so than we felt as individuals: we identify with all of mankind.

There are forces therefore that work toward the survival of mankind as a whole. Instead of being limited by individual forces, they set limits for them. It is the law of these forces, the law of justice, the law of morality, the law that intends that everyone should be respected, honored, and allowed to safely pursue his chosen career, earning himself the love and admiration of his fellowman. This law intends that everyone should be cared for as a precious jewel, for each human being is a precious jewel for all other humans. This law is found wherever men live together, and it is demonstrated when men act in relation to each other. It consists of the love of husband and wife for each other; the love of parents for children and children for parents; the love of siblings and friends, the sweet attraction between the sexes; the industriousness that supports us, the diligence with which men work in their own sphere, for those far away, for humanity—and finally it consists of the order and form with which whole societies and states surround their existence and complete it. Older as well as modern poets have often used these themes to make their works more appealing to races near and far. The scientist sees nothing but this law wherever he looks, because it is the only general law, the only one that is always valid. He sees it in the lowest hut as well as in the highest palace; he sees it in the devotion of a poor woman and in a hero's calm contempt of death as he thinks of his homeland and humanity.

Certain movements in the human race have directed our spirits toward a goal, and these have changed the form of whole eras. When the law of justice and morality is recognizable in these movements, when they are introduced and carried on according to this law, then we feel that humanity as a whole has been elevated. We feel ourselves more generally human. We feel the sublime settling in our souls, as it always does when immeasurably great forces work together in time or space to shape a whole according to the principles of reason. But when the law of justice and morality is not visible in these movements, when they wrestle for one-sided and self-centered goals, then he who would study mankind turns away from it in disgust, no matter how powerful and formidable it may be, and considers it to be trivial and unworthy of mankind. The power of this law of justice and morality is so great that it has always left the battlefield victorious and splendid, whenever it has been challenged. Yes, even though individuals or whole races have perished fighting for justice and morality, we do not see them as conquered; we see them as having triumphed. Jubilation and ecstasy are mixed with our sympathy because the whole is greater than the part, because righteousness is greater than death. We say in such cases that we perceive tragedy, and are elevated with a shudder into the purer ether of the moral law. When we see humanity approach a great, eternal goal in history like a peaceful silver stream, we experience that which is noble and can be thought of as epic.

But no matter how powerfully and deeply the tragic and epic affect us, no matter what excellent tools they are for art, it is above all the ordinary, daily, constantly recurring actions of men in which this law reveals itself most clearly. These are the long-lasting, basic actions, like a million little roots of the tree of life. In Nature general laws work quietly and unceasingly, and whatever is conspicuous is merely a single expression of these laws. The moral law likewise works quietly, refreshing the soul, through the endless contact of man with man. The ephemeral miracles we see in individual events are only minor manifestations of this general force. So it is this law that preserves mankind, while the natural law preserves the world.

Just as in natural history notions of what is great have been constantly changing, so it has been in the moral history of man. At the beginning men were affected by whatever was closest at hand. Physical strength and victories in wrestling matches were praised. Then came bravery and a warlike spirit, aimed at expressing and carrying out powerful feelings and passions against enemy hordes and confederations. Next men sang of the greatness of the clan and the power of the family; praised beauty and love as well as friendship and devotion. But then a general perspective on something greater appeared. Entire areas of human life and their interrelationships were classified; the right of the whole was united with that of the part. Generosity to the enemy and suppression of one's feelings and passions for the sake of justice were found to be noble and splendid. Indeed, moderation was thought even by the ancients to be the primary manly virtue. And finally, ties joining all peoples came to be thought desirable, for the purpose of exchanging all the talents of one people with those of another, encouraging science to reveal its treasures for all men, and leading art and religion to that which is simple but noble and divine.

The human race declines just as it rises. Decadent nations begin by losing their sense of proportion. They seek the individual; they throw themselves shortsightedly into the limited and insignificant; they set the conditional and the restricted above the general. Then they seek pleasure and the sensual. They seek satisfaction for their hate and envy of their neighbors. The one-sided is depicted in their art, that which is valid from only one standpoint; then the decaying, dissonant, fantastic; finally the sensual and exciting; and last of all immorality and vice. In religion, inwardness sinks to mere formality or to luxurious daydreaming. The distinction between good and evil disappears; the individual despises the whole and pursues his pleasure and his ruin. And thus a people becomes a victim of its inner chaos, or that of an external, more primitive, but more powerful enemy.

TRANSLATED BY MARGARET WOODRUFF

## (68) Silent cold

DETLEV VON LILIENCRON, "Acherontic Chill"

The impressionist technique of omission evokes aspects of the underworld. The apparently smooth-flowing parlando is the vehicle for cold silence, a melody of not-yet-but-soon.

At harvest feasts the fiddles jubilated,
But now the starling eats the rowan berries.
And only wait, for all the leaves are fated
To fall beneath the scissors autumn carries.
With emptiness the woods are penetrated.
I'll see through branches naked then and airy
A stream and on it, long anticipated,
My transport into silent cold, the ferry.

TRANSLATED BY SHARON JACKIW

## (69) Birth and death belong equally to life

ARTHUR SCHOPENHAUER, The World as Will and Representation

The myth of chthonic power has its origin in the horror of death. Schopenhauer's text expresses thoughts also characteristic of Johann Jacob Bachofen's works (for example: *The Law of the Mothers: Gynecocracy in Antiquity, Symbolism on Graves in Antiquity*). "When man has been deserted by everything, the earth and its growing things still lovingly embrace the petrifying house."

As the will is the thing-in-itself, the inner content, the essence of the world, but life, the visible world, the phenomenon, is only the mirror of the will, this world will accompany the will as inseparably as a body is accompanied by its shadow; and if will exists, then life, the world, will exist. Therefore life is certain to the will-to-live, and as long as we are filled with the will-to-live we need not be apprehensive for our existence, even at the sight of death. It is true that we see the individual come into being and pass away; but the individual is only phenomenon, exists only for knowledge involved in the principle of sufficient reason, in the *principium individuationis*. Naturally, for this knowledge, the individual receives his life as a gift, rises out of nothing, and then suffers the loss of this gift through death, and returns to nothing. We, however, wish to consider life philosophically, that is to say, according to its Ideas, and then we shall find that neither the will, the thing-in-itself in all phenomena, nor the subject of knowing, the spectator of all phenomena, is in any way affected by birth and death. Birth and death belong only to the phenomenon of the will, and hence to life; and it is essential to this that it manifest itself in individuals that come into being and pass away, as fleeting phenomena, appearing in the form of time, of that which in itself knows no time, but must be manifested precisely in the way aforesaid in order to objectify its real nature. Birth and death belong equally to life, and hold the balance as mutual conditions of each other, or, if the expression be preferred, as poles of the whole phenomenon of life. The wisest of all mythologies, the Indian, expresses this by giving to the very god who symbolizes destruction and death (just as Brahma, the most sinful and lowest god of the Trimurti, symbolizes generation, origination, and Vishnu preservation), by giving, I say, to Shiva as an attribute not only the necklace of skulls, but also the lingam, that symbol of generation which appears as the counterpart of death. In this way it is intimated that generation and death are essential correlatives which reciprocally neutralize and eliminate each other. It was precisely the same sentiment that prompted the Greeks and Romans to adorn the costly sarcophagi, just as we still see them, with feasts, dances, marriages, hunts, fights between wild beasts, bacchanalia, that is with presentations of life's most powerful urge. This they present to us not only through such diversions and merriments, but even in sensual groups, to the point of showing us the sexual intercourse between satyrs and goats. The object was obviously to indicate with the greatest emphasis from the death of the mourned individual the immortal life of nature, and thus to intimate, although without abstract knowledge, that the whole of nature is the phenomenon, and also the fulfillment, of the will-to-live. The form of this phenomenon is time, space, and causality, and through these individuation, which requires that the individual must come into being and pass away. But this no more disturbs the will-to-live—the individual being only a particular example or specimen, so to speak, of the phenomenon of this will—than does the death of an individual injure the whole of nature. For it is not the individual that nature cares for, but only the species; and in all seriousness she urges the preservation of the species, since she provides for this so lavishly through the immense surplus of the seed and the great strength of the fructifying impulse. The individual, on the contrary, has no value for nature, and can have none, for infinite time, infinite space, and the infinite number of possible individuals therein are her kingdom. Therefore nature is always ready to let the individual fall, and the individual is accordingly not only exposed to destruction in a thousand ways from the most insignificant accidents, but is even destined for this and is led toward it by nature herself, from the moment that individual has served the maintenance of the species. In this way, nature quite openly expresses the great truth that only the Ideas, not individuals, have reality proper, in other words are a complete objectivity of the will. Now man is nature herself, and indeed nature at the highest grade of her self-consciousness, but nature is only the objectified will-to-live; the person who has grasped and retained this point of view may certainly and justly console himself for his own death and for that of his friends by looking back on the immortal life of nature, which he himself is. Consequently, Shiva with the lingam is to be understood in this way, and so are those ancient sarcophagi that their pictures of glowing life exclaim to the lamenting beholder: *Natura non contristatur.*

TRANSLATED BY E. F. J. PAYNE

## (70) The horizon

ALEXANDER VON HUMBOLDT, Journey to the Equinoctial Regions of the New Continent

Alexander von Humboldt, the younger brother of Wilhelm von Humboldt, was born in Berlin in 1769. Georg Forster, who earlier had accompanied his father on James Cook's second trip to the South Seas, was of great importance in Alexander von Humboldt's scientific development. Humboldt also accompanied Forster in 1790 on a trip up the Rhine via Cologne and Holland to England. Humboldt was in his thirties when he visited Latin America; he subsequently traveled to many countries. Charles Darwin believed him to be the most important scientific traveler of all time. His broad education made him capable of a universal perspective: "My eyes must constantly be focused on the cooperation of forces, on the influence of inanimate creation on the living world of animals and plants."

The description of the trip into the equinoctial regions of the new continent comprises thirty volumes.

What the seafarer observes as he approaches a new country, the traveler also notices along the edge of the steppes. The horizon begins to widen toward the north where the vault of heaven no longer seems to rest on the grass-covered soil at the same distance.

A *llanero* or dweller of the steppe only feels at ease when he "can see all around him," as the naive popular saying has it. What seems to us a grass-covered, slightly undulating, occasionally barely hilly country is, for him, a horrible land full of mountains. Our judgment about the uneven-ness of the terrain and the nature of its surface is a completely relative one. When one has spent several months in the dense forests along the Orinoco and has become used to being able to see the stars only close to the zenith, and as if one were looking at them from inside a well, the moment one moves away from the river, traveling across the steppes has something pleasant and attractive about it. The new sights one takes in make a great impression. Like the llanero, one feels at ease because one can see so well in all directions. But this satisfaction is short-lived (we had personal experience of this). True, the prospect of an endless horizon is a serious and grandiose thing. The spectacle fills us with admiration, whether we find ourselves on a peak in the Andes, or in the Alps, or somewhere on the infinite ocean, the extensive plains of Venezuela or in Tucumán province. The immensity of the space (poets have spoken of this in all languages) reflects itself in us. It combines with ideas of a higher order, it expands the soul of the person who finds his pleasure in the stillness of solitary contemplation. Yet the sight of unlimited space varies in character from place to place. The spectacle one enjoys on a free-standing mountain peak shifts, depending on whether the clouds below spread out in layers, gather in masses or allow the surprised glance to drop through broad cracks onto the homes of human beings, the tilled soil, the whole green floor of the ocean of air. A gigantic expanse of water, inhabited down to the bottom by thousands of different creatures, changing in coloration and appearance, mobile at the surface like the element which stirs it, has a considerable attraction for the imagination during a long voyage; but the steppe, which is dusty and cracked for much of the year, makes one melancholy through its unending monotony. If, after an eight- or ten-day march one has become accustomed to the play of mirages and the glossy green of the Mauritia bushes that appear every mile or so, one feels the need for more variegated impressions; one longs for the sight of the powerful trees of the tropics, wild mountain torrents, the regions and valleys tilled by the peasant's hand. If, unluckily, the phenomenon of the African deserts and of the llanos or savannahs of the new world (a phenomenon whose origin is lost in the darkness of the earliest history of our planet) were to occupy an even more extensive area, nature would be without some of those splendid products which are indigenous to the tropical zones.

TRANSLATED BY MICHAEL SHAW

## (71) The village and its mountain

ADALBERT STIFTER, Rock Crystal

The children of the shoemaker of Gschaid visit their grandmother in Millsdorf on the day before the Christmas celebration. On their way home they are surprised by a severe snow storm. They lose their way and wander into the icy regions of the snow-capped mountain. They seek protection in a cave, but the sound of the cracking ice keeps waking them up, which is what saves their lives.

The village stands for the cosmos, security, homeland. The snow-covered mountain and its "icy severity" stands for the implacability of Aorgic nature.

In the high mountains of our fatherland lies a little village with a small but very pointed church steeple, which stands out among the green of abundant fruit trees because of the red color of its shingles. Because of the same red color, it is visible from afar in the fragrant and blue twilight of the mountains. The little village lies in the middle of a rather broad valley, which is shaped almost like an oval. In addition to the church there are a school, a village hall, and several other stately houses which form a square, upon which four lindens stand, with a stone cross set in the middle. These houses are not only farm houses, but they also shelter those trades which are indispensable to mankind and which are intended to fulfill the highlanders' only demand for man-made goods. In the valley and upon the mountains there are many other cottages scattered about, as is customary in the highlands, which do not all belong to the church and the school, but also to those trades mentioned earlier, by virtue of selling goods to pay their debt. Other cottages also belong to the village, which cannot be seen at all from the valley because they are hidden deep in the mountains; their dwellers seldom come out to visit their fellow villagers, and in winter they must often store their dead away, in order to bring them to burial after the melting of the snows. The greatest personage whom the villagers see during the course of a year is the pastor. They revere him greatly, and it usually happens that he becomes accustomed to solitude from his long sojourn in the village, and that he does not stay reluctantly and simply survive. At least as far back as anyone can remember, it was not witnessed that the village pastor had been an excessively roving man, or one unworthy of his station.

No roads lead through the valley. They have their double-trcked trails, which are used to convey produce from the fields to their homes in little one-horse carts. For this reason few people come to the valley, but among these few an occasional hiker who is a lover of nature and lives for a time in the painted upper story of the inn, and watches the mountains; or even a painter who sketches, on the small easel from his portfolio, the little pointed steeple and the beautiful peaks of the crags. So the inhabitants constitute a separate world, they all know one another by name and by the individual histories of grandfather and great-grandfather; they mourn together when someone dies, know his name; know when someone is born; have a language that deviates from the plain outside; have their quarrels, which they settle; stand by one another and get together when something extraordinary occurs.

They are quite constant, and things always stay the same. If a stone falls from a wall, it is put back again; the new houses are built as the old, the damaged rooftops are repaired with the same shingles, and if one household has dappled cows, the same calves are raised, and the color remains with the household.

Toward the south from the village one can see a snow-capped mountain, which seems to be just above the rooftops with its gleaming horns, but in fact it is not so near. The whole year round, summer and winter, it looks down into the valley with its jutting cliffs and its white surfaces. As the most notable thing that the inhabitants have in their environment, the mountain is an object of consideration among them, and it has become the focus of many stories. There is no man young or old in the village who could not speak of the mountain's peaks and crags, crevasses and caves, of its streams and rubble slides, which he has experienced on his own or heard about from another. This mountain is also the pride of the village, as if they had made it themselves, and it is not quite certain that the inhabitants of the valley, in spite of their highly acclaimed uprightness and love of truth, do not on occasion tell a lie for the honor and glory of their mountain. In addition to being the local curiosity, the mountain also provides a real use; for when a party of travelers comes along, in order to climb the mountain from the valley, the villagers serve as guides. To have once been a guide, to have experienced this or that, to have known this or that spot is a distinction that everyone gladly acknowledges. They often talk about it when they sit together in the inn tavern and recount their daring and wonderful experiences, and they never fail to mention what this or that traveler had said, and what they had received from him as a payment for their efforts. And the mountain sends its water down from the snowfields, which feeds into a lake in the timber forests and creates a brook which flows merrily through the valley, turning the sawmill, the grinding mill and other small works, cleaning the village and watering the livestock. Wood is taken from the forests on the mountain, and they also hold back the avalanches. The water seeps through inner passages and cavities of the heights, then it flows in arteries through the valley and appears as little springs and wells from which the people drink, and offer their highly praised water to visitors. But they do not think about these uses, and simply believe things had always been this way.

If one were to observe the annual calendar of the mountain, then in winter the two crags of its pinnacle, which they call horns, are snowy white and stand dazzling in the dark blue of the air. If they are visible by daylight, all the surfaces lying around these peaks are then white, all the slopes, even the steepest walls, which the inhabitants call palisades, are covered with a sprinkling of white hoar and with fragile ice like a varnish, so that the entire mass towers forth like a magic palace from the hoary gray of the forest base, which spreads heavily about its feet. In the summer, when sun and warm wind erase the snow from the steep sides, the horns, according to the expression of the inhabitants, tower up black against the sky and have beautiful white veins and speckles on their backs, but in fact they are of a delicate distant blue, and what they call veins and speckles is not white, but has the milky blue of the distant snow against the darker blue of the crags. The surfaces around the horns do not lose their perpetual snow on the upper parts even when it is really hot, and precisely then it shines down very white upon the green of the valley trees. The winter snow, which had only been a down, recedes from the lower parts. The vague iridescence of blue and green becomes visible then; it is the detrital ice which lies exposed and looks down upon the inhabitants. At the edge of this iridescence, where from a distance it looks like a border of gem fragments, there lies close by a confusion of wild, gigantic boulders, sloping rocks and debris, which crowd against one another and are forcibly entangled. If a summer is quite hot and long, the ice fields are exposed far upward, and then a much larger surface of blue and green looks into the valley. Many summits and spaces which are otherwise only to be seen in white are exposed, the dirty fringe of the ice grows visible where crags, earth and mud are pushed along, and much more copiously than usual the water flows into the valley. This goes on until finally the autumn comes, the water diminishes, and at some time a gray and lasting rain covers the entire plain and valley. When the fog lifts from the heights, the mountain has once again donned its soft cover, and all the crags, cones and peaks stand there dressed in white. Thus one year after the other drifts by with only minor changes, and will continue to drift by as long as nature remains as it is, and there is snow on the mountain and people in the valley. The valley people call the minor changes big, note them well and reckon the progress of the year by them. They designate the heat and exceptions of the summers by the bare surfaces.

As concerns the climbing of the mountain, this is done from the valley. One walks in a southerly direction along a good, clear path which leads across a so-called neck into another valley. Neck refers to a fairly high ridge that connects two larger and important mountains. Upon the neck, which connects the snow-capped mountain with an adjacent large mountain chain, there is nothing but pine forest. At about the highest elevation of this forest, where the path into the valley beyond eventually begins to slope downward, stands a so-called accident post. Once a baker who carried bread in his basket across the neck was found dead in this spot. The dead baker with his basket and the surrounding pines were painted into a picture, inscribed below it were an explanation and a request for prayers, the picture was mounted on a wooden post painted red, and the post was erected at the site of the accident. At this post one turns off the path and walks along the length of the neck, instead of hiking across its breadth into the valley beyond. The pines form a pass there, as if a road passed between them. Sometimes there is a path leading in this direction, for the purpose of bringing wood from the higher regions down to the accident post, but it grows over again with grass. If one walks along this path, which gently slopes upward, one arrives at length at a clear space bare of trees. This is parched heath soil, without so much as a shrub, but overgrown with feeble Scotch heather, dried mosses and parched creeping plants. The space becomes steeper and steeper, and one walks uphill for a long time, but always within a furrow like a rounded ditch, which has the advantage that one cannot become easily lost in the large, treeless and monotonous space. After a time cliffs appear, which rise straight up from the grassy ground like churches, and between whose walls one can continue to walk uphill. Then bare, almost plantless ridges appear, towering into the airy spaces of the higher regions and leading directly to the ice. On both sides of this path are steep walls, and by this dam the snow-capped mountain is connected with the neck. In order to conquer the ice, one walks for a long time along its edge, where it is encircled by the cliffs, until one gets to the older, perpetual snow that bridges the crevasses and during most times in the year will support the wanderer. At the highest point of the perpetual snow, the two horns rise up, of which one is the higher and therefore the summit of the mountain. These peaks are very hard to climb. Because they are encircled by a now broad, now narrow furrow of snow—the perpetual snow crevasse—which must be leapt across, and because their steepest walls have only small ledges for footholds, most mountain climbers are content to reach the perpetual snow crevasse, and to enjoy the panorama from there as far as it is not obstructed by the horn. Those who would climb the peak must do this with the help of climbing irons, ropes and clamps.

In addition to this mountain there are others on the southern side, but none is as high, even if they are covered with snow early in autumn and keep it until deep into spring. The summer always takes it away, and the crags gleam cordially in the sunshine, and the woods lying lower display their gentle green shot through with broad, blue shadows which are so beautiful one cannot get enough to see in an entire lifetime.

On the other sides of the valley, namely north, east and west, the mountains are elongated and lower, some fields and meadows rise rather high, and above them one sees various clearings, alpine cottages and such. These have their perimeter high against the sky at a finely indented forest, and it is precisely this indentation which designates their lesser height. The southern mountains, even though they harbor still more magnificent forests, nonetheless reach up to the brilliant sky with a perfectly smooth border.

If one stands more or less in the center of the valley, one has the impression that nowhere does a path lead into this basin, and nowhere does one lead out; only those who have spent a lot of time in the mountains are familiar with this illusion: in fact, not only do various paths lead out into the northern plains, and among them even some which are on level ground due to the shifting of the mountains, but toward the south, where the valley seems to be almost closed by precipitous walls, a path leads across the above-mentioned neck.

The little village is called Gschaid, and the snow-capped mountain which gazes down upon its houses is called Gars.

TRANSLATED BY ADRIAN DEL CARO

## (72) The miracle is the law

RUDOLF VIRCHOW, Four Speeches on Life and Illness

The discovery of the cell as the building block of both plant and animal organisms occurred in 1838 and 1839. Drawing on that knowledge, Rudolf Virchow (1821–1902) recognized that both morbid processes and normal life constitute a biological event that takes place in the cell. Medicine in the second half of the nineteenth century was characterized by a preoccupation with cellular pathology that led to the therapeutic benefits of pharmacology.

Virchow championed socialization of medical services that would entitle rich and poor alike to the same claim to treatment. An expanded health-care system was to be used in combatting epidemics (tuberculosis, cholera, trichinosis). However, Virchow worked mainly in anthropology, folklore, ethnology, prehistory, and archaeology. He was politically committed to the 1848 movement. He was the city commissioner of Berlin and co-founder of the progressive party, and he served in the Prussian house of deputies after 1861. "His quick-wittedness and sarcasm in parliamentary debate created great difficulties for his opponents. He made trouble for Bismarck, even to the point of personal enmity, not because he wanted anything for himself but because he simply defended what he considered right. His parliamentary speeches also revealed him to be a doctor and a friend of man. He opposed the death penalty and fought anti-Semitism, supported the amity of peoples, and was particularly energetic in promoting good relations between the new German Reich and France. His social programs included the introduction of a 'normal working day' to leave workers enough time to obtain further training; educational reforms to facilitate the training of young people to think; the removal of financial barriers to secondary school and university education for talented students; state guarantee of medical treatment for the ill; and financial assistance for the poor and disadvantaged elderly." (Paul Diepgen)

Life is the activity of the cell and its peculiarity is the peculiarity of the cell. The cell is a living body made up of certain chemical substances and structured according to a specific law. Its activity changes with the substance which forms it and which it contains. Its function changes, intensifies and abates. It begins and ends with the change, the accumulation and the decrease of this substance. But in its elements, this substance does not differ from the matter of the inorganic, inanimate world from which it rather continually replenishes itself and into which it subsides again after it has fulfilled its special purpose. It is only its makeup that is distinctive, the particular arrangement of the smallest particles; and yet it is not so peculiar as to form a contrast to the kind of order or arrangement inorganic chemistry tells us about. The kind of activity, the special work of the organic substance, seems curious to us; and yet it does not differ from the activity and work which is known to the physics of inanimate nature. What is distinctive is no more than that the greatest variety of combinations of the substance is pressed together into the smallest space; that every cell constitutes a center of the most intimate workings of the most manifold combinations on each other; and that therefore successes are obtained which occur nowhere else in nature since a similar impingement of reciprocal effects is known nowhere else.

But although life is very special and distinctive and inward, it yet does not escape the rule of chemical and physical laws. Rather, every new step on the path of knowledge takes us closer to the understanding of those chemical and physical processes which are the bases of life itself. Every peculiarity of life finds its explanation in special anatomical or chemical arrangements, in special dispositions of the substance which expresses, through this disposition, the properties that everywhere attach to it though in a way that seems quite different from what it is in the inorganic world. But this difference is merely apparent, for the electric event in the nerve does not differ in kind from that in the telegraph cable or in the cloud during a thunderstorm. The living body produces its warmth just as warmth is produced in a stove. Starch in plants and animals is converted into sugar as in a factory. These are not diametrically opposite but rather distinct processes.

The living cell is thus only a part that exists for itself in which known chemical substances with their ordinary properties are combined in a special way and become active in a manner that corresponds to this combination and their properties. This activity can only be a mechanical one. It is vain to try to show that life and mechanics are opposites. All experience leads to the same conclusion, that life is a special kind of movement of certain substances which become active through an inner necessity when they are excited, when they receive an "impulse." Their living activity brings a change of the living parts or, rather, as long as the parts are still living, their every change presents itself to us as the impulse of an activity, as something that stimulates an expression of life. When a muscle contracts, the smallest parts inside it arrange themselves differently from the way they do during a state of rest.

At the same time, chemical changes occur through which certain of these small parts are destroyed. But the muscle does not contract on its own—it is not its own impulse to inner change, to activity—but receives the stimulus from outside and cannot choose whether to contract or not. It must contract if the outer stimulus is sufficient to rouse its inner parts from their rest.

### The law of causality also applies to organic nature

Is this not materialism pure and simple? That is the question that is customarily raised these days, and its very formulation contains a judgment. How small the number of those who will just take the trouble to wait for an answer! As if it were obvious that the judgment would have to be damning if the answer should be affirmative! Though it strongly contradicts traditional prejudices, might experience not prove a better guide and might it not be more justifiable to demand the sacrifice of prejudices than to pronounce sentence on experience? But the mechanical conception of life is not in fact materialism. For what can be meant by this word except the tendency to want to explain everything that exists and happens from the matter known to us? Materialism goes beyond experience: to every phenomenon, it applies the narrow yardstick of its knowledge. It constitutes itself as a system.

Systems have great significance in the natural sciences but only when they are derived from experience. But most systems are much more the result of speculation than of experience because they carry within them the need for completeness and this need can be satisfied only by speculation. For all experiential knowledge is incomplete and fragmentary. That is why in today's natural science there is such aversion to and, in some of its branches, even a certain fear of, systems. They are countenanced for purposes of ordering and classifying known material but only with extreme caution when explanation is at stake. The worry that one might go beyond the limits of experiential knowledge is so widespread that even the writers most often accused of materialism carefully avoid constructing a system.

The mechanical view is so unmaterialist that even religious conceptions cannot dispense with it. The Old Testament states specifically: "And the Lord God formed man of the dust of the ground, and breathed into his nostrils the breath of life," and ". . . the rib which the Lord God had taken from man, made he a woman . . ." Indeed, this idea of the earthly, mechanical creation of man who will again turn to the dust from which he was taken, so completely dominates the religions that have come down to us that today's natural science certainly cannot be reproached with being more mechanical. Rather, its mechanics is less crude. It does not stop at the roughest, most general expression but attempts to use the more advanced experiences of our time to discover how even the smallest events fit into the overall scheme of creation.

There are those who pretend that all ideal conceptions, all poetic fragrance, are being destroyed in this way. One feels sorry for the researcher who frees himself of the illusions of childhood. One timidly turns away from an investigation that no longer stops at the superficial appearance of things but penetrates their inner nature. People imagine that the heart of the scientist closes itself to the moving images of heaven and earth; that it is for nought that nature clothes itself in its most beautiful colors; for nought that it appears in surprising shapes: Before the cold eye of the scientist, color and shape dissolve and all he sees are the atoms of the substance which move without freedom and meaning. It is only itself and its triumphs that natural science admires. Making a divinity of itself, it feels no admiration, no adoration for a greatness that is alien to it. What confusion! One need not be a scientist to have a cold heart or a closed mind, to be so self-infatuated that one becomes hardened and incapable of any kind of regard for the merit of others or any stirrings of admiration. The philosophical schools of antiquity already enjoined us: *nil admirari!*

It is in the nature and mood of the individual and in the education of the masses that we must look for the reason why individuals at a given time, and masses at various times, differ so much in their inclination to now see the world of phenomena in images, now more objectively; indeed why at various times even the individual will tend to feel or to think, to be a poet or a scientist. During earlier times of the history of nations, the voices of the gods themselves spoke from the thundercloud and the rainbow was the real bridge between heaven and earth. In our later times, the child, the more delicate female, the enthusiastic poet, may follow the course of the "cloud's messenger" with hopeful or hesitant glance, or discern all sorts of strange or familiar shapes in the formless mist: ghosts or animals, human faces or distant mountains. Is a calm man to follow such dreamers? Must the supernatural be invoked every time, or need one surrender to every whim of an unbridled imagination to discover the charms nature holds?

There is a comet in the skies, more splendid and radiant than any that has been seen in a long time. Are we again to interpret it as a warning or as a threat to the sinful tribe which heralds difficult times, famine and pestilence? Or should we take it as the cheerful prognosis of a good year for wine? Heaven no longer has the sort of messengers whom it can send forth whenever it pleases and who serve this or that end. The astronomer calculates even the path of the comet and determines its period of revolution. Someday it will return, and *must* return at that specific moment.

Yet, when human eyes contemplate it at that future time, when another generation with much wider knowledge perhaps awaits its appearance, will the blaze of its powerful sheaf of fire arouse less admiration? Won't the appearance of this wanderer from afar even then produce in feeling beings that sense of trepidation and wonder which every sight of what is great calls forth in us?

No, science does not dim the sense of the beautiful, it does not dull the impression of the sublime, it does not deaden the emotion which the recognition of the good and the purposeful arouses in us. Even our hearts take delight in the snowy ridges of the mountains, the blue lines of the hills, the succulent green of the plain, the rippling wave of the brook or the ornament of the flower. We also are driven out of doors by the longing for the pure enjoyment a calm contemplation of nature can bring. Our imagination also is busy painting pictures of distant affairs, magically evoking for us events of the past and the future, projecting into the present new combinations and forms.

But our imagination has no need of illusions. Why conceive of every tree as inhabited by a dryad when we know from experience that there is a much ampler life than imagining what such a subordinate deity would offer us? Why people every cleft with trolls when the forces of the rocks, the waters and the air, the antagonistic and cooperative workings of warmth, of plant and animal life disclose for us so vast and rich a picture of activities? Is it that the knowledge of the operation of the law is inimical to every emotion, every sentiment? On the contrary, it heightens the excitement, and it merely depends on our mood whether this excitement will direct itself to the beautiful, the sublime or the touching. The scientist has no need of the thunderstorm, the comet or the uncommon natural phenomenon to have such feelings. Even the overcast sky of an autumn day, the daily rising and setting of the sun, the most ordinary and most humble events of his own life offer him unending material not only for the mind but also for the soul. And if the miracle loses the quality of illusion, if it appears to us as the revelation of the law itself, is the law therefore less miraculous, the miracle less astonishing? Can one really believe that the human soul would lose a source of exhilaration if the illusion, that the miracle is a unique act, were to be destroyed? That it is intended only in this particular instance? Isn't it much more moving to suddenly see in the miracle the law in a blinding brightness, the law which the veil of mystery ordinarily hides from our spirit? ·

The miracle is the law and the law works mechanically, through causality and necessity. The cause is necessarily followed by the effect and the effect in turn becomes the cause of a new effect. One brings about the other in an ordinary or an extraordinary manner, but equally miraculous in either case. However, the unusual does more to stimulate not just our soul but also our mind; it produces more lasting impressions and advances us further when we are capable of understanding it. But we understand it only in its mechanical progress, from cause to effect. For the human mind is incapable of any other kind of understanding.

TRANSLATED BY MICHAEL SHAW

## (73) Creature

GEORG BÜCHNER, Woyzeck

The dramatic fragment *Woyzeck* was written in 1836–37. The three extant manuscripts do not provide conclusive indications of the planned final version. The poet Büchner was inspired by several criminal cases of the time, and the content derives from reality. A certain Johann Christian Woyzeck had stabbed his lover in 1821, in Leipzig. The motive was jealousy, caused by general delusions of madness. The privy councilor J.C.S. Clarus declared Woyzeck to be sound of mind. Woyzeck was condemned to death and, after a refusal to pardon him on the basis of a second judgment by Dr. Clarus's that was confirmed by the medical faculty of the University of Leipzig, Woyzeck was beheaded in the Leipzig marketplace.

In Büchner's work Woyzeck is the victim. The external circumstances of an oppressive series of events and his own increasing confusion are mutually determined, driving Woyzeck to the destruction of his happiness and of his existence. "However, he is unable to distinguish between the causes and their consequences. At this point the moralist Büchner provides only an intimation. Particularly in view of the fact that the text remained incomplete, it is necessary to keep in mind the view expressed by him earlier in a letter to his parents in February 1834: . . . in view of a greater guilt, the innocence of the involved (simply . . . 'because it lies in no one's power to avoid becoming a fool or a criminal'). The guilt is neither the fault of the murderer Woyzeck nor of his victim. Nor of the tormentors either, who after all are themselves tortured in the end. It is inherent in the givens of a social and economic order that sends the love between Woyzeck and Marie to ruin, that threatens a human and dignified existence, and that must ultimately destroy the driven and inwardly menaced existence of a Woyzeck." (Gerhard P. Knapp)

*Doctor:* What's this I find, Woyzeck? A man of your word!

*Woyzeck:* What is it, Doctor?

*Doctor:* I saw you, Woyzeck. You pissed in the street, you pissed against the wall like a dog! Two groschen a day, and you do that to me! Woyzeck, that's bad. The world's getting bad, very bad.

*Woyzeck:*   But Doctor, when Nature calls!

*Doctor:*   When Nature calls, when Nature calls! Haven't I shown you
that the *musculus constrictor vesicae* is subject to the will? Nature! Man's
free, Woyzeck, individuality's transformed into freedom in man. Not
to be able to hold your urine! (Shakes his head, puts his hands behind
his back, and paces up and down) Did you eat your peas, Woyzeck?
Well, there'll be a revolution in science, I'm going to blow it sky high.
Urea 0/10, *hydrochloraton ammonium,* hyperoxydic.

    Woyzeck, don't you have to piss again? Please go in and try.

*Woyzeck:*   Can't, Doctor.

*Doctor* (with fervor):   But you can piss against a wall! I've got it in writing, I've got the contract in my hand! I saw it, with my own eyes I
saw it. I had just stuck my nose out the window and given it some
sunlight in order to observe the process of sneezing. (Approaches him)
Don't worry, Woyzeck, I'm not angry, anger's unhealthy, unscientific.
I'm calm, quite calm. My pulse is its normal 60 and I'm telling you
with the utmost composure. Woe to the man who'd get angry at a
human being—a human being! Not if it were a Proteus ready to croak!
But you shouldn't have pissed against the wall—

*Woyzeck:*   Look, Doctor, sometimes you got a certain character, a certain . . . structure. But it's different with Nature, with Nature, see
(cracking his knuckles), it's like, oh,—how should I say?—for instance . . .

*Doctor:*   Woyzeck, you're philosophizing again.

*Woyzeck:* (confidentially)   Listen, Doctor, did you ever see double nature?
When the sun stops dead at noon and it's like the world's going up in
flames, a horrible voice has spoke to me!

*Doctor:*   Woyzeck, you've got an *aberratio.*

*Woyzeck:*   (puts his finger to his nose)   Toadstools, Doctor, that's what
it is. Did you ever see what shapes those toadstools make on the
ground? That would be something to figure out!

*Doctor:*   Woyzeck, you've got a fine case of *aberratio mentalis partialis,*
second species, very well advanced! You'll get a raise for that! Second
species, *idée fixe,* generally rational state of mind. Doing everything as
usual? Shaving the captain?

*Woyzeck:*   Oh, yes, sir.

*Doctor:*   Eating your peas?

*Woyzeck:*   Same as ever, Doctor. Housekeeping money goes to my wife.

*Doctor:*   Going on duty?

*Woyzeck:* Yes, sir.

*Doctor:* You're an interesting *casus.* Woyzeck, my subject, your're due for a raise! Now just behave and show me your pulse! Uh huh.

*Scene: Captain, Doctor*

*Captain:* Doctor, horses make me nervous. When I think that the poor beasts have to get around on foot! Don't run away like that. Don't paddle your cane in the air like that. You know you're courting death that way. A good man with a clean conscience doesn't walk that fast. A good man. (He grabs the doctor by the coat) Doctor, permit me to save a human life, you're aiming . . . Doctor, I've been so melancholy, there's something excitable about me; I always have to cry when I see my coat hanging up on the wall, how it hangs.

*Doctor:* Hmm! Neck's swollen up, thick, fatty. Apoplectic constitution. Well, Captain, it looks like you're developing *apoplexia cerebralis,* but you may get it only on one side, and then be paralyzed on that side, or else at best be brain-damaged and then just vegetate. Those are roughly your prospects for the next 4 weeks. Also I can assure you that you promise to be a most interesting case, and God willing, your tongue is part paralyzed too. We'll make some quite immortal experiments.

*Captain:* Doctor, don't frighten me, you know there are people who've died from fright, from sheer and utter fright!

*Doctor* (holds out his hat): What's this, Captain? A numbskull!

*Captain* (puts a fold in it): What's this, Doctor? A fool's fold?

*Doctor:* Good day, worthy Drillmasterprick.

*Captain:* To you too, my dear Master Coffinnail.

TRANSLATED BY DAVID JACOBSON

## (74) Temples drifting

GOTTFRIED BENN, Brains

The motifs of death and decomposition characterize Gottfried Benn's early expressionist poetry. Benn, the son of a Protestant minister, was born in 1886. He first studied theology and then medicine. Starting in 1917, he worked as a specialist in skin and venereal diseases. He died in Berlin in 1956. His volume of poetry entitled *Morgue* was published in 1912; the novel *Brains,* written before World War I, in 1915. In a prose work of the year 1913, it is stated: "For years I lived only in the echo of my screams, starving and on the brink of nothingness. Beyond good and evil—stupid literary phrase. Beyond cancer and syphilis and heart attack and suffocation—it was that whole horrible life of the gods before they created their earth. In my village everything was formerly related to God and death, never to anything earthly. Things then stood firmly where they belonged and reached down into the earth's heart.

"Until I was felled by the plague of knowledge: nothing happens except in my brain. Then things started to vacillate, became contemptible, and hardly worth looking at. And even the big things: who is God? And who is death? Trivialities. Heraldic animals. Words from my mother's mouth. Now there was no longer anything that sustained me. Above all depths there was only my breath. The thou was now dead. Now everything was dead— redemption, sacrifice, and extinction. Until I found the exit from myself: in colonies from my blood. They ought to become homeland. Comfort, earth, heaven, revenge, dialogue."

*Anyone who thinks we can lie with words*
*might think that's what was going on here.*

Rönne, a young doctor who had previously done a lot of autopsies, was traveling from southern Germany to the north. He had spent the last few months idly. For two years he'd been employed at a pathology institute, meaning that approximately two thousand corpses had passed mechanically through his hands, and this had worn him out in some odd, obscure way.

Now he was sitting in his corner seat, staring into his journey: so, it goes over vineyard country, he said to himself, rather flat, by fields of scarlet burning with poppies. It's not very hot out; the sky's a flood of deep blue, humid, blown in from the coast. The houses here look like they're leaning against the rose bushes, some look quite submerged. I think I should buy a notebook and a pencil. I should jot down as much as possible now, to keep it all from flowing away. All these years I've been living, and everything's gotten submerged. Did things stick with me when I was starting out? I can't tell anymore.

And then in a series of tunnels his eyes would wait to take in light again. There were men working in the hay; wooden bridges, stone bridges; a town and a wagon, over the hills, in front of a house.

Verandas, lodges, carriage houses, built into the woods, on hill tops— here was a place where Rönne would have liked to take over as chief physician for a few weeks. Life is so all powerful; this hand of mine will never be able to thwart it, he thought, staring down at his right one.

At the hospital site there was no one but the staff and the sick. The

institute was high up. Rönne was in a solemn mood; haloed in his loneliness, he discussed official business with the nurses, cool and aloof.

He left all the work to them. The switching of levers, fastening of
lamps, motor propulsion, lighting this and that with a mirror—it relieved him to see science reduced to a series of maneuvers, somewhere
between a blacksmith's and a clockmaker's. Then picking up his own
hands he passed them over an x-ray tube, shifted the mercury of a quartz
lamp, opened or tightened an aperture that cast light on someone's back,
stuck a funnel into someone's ear, took some cotton, propped it in the
auditory canal, and in so doing was raised in the estimation of the ear's
owner. The way images formed of the helper, of healing, of the good
doctor, of general trust and life-affirmation, and distance from superfluous
things got confused with something spiritual. Then there was an accident, and he took a small wooden splint, padded with cotton, pushed it
under the injured finger, wound a heavy bandage around it, and mused
how like this finger he seemed; how, in the leap over a grave or over
disregarded roots, through pride or recklessness, in every connection he
was broken off from the course and the fate of this life, having to maintain it now like an alien or a fugitive. He listened in the distance for a
dim voice that was becoming audible, as in the moment when pain set
in.

It was common practice in the institute to discharge the terminally ill
and send them back to their families without informing them of their
true condition, in order to avoid all the red tape and the filth that death
entails. Rönne was with one of these patients now, examining him: an
artificial opening on his front side, a back incision, some decaying flesh
between. He congratulated him on his successful cure and watched the
man trudge off. Now he'll go home, thought Rönne, treating his pains
as an awkward side effect of recovery, laboring under a notion of renewal,
ordering around his son, teaching his daughter, respecting his neighbors,
going along with local opinion, till the blood comes up in his throat one
night. Anyone who thinks we can lie with words might think that's what
was going on here. But if I could lie with words I wouldn't be here.
Everywhere I look it takes some word to keep on living. I certainly would
have been lying if I'd wished this man "Good luck!"

One morning he was sitting in front of his breakfast table, deeply
troubled, sure that the chief physician would leave, and a replacement
come who right then and there would rise out of bed and steal his breakfast roll. We think, we eat, and our food takes effect on us. All the same

though he carried on his work, taking care of whatever questions and orders pertained to him: tapped with the fingers of his right and left hands, someone's lung beneath him; visited bedsides. Good morning, how's the body behaving? But now and then it would also seem to him that he was going through the wings without asking a single routine question, be it the frequency of someone's coughs or the warmth of someone's bowels. When I walk through the open-air decks—and this concerned him too deeply—no matter what set of eyes I encounter, I'm absorbed by them and judged. They associate me with generous and earnest things. Perhaps some anxious household receives me, perhaps it's a bit of tanner's wood that somebody took a taste of once. And once I too had a pair of eyes: they trailed behind me, backward, following these glances. Oh yes, I was always at their service, calm and unquestioning. Where have I come to? Where am I? A small flutter, a breeze.

He speculated when it might have begun, but he couldn't remember: I walk down a street and see a house and remember a palace in Florence that was like it, but then they both get struck with a glint of light and go out.

Something's weakening me from up above. I have no more control over my eyes. Space looms up so endlessly; once it used to flow in a fixed place. The cortex that used to support me has fallen to pieces.

Often, when he had returned to his room after these walks, he would twist and turn his hands and stare at them. And once too a nurse noticed how he sniffed at them, or rather, how he went over them as though testing their breath, and how he clasped his gently curved palms, open at first, to his small shut fingers, and kept moving them together and apart, as though he were breaking open a large soft fruit or bending something apart. She told the other nurses about it; but none of them knew what to make of it. Until it happened that a rather large animal was slaughtered in the institute. Rönne came in, seemingly by accident, as the head was being cut open, but then he took the contents into his hands and split both halves apart. The nurse realized then that this had been the same motion she had seen on her rounds. But she didn't know how to fit the two things together and soon forgot about it.

Rönne, for his part, went on a walk through the gardens. It was summer; the blue sky was shaking the adder's-tongues, the roses were in bloom, daintily trimmed. He felt the earth's pull to the soles of his feet, and the surging of great forces, no longer in his blood. He made a point of following paths that were shady and had enough benches. Often he had to rest from the merciless sunlight; he felt he'd been abandoned to a sky without air.

Gradually he began to tend to his duties only erratically. Mainly though, if he had to speak of some matter in conversation with the director or with his supervisor, whenever he felt he should make some appropriate comment on the matter in question, he would be virtually paralyzed. What was there to say to an event? If it didn't happen one way, it would happen a little differently. Its place certainly wouldn't go unfilled. All he wanted now was to look out serenely from this and rest in his own room.

But when he lay down, he wasn't at all like a man who had come only a few weeks ago from a lake or over the hills. Instead it was as though he himself had sprung up with the place where he lay and all these years it had burdened and sapped him. And there was something on him now that was stiff and waxy, as though taken from the bodies that had been his company for so long.

Later on too his hands engrossed him. The nurse who worked under him loved him very much; he always spoke so fervently to her, though she never quite knew why. Often he would start in rather scornfully, saying that he understood these strange figures, that his own hands had held them. Then he would fall apart again: they lived in laws that were not our own and their fates were as foreign to us as that of a river we travel on. And then utterly snuffed out, nothing but a night-vision, it involved a dozen chemical elements that would fuse together without his bidding, and break apart again without asking him. The question to ask was where they went. It would just blow over them.

He no longer seemed to face anything. As though he no longer had any power over space, he once declared; he rested almost constantly now, seldom stirred.

He kept his room locked so that no one could assail him. He wanted to be able to open the door and look out calmly.

He ordered that the ambulances could drive up and down the highway. He'd noticed that the sound of moving vehicles agreed with him, all so remote, like something from before, going into a distant city.

He always rested in the same position, stiff on his back. He lay in a long chaise, which stood in a rectangular room, which stood in a house, which stood on a hill. Except for a few birds, that made him the highest creature around. So the earth carried him gently through the ether, spinning him serenely past all the stars.

One evening he went down to the open-air wings. He gazed over the deck chairs, watching all the patients waiting under their blankets to be cured. He studied them as they rested there, all from hometowns, from dream-filled sleeps, from homecomings at evening, from songs handed down from father to son, between happiness and death. He looked down the wing and withdrew.

The chief physician was recalled, a friendly man. He mentioned that his daughter had taken ill. Rönne, however, said: Look, I held them here in my very own hands, a hundred or even a thousand pieces; many of them soft, many of them firm, and all of them quite decomposed, men, women, bloody and rotting. Now I constantly hold my own in my hands, probing all the time to see what can become of me. If the obstetric forceps had pressed a little harder at the temples . . . ? If I'd been beaten continually at a certain spot on my head . . . ? What is it about brains? I've always wanted to fly away like a bird from a chasm; now I live beyond, in crystal. But please, just set me free again, and I'll soar once more—how tired I was!—on a path only for wings—with my blue anemone sword—in a blaze of light at high noon—in the ruins of the South—in crumbling cloud banks—pulverized foreheads—temples drifting.

TRANSLATED BY DAVID JACOBSON

# ERRORS
# AND
# CONFUSIONS

# OBSERVING
# THE
# WORLD

*The basis of the world is no longer considered to be something "concealed." In viewing phenomena, especially social issues* parterre, *what is perceived are "the mechanisms of life."* Society seen from below: *the base is more important than the superstructure; perceptions should be turned right side up.*

*At the beginning of the era the proletariat—farm workers, day laborers, artisans, is "discovered" by the Romantics. The suffering of the masses comprising the industrial labor force soon led to revolutionary demands that subsequently formed the basis for Marx and Engels' comprehensive, critical analysis of the system. Socialism in Germany, however, took an evolutionary course. In the arduous process of raising consciousness and changing institutions, people made an attempt to conquer a share in a dignified life for themselves.*

*People at the close of the nineteenth century got into a state of neurasthenic confusion from the hectic quality of incipient "modernity," which was primarily characterized by rapidly spreading materialism and a supremely confident belief in progress.*

*Emotional development does not keep pace with industrial and economic change. The regressive longing for "the good old times forms a steady counterpoint to the Americanization of life." The sexual obsession that characterizes the era (concealed behind middle-class "propriety" and accompanied simultaneously by the unimpeded use of all manner of moral outlets), this ambiguity of the epoch, gives rise to psychological and psychoanalytic interpretations that determine science, literature, and philosophy.* Modern nervousness, *accompanied by expansionist zeal and decadence, prepared the "sickness unto death" that climaxed during World War I. Even before 1914 the* dark vision *anticipated the apocalypse, the disaster prophesied mainly by poets and socialists. The paternalistic society based on command and obedience was over; the rise of an attitude of brotherhood was uncertain.*

# SOCIETY SEEN FROM BELOW

Romanticism and Classicism are synonymous with a transported world. The mild glow of humanity is everywhere. Beautiful souls wander in the distance. What happens in the foreground and beneath the surface is mostly outside the perspective.

The Biedermeier era and a part of the period of realism are directed inward. What is contemporary lags behind in comparison with the "ultimate question" of human existence: people feel themselves more "hurled" into being than into being-there. Even though Young Germany had been concerned with immediate and real issues, there had been altogether a belief in the necessity of tracking down a basis for the world that lay deep underneath mere social conditions.

But now it is a question of observing the world, of dedicated concern with surface phenomena, primarily with social reality. What occurs *parterre* becomes clear: a confused world that has gone astray. Class divisions within society had been widened by industrialization, and people began to realize that hardship was boundless.

The social question of the nineteenth century emerges even before the beginning of the machine age. In the early period of industrialization the proletariat constitutes a rural substratum which, although freed, by the Stein-Hardenberg agrarian reforms from the chains of feudal obligations, had become extremely poor in the absence of seignorial concern and protective duty. For the rural lower class there was hardly any escape from a miserable existence until the middle of the century; the weak beginnings of industrialization in the western part of Germany did not produce an adequate number of jobs.

The excess labor force, a result of economic and social factors, was swelled significantly by an unusually large population growth. This was due to a sinking mortality rate, and substantially higher birthrates, which were a result of hygienic and medical progress as well as of earlier marriage. Thus

297

the population of Germany increased between 1800 and 1900 from approximately 24 to 56 million. While the mercantile state in the seventeenth and eighteenth centuries had still attempted to cope with a shortage of population and the resulting labor shortage by a planned *"Peuplierungspolitik,"* many governments during the nineteenth century resorted to "adjusting the population to the economic volume" by restricting marriage licenses. The introduction of freedom of occupation increased the social consequences of agrarian reforms and the population explosion. Following the granting of freedom of occupation, the restrictive guild, which had permitted only a small privileged class to become master craftsmen, and forced the majority of journeymen into dependence upon the master craftsmen without any possibility of establishing their own families—this restrictive guild was suspended. Many apprentice artisans now set themselves up as independent craftsmen, leading to an oversupply in many trades and to crises for many of the artisans due also to the increasing pressure of industrial competition. Actually most of the so-called independent craftsmen either worked at home in cottage industry or in stores, factories, etc., if indeed they avoided sinking into the lower class of unemployed craftsmen. Only a few managed to become small factory owners, middlemen, or traveling salesmen. (Wilfried Gottschalch)

Even by the end of the eighteenth century there was a depression due to shortages and distribution problems in skilled trades that had flourished since the end of the Thirty Years War. Senator Johann Weiss of Speyer mentioned the following reasons for the lack of turnover and the decline of crafts in his 1795 "Prize Essay Concerning the Advantages and Disadvantages, Improvements, or Total Elimination of Guilds":

• Satiation of the need for handmade products;
• Lack of fluid capital;
• Excessive tax burdens, especially in rural areas;
• Oversupply of agriculture workers;
• Slowdown in exports abroad;
• Cutbacks in jobs as a result of rationalization in factories;
• Diminished need for replacement as a result of humanization of the conduct of war;
• Consumer preference for simple and functional items, especially for imported objects in this category.

In view of such a difficult situation, the craftsman had to develop special virtues to survive in the trade at all. Diligence, thrift, upright business practices and, above all, strict adherence to the middle-class moral code offered security in a swiftly changing, confusing world. The work place was to be the bastion of stability and uprightness, providing crafts-manlike solidity as an alternative to the alienation of mass production. While the craftsman was excluded or at best derived only minimal bene-fits from the general economic upswing, he sought to compensate for the material deficit through the help of intellectual, spiritual, and cultural values. Thus in a positive sense craftsmen upheld many of the middle-class values that had gotten lost after the Biedermeier era in the wake of industrialization, expansion of wholesale trade, and the increasing orien-tation toward profit.

In the craftsmen's homes middle-class virtues increasingly slipped into second place. Idealistic strength of conviction and tenacity were turned into a rigid creed. Craftsmen adapted to the situation by becoming power-oriented. Industry and wholesale operations resulted in utilization of world markets and promoted urbanity and cosmopolitanism; the status of the craftsman regressed to provincialism, narrow-mindedness, petit bourgeois values. Middle-class ideology was entrenched in Seldwyla. Mas-ter Joiner Anton in Friedrich Hebbel's tragedy *Maria Magdalena* (large, bony, upright, an almost stiff posture, an abrupt manner of speaking, commandeering, self-righteous but given, too, to masochism, brooding, irritably concealing any gentler impulse) says in the end when everything has gone to ruin: "I no longer understand the world." If this work is understood as a historical social drama, middle-class virtues of craftsman-ship, particularly the concept of honor, have petrified. Kurt May calls Anton a "phantom and a distortion of personality;" his value judgments are unequivocally determined by a deteriorated bourgeois Christian mo-rality. This hero in shirtsleeves represents the Protestant Christian ethic whose development has petrified in the narrowness of a North German small town. The setting is a petit bourgeois circle in an era of crippled moral sensitivity and diminished piety that had to be liberated by a more genuine, healthy, vital moral and religious epoch that was more respon-sible to the individual. The daughter, Klara, escapes from the dependen-cies and taboos of provincial narrowness by suicide. Privation endured in composure has yielded to the despair of being alone (75).

Friedrich Hebbel himself grew up in the poorest of circumstances. His father had been a mason.

How dreary and barren my childhood was. My father actually hated me, and I was unable to love him. He was a slave of marriage, bound with iron chains to poverty, to bare need, unable despite the expenditure of all his energies and immoderate exertion to get even a step ahead. But he also hated pleasure, to which his heart was blocked by thistles and thorns. He was unable to tolerate it even on his children's faces. Merry, hearty laughter he considered a sacrilege, perceiving it as a mockery of himself. A tendency toward playfulness indicated frivolity and uselessness. Reluctance toward hard manual labor pointed to innate ruin and a second fall from grace. My brother and I were called his wolves; our appetite banished his own; rarely could we eat a piece of bread without having to hear that we did not deserve it. Nonetheless my father was a genuinely good, faithful, well-meaning man (if I were not deeply convinced of that, I would never have written such a thing about him). But poverty had replaced his soul.

Hebbel had to go through an arduous process to acquire an education. The drudgery of writing in a parish beadle's house was followed by a short stay in Hamburg. His studies in Heidelberg and Munich were partially financed by Elisa Lensing, a seamstress from Hamburg whom he loved. Nonetheless he abandoned his study of law, thereby losing a stipendium. After his mother died, he had to return to Hamburg on foot. The *Travel Journal from Munich to Hamburg* conveys a realistic impression of life on the highway of that era. Germany is still a province. Industrialization has gained hold only in certain areas. The rural scene is observed from below with no trace of the Biedermeier spirit or of the "green ethos" (76).

Karl Marx wrote that the division of work between the various cities resulted in the creation of factories ("facilities in the main for finishing fabrics, weavings, threads"), i.e., branches of production that were an outgrowth of the guild system.

> Work that at the outset presupposes a machine, even if only in the crudest form, very soon proved to be the kind that best lent itself to development. Weaving, previously a sideline enterprise of peasants to enable them to acquire the clothing they needed, was the first form of work to receive a stimulus and to be expanded by improved transportation facilities. The rising demand for material for clothing resulting from increased population, the incipient accumulation and mobilization of indigenous capital by more rapid circulation, the resulting need for luxury encouraged also by the gradual expansion of transportation in general gave weaving both quantitatively and qualitatively an impulse that freed it from its previous mode of production.

Manufacturing also brought about a changed relationship between worker and employer. In effect, a patriarchal relationship continued in the guilds. In manufacturing, however, the patriarchal relationship was replaced by a money relationship between worker and capitalist, and although the old patriarchal "relationship continued or was simulated in the country and in small cities, it was soon almost completely eliminated in larger actual manufacturing sites." In reality the automatic loom, the "spinning machine," assisted manufacturing to the breakthrough when the form of driving power was changed: the steam engine replaced the water wheel (typically used in preindustrial manufacturing such as paper mills, wire-pulling, and forging). Turnover then started to occur with increasing rapidity—the needs of the increasing population led to mass production in factories; factory construction was mostly financed by business people with control of fluid capital which, in contrast to indigenous and estate capital, was capital in the modern sense.

In a certain sense the factory worker during the thirties and forties of the nineteenth century was still considered a member of a more privileged class (in comparison, for example, with the rural proletariat); he is now increasingly exploited and driven into the greatest misery. The ruling upper class whose feudal-aristocratic or patrician-patriarchal tradition formerly made them feel obligated to fulfill their "seignorial" virtues toward the poor is now replaced by the capitalist, the *homo economicus,* in whose new scale of value material or economic wealth is primary. The productive capacity of the person is in any case to be fully and ruthlessly exploited. The worker appears merely as a cost factor. Inhuman working conditions, excessively long work hours, inadequate work space, and extremely heavy labor are considered to some extent as productive factors. This is particularly the case with child labor.

> The most important reason for the entrepreneur to employ children undoubtedly was the question of wages. The attitude expressed by manufacture in general was that workers' wages must be kept as low as possible, otherwise they would not work enough. Children were basically treated as the cheapest labor force. They were hence "indispensable" to the enterprise as a cost-saving factor in production. The parents were equally interested in child labor because of material need. The interest in child labor by entrepreneurs, governmental authorities, and educators had as its origin two sets of goals: those reflecting economic and competitive considerations and trade policy, and those reflecting social and so-called pedagogical and ethical considerations—i.e., as the kind of palliation of profit interests that was typical of the era. (Erna M. Johansen)

When Bettina von Arnim dedicated her description of poverty to the king, the target was the ruling class altogether, which only sought to exploit but not to concern itself with the poor (77). The sister of Clemens von Brentano, and along with Rahel Varnhagen the most prominent woman of the Romantic period, Bettina was distinguished by her clear perspective on social reality. Above all, she was deeply moved by the suffering of the weavers in Silesia, where conditions in 1844 subsequently led to the first worker uprising, which was brutally put down. A contemporary reported:

> As a consequence of three salvos, three people were killed. Blood and brains splattered. One man's brains spilled out above one of his eyes. A woman standing in the door of her house two hundred steps away sank down motionless. The side of one man's head was torn away. The bloody top of his skull lay some distance from him. A mother of six children died that same evening from several shot wounds. A girl on her way to a knitting lesson was hit by bullets and sank to the ground.

Heinrich Heine wrote his song of the weavers in bitter fury in Paris (78).

The proletarian, although legally free, owned nothing; he was constantly compelled to seek employment but unable to find a secure job. Basically, wages covered only survival and offered no prospects of ameliorating a situation that was accordingly passed on to the next generation. The proletarian had only himself to rely on. Philanthropic and organized religious efforts in the first third of the nineteenth century were either "alms socialism" or were related to the erroneous idea that increased religiosity would bring about an improvement in the circumstances of life. Georg Büchner was among the first who emphatically propagated an open political struggle by the poor against the rich as the solution to social need (79). Along with Peter Friedrich Ludwig Weidig, head of a secret republican organization, Büchner attacked the power of the princes. In a letter to his family, he states: "I will always act in accordance with my principles, but have recently learned that only the need of the great masses can bring about changes, that all agitation and writing by lone individuals is the futile work of fools. They write—it is not read; they scream—they are not heard; they act—no one helps them . . ."

Büchner's position anticipated the standpoint from which Karl Marx and Friedrich Engels later developed a systematic theory of social revolution. Philosophers had previously only interpreted the world; the task now was to change it. *The Communist Manifesto,* which was written in December 1847 and published in February 1848 in London, pointed the road to revolution for the socialist movement:

The communists disdain concealing their views and intentions. They openly state that their purposes can only be achieved by the forceful overthrow of all previous social orders. May the ruling classes tremble before a communist revolution. The proletarians have nothing to lose from a communist revolution but their chains. They have a world to gain. Proletarians of all countries, unite!

The communists directed their main attention to Germany, because it was on the brink of a bourgeois revolution that would be accomplished under more progressive conditions of European civilization in general and with a much more developed proletariat than that of England in the seventeenth century or France in the eighteenth. The German middle-class revolution was only the "immediate prelude to a proletarian revolution."

Developments in Germany assumed, however, a different course than that in Marx's prognosis. Here the working class's battle for emancipation was won in the parliaments instead of on the barricades. Decisive stations along the route were the founding of the German Workers' Union (*Allgemeiner Deutscher Arbeiterverein*) by Ferdinand Lassalle (1863), the Social Democratic Workers' Party (*Sozialdemokratische Arbeiterpartei*) by Wilhelm Liebknecht and August Bebel (in Eisenach in 1869), as well as the unification of the Lassalle faction and the Marxist-oriented *Eisenachs* into the Socialist Workers' Party of Germany (*Sozialistische Arbeiterpartei Deutschlands*, 1875), which in 1893 became the strongest party.

Ferdinand Lassalle, unlike Heine, was not content with a curse on the "false Fatherland." Influenced by Karl Marx and impressed by events of the March Revolution of 1848, he demanded the development of a social consciousness characterized by solidarity. On April 12, 1862, in the Artisans Union in Oranienburg, a Berlin suburb, Lassalle delivered a long speech that came to be known as the "Workers' Program." To a group of machine construction workers, he explained, among other things, that the bourgeois state, characterized by profound immorality, had led to a situation in which the stronger, shrewder, and wealthier exploited and controlled the weaker. The moral idea of the working class, in contrast, was that the unimpeded and free use of individual energies did not suffice. On the contrary, he stated, what was also necessary in a morally ordered community was solidarity of interests, possession of goods in common, and reciprocity of development. The "nightwatchman government of the bourgeoisie" (". . . a nightwatchman idea for the reason that the bourgeoisie can conceive of the state only in the image of a nightwatchman whose entire function consists in impeding robbery and thievery . . .") had to be replaced by a state that would promote the positive development of the human being.

> The purpose of the state is hence that of bringing about the positive, on-going development of the human being—i.e., of embuing human destiny, or the civilization of which the human race is capable, with real existence. The purpose is the training and development of the human race for freedom.

Lassalle was the son of a modest Galician Jew who settled in Breslau after the Prussian Edict of Toleration of 1812, retaining his family name (Heyman Lassal, after his birthplace, Loslau). Lassalle, both a Romantic and a fanatic as well as forensically brilliant social revolutionary whose lifestyle was that of a "dissolute youth," occupied the fantasy both of his contemporaries and his successors to an unparalled degree. A diary entry (April 1, 1841) when he was sixteen (he adopted the French form of his name only after his 1846 sojourn in Paris) reports a conversation between father and son:

> My father asked me why I did not want to study medicine or law. "Both the doctor and the lawyer," I replied, "are business people who do business with their knowledge!" . . . I wanted to study something for the sake of its effectiveness. My father asked whether I believed I was a poet. "No," I answered, "but I want to dedicate myself to mass communication. Now is the time when people are fighting for mankind's most sacred purposes. Up to the end of the previous century the world was kept in chains of stifling superstition. A material force then came into being which, stimulated by the power of intellects, bloodily toppled the existing order into ruins." The father warns the son against martyrdom: "Freedom must be achieved, but without you. Stay with us!" But the son is resolved on revolt and departure: "Why? Because God put a voice in my breast that summons me to battle, because God gave me the strength—I feel it—that makes me capable of battle. Because I can fight and suffer for a noble purpose. Because I do not wish to swindle God out of the strengths he gave me for definite purposes. Because, in a word, I can do nothing else."

His own staging is already perfect in this document. In many roles—as publicist, poet, philosopher, jurist, ultimately as labor leader—Lassalle led the "battle for the noblest purpose in the noblest manner." Affairs and love adventures constantly nourished the gossip of the Biedermeier era and provided his person with the aura of the "human, all too human." At home in salons, prisons, and on the barricades (mainly intellectual barricades), he remained the topic of discussion: from his final examination before graduation in Breslau, which the rebellious student was at first not permitted to take, while studying in Breslau and Berlin up to his stay in Paris, during his trials and arrests in Düsseldorf, and his move to Berlin (the highpoint of his activity as a writer), from the founding and direction of the German Workers' Union and to the duel in the woods of Carronge (Switzerland) where he was mortally wounded (1864). Viewed from his demise, the paradoxes of his life become particularly clear. An antibourgeois, undogmatic socialist who was even able to impress Bismarck, Lassalle was consumed by passion for the moody, spoiled, extravagant Helen von Dönniges. Although disappointed by her "fickleness" (he even calls her an "outcast and a prostitute"), he remains her gallant suitor. Her family considers Lassalle, as a communist and a Jew, unbearable. Lassalle wants to avenge such an insult. Helen's father considered himself too old for a duel. A tubercular young student, Janko von Racowitza, who was considered suitable for marriage to Helen, assumed the defense of the family honor and shot Lassalle in the lower abdomen. By this time Lassalle was virtually "used up"—worn out from efforts to achieve worker solidarity, alienated from Sophie von Hatzfeld, his friend of over two decades (as her economic and legal adviser, he handled her divorce and settlement, his "share" in which made possible his financial independence). Mainly, however, his health was ruined, not least of all by the syphilis that he had contracted in 1848.

Heinrich Heine accurately stated in a letter to Karl August Varnhagen von Ense that with Lassalle a new race had tried to come into its own (80).

In the same year that the "comet Lassalle" vanished, August Bebel was appointed to the "Committee for Ongoing Business" at the second convention of the German Workers' Union. In the years 1864–1870, the rise of German social democracy was prepared by three men: Jean Baptist Schweitzer, Wilhelm Liebknecht, and August Bebel. Schweitzer, a South German lawyer who carried on the Lassalle tradition, sought, by means of shrewd tactics and a readiness to compromise, to unite various socialist groups, to make concessions to public opinion and the government, and to deal with practical questions in the parliament of the North German Confederation.

Wilhelm Liebknecht's goal was the creation of a socialist party as conceived by Marx. He supported the doctrine of class struggle, strictly adhering to this position without regard for public opinion.

The third in the Confederation [August Bebel] became a member of the Reichstag at age twenty-seven. He quickly recognized his big opportunity: to adhere to the principles of the Marxist doctrine proclaimed by Liebknecht but to use Schweitzer's tactics. As the son of a Prussian noncommissioned officer, he is not burdened by the fundamental aversion toward Prussia and its army, and as a turner he is closer to the workers than Liebknecht and Schweitzer. His strength of conviction, his unusually strong pedagogical drive, and his talent as an orator won him even as a young man the esteem of his opponents, who were soon fighting him as their most dangerous enemy, thereby strengthening his position among the proletariat. (U. Schulz) (81)

Following two attacks on the life of Kaiser Wilhelm I (1878), Bismarck opposed the worker movement with the aid of a law that defined social democratic goals as inimical to the public interest. Police pressure only made the social democrats stronger, however, and the attempt to detach the working class from their leaders by social reform from above failed. The working class increasingly formed a state within a state. The unions, too, which were organized starting in 1868, gained increasing influence. The strike became an important tool in the struggle for the improvement of material and political conditions, confirming what Georg Herwegh had expressed in 1864 in the "Song for the General League of German Workers":

> Man of labor, do wake up!
> Recognize your awesome might!
> All the wheels will grind to a halt
> If your strong arm so decides.   (82)

When August Bebel died on August 13, 1913, an epoch ended that had brought decisive social progress to many sectors of the population. Bebel's splendid life, according to the *Vorwärts,* the social democratic party newspaper, had abounded in activity and work in the service of a great idea.

And if in the battle for these fine socialist ideas about civilization he also had to endure much difficulty, on the other hand in serving as a pathfinder toward a better future, he had attained his satisfaction and the joy of his life. His name belongs to history forever, and those for whom he fought and suffered will not forget him. He survives in our faithful hearts, for he placed his life in the service of the suffering and dispossessed.

The socialist movement, from its perspective of society seen from below, developed a commitment to the necessity of moving "forward" and "upward." It was moved by the conviction that the human race will achieve freedom and humanity. Hence, with all its realism, it was idealistically oriented. The great writings of German idealism were considered the guiding star along the route to social amelioration, and socialist literature is permeated by love of one's fellow human beings and sentiments of brotherhood. While later bourgeois sensibility peered "from above" on those "down there" with refined aestheticism, and sought by means of poetic ciphers to suppress its helpless, beauty-ridden melancholy about human misery (83), expressionist socialism, or socially committed expressionism, was charged with a four-pronged cry: Revolt and scream! Awakening of the heart! A call to indignation! Love of mankind! (84)

Kurt Pinthus compiled a poetry anthology, *Twilight of Mankind: A Document of Expressionism* (1919), a collection of the convulsions and passions, the yearnings and torments of the epoch. In it he said that the political art of this period must not be versified editorials, but must attempt to aid mankind and bring about the completion and realization of the idea itself. "The fact that literature simultaneously contributed to going against the madness of *Realpolitik* and a degenerate social order was merely an obvious and small service. Its greater and suprapolitical significance is that it repeatedly pointed remonstratingly and resoundingly to the human being himself. It restored, in the realm of the spirit, relatedness of people among and with each other and a bond of the individual with the infinite." From the errors and confusions, defeats and miseries of the era, the person, the pure, radiant person, was to arise anew like a phoenix from the ashes.

## (75) Honestly paid

FRIEDRICH HEBBEL, Maria Magdalena

*Maria Magdalena* (1844) is considered the first modern bourgeois tragedy. While Lessing and Schiller were still concerned with the unbridgeable cleavage and all the consequences of an unequal collision between the world of the nobility and the middle class, Hebbel is solely preoccupied with the dull, prudish world of the petit bourgeois whose prejudices, concepts of honor, and inhuman morality he castigates. His social indictment anticipates the preoccupations of Gerhard Hauptmann and Henrik Ibsen. Quite apart from all manner of oppression, he is also in quest of a new morality for countering the decline of the bourgeois world.

Klara, the daughter of the master joiner Anton, has been intimate with her fiancé, the
clerk Leonhard, whom she does not love. Although she has become pregnant by him,
Leonhard deserts Klara when her brother is accused of theft. The friend of her youth who
has just returned home after a long absence fells Leonhard in a duel, but is nonetheless
unable to decide in favor of Klara: "No man can disregard *that!*" In despair Klara leaps
into the well, wishing to spare her father—her mother has meantime died—the shame.
Master Anton remains behind in tragic loneliness and, having sacrificed everything for his
unconditional morality, complains: "I no longer understand the world!"

*Master Anton:*    When I was young things went poorly. I came into the
world no more a spiny porcupine than you, but eventually I became one.
At first my spines pointed inward, people pinched and pressed them into
my tender smooth skin to their heart's content, and were glad when I
winced, because the quills dug into my heart and my guts. But I didn't
like it, I turned my skin inside out, now the quills stuck in their fingers
and I had some peace.

*Leonhard [aside]:*    Before the devil himself, I'll bet!

*Master Anton:*    My father worked himself to death when he was thirty
years old, because he gave himself no rest day and night; my poor mother
supported herself as well as she could by spinning. I grew up without
learning a trade. As I grew older and still couldn't earn any money, I
would have liked to get over the habit of eating, at least, but even when
I sometimes pretended to be sick in the afternoon, and pushed my plate
aside, what good did it do me? By evening my stomach forced me to
declare myself healthy again. My biggest anguish was that I stayed so
clumsy. I could take myself to task for it as though it had been my own
fault, as though I had provided myself in the womb with nothing but
devouring teeth, and left all useful traits and skills behind on purpose. I
could get embarrassed just walking out into the daylight. Right after my
confirmation, the man they buried yesterday, Master Gebhard, walked
into our living room. He wrinkled his brow and made a grimace, as he
always did when he had something good on his mind. Then he said to
my mother: "Have you brought your boy into the world so that he can
eat you out of house and home?" I felt ashamed, for I was just about to
cut a piece of bread, and quickly put it back into the cupboard. My
mother got angry at his well-meant words; she stopped her wheel and
answered crossly that her son was honest and good. "Well, let's see about
that," said the master. "If he wants, he can join me in the shop right
now, just as he is. I'll demand no apprenticeship fee; he'll get free board
and I'll even take care of clothes, and if he wants to rise early and go to
bed late, then he'll miss no opportunity for earning some nice pocket

money now and then for his old mother." My mother began to cry, I to dance. When we finally tried to thank him, the master just covered his ears, motioned to me and walked out. I didn't need to put on my cap because I had none, and without saying good-bye to my mother I followed him out. When I got to visit her on the following Sunday, for the first time and barely for an hour, he gave me a half a ham for her. God's blessings on the good man's grave! I still hear his half-gruff "Tony, boy, stick it under your jacket so my wife doesn't see it!"

*Leonard:* Why, you're crying!

*Master Anton [dries his eyes]:* Yes, I better not think about it. The tear well is pretty blocked up in me, but every time it leaks again. Well, that's good, too; if I ever get dropsical, then at least these drops won't have to be drained off. *[with a sudden turn]* Tell me what you think. If on a Sunday afternoon you had wanted to visit the man to whom you owed everything, just to have a pipe of tobacco, and you found him looking all disordered and wild, with a knife in his hand, the same knife that he had used a thousand times to slice your evening bread—bloody against his throat, terrified and drawing a cloth up to his chin—

*Leonard:* That's how he walked around until the end!

*Master Anton:* Because of the scar. And if you came just in time, you could save him and help, but not only by tearing the knife out of his hand and bandaging the wound; you also had to pay out the miserable thousand thalers which you had saved, and that had to be done on the sly, simply in order to get the old man to accept it. Well, what would you do?

*Leonard:* Unmarried and free as I am, without wife and child, I would sacrifice the money.

*Master Anton:* And if you had ten wives, like the Turks, and as many children as were promised to father Abraham, and if you could think about it for only a minute, then you would be—hmmm, my son-in-law! Now you'll know where the money is, today I can tell you, because my old master is buried, but a month ago I would have kept it to myself even on my death bed. Before they nailed the coffin shut, I put the written promise under the dead man's head. If I had actually been able to write, I would have written underneath: Honestly paid! But being unlettered, I had no choice but to make a tear through the length of the paper. Now he'll sleep peacefully, and I hope I will, too, when someday I lie down next to him.

TRANSLATED BY ADRIAN DEL CARO

## (76) Travel journal from Munich to Hamburg

FRIEDRICH HEBBEL, Diaries

Friedrich Hebbel mentioned in his diary before again leaving Munich that he had revisited the English Gardens and prayed ". . . for blessings on Munich, which received me in such a friendly manner, and for blessings for myself. 'Make something of my life,' I called, 'whatever it be!' For my beloved Beppi, too, I appealed to heaven for blessings. And, since this page must be concluded, why should I not close it with my name?" The reference to Beppi is to Josefa Schwarz, the daughter of a carpenter. Along with Elise Lensing, the Hamburg seamstress who had selflessly supported him, and Christine Enghaus, an actress at the Vienna Burgtheater who had been his understanding friend and permanent companion since 1846, Josefa Schwarz was one of the most important women in Hebbel's life. (The situation of the Schwarz family, in whose house Hebbel had lived during his Munich period, is later recalled in *Maria Magdalena*.)

The next morning at 10:30 I arrived in Nüremberg. The weather was fine, but perceptibly cold. I decided to stop over for a day, and regret this now. I didn't need a day of rest, but in order to get to know such a city, one day is not enough. In the afternoon I rode on by steam rail to Fürth, the little dog Hans in my lap. The movement is one of increasing velocity: one notices how fast it is when one speeds by some object—milestones, trees, houses all disappear as they pop up. The Albrecht Dürer house in Nüremberg was also viewed. This stirred annoying sensations in me later when I learned that it was a modern antique, a restored relic. The next day I visited the city library—unwillingly, for I had to leave because of the bad weather, and because the coachman did not leave until two o'clock. An old, very likable librarian, who is spending his life on the composition of a catalog, guided me about; the books were poorly shelved in unheatable places, and the cold was so penetrating that I couldn't stay long. I saw some interesting things, many incunabula, a first draft of a manuscript by Luther, handwritten manuscripts by Frischlin, Regiomontanus and others.

At 1:30 I departed for Bamberg. With me in the coach was a family of traveling performers; the children were crowded against the adults and the dogs against the children. The father was coarse in manners and conversation; he liked all the tobacco that had been planted in Nüremberg. The sons, one of whom had a swollen eye, stood a couple of steps higher; the smaller boys, the *Wunderkinder* of the concerts, were tolerable. A poorly concealed quarrel among them all. On the way a loaf of peasant's bread was eaten, and there was a good deal of showing off in front of me.

They remained in Erlangen. There a retired gendarme got into the coach; he cursed his position, but probably only because he was about to enter another one. I saw nothing of the Ludwig Canal and the region; the weather was murderous and I vomited continually—though it had never happened before, the traveling was getting to me. We rode into Bamberg by dark night. In the morning I went out early, the city seemed quite spread out. It had a festive appearance because it was Sunday.

A very long way from Bamberg to Koburg. Two hours from Koburg I met up with an empty postal wagon which picked me up for a small fee. The driver told me I could ride cheaply from Koburg to Gotha with the mail trunks. I accepted and departed at three in the morning. A tiny wagon upon which I could hardly sit; biting cold; without a coat, boots wet; a real torture. Almost more than myself, I pitied my poor little dog, which I had tried in vain to keep warm in my lap. His little feet had become raw and bloody from the walking; he was so cold that he had to pass water nearly every minute. It was cold atop the wagon. In Hildburgshausen I abandoned the vehicle and walked to Suhl by way of Schleusingen. In addition to the highway, a footpath winding through the woods and across the snowy mountains led to Suhl. Shortly before I got to it, I was joined by a red-haired, most repugnant fellow who asked if he could accompany me. I explained to him that I wanted to walk alone, but he arranged it so that he was always near me. Once he stood and looked at one of the mountains which he must have seen a thousand times, being a native; then he accosted someone along the way and asked for directions which he doubtlessly knew already, since he had offered me his services as guide and pack carrier; another time he fumbled around with something on his tattered shoes. Then as he was walking along he brandished his club about his head. I couldn't risk taking the detour over the highway, so I just made sure the weird stranger did not get too close behind. This would have been dangerous in the narrow pass, piled up to the sky on both sides with snowbanks; there was not even enough room for two people to walk side by side. Whole flocks of ravens were building their eyries in the treetops. I made my way through the wood, continually watched with impudence by the fellow who looked back frequently over his shoulder; I had removed my gloves in case I should have to draw my sword, and truly I was disappointed at not finding an opportunity to use it.

In Suhl I was afraid I would have to be satisfied with a pub, and was surprised to find the best inn that I had encountered on the whole journey. The strange fellow once again crossed my path, this time as a beggar and very humbly, but I gave him nothing. I was given a room which had been heated in advance; an accommodating waiter attended amicably to the needs of the obviously happy guest. Since it was my birthday and I had arrived early, in mid-afternoon, I ordered coffee. It was deliciously prepared, and warmed me body and soul. Then I wrote a poem. In the evening a very nice supper, the first good potatoes in a long time, pike and roast veal; but unfortunately along with it I had the intolerable company of boastful shopkeepers' servants. I was invited to a concert and ball later on by the innkeeper, who participated in the concert as the director, while the waiter played an instrument. But as I had no evening dress, and had not even brought along a decent pair of boots, I declined.

From Suhl to Gotha by way of Zella and Ohrdruf. I had to climb the highest elevation of the Thuringian Forest (2,500 feet), and would have caught sight of the snow-capped summit in clear weather, but it snowed and the sky was overcast. And old woman with whom I walked for a while instructed me about how the inhabitants could live off the forest for lack of pasture and arable land: wood cutting, board cutting; a couple of cows to yield butter and cheese which they later sold. Much snow up there, and a memorial which the builder of this truly excellent road, the Duke of Saxony-Koburg, had apparently erected for himself. I was strangely moved by the black woods as they emerged from the white background; in spite of the winter cold a divine sight. I saw nothing of Gotha but my inn, a large palace across the way and, when leaving, a pretty baker's girl from whom I bought very good bread. In the inn a droll doctor confessed an uncommon pity for the wretchedness of dogs.

Now I came into Prussian territory and was amazed by the size of the villages and cities. I stayed overnight in Mühlhausen, the former independent imperial city; from there to Heiligenstadt. I arrived in Göttingen in rainy weather, and a student whom I had once helped out of financial difficulty in Munich offered me lodging at his place. While he went to his lecture, I wrote a letter to Elise. At first my host was the personification of kindness; in the afternoon he asked if he should invite acquaintances over and arrange for a game of cards. When I replied that this would be quite all right by me, but that I myself did not play and therefore could not take part in the game, he became noticeably depressed. From Göttingen to Einbeck, where I arrived dry at about three in the afternoon in spite of the heavy downpour. From Einbeck to Elze, and on until Alfeld in the company of a swaggering student from Hanover. This man disgusted me; he had a half-starved dog with him, to which he gave not even the slightest morsel to eat. Shortly before Elze I encountered a candidate in theology who went by the name of Klingsohr; a face dunked in honey, long pipe in his mouth. He stayed in Elze, as I did, and I was pleased because I looked forward to his conversation through the long evening. But he was uninteresting to the point of transparency, and, as I convinced myself next day, vulgar as well.

The innkeeper's wife came up to my room the next morning, after Klingsohr had gone downstairs, and asked whether I were paying for him. When I denied this in astonishment, she replied that she had suspected as much. Yet Klingsohr had maintained that she should not bother to itemize the bill, but simply give me the whole sum to avoid any fuss. This sounded suspicious to her. When my ecclesiastic friend came upstairs again, I confronted him with his dirty trick, but of course he said the woman had merely misunderstood him. However, when he had to hand over the few pennies, he grew pale as a sheet with rage, complained about the monstrously high prices and poured his venom into the hotel register. I, in contrast, found the bill to be extremely reasonable, and mentioned this in the register. He had tried to contrive the deception on the previous evening, by saying to me several times, since we were sharing a room: I am lodging, so to say, with you; whereupon I replied, suspecting nothing foul: and I with you!

From Elze to Hanover by way of Tiedemannswiese and in the morning a violent snowstorm. My poor little dog, which had followed behind me so faithfully, finally despaired and lay down as if to die in a deep wagon rut. Things got better in the afternoon. In Hanover I got a haircut. My hair had grown so long that I was beginning to attract attention. From Hanover to Celle; a lovely morning, in the afternoon heavy rain. On one side of the highway stones had been piled; my little dog ran along behind the stones, which protected him against the rain like a wall, but every minute or so he raised his little yellow head above the stones, in order to convince himself that I was still there, then wagged his tail and marched onward. Seldom has anything moved me so much. In Celle an excellent inn and not overly expensive; I wrote the final version of a couple of poems conceived along the way.

From Celle to Soltau. In Soltau I got some milk for little Hans, which must have been sour, because afterward he began to vomit and this went on through the night. From Soltau to Welle. The little dog was quite miserable; along the way I turned into a farm and got some broth for the

poor little fellow; he would not eat. I asked the farmer if he thought
Hans would pull through. "No," he replied, puffing, while he pushed
his brass spectacles higher on his nose, "I don't think so. You would be
better off leaving him with me, then he wouldn't hinder you anymore.
I'd watch him today and kill him tomorrow if he didn't improve." I
didn't answer but left his house; it was an unspeakably agonizing thought
that the faithful little dog should have to die along the way. I couldn't
hold back my tears, took him into my arms, heedless of the heavy pack
which I had to carry already, covered him as well as I could with my coat
and promised him, as though he could understand me, the best of lives
in Hamburg.

TRANSLATED BY ADRIAN DEL CARO

## (77) Documents on poverty

BETTINA VON ARNIM, This Book Belongs to the King

In an imaginary conversation with Goethe's mother the author describes two visits of the
councilor's wife with Queen Louise in the Darmstadt Palace in the years 1799 and 1803.
The conversations contain a blend of political, social, and philosophical concepts and
ideas. Bettina von Arnim advocates political freedom and the elimination of privileges.
King Friedrich Wilhelm IV of Prussia is implored to make an end of the suffering of the
masses and to make possible the general well-being of the people. The Romantic tendency
of the book caused it to be poorly received at first. Only when the publicist Adolf Stahr
spoke of the "spiritual Bible of the future" and summarized the most important ideas in
his own writing was attention drawn to the dangerous ideas contained in the work.

Weaver *Naumann* has been in debtor's prison already for seven weeks
because of a debt in the amount of 3 talers, 15 groschen. The executor
personally went with him to see the director of the welfare agency and
called the director's attention to the fact that if the agency could not
bring itself to pay this debt, it would then be saddled with the burden of
having to support a wife with six small children. But to no avail: they let
the poor man stay in prison and they handed out 4 talers per month to
his penniless family. This example demonstrates clearly how ineptly welfare funds are administered. Instead of recognizing and utilizing the
proper time for the right kind of support, the administrators use the
funds for *alms, which have never really improved the situation of a man in
financial straits.* The alms in question take care of the rental payments,

but whatever money is left over is not sufficient to keep the family from starving. The young wife of the landlord told me that the children are without any food for days on end and that she herself had often breast-fed the youngest of them.

*Schneider,* from Hirschlanden near Zurich, took part in the Russian campaign, and has lived in Berlin since 1813. The two youngest of his nine children are at home. He suffers from a double hernia. His wife is old and sickly. Both of them gather bones and paper. Today, their combined labor yielded them the sum of 2 groschen 4 pfennigs. A year ago they received welfare support in the amount of 2 talers from the welfare agency. Two years ago, *Schneider* begged somebody for a little money; he received 3 pfennigs, was caught in the act by a police officer, and was incarcerated for six months.

An old widow, who also gathers bones, lives with them in the same room.

*Kornewitz* was the child of a soldier, and in his youth he took part in several military campaigns. Later on, he was employed with the postal service as a head ostler. He was dismissed eight years ago, however, allegedly because he had become insane as a result of a nervous fever. Both he and his wife claim that his dismissal had been brought about by a certain government councilor B. who once had been informed by *Kornewitz* that he was carrying excess baggage with him. The postal service had settled on Kornewitz a pension of 8 talers per month. Of their thirteen children, six are living; five are still minors and at home with their parents.

Weaver *Weber* is fifty-eight years old, and has been out of work since mid-November of last year. Household articles and clothes have been sold. His children are pallid with hunger.

Weaver *Beneke* has been out of work for fourteen weeks. He is sick and bedridden. Their four children appear to suffer great hardship. His wife confided to me that she was feeding her family by means of begging. Once she received 2 talers from the welfare agency. Old *Warich* lives in the same room with them, rent free. He gathers bones and paper.

Those people have bad feelings about both the police and the welfare agency. They say that the police want the poor to be thrown out into the streets so that they can be taken to the *Ochsenkopf.* They say that the director of the welfare agency declines to get involved where many poor people live next to each other. They find it remarkable that one welfare director hanged himself, and that his successor was dismissed on account of embezzlement of funds, and now had become a beggar himself.

TRANSLATED BY PETER SPYCHER

## (78) The false Fatherland

HEINRICH HEINE, "The Silesian Weavers"

Heine's poem "The Silesian Weavers" was published in 1844 under the title "The Poor Weavers" in the Paris *Vorwärts.* The title comes from an 1831 French song.

"Heine's fame in the workers' movement as a political author was based primarily on his poetry rather his prose, and his poems served social-democratic authors as a model of mockery, irony, and satire. Traces are to be seen in *Wahrer Jakob,* the satirical socialist paper, and in other satirical newspapers starting in the seventies. Particularly while the law made public admission of socialist goals dangerous, satirical and humorous writing sustained and made accessible social-democratic criticism of the Reich and the ruling powers. Drawing on Heine as a model, there was also much contact with oppositional bourgeois authors.

"Nonetheless Heine is by no means regarded as *the* political poet of the working class, and he surely would have agreed with this. The literary perspective of German socialists ascribed greater importance to an appeal for support and ritualized commitment than to a reflected, ironic approach . . ." (Frank Trommler)

No tears betray their tribulation,
They sit at their looms with a grim resignation:
Deutschland, we're weaving your winding-sheet,
Three curses we weave to make it complete—
 We're weaving, we're weaving!

A curse on the God who did not hear our prayer
On cold winter nights when our cupboards were bare;
We patiently waited and hoped all in vain,
He mocked us and fooled us and shrugged at our pain—
 We're weaving, we're weaving!

A curse on the king for his selfishness,
Whose heart was not softened by our distress,
Who grabs the last penny with which we could eat
Then has us shot down just like dogs in the street—
 We're weaving, we're weaving!

A curse on the treacherous fatherland,
Where shame and dishonor remain in command,
Where every flower is nipped in the bud,
Where rot and decay feed the worms in the mud—
    We're weaving, we're weaving!

The shuttle flies, the loom creaks on,
We're weaving through the dusk and dawn—
Old Deutschland, we're weaving your winding-sheet,
Three curses we weave to make it complete,
    We're weaving, we're weaving!

TRANSLATED BY ADRIAN DEL CARO

## (79) Peace to the cabins, war on the palaces

GEORG BÜCHNER, The Hessian Courier

This text was published in 1834. The co-author was Friedrich Ludwig Weidig (1797–1837). Tension developed between the two authors, as Weidig was more sympathetic to the liberal-bourgeois branch of the revolutionary movement, placing hope in the liberal upper class. Büchner stressed the interrelationship of political and economic conditions and was more radical. The flyer was provided with practical instructions to the reader.

Darmstadt, July 1834

This paper is meant to report the truth to the province of Hesse, but whoever speaks the truth gets hanged; and even someone who reads the truth risks punishment at the hands of perjuring judges. So that those who have received this paper should observe the following rules:

1. They must carefully keep this paper outside their houses and away from the police;

2. they should share it only with trustworthy friends;

3. to those they trust less than themselves, they should pass it on only by secret means;

4. if this paper nevertheless is found on the person of someone who has read it, he must swear that he was just about to turn it over to the district council;

5. anyone who has not read this paper when it is found on him is, of course, guiltless.

### Peace to the Cabins, War on the Palaces!

*In the year 1834 it appears as though the Bible has been given the lie. It appears as though God created farmers and manual laborers on the fifth day and princes and noblemen on the sixth; and as though the Lord told the latter two: "Have dominion over all creatures that crawl upon the earth," and counted farmers and commoners among the vermin and reptiles.* The life of the "noblemen" is one long Sunday. They live in beautiful homes, they wear exquisite clothes, they have well-fed faces and they speak a language all their own. Meanwhile the people lie at their feet like dung on a field. The farmer walks behind his plow, but the "noblemen" walks behind him *and* the plow and drives him along with his oxen, taking away the grain and leaving him only stubble. The life of the farmer is one long workday. Before his very eyes strangers devour his fields; his body is one large callus; his sweat is the salt on the "nobleman's" table.

There are 718,373 inhabitants in the Grand Duchy of Hesse, and they contribute 6,363,436 gulden annually to the state, in the form of

1. Direct taxes ........................... 2,128,131 gulden
2. Indirect taxes .......................... 2,478,264 gulden
3. Domains ............................... 1,547,394 gulden
4. Royalties.............................. 46,938 gulden
5. Monetary fines ........................ 98,511 gulden
6. Various other sources .................. 64,198 gulden

6,363,436 gulden

This money is the blood-tithe taken from the body of the people. Nearly 700,000 of them sweat and groan and starve for it. It is extorted from them in the name of the state; the extortionists appeal to the government, and the government declares it necessary for keeping order in the state. Now just what sort of mighty entity is this state? When a certain number of people live together in a certain place, and certain ordinances or laws exist, to which each of them has to conform, then it is said that these people comprise a state. The state therefore is everyone; the governors of the state are the laws by which the well-being of everyone is assured and which should proceed from the well-being of everyone. But see what passes for a state in this grand Duchy; see what is meant by "keeping order in the state"! 700,000 people pay for 6 million, meaning that they are turned into plow horses and oxen so that they can live an "orderly" life. Living in order means starving and being flayed alive.

Who are they, then, who have created this order, and who intend to maintain it? They are the grand ducal government. This government is made up of the Grand Duke and his chief officials. The other officials are men who are called up by the government to maintain the strength of their order. Their number is legion: state boards and administrative boards, provincial councils and district councils, spiritual assemblies and school assemblies, finance commissions and forestry commissions, etc., with a whole army of secretaries, etc. The people are their herds, and they its shepherds, milkers, and fleecers. For clothing they wear the hides of farmers, they hoard loot from the poor in their houses; the tears of widows and orphans are the grease on their faces; they rule freely, and exhort the people to bondage. You give them 6 million gulden in taxes, for which they have the trouble of governing you, that is, of helping themselves to feed off you and stripping you of your human and civil rights. Behold the harvest of your sweat!

1,110,607 gulden go to the Ministry of the Interior and the Justice Department. For which you get a jumble of laws heaped up from the capricious ordinances of all centuries, most of them written in a foreign language. The absurdity of all past races is thereby bequeathed to you, and the burden that crushed them rolls onto your shoulders. The law is the property of an insignificant class of "noblemen" and scholars that bestows authority upon itself through its own handiwork. This authority is simply a means of keeping you in check, so that they can fleece you more easily. It invokes laws you don't understand, principles you've never heard of, sentences you could not possibly comprehend. It is incorruptible, because it sees to it that it's paid well enough not to need bribes. Yet most of its servants are bought off body and soul by the government. Their easy chairs rest on a money heap of 461,373 gulden (the total expenditures for courts of law and penal institutions). The tailcoats, walking sticks and sabers of these unassailable servants are studded with the silver of 197,502 gulden (the cost of maintaining the entire police force, gendarmerie, etc.). For centuries now justice in Germany has been the whore of the German princes. You've had to pave every step of the way to her with silver, you've had to purchase her every sentence with poverty and humiliation. Think of the stamp duties, think of your kowtowing in offices, and think of your standing watch outside them. Think of the gratuities for scribes and court clerks. You may sue your neighbor when he steals a potato from you; but just try once to complain of the theft committed daily against your property in the guise of levies and taxes, by which a legion of useless officials glut themselves on your sweat. Just once complain that you're prey to the whims of a few pot-bellies and that these whims are referred to as "the law!" Complain that you're the plow horses of the state, complain of your lost human rights; but where are the courts that will listen to your grievances? Where are the judges who will mete out justice? The chains of your Vogelsberg compatriots hauled off to Rockenburg will give you an answer.

*And if some judge or other official from among the few who really prefer justice and the common good to satisfying Mammon and their own bellies were to be a true counsel to the people instead of their oppressor, he too would be hounded by the Prince's chief advisors!*

TRANSLATED BY DAVID JACOBSON

## (80) The new generation wants to be heard

HEINRICH HEINE, Letter to Karl August Varnhagen von Ense

The diplomat Varnhagen von Ense (1785–1858) was a known writer during his lifetime. Primarily as the result of the influence of his wife, Rahel Levin (1771–1833), a baptized Jew, his house became a center of the Romantic movement. It was here that the Schlegels, Wilhelm von Humboldt, Fichte, Henrich von Kleist, Schleiermacher, and later Heinrich Heine met.

Paris, January 3rd, 1846

Dearest Varnhagen!

This is the first letter I shall write in the new year, and I'm beginning it with the happiest wishes. May physical as well as mental well-being be yours in this year! That you are often oppressed by physical suffering is something I hear with great sadness. I would gladly have shouted out an occasional word of consolation, but Hecuba is a poor consoler. My health in recent days has been disgracefully poor, and even writing constantly reminds me of my physical affliction; I can barely see my own handwriting, because one eye is totally shut and the other is closing, and every letter is an agony! It is therefore with sincere joy that I seize the opportunity of bringing you verbal news of myself through a friend, and since he is privy to all my sufferings, he can inform you in detail about how horribly I have been tricked by my own flesh and blood, and perhaps about what could still be done for me in this regard. My friend Herr Lassalle, who brings you this letter, is a young man of the most outstanding intellectual gifts, of the most thorough learning, of the most expansive knowledge and of the greatest sagacity which has ever confronted me. He combines the richest talent for expression with an energy of knowing and an *habileté* for taking action, all of which astonish me, and if his sympathy for me does not fade, then I expect the most energetic support from him. Anyway this combination of knowledge and ability, of talent and character, was a delightful boon to me, and you, with your versatility of appreciation, will certainly do complete justice to it. Herr Lassalle is simply a distinguished son of modern times, who will hear nothing of that resignation and modesty with which we, more or less hypocritically, hungered and driveled ourselves through *our* days. This new generation wants to enjoy, and to assert itself visibly; we, the old ones, bowed humbly before the invisible, snatched after shadowy kisses and blue garden fragrances, relinquished and whined and yet were perhaps happier than those stern gladiators who confront death so proudly. The millennium reign of romanticism is at end, and I myself was its last and abdicated fairy king. Had I not torn the crown off my head and donned an apron, they would have beheaded me. Four years ago, before I revolted against my own self, I had the urge to go romping once more in the moonlight with my dream companions—and I wrote *Atta Troll,* the swan song of my declining period, and I dedicated it to you. That was fitting, for you have always been my most kindred comrade in arms, in play and in earnest; like me you helped to bury the old times and helped in the midwifery of the new—yes, we brought it to light and we are afraid. We're like the poor hen who has hatched duck eggs and watches horror-stricken as the young brood plunges into the water and swims complacently!

I am bound by a publisher's contract to publish *Atta Troll,* which should happen in a few months, but cautiously, so that they don't put me on trial and behead me.

You notice, dear friend, how vague, how uncertain I feel. Such a weakling mood, however, is rooted mostly in my illness; if the pressure of paralysis lets up, which squeezes my chest like an iron hoop, then my good old energy will fledge once more. Yet I fear that will still take a long time. The treachery which was committed against me in the bosom of my family, where I was unarmed and trusting, struck like lightning from the clear blue sky and nearly killed me; whoever weighs the circumstances will see an assassination attempt in all this; creeping mediocrity, which waited twenty years, grimly jealous of the genius, finally achieved its hour of victory. Basically that, too, is an old story which always repeats itself.

Yes, I am quite ill physically, but my mind has suffered little; a weary flower, it is bowed a bit, but in no way withered, and still it is rooted firmly in truth and love.

And now farewell, dear Varnhagen; my friend will tell you how much and how constantly I think of you, which is all the more understandable, since now I cannot read at all, and cheer myself up in the long winter evenings only by recollecting.
*Heinrich Heine*

TRANSLATED BY ADRIAN DEL CARO

### (81) Joining the workers' movement

AUGUST BEBEL, My Life

The liberal politician Friedrich Naumann wrote in his obituary of August Bebel (1840–1913): "What would have become of Marxist theory in Germany if Liebknecht had not found this man and involved him? He was not a creative thinker like Marx, was not equipped with the weapons of the century like Lassalle, did not have Liebknecht's tenacity of principles, and was a not cunning, talented diplomat like Schweitzer, whom he despised to the end. But he was more than all of them, for he was flesh and blood from the flesh and blood of the people, a child of the elementary school. He himself had been an apprentice and journeyman, working with his hands—robust, fanciful, intuitive, German. The greatness of German social democracy is based in part on the boundless trust enjoyed by 'August' among the masses. In no other country had the proletariat found such a person. For this reason, the social democrats of neighboring countries regarded him as a father."

On February 27, 1860, I set out on my journey back home. At that time there were no railroads yet in southeastern Bavaria; besides, a journeyman in those days traveled most cheaply on foot, provided he also did a little scrounging. The weather was miserable, again. One day, when it was snowing and the wind was whipping me in the face, I was trudging along on the road across the Franconian ridge, my hands in my pants pockets, my stick under my arm and my hat pulled onto my face. Suddenly, I was seized by the arm and hurled into the ditch along the side of the road. Surprised, I looked up and saw that it was the horse pulling a cart coming toward me that had been smart enough to take me by the arm and thrust me aside. In the stormy weather, I had neither seen nor heard the approaching vehicle.

This was the third time I had come through Munich and from there to Ingolstadt, Eichstätt, Nüremberg, Fürth, Würzburg, Aschaffenburg and

Frankfurt from there. Between Würzburg and Aschaffenburg, I spent more than four hours walking through a magnificent beech forest which was part of the Spessart and where I did not encounter a soul. My footsteps were the only sound I heard. Even the forester's hut, which lay in the middle of the forest and off to one side of the road, looked uninhabited. I breathed more easily when I had the seemingly endless forest behind me. Böcklin's painting *Silence in the Forest,* which I came to know years later, brought back again for the first time the mood that had crept over me on that solitary march through the ghostly silence of the beech forest. When I was finally approaching Wetzlar, I began to feel rather odd. I rushed up a low hill ahead from where I saw first the tip of the cathedral and soon thereafter the entire little town. It was the middle of March and after an absence of more than two years I saw my second home again. At the house of one of my aunts, the miller's wife, I found temporary quarters.

Because of general physical weakness, the army deferred me for one year. The same thing happened the next few years when I reported in Halle am Saale, where I journeyed twice from Leipzig. I was finally let go as unfit for military service. Because I could not find work in Wetzlar, I took a temporary job with a Jewish master wood turner in Butzbach, two miles from Wetzlar. The season became more and more beautiful and one day three of my friends from school, with knapsacks on their backs, came into the shop. They told me that they were walking to Leipzig, and "it drew me powerfully on" as the journeymen's song says. I promised my friends to follow within three days and hoped that I would catch up with them, provided their daily marches were not too long. I could risk this proposal since in those days, no one marched better than I.

Up to this time I had not had the slightest desire to visit Leipzig and Saxony and if it had been up to me, I would have seen neither at the time. And yet this journey was decisive for my entire future in more than one respect. Thus chance often rules man's fate.

I should like to mention here parenthetically that I think next to nothing of the proverb that tells us that "everyone is the architect of his own fortune." Man invariably yields to the circumstances and conditions in which he finds himself and which coerce him to act as he does—this is why there is nothing to the so-called freedom of action either. In most cases man cannot foresee the consequences of what he does at a given moment. It is only later that he realizes where that action led him. One step to the left instead of the right or vice versa would have landed him in altogether different circumstances which might have been better or worse than those he found on the path he did take. As a rule, it is only by its results that he recognizes whether he took the smart or the wrong step. But it also happens often that he does not become aware of the right or wrong nature of his actions because he lacks the chance to compare. The self-made man exists only to a very limited degree. Hundreds with much greater qualities than the one who makes it to the top remain anonymous, live and die because unfavorable circumstances prevented their getting ahead, i.e., the correct application and exploitation of their personal qualities. "Fortunate circumstances" are necessary to give the individual a privileged place in life. For that infinite number that does not reach that place, life's table is not laid. If circumstances are favorable, however, it is true that adaptability is needed to exploit them, and that can be seen as the personal merit of the individual.

I caught up with my three friends before they had reached Thuringia and was just in time to help one of them whose feet were already sore by taking him under my arm. As we walked through the villages, this repeatedly provoked the amusement of the inhabitants. We passed through Ruhla, Eisenach and Gotha and arrived in Erfurt. This was the first time we were spending the night in the hostel of a Christian Youth association. It was also the last. The unctuous, creepy manner of the warden disgusted me. Sometime during the evening, he ordered all of us to bed. When we had climbed the stairs to the second floor, the door to a small hall opened and a choral melody came toward us which a youth with smoothly combed blond hair was playing on a harmonium. We entered, surprised, and curious what would be next. The warden now mounted a podium and read out an entire stanza from a book of songs. Accompanied by the harmonium, we had to sing each line as he recited it. Nothing of the sort had ever happened to me in a Catholic apprentices' association. In Munich, for example, where we slept two to a room, a printed prayer had been nailed to the wall which contained the request to recite it before one went to bed. But there was no trace of moral compulsion. But I repeat that I do not know if anything has changed since that time in Catholic apprentices' associations.

Here, in Erfurt, the procedure was beginning to amuse us. Roaring like lions, we went through the melody and text. Then we walked up to the sleeping quarters. After our shirt collars had been inspected for undesirable visitors as the regulations demanded, we climbed into bed. The warden left with his candle, and utter darkness fell. But among the dozens of young people who represented almost all the regions of Germany, there now set in a jesting and bantering such as I had never heard before. The hilarity reached its high point when, in the most remote corner of the dormitory, a fellow from Württemberg began making humorous comments in the purest Swabian. The noise did not die down until late. The following day, we marched on to Weimar. Here my companions declared that they would walk no farther, their feet being too sore. They proposed going on to Leipzig by train. I protested, for I had very little money. And what if there were no work to be found in Leipzig? But my protest was of no avail. If I did not care to continue alone, I would have to go with them. On May 7, 1860, at eleven o'clock at night, we arrived in Leipzig and asked our way to the inn in the Grosse Fleischergasse.

The next day it was the most splendid May weather, and as we went sightseeing in the town and along the promenades in their spring splendor, I found Leipzig very pleasant indeed. Also, I was lucky and found work in a shop where I learned to make the article whose manufacture later enabled me to go into business for myself. Had I arrived in Leipzig twenty-four hours later, the opening would have been taken by someone else. Here again, "a moment's good luck" decided my future. It was the second time I was working in a fairly large shop where five journeymen and an apprentice were employed beside myself. I liked the master and my fellow workers. I also liked the work because it gave me a chance to learn something new. What I did not care for was the bad coffee we were given in the mornings. And the quantity and quality of our midday meal were both inadequate. We had to provide our own breakfast, late-afternoon snack and evening meal. The seven of us slept in a roomy attic in the master's house.

I soon started rebelling against the food. Within a few weeks, I had got my colleagues to agree to a joint complaint. We told the master that all of us would stop working unless there was a change. Which means that we threatened a strike before any of us had ever heard the word; the form of our resistance developing from the nature of the situation. The master was extremely embarrassed and told us that he could not understand our complaint, and that he found the food excellent. That was only natural. He ate with his family after we did and the food he was served was not the same as ours. He had been unaware of this. After repeated negotiations, we got him to agree to an appropriate contribution to our meals which we would purchase ourselves; an arrangement which he claimed he found profitable for he had to give his wife more money for our food than we were demanding. Later, by stubbornly refusing to get out of bed, we persuaded him to put off the start of the working day from five to six. Later still, we insisted on piecework, to which he did not wish to agree at first because he was afraid our work would be poor. But he later saw that he had been mistaken. Finally, we also obtained permission to find our own living quarters.

TRANSLATED BY MICHAEL SHAW

## (82) Working man, awake!

GEORG HERWEGH, "Song for the General League of German Workers"

Herwegh (1817–1875) studied theology at the seminary in Tübingen. His *Poems of a Living Person* (1841–1843) became a great success. The volume contained songs of love and of hate (among others, "We Have Loved Long Enough, We Want Finally to Hate"). Along with August Heinrich Hoffmann von Fallersleben (1798–1874), who published *Unpolitical Songs* in 1840 (containing "Deutschland, Deutschland über alles," which later became the German national anthem), he was the most popular political poet in Germany. In his poem "The Party" of 1842 he challenged poets to become politically involved. Herwegh was a friend of Ferdinand Lassalle.

> Pray and work! the world demands,
> Pray succinctly! for time is money.
> Need and poverty knock at the door—
> Pray succinctly! for time is bread.
>
> And you till and then you seed,
> And you rivet and you sew,
> And you hammer and you spin—
> Tell me, folks, what do you gain?
>
> You work at the loom day and night,
> Dig for ore or coal in the mines,
> Fill the cornucopia,
> Fill it up with wine and grain.
>
> But where do you get *your* meal?
> But where is *your* holiday dress?
> But where is *your* warming hearth?
> But where is *your* sharpened sword?

All your own work! Think of it:
All; but nothing is meant for you!
And of all those marvelous things
Only the chain you forge is yours?

The chain with which the body is fettered,
With which the wings of the spirit are broken,
With which already the foot of the child
Is tied—ah, folks, this is your wage.

What you lift to the light of day,
Are the treasures for the crooks;
What you weave into colored cloth,
Is the curse for you yourselves.

What you build does not provide
Roof and shelter for yourselves;
Those who get clothes and shoes from you
Trample wantonly on you.

Human bees! Has nature ever
Left the honey for *your* use?
Take a look at the drones around you!
Have you actually lost your stings?

Man of labor, do wake up!
Recognize your awesome might!
All the wheels will grind to a halt
If your strong arm so decides.

Your tormentors will turn pale
If you, weary of your toil,
Lean your plow against a wall,
If you shout: Enough of this!

Break the double yoke in two!
Break the plight of slavery!
Break the slavery of need!
Bread is freedom, freedom's bread!

TRANSLATED BY PETER SPYCHER

## (83) Below and above

HUGO VON HOFMANNSTHAL, "Some, of course"

Life, dream, and death form the great triad that characterizes the work of Hugo von Hofmannsthal (1874–1929). His late Romantic poetry made him a "noble symbol" for Austria. "It was all too clear to him that absolutely everywhere he stood for lost causes. There were no prospects for the continued existence of the Austrian monarchy that he had loved and never ceased to love; there were no prospects for his inclination toward the nobility, which still led merely a caricaturelike, hollow existence; there were no prospects for his fitting into the style of a theater whose greatness was sustained only by a few surviving actors; there was no prospect for his succeeding in his wish to restore all the vanishing legacy of the glories of Maria Theresa's reign now in the process of becoming a Baroque-influenced grand opera. Hofmannsthal's life was a symbol, a noble symbol of a vanishing Austria, of a vanishing nobility, of a vanishing theater—a symbol in a vacuum, but nonetheless not the vacuum." (Hermann Broch)

Some, of course, must perish down below,
Where heavy oars of ships graze one another,
While others live up above by the helm,
And know the flight of birds and the lands of stars.

Some always lie with heavy limbs
By the roots of tangled life,
For others, chairs are set up
Among the Sibyls, the queens,
And there they sit making themselves at home,
With light heads and light hands.

Yet a shadow is cast from those lives
Into the other lives.
And the light are bound to the heavy
As though to air and to earth.

The wearinesses of forgotten nations—
I cannot lift them from my eyelids,
Nor can I keep from my terrified soul
The silent falling of faraway stars.

Many destinies teem next to mine,
Existence plays them all into a tangle,
And my part is more than this life's
Slender flame or narrow lyre.

TRANSLATED BY JOACHIM NEUGROSCHEL

## (84) Dingy Prometheus

KARL OTTEN, "Worker!"

"I can only say of my life that it was dedicated to the struggle for the success and victory of the poor—i.e., the proletariat," wrote Karl Otten (1889–1963). Otten studied in Munich, Bonn, and Strassburg, and was arrested during World War I because of his pacifist sympathies. During the twenties he wrote novels and plays. In 1933 he left Germany, going first to Spain and then to England.

Worker! You chained to the wheel, lathe, hammer, pick, plow
Dingy Prometheus I summon you!
You with the harsh voice, the coarse mouth.
You man full of sweat, wounds, soot and filth
Who must obey.
I do not ask what you are working on,
What good it is, whether right or wrong, well or poorly paid,
Whether any pay can reward your dismal work.
Whether money is even the right word or the sop
Which makes this work innocent, meaningful, worthy of pay.
This night lasts long, for years, blackest gloom,
It stuffs its damp shirt before our silent mouths.
I do not see whether you blush.
No one can look into your heart.
You know nonetheless, nonetheless
That you are numbers!
Wherever: in the factory, in jail, the field hospital, the barracks,
            in the cemetery,
You exist for the statistics whose sum, whose rise and decline, wavering
Can be read in every newspaper.
Likewise your children, your wives, your parents, sisters and brothers.
Your lot is improving, one sees it in the statistics.
You are freer, one hears it in the unions.
You are full, one notes this from the flags and music.
You work hard, one feels it in the good cloth of your suits,
            the shoes of your wives.
You understand me? In your heart, deep in the last shaft
You are awake, dissatisfied, philosophical, rebellious.
Deep in your blood you have the bitterness of punishment,
            of regimentation.
Like an angel, immensely strange and unspeakably

You suffer in silence the riddle of this meaningful servitude.
Worker, proletarian, son of the factory, the backyard, the movies,
   Nick Carter and the brothels!
You who live off potatoes and bread, twelve people in two rooms,
Whose childhood horizon was darkened by envy and beatings.
You who strive brutally, maliciously only to avenge yourself on yours,
You who dream of the parcelling out, of the sea, the Alps,
   the palaces and gardens of the rich.
You who are hungry for glittering lamps, mirrors, curls,
   chairs and women—
You await the day! The light! The requital! The day of secret payment:
Eye for an eye, tooth for a tooth!
Gloriously it will dawn, solemn eternal sun above that church steeple
And your triumphal cry will drown out the deepest death rattles!
You have your programs, you have your prophets, yours is the triumph!
It must come for it can be calculated!
Calculated! And I hear your footsteps there
Shuffling forever around the machine
Which is deaf to every entreaty and prayer.
In silence you suffer this brutal routine.


Your heartbeat grew faint with the passing of years
Running down in the passage of time.
It pulsed to the rhythm of pistons and gears
And you just went along with the crime.


The throb of the hissing machines won't abate
They lull you to sleep in the rust.
The iron and money god which they create
Is your own, in him do you trust.


You pray to the same old god of profanity
Erected with newspapers, numbers and war,
Whose visions of bloodshed torture humanity
With stock markets, medals and battlefield gore.


The day will arrive, for come it must
When your eyes will open to bloody awareness,

Your last bit of heart, the spoils of disgust
Will stream from your throat, O horrid awareness!

I summon you son of the galleys of steam,
I hold you on this island of dread
In a bloody and fearful and fiery stream
In the storm of the final cries of the dying
Of mothers and brides and suckling babes
Of curses, begging, feverish crying
Of the wounded, the burned and the poisoned
Of the buried alive and mutilated
The demented by fear, poison, hunger—
You are as I am!
You should and can reason!
You must account for each pull of the lever,
Each hammer blow, every penny you'll earn,
Each word you squander, untruthful, malign!
Do you know it is your duty
To be human, mortal, to have a soul, a heart!
Worker, my dingy brother, you have a heart!
Your heart obligates you to mankind.
From your heart all suffering will find
Its way into all hearts.
Your heart beats in time with the hearts of men
Gives life and atones, then takes life again,
Tears it from the mechanical chest.
Hurry, blood flows and you must do your best.
Blood flows, but you can save humanity!
You son of mankind, whose callouses all masters slavishly lick,
On your heart, your goodness and being, too,
Only on you
Son of a maid, brother of Christ
Depends whether light shall enter this sea of blood and murder!
Your goal, your triumph, your joy is inside!
Within your heart, it is, it is! sure as your heart beats.
Only the heart can decide
The battle which is being waged against you.
Your heart is that which the bullet cuts through
Indifferent of whom: it suffered and feared,

Hoped, sang, was small and poor,
And the heart of a man, of your brother.


They gave you bread, money, work and permission—
I give you your heart!


Believe in your heart, in your feelings, in your goodness,
              in *the* good, in justice!
Believe that there is meaning in belief,
To believe in the eternity of good,
In humanity, whose heart you are.
Only the good will triumph, love, gentleness,
The strong unerring will to truth,
The stiff-necked resolve to say what you feel
And that nothing makes happy like truth.
Be brothers of man! Be human! Be heart! Workers!

TRANSLATED BY ADRIAN DEL CARO

# MODERN NERVOUSNESS

The fever of incipient modernity, characterized primarily by rapidly spreading materialism and a confident belief in progress, placed people in a state of neurasthenic confusion at the end of the nineteenth century. Spiritual development does not keep pace with industrial and economic developments; the "good old days" permeate the "Americanization of life" as regressive longing. Confronted with the demands of an outmoded taste that was predominant precisely because it was outmoded (the taste of the ruling classes), with emphasis dogmatically placed on affirmative civilization and goaded by capitalism's profit-maximizing drive toward accumulation, "modern nervousness" means a condition of innovative cultural agitation. People turn against the moral code that is propped up in facade fashion and which, idealized and romanticized by epigones, offers inadequate protection against emotional conflict. People want to break away, but they do not get free; people want to start something new but are chained to the old. Flight from the world is balanced off against longing for the world. Modern life produces a neurotic sensitivity that, according to Sigmund Freud, arose from the unresolved contradictions of a driven civilization (85).

Freud put his mark on his epoch by analyzing it. Not only was the soul of the individual unveiled on the psychoanalyst's couch; the depths of the individual subconscious were probed. Freud also investigated the emotional landscape of his century, which he surely believed simply to be the expression of the collective emotional structure. What he discovered was expressed in many forms. His consciousness penetrated historical being, which in turn also determined his consciousness. Freud was a citizen of the era, and as such he interpreted the era.

The view of society from below—from the standpoint of psychology, psychoanalysis, and psychological literature at the turn of the century—is less a look at social conditions than it is a look into the depths of the soul of both the individual and the collective subconscious. The errors and confusions, drives and strivings, are consequently also ferreted out in deviations and perversions. The era was characterized by an obsession with sex. People were believed to be sexually obsessed, and this obsession had to be concealed by a facade of propriety. The unmasking of this condition was conceived to be a process of release from such deterioration. The ambiguous aspect of society was accordingly analyzed or exhaustively discussed.

"I have often asked myself in astonishment whence they could obtain this or that secret knowledge which I acquired by arduous examination of the subject, and finally I came to envy the poet whom I otherwise admired," Freud stated in a letter to Arthur Schnitzler in 1906. Schnitzler's melancholy-mocking erotic vignettes, borne by the flair of old Vienna (with its cafes and casinos, parks and theaters, boudoirs and stores, promenades and attic rooms) are the literary counterpart to Freud's theoretical writings. The profile of a luxurious demimonde managed to be a family idyll as well as a flirtation, cultural refinement as well as hysteria, code of honor as well as deviations (86).

The greatest neurasthenic of the era was Friedrich Nietzsche. The various aspects of the spirit of the time coalesced in him.

> The work that he left behind in January 1889 when he became insane is the most comprehensive diary of the soul, the most open confession, the most merciless journal (merciless even to the point of shamelessness) ever written. From *The Birth of Tragedy* to the convolutions of the eighties: a sum of interpretations of the self. This is not philosophy that is being developed; rather, a person is speaking freely—primarily as an aesthete, then as a scientist, ultimately as a prophet . . . What is involved are crises and triumphs, plans and disappointments, i.e., that "passionate emotional story," a "novel with its crises and catastrophes" whose formulation in the form of a psychological biography constituted Nietzsche's actual goal. A four-thousand-page self-analysis through which Nietzsche wanted to overcome Kant and Schopenhauer: i.e., the artist of the soul wanted to overcome the thinkers . . . The explorations in the regions of the soul—cold analyses of depressions, states of intoxication, precipitous illumination, and enduring anxiety anticipate case histories as Freud taught they should be written. (Walter Jens)

Nietzsche was a German who hated Germany; a man who, reared in middle-class prudishness, was made neurotic by overly tender women and was devoured by anxiety; who from weakness professed to have the strength of the "superman," but who also knew how to sublimate suffering through knowledge. *Ecce homo!* (87) His heightened sensitivity made him capable of vision that described the emergence of both the new man and the barbarian. "Great things demand that one either speak grandly or maintain silence about them. Grandly—i.e., cynically and with innocence." Nietzsche, who abandoned himself to Dionysiac intoxication and longed for Apollonian clarity, predicted the plunge into the depths and into the emptiness of the depths. Nihilism was no longer tenable. "Our entire European civilization has long moved in torturous tension that increased from century to century as if toward a catastrophe—restless, powerful, precipitate, like a stream that wants to reach the end, no longer thinking, and fearing thinking."

Anticipating civilization's pessimistic interpretation of the revolt of the masses, Nietzsche feared the rule of the "rabble." He was disturbed by the low niveau of the masses and also by the low level of what called itself bourgeois civilization. The democratic movement was the legacy of a Christian slave morality in any case, and this included the "emancipation of women," anarchism, socialism—phenomena of the "entire degeneration of mankind." By "sacrificing" religion and art to his belief in science, however, he became the spokesman of a scientifically emancipatory mass culture that sought to replace transcendence by immanence. To decadence he contraposed the healthy life, which meant overcoming neurasthenia as both an individual and a collective manifestation. At the same time, he considered decadence a necessary consequence of life and of the growth of life. He thereby indirectly affirmed the antinomies of his era from which he suffered: the culturally immature oscillation between an afterworld mood and longing for change, repression of death and debauchery of suffering, nervous sensitivity and antiemotional materialism.

> The appearance of decadence is as necessary as any ascent and forward motion of life: it is not given to us to eliminate it. Reason wishes, on the contrary, its due, maintaining that it is an outrage for social system-builders to believe there could be circumstances, social combinations in which vice, illness, crime, prostitution, and need would no longer thrive . . . But that means condemning life . . . A society does not have the choice of remaining young. And even at its strongest it must produce garbage and trash. The more energetically and boldly it proceeds, the richer it will be in failures, deformations, and the closer it will be to decline . . . Age is not eliminated by institutions. Neither is illness. Nor vice.

Nietzsche, decadent himself, did not consider decadence something to be combatted; decadence was fate that was overcome by being accepted.

Decadence—i.e., skepticism, libertinage of the mind, corruption of morals, weakness of the will, the need for stronger stimuli. The course of decadence could certainly not be stopped by treatment. Diseases, especially those of the nerves and of the head, were signs that the defensive force of the strong nature was lacking. Yet in the midst of weakness the unchecked breakthrough to new strength occurs. The swan song of emerging nihilism is defiantly sounded in Nietzsche's work, but his constitution was not up to such a glance into the abyss.

Rainer Maria Rilke was also anemic and neurasthenic. Existential anxiety and the feeling of insecurity permeate his work, and repeatedly there is an attempt to find support in the desperate quest for the "divine" by making visible what lies beyond. What was fascinating about him, this "Orpheus in the world of the masses," was his weakness, his stylized sensitivity which led to incredibly widespread admiration of the poet among devotees who perceived in the endurance of anxiety the expression of great courage. The cult of the beautiful was the counterposition to a world that was constantly becoming uglier.

In the *Notebooks of Malte Laurids Brigge,* which Rilke began in 1904 and published in 1910, the poet registered associatively and impressionistically urban reality, especially its horrible and dreadful aspects—sickness, need, death, poverty. The nervous flickering of film is anticipated in language, especially in the first part in which Malte "learns to see," which for him means the simultaneous acceptance of environmental stimuli that everywhere signalize man's homelessness and lost condition. While bourgeois class consciousness idolized dwelling (and the living room) as the place of refuge from the era's storms and attempted to cure modern nervousness by old-fashioned interiors, Rilke, by giving in to neurotic illusion in the flight from the "view downward," proves to be the anatomist of a disintegrating society. Things become the symbol of the transitoriness of man and history. The citizen's well-protected house collapses into ruins in the visions of a "difficult person"—i.e., of Malte, who is equally driven by anxiety about and longing for death. The sight of a torn-down row of houses is a cipher of such modern endangerment (88).

Adhering more emphatically and impressionistically to the phenomenon, Detlev von Liliencron illustrated the endangerment of the era by technological catastrophes. But "Lightning Train" (89) also has a surrealist dimension: the on-and-on-and-on of catapulting technological development races to the abyss; the stop signals are overlooked, the view of society from below is shown in the hybris of a society condemned to ruin. "Trinket, trinket is the symbol of the human hand!" as it is stated in Theodor Fontane's ballad "The Bridge at the Tay." The ballad is a prophetic warning made evident through a dreadful catastrophe caused by the collapse of the middle portion of the bridge over the Firth of Tay in Scotland during a hurricane on December 28, 1879; 200 persons were hurled to the depths.

Just as the Lisbon earthquake had once shattered many people's enlightened belief in theodicy, according to which our world was the best of all possible worlds, the new belief during the era of industrialization in the irrepressibility of progress ran aground when the luxury steamship *Titanic* sank in 1912. A technological spectacle ended in a catastrophe that was justly registered by many contemporaries as the herald of many greater misfortunes still to come.

The steamship *Titanic,* weighing 46,329 net tons, set sail from Stapel in 1911. At that time it was the largest ship in the world. Carrying a crew of 900, it could accommodate 2,203 passengers in first class, 564 in second class, 1,134 in third. It was comparable to a floating city with many palaces and tenement apartments. By setting a record for speed, it was supposed to win the "Blue Band" trophy for the fastest Atlantic crossing.

Pressed for time and vibrating with speed, it disregarded five ice warnings. Racing ahead at full speed, or 21 knots, it ran against an iceberg in the Banks of Newfoundland on April 14, 1912, at 11:40 P.M. The iceberg made an almost 90-meter gash in the ship from the bow to the boiler room. At 2:18 A.M. the lights went out, and shortly thereafter the ship sank. The Cunard Line's *Carpathia* traveled at full steam to rescue 703 survivors, but 1,503 people perished.

In Elias Canetti's recollections of his youth, *The Tongue Set Free,* he tells of the personal shock and mass mourning that followed the sinking of the *Titanic:*

> I cannot remember who first spoke of the sinking of the *Titanic.* But our governess, whom I had never before seen cry, wept at breakfast. And Edith, the maid, joined us in the nursery, where we otherwise never saw her, and the two of them cried together. I heard of the iceberg and of the many people who drowned, and what impressed me most was the band, which went on playing as the ship sank. I wanted to know what they had played, but got a gruff answer. I understood that I had asked something inappropriate and now began to cry, too, so all three of us cried together. When

Mother called up to Edith, she herself may have just heard about the disaster. We then went down, the governess and I, and found Mother and Edith crying together.

We must then have gone out, for I see before me the people on the street. It was all very changed. People stood together in groups and spoke excitedly, others joined them and had something to say. My small brother in the carriage, whose beauty otherwise attracted an admiring word from all passersby, was noticed by no one. We children were forgotten, and yet people spoke of children who had been on board and how children and women were rescued first. The captain, who had refused to abandon ship, was repeatedly talked about. But the most frequent word that I heard was "iceberg." It impressed itself on me like "meadow" and "island." Although I did not learn my third English word from my father, the fourth was "captain." I do not know exactly when the *Titanic* sank. But in the excitement of those days, which did not subside so quickly, I sought in vain for my father. He would have spoken to me about it and would have found a comforting word. He would have protected me from the catastrophe that sank into me with full force. Each of his movements has remained dear to me, but when I think *"Titanic"* I do not see him, I do not hear him, and nakedly I feel the anxiety that overcame me when the ship ran aground on the iceberg and sank in the cold water in the middle of the night while the band played on.


Theodor Fontane faced the errors and confusions and catastrophes of the nervous era with composure. In a sober, clear-sighted, realistic manner marked by impressionistic and naturalistic touches, he describes—*sub specie aeternitatis*—the tension between the old and the new, the inhuman correctness and the upper class's facadelike concept of honor. He looks at society from below. "What is great style? Great style in effect means passing by everything that actually interests people." He subtly captured in literary snapshots as well as in the total panorama of epic flow the deception and appearance of an outmoded world, a world that walked on stilts. Fontane observes the world without *Weltanschauung*. He shows the era as it is, and he shows the hearts of people living in the era. "My entire production is psychology and critique," he explained concerning his writing. He knows no transcendence, not even special instances and borderline situations. The only thing that matters in life is to fill one's allotted span of time and to play one's role in a particular place. There is no place for pathos or metaphysical speculation, not even for pedagogical or meliorative purposes (90). "Morality is valid and must be valid. And because things are as they are, it is best not to go too near and to keep hands off." Relativism and resignation, the feeling of somehow being at the end, replace the absolute and the ideal. Wise humanity commends the poet to keep a distance and to observe things from a distance, to let mildness and goodness have their way where society's dubiousness actually deserves harsh condemnation. There is no programmatic start toward achieving the new man, only an accommodation to that which cannot be changed (91). "Stay still, remain silent. Just don't ask: Why? Why?" Life offers no illusions; each person is alone with himself. "Much joy, much suffering. Errors, confusions. The same old song."

## (85) Rushing and racing. Double morality

SIGMUND FREUD, "Civilized" Sexual Morality and
Modern Nervous Illness

Sigmund Freud was born on May 6, 1856, in Freiberg, Moravia. It was believed that his father's family had long lived in Cologne, having fled to the East as a result of Jewish persecution in the fourteenth or fifteenth century, and back from Lithuania via Galicia to Austria in the course of the nineteenth century. Freud lived in Vienna for seventy-nine of his eighty-three years. Vienna was the city that he hated and disdained but which he also loved and in which, by hard work, he achieved respect and international importance. The National Socialists drove him from his homeland, and he died in London in 1939.

Freudian psychoanalysis produced an intellectual revolution. A rigorous thinker, Freud destroyed the well-established, dominant moral edifice of the era. He demonstrated the significance of impulses and proved to be an archaeologist of the individual as well as the collective soul. "The thinking and understanding of each of us in the 20th century would be different without him. Each of us would think, judge, and feel more constrictedly, less freely and less justly without the background of his thinking, without that powerful inner impulse he provided." (Stefan Zweig)

In his recently published book, *Sexual Ethics,* von Ehrenfels (1907) dwells on the difference between "natural" and "civilized" sexual morality. By natural sexual morality we are to understand, according to him, a sexual morality under whose dominance a human stock is able to remain in lasting possession of health and efficiency, while civilized sexual morality is a sexual morality obedience to which, on the other hand, spurs men on to intense and productive cultural activity. This contrast, he thinks, is best illustrated by comparing the innate character of a people with their cultural attainments. I may refer the reader to Von Ehrenfels's own work for a more extensive consideration of this significant line of thought, and I shall extract from it here only as much as I need as a starting point for my own contribution to the subject.

It is not difficult to suppose that under the domination of a civilized sexual morality the health and efficiency of single individuals may be liable to impairment and that ultimately this injury to them, caused by the sacrifices imposed on them, may reach such a pitch that, by this indirect path, the cultural aim in view will be endangered as well. And Von Ehrenfels does in fact attribute a number of ill-effects to the sexual morality which dominates our Western society to-day, ill-effects for which he is obliged to make that morality responsible; and, although he fully acknowledges its high aptitude for the furtherance of civilization, he is led to convict it of standing in need of reform. In his view, what is characteristic of the civilized sexual morality that dominates us is that the demands made on women are carried over to the sexual life of men and that all sexual intercourse is prohibited except in monogamous marriage. Nevertheless, consideration of the natural difference between the sexes makes it necessary to visit men's lapses with less severity and thus in fact to admit a *double* morality for them. But a society which accepts this double morality cannot carry "the love of truth, honesty and humanity" (Von Ehrenfels, *ibid,* 32 ff.) beyond a definite and narrow limit, and is bound to induce in its members concealment of the truth, false optimism, self-deception and deception of others. And civilized sexual morality has still worse effects, for, by glorifying monogamy, it cripples the factor of *selection by virility*—the factor whose influence alone can bring about an improvement of the individual's innate constitution, since in civilized peoples *selection by vitality* has been reduced to a minimum by humanity and hygiene (*ibid.,* 35).

Among the damaging effects which are here laid at the door of civilized sexual morality, the physician will miss a particular one whose significance will be discussed in detail in the present paper. I refer to the increase traceable to it of modern nervous illness—of the nervous illness, that is, which is rapidly spreading in our present-day society. Occasionally a nervous patient will himself draw the doctor's attention to the part played in the causation of his complaint by the opposition between his constitution and the demands of civilization and will say: "In our family we've all become neurotic because we wanted to be something better than what, with our origin, we are capable of being." Often, too, the physician finds food for thought in observing that those who succumb to nervous illness are precisely the offspring of fathers who, having been born of rough but vigorous families, living in simple, healthy, country conditions, had successfully established themselves in the metropolis, and in a short space of time had brought their children to a high level of culture. But, above all, nerve specialists themselves have loudly proclaimed the connection between "increasing nervous illness" and modern civilized life. The grounds to which they attribute this connection will be shown by a few extracts from statements that have been made by some eminent observers.

W. Erb (1893): "The original question, then, is whether the causes of nervous illness that have been put before you are present in modern life to such a heightened degree as to account for a marked increase in that form of illness. The question can be answered without hesitation in the affirmative, as a cursory glance at our present-day existence and its features will show.

"This is already clearly demonstrated by a number of general facts. The extraordinary achievements of modern times, the discoveries and inventions in every sphere, the maintenance of progress in the face of increasing competition—these things have only been gained, and can only be held, by great mental effort. The demands made on the efficiency of the individual in the struggle for existence have greatly increased and it is only by putting out all his mental powers that he can meet them. At the same time, the individual's needs and his demands for the enjoyments of life have increased in all classes; unprecedented luxury has spread to strata of the population who were formerly quite untouched by it; irreligion, discontent and covetousness have grown up in wide social spheres. The immense extension of communications which has been brought about by the network of telegraphs and telephones that encircle the world has completely altered the conditions of trade and commerce. All is hurry and agitation; night is used for travel, day for business, even 'holiday trips' have become a strain on the nervous system. Important political, industrial and financial crises carry excitement into far wider circles of people than they used to do; political life is engaged in quite generally; political, religious and social struggles, party politics, electioneering, and the enormous spread of trade unionism inflame tempers, place an ever greater strain on the mind, and encroach upon the hours for recreation, sleep and rest. City life is constantly becoming more sophisticated and more restless. The exhausted nerves seek recuperation in increased stimulation and in highly spiced pleasures, only to become more exhausted then before. Modern literature is predominantly concerned with the most questionable problems which stir up all the passions, and which encourage sensuality and a craving for pleasure, and contempt for every fundamental ethical principle and every ideal. It brings before the reader's mind pathological figures and problems concerned with psychopathic sexuality, and revolutionary and other subjects. Our ears are excited and overstimulated by large doses of noisy and insistent music. The theatres captivate all our senses with their exciting performances. The plastic arts, too, turn by preference to what is repellent, ugly and suggestive, and do not hesitate to set before our eyes with revolting fidelity the most horrible sights that reality has to offer.

"This general description is already enough to indicate a number of dangers presented by the evolution of our modern civilization. Let me now fill in the picture with a few details."

Binswanger (1896): "Neurasthenia in particular has been described as an essentially modern disorder, and Beard, to whom we are indebted for a first comprehensive account of it, believed that he had discovered a new nervous disease which had developed specifically on American soil. This supposition was of course a mistaken one; nevertheless, the fact that it was an *American* physician who was first able to grasp and describe the peculiar features of this illness, as the fruit of a wide experience, indicates, no doubt, the close connections which exist between it and modern life, with its unbridled pursuit of money and possessions, and its immense advances in the field of technology which have rendered illusory every obstacle, whether temporal or spatial, to our means of intercommunication."

Von Krafft-Ebing (1895): "The mode of life of countless civilized people exhibits nowadays an abundance of antihygienic factors which make it easy to understand the fateful increase of nervous illness; for those injurious factors take effect first and foremost on the brain. In the course of the last decade changes have taken place in the political and social—and especially in the mercantile, industrial and agricultural—conditions of civilized nations which have brought about great changes in people's occupations, social position and property, and this at the cost of the nervous system, which is called upon to meet the increased social and economic demands by a greater expenditure of energy, often with quite inadequate opportunity for recuperation."

The fault I have to find with these and many other similarly worded opinions is not that they are mistaken but that they prove insufficient to explain the details in the picture of nervous disturbances and that they leave out of account precisely the most important of the aetiological factors involved. If we disregard the vaguer ways of being "nervous" and consider the specific forms of nervous illness, we shall find that the injurious influence of civilization reduces itself in the main to the harmful suppression of the sexual life of civilized peoples (or classes) through the "civilized" sexual morality prevalent in them.

TRANSLATED BY JAMES STRACHEY

## (86) Sweet young things

ARTHUR SCHNITZLER, Youth in Vienna

While Sigmund Freud analyzed the bourgeoisie's ambivalence, which vacillated between the learned morality of the obligation to procreate and the escapist morality of pornography and prostitution, Arthur Schnitzler (1862–1931) described the world of the dandy who gallantly and dreamily dawdles through a society in which "sweet young things" flourish, their sensitivity mundanely cultivated by melancholy males.

Schnitzler worked as a doctor, and his autobiography reflects the fact that his writing is based on life experience. As characterized by Theodor in the play *Frivolous Affair* which was first performed in 1895: "Women don't have to be interesting, just agreeable. You must seek your fortune where I have thus far sought and found mine—where there are no big scenes, no dangers, no tragic complications, where the beginning is not marked by any particular difficulties and the end is free of torment; where the first kiss is received smilingly, and separation occurs with tender emotion."

It was near the end of Carnival when I accompanied my friend Louis to a small suburban gathering in which he'd been dispatched by the pretty wife of a coffeehouse-proprietor. Her favors—or so it had seemed in the coffeehouse, where the affair began—he was seeking a little less passionately than she his. Three Angels Hall, in which this "house party" (for so these events were called, even if, for a nominal fee, any stranger could purchase a ticket at the door) was taking place, was distinguished less for its brilliance and refinement than for a certain old-time congeniality. There was dancing in the main hall, and in the adjacent tavern-rooms the local notables sat at food and drink. All were done up in their Sunday best—fathers, mothers, and various relatives, most of them solidly, comfortably middle-class. Everywhere the odor of beer and cigarettes mingled with the fragrance of flowers and bland perfume which their daughters were spreading as they danced in their bright and colorful summer dresses. There was no lack of propertied native sons and suburban swells among the dancers; and so we two one-year volunteers stepped into this society in our officer-like uniforms, relieved of an odious Moses-dragoon-hood, if not exactly like fairy-tale princes, still, I think, like apparitions

from another, loftier world. Whether in this regard we were viewed with
respect or disgruntlement by the well-established, well-heeled gentlemen,
there was nothing more sensible for us to do than to mix with the people
and plunge ourselves in among them with the utmost friendliness. For
my part I lost no time in asking a very pretty little blonde to dance with
me; and when, strolling aimlessly during a break, we wound up in an
adjoining room that was actually like a giant store room. Unlighted,
filled with overturned chairs and a long, bare table, it evidently was used
on other days as a sort of private clubhouse. In here our discussion became
so animated that after a few minutes we left the room far more intimate
than we'd entered it. During every break that followed we repeated our
visit, also stopping occasionally at the tavern, where Anni's father, a small
gray-bearded gentleman in a Prince Albert, was solemnly downing one
beer after another and smoking a cigar in a long white holder. Anni's
mother, whose appearance I can't remember, watched these goings-on of
youth, utterly unconcerned if her daughter vanished from sight, or from
the ballroom, for a long time or a little while, and always with the same
partner. Whether Louis enjoyed himself as much with the proprietor's
wife as I did with this new acquaintance, I really can't say; indeed, I
don't even recall if the woman showed up. All the figures of this happy
Carnival night have become like shadows to me, shadows among which
blonde Anni and I hover, dancing, the only living creatures, kissing and
caressing one another in a dark corner, while her gray-bearded father,
solemn and bleary-eyed, his cigar cold and his beer going flat, contents
himself with his remote and indifferent minor role.

That Anni, despite her innocent little face and childlike figure, had in
fact already tasted life considerably, was a fact I had to assume, in the
very first hours of our acquaintance, from the way she responded to my
endearments, from the ardent expertness of her kisses. A few days later,
on our first evening stroll together, she confided to me, with the half-
sincerity that inevitably attends accounts of such relationships—and
which at the same time adds significantly to their charm—that she had
indeed been very close to a number of men. But she had truly loved—
and would continue to love—only one, the conductor of a small orchestra.
Rather popular at the time and, incidentally, married, the fellow performed for dances in taverns, or just for entertainment. This suburban
Don Juan had left her expecting, but she had preferred to put a violent
and premature end to her new situation: and so, in the cautionary memory of that painful interlude, yet driven all the same by her temperament

to further love-intrigues, she belonged to that almost lamentable variety of female creature that is doomed to live from one month to the next in a constant round of gaiety and anxiety. Yet gaiety was the stronger element in her soul; and so our brief affair passed almost without any trouble, except for a few unquiet days in which she swore, with an oath quickly broken, never to be mine again. And as I, for my part, felt absolutely carefree, and moreover, despite my infatuation, was not yet pained with the jealousy of the past and future that would afflict me on later occasions, I can count the few scant hours given me to spend in Anni's arms, if not among the most passionate and profound, in any event among the pleasantest and serenest memories of my youth. And if I were obliged, in some dream-examination given by a pendantic professor of literature, to identify the true prototype of the "sweet young thing" from among all the girls I knew, it could only be blond little Anni, the one I found by chance and came to know at the family ball at Three Angels Hall; who was tainted without being sinful, innocent without being chaste, passably sincere and a little mendacious, most of the time quite good-spirited and yet sometimes riddled with fleeting traces of worry; not entirely exemplary as the good little middle-class daughter, and yet, as a sweetheart, the most selfless and respectable creature imaginable. And even if she had just been the exuberant and tender paramour, blissfully lost in the charmed hour of a snug, well-heated little room into which she had followed me after some initial hesitation, still she had only to cross the dim corridor past dimmer stairs, and then a secluded, twilit alley, and enter the pale yellow lamplight of the main street; to merge herself with the evening bustle of shoppers, strollers, and home-bound people; to be changed into an unobtrusive, acceptable young lady with bright, ingenuous eyes, one among many. And I don't doubt that she would show up a quarter of an hour after at the family dinner table, a little late, it was true, but innocently merry and spreading her mirth, the good, and bad, little daughter, bringing back, whether anyone believed it or not, greetings from the merchant from whom she had just bought something, or from some girl friend with whom she had spent a little too much time chatting. And while this charming child eagerly devoured the dinner that had been reheated for her, her mother might well have noticed that her braids were not arranged quite the way thay had been that afternoon, when she had been in such a hurry to leave right after coffee. The woman would refrain, however, from the obvious remarks and questions, cast a glance at the girl's father, always so trusting, who would just then be fixing his cigar into its white paper holder, and think, probably not without nostalgia, but hardly with regret, of the time when she too was young, and perhaps even a sweet young thing.

TRANSLATED BY DAVID JACOBSON

## (87) Symptoms of decadence

FRIEDRICH NIETZSCHE, Ecce Homo. Why I Am So Wise

Four types of decadence are distinguished by Nietzsche in a note found among his posthumous works of the 1880s.
"1.   One chooses, in the belief that one is choosing a cure, something which hastens exhaustion—which is where Christianity belongs (to mention the greatest instance of misguided instinct), which is where 'progress' belongs;
2.   One loses the strength of resistance to stimuli—one is conditioned by coincidence; experiences are made crude and monstrously magnified . . . a 'depersonalization,' a disintegration of the will, which is where altruism, a complete system of morality, belongs; altruism, which focuses on talk of sympathy, and whose essential feature is the weakness of personality, causing it to vibrate sympathetically and to quiver like an overstimulated string . . . an extreme irritability . . .
3.   Cause and effect are confused: decadence is not understood to be physiological and its consequences are perceived as the actual cause of feeling bad—which is where all religious morality belongs . . .
4.   One longs for a condition in which there will no longer be suffering; life is literally perceived to be the basis of evils—states of unconsciousness and lack of feeling (sleep, unconsciousness) are rated incomparably more valuable than conscious states; from this a methodology . . ."

The good fortune of my existence, its uniqueness perhaps, lies in its fatality: I am, to express it in the form of a riddle, already dead as my father, while as my mother I am still living and becoming old. This dual descent, as it were, both from the highest and the lowest rung on the ladder of life, at the same time a *decadent* and a *beginning*—this, if anything, explains that neutrality, that freedom from all partiality in relation to the total problem of life, that perhaps distinguishes me. I have a subtler sense of smell for the signs of ascent and decline than any other human being before me; I am the teacher *par excellence* for this—I know both, I am both.

My father died at the age of thirty-six: he was delicate, kind, and morbid, as a being that is destined merely to pass by—more a gracious memory of life than life itself. In the same year in which his life went downward, mine, too, went downward: at thirty-six, I reached the lowest point of my vitality—I still lived, but without being able to see three steps ahead. Then—it was 1879—I retired from my professorship at Basel, spent the summer in St. Moritz like a shadow, and the next winter, than which not one in my life has been poorer in sunshine, in Naumburg *as* a shadow. This was my minimum: the *Wanderer and His Shadow* originated at this time. Doubtless, I then knew about shadows.

The following winter, my first one in Genoa, that sweetening and spiritualization which is almost inseparably connected with an extreme poverty of blood and muscle, produced *The Dawn*. The perfect brightness and cheerfulness, even exuberance of the spirit, reflected in this work, is compatible in my case not only with the most profound physiological weakness, but even with an excess of pain. In the midst of the torments that go with an uninterrupted three-day migraine, accompanied by laborious vomiting of phlegm, I possessed a dialectician's clarity *par excellence* and thought through with very cold blood matters for which under healthier circumstances I am not mountain-climber, not subtle, not *cold* enough. My readers know perhaps in what way I consider dialectic as a symptom of decadence; for example in the most famous case, the case of Socrates.

All pathological disturbances of the intellect, even that halfnumb state that follows fever, have remained entirely foreign to me to this day; and I had to do research to find out about their nature and frequency. My blood moves slowly. Nobody has ever discovered any fever in me. A physician who treated me for some time as if my nerves were sick finally said: "It's not your nerves, it is rather I that am nervous." There is altogether no sign of any local degeneration; no organically conditioned stomach complaint, however profound the weakness of my gastric system may be as a consequence of over-all exhaustion. My eye trouble, too, though at times dangerously close to blindness, is only a consequence and not a cause: with every increase in vitality my ability to see has also increased again.

A long, all too long, series of years signifies recovery for me; unfortunately it also signifies relapse, decay, the periodicity of a kind of decadence. Need I say after all this that in questions of decadence I am *experienced?* I have spelled them forward and backward. Even that filigree art of grasping and comprehending in general, those fingers for *nuances,* that psychology of "looking around the corner," and whatever else is characteristic of me, was learned only then, is the true present of those days in which everything in me became subtler—observation itself as well as all organs of observation. Looking from the perspective of the sick toward *healthier* concepts and values and, conversely, looking again from the fullness and self-assurance of a *rich* life down into the secret work of the instinct of decadence—in this I have had the longest training, my truest experience; if in anything, I became master in *this*. Now I know how, have the know-how, to *reverse perspectives:* the first reason why a "revaluation of values" is perhaps possible for me alone.

Apart from the fact that I am a decadent, I am also the opposite. My proof for this is, among other things, that I have always instinctively chosen the *right* means against wretched states; while the decadent typically chooses means that are disadvantageous for him. As *summa summarum,* I was healthy; as an angle, as a specialty, I was a decadent. The energy to choose absolute solitude and leave the life to which I had become accustomed; the insistence on not allowing myself any longer to be cared for, waited on, and *doctored*—that betrayed an absolute instinctive certainty about *what* was needed above all at that time. I took myself in hand, I made myself healthy again: the condition for this—every physiologist would admit that—is *that one be healthy at bottom.* A typically morbid being cannot become healthy, much less make itself healthy. For a typically healthy person, conversely, being sick can even become an energetic *stimulus* for life, for living *more.* This, in fact, is how that long period of sickness appears to me *now:* as it were, I discovered life anew, including myself; I tasted all good and even little things, as others cannot easily taste them—I turned my will to health, to *life,* into a philosophy.

For it should be noted: it was during the years of my lowest vitality that I *ceased* to be a pessimist; the instinct of self-restoration *forbade* me a philosophy of poverty and discouragement.

What is it, fundamentally, that allows us to recognize *who has turned out well?* That a well-turned-out person pleases our senses, that he is carved from wood that is hard, delicate, and at the same time smells good. He has a taste only for what is good for him; his pleasure, his delight cease where the measure of what is good for him is transgressed. He guesses what remedies avail against what is harmful; he exploits bad accidents to his advantage; what does not kill him makes him stronger. Instinctively, he collects from everything he sees, hears, lives through, *his* sum: he is a principle of selection, he discards much. He is always in his own company, whether he associates with books, human beings, or landscapes: he honors by *choosing,* by *admitting,* by *trusting.* He reacts slowly to all kinds of stimuli, with that slowness which long caution and deliberate pride have bred in him: he examines the stimulus that approaches him, he is far from meeting it halfway. He believes neither in "misfortune" nor in "guilt": he comes to terms with himself, with others; he knows how to *forget*—he is strong enough; hence everything *must* turn out for his best.

Well then, I am the *opposite* of a decadent, for I have just described *myself*.

TRANSLATED BY WALTER KAUFMANN

## (88) Automobiles run over me

RAINER MARIA RILKE, The Notebooks of Malte Laurids Brigge

Rilke's novel, in the form of a diary begun in Rome in 1904 and completed in Paris in 1910, deals with an aristocratic young Dane who, homeless and without means following the death of his parents, lives in Paris as a poet. "Even his first entries testify how this extremely impressionable young person from an urban reality, which appears almost everywhere to show its ugly, even dreadful side, is virtually overwhelmed. Images of disgust, illness, poverty, death intrude on the unprotectedly exposed person, releasing in him profound existential anxiety nourished on childhood anxieties that are revealed here for the first time as a basic mood of the century, long before their investigation by existential philosophy. . . . In the world of childhood, which formerly seemed to Malte 'as if buried,' there simultaneously comes into being a counterpart to oppressive urban reality. Numerous recollections juxtaposed to the Parisian experiences yield a picture of the two most important childhood environments and the persons involved in them: Ulsgaard, the Brigges' palace, and Urnekloster, the family home of his maternal family Brahe. 'Maman,' Malte's only confidante during his childhood, is the focus of the most intimate recollections." (Joachim W. Storck)

To think that I cannot give up sleeping with the window open. Electric street-cars rage ringing through my room. Automobiles run their way over me. A door slams. Somewhere a window-pane falls clattering; I hear its big splinters laugh, its little ones snicker. Then suddenly a dull, muffled noise from the other side, within the house. Someone is climbing the stairs. Coming, coming incessantly. Is there, there for a long time, then passes by. And again the street. A girl screams: Ah tais-toi, je ne veux plus. An electric car races up excitedly, then away, away over everything. Someone calls. People are running, overtake each other. A dog barks. What a relief: a dog. Toward morning a cock even crows, and that is boundless comfort. Then I suddenly fall asleep.

These are the noises. But there is something here that is more terrible: the stillness. I believe that in great conflagrations there sometimes occurs such a moment of extreme tension: the jets of water fall back, the firemen no longer climb their ladders, no one stirs. Noiselessly a black cornice thrusts itself forward overhead, and a high wall, behind which the fire shoots up, leans forward, noiselessly. All stand and wait, with shoulders raised and faces puckered over the eyes, for the terrific crash. The stillness here is like that.

I am learning to see. I don't know why it is, but everything penetrates more deeply into me and does not stop at the place where until now it always used to finish. I have an inner self of which I was ignorant. Everything goes thither now. What happens there I do not know.

Writing a letter today, I was struck by the fact that I had been here only three weeks. Three weeks elsewhere, in the country for example, would be like a day; here they seem like years. And I mean to write no more letters. What's the use of telling anyone that I am changing? If I am changing, then surely I am no longer the person I was, and if I am something else than heretofore, then it is clear that I have no acquaintances. And to strange people, to people who do not know me, I cannot possibly write.

Have I said it before? I am learning to see. Yes, I am beginning. It still goes badly. But I intend to make the most of my time.

To think, for instance, that I have never been aware before how many faces there are. There are quantities of human beings, but there are many more faces, for each person has several. There are people who wear the same face for years; naturally it wears out, it gets dirty, it splits at the folds, it stretches, like gloves one has worn on a journey. These are thrifty, simple people; they do not change their face, they never even have it cleaned. It is good enough, they say, and who can prove to them the contrary? The question of course arises, since they have several faces, what do they do with the others? They store them up. Their children will wear them. But sometimes, too, it happens that their dogs go out with them on. And why not? A face is a face.

Other people put their faces on, one after the other, with uncanny rapidity and wear them out. At first it seems to them they are provided for always; but they scarcely reach forty—and they have come to the last. This naturally has something tragic. They are not accustomed to taking care of faces, their last is worn through in a week, has holes, and in many places is thin as paper; and then little by little the under layer, the no-face, comes through, and they go about with that.

But the woman, the woman; she had completely collapsed into herself, forward into her hands. It was at the corner of rue Notre-Dame-des-Champs. I began to walk softly as soon as I saw her. When poor people are reflecting they should not be disturbed. Perhaps their idea will yet occur to them.

The street was too empty; its emptiness was bored; it caught my step from under my feet and clattered about with it hither and yon, as with a wooden clog. The woman startled and pulled away too quickly out of herself, too violently, so that her face remained in her two hands. I could see it lying in them, its hollow form. It cost me indescribable effort to stay with those hands and not to look at what had torn itself out of them. I shuddered to see a face from the inside, but still I was much more afraid of the naked flayed head without a face.

I am afraid. One has to take some action against fear, once one has it. It would be very nasty to fall ill here, and if it occurred to anyone to get me into the Hôtel-Dieu I should certainly die there. This hôtel is a pleasant hôtel, enormously frequented. One can scarcely examine the facade of the Cathedral of Paris without danger of being run over by one of the many vehicles that must cross the open space as quickly as possible to get in yonder. They are small omnibuses that sound their bells incessantly, and the Duke of Sagan himself would be obliged to have his equipage halted if some small dying person had taken it into his head to go straight into God's Hôtel. Dying people are headstrong, and all Paris is at a standstill when Madame Legrand, brocanteuse from the rue des Martyrs, comes driving toward a certain square in the Cité. It is to be noted that these fiendish little carriages are provided with uncommonly intriguing windows of opaque glass, behind which one can picture the most magnificent agonies; the fantasy of a concierge suffices for that. If one has even more power of imagination and it runs in other directions, conjecture becomes simply boundless. But I have also seen open cabs arriving, hired cabs with their hoods folded back, plying for the usual fare: two francs for the hour of agony.

Will anyone believe that there are such houses? No, they will say I am misrepresenting. This time it is the truth, nothing omitted, and naturally nothing added. Where should I get it from? Everyone knows I am poor. Everyone knows it. Houses? But, to be precise, they were houses that were no longer there. Houses that had been pulled down from top to

bottom. What *was* there was the other houses, those that had stood alongside of them, tall neighboring houses. Apparently these were in danger
of falling down, since everything alongside had been taken away; for a
whole scaffolding of long, tarred timbers had been rammed slantwise between the rubbish-strewn ground and the bared wall. I don't know
whether I have already said that it is this wall I mean. But it was, so to
speak, not the first wall of the existing houses (as one would have supposed), but the last of those that had been there. One saw its inner side.
One saw at the different storeys the walls of rooms to which the paper
still clung, and here and there the join of floor or ceiling. Beside these
room-walls there still remained, along the whole length of the wall, a
dirty-white area, and through this crept in unspeakably disgusting motions, worm-soft and as if digesting, the open, rust-spotted channel of
the water-closet pipe. Gray, dusty traces of the paths the lighting-gas had
taken remained at the ceiling edges, and here and there, quite unexpectedly, they bent sharp around and came running into the colored wall and
into a hole that had been torn out black and ruthless. But most unforgettable of all were the walls themselves. The stubborn life of these rooms
had not let itself be trampled out. It was still there; it clung to the nails
that had been left, it stood on the remaining handsbreadth of flooring, it
crouched under the corner joints where there was still a little bit of interior. One could see that it was in the paint, which, year by year, it had
slowly altered: blue into moldy green, green into gray, and yellow into
an old, stale rotting white. But it was also in the spots that had kept
fresher, behind mirrors, pictures, and wardrobes; for it had drawn and
redrawn their contours, and had been with spiders and dust even in these
hidden places that now lay bared. It was in every flayed strip, it was in
the damp blisters at the lower edges of the wallpapers; it wavered in the
torn-off shreds, and sweated out of the foul patches that had come into
being long ago. And from these walls once blue and green and yellow,
which were framed by the fracture-tracks of the demolished partitions,
the breath of these lives stood out—the clammy, sluggish, musty breath,
which no wind had yet scattered. There stood the middays and the sick-
nesses and the exhaled breath and the smoke of years, and the sweat that
breaks out under armpits and makes clothes heavy, and the stale breath
of mouths, and the fusel odor of sweltering feet. There stood the tang of
urine and the burn of soot and the gray reek of potatoes, and the heavy,
smooth stench of ageing grease. The sweet, lingering smell of neglected
infants was there, and the fear-smell of children who go to school, and
the sultriness out of the beds of nubile youths. To these was added much

that had come from below, from the abyss of the street, which reeked, and more that had oozed down from above with the rain, which over cities is not clean. And much the feeble, tamed domestic winds, that always stay in the same street, had brought along; and much more was there, the source of which one did not know. I said, did I not, that all the walls had been demolished except the last—? It is of this wall I have been speaking all along. One would think I had stood a long time before it; but I'm willing to swear that I began to run as soon as I had recognized that wall. For that is the terrible thing, that I did recognize it. I everything here, and that is why it goes right into me: it is at home in me.

TRANSLATED BY M. D. HERTER-NORTON

## (89) Another train smashes into its side

Detlev von Liliencron, "Lightning Train"

The "dream of a network" presented by the railroad system becomes a nightmare in this poem. The rhythm of the impressionistically structured verse repeats the express train's hurried rhythm. This "reporter poetry" is characterized by visual and auditory sensations that are superimposed above the staccato sound of the divisions in the tracks. In the midst of the general belief in progress the demonism of technology is suggested.

> Straight across Europe through country and city
> Rattles and clatters the rail melody.
> Is it to savor some rapture more quickly?
> Is someone late for the judgment day tea?
> > On and on on and on big wheels revolving,
> > Streaking along with the distance dissolving,
> > Smoke is the monster's ephemeral mane,
> > Whistles are blown by conductor and train.

> Countries fly past and the cities are absent,
> Hours and days are engulfed in retreat,
> Valleys and mountains are gone in an instant,
> Fantasies, longing and mental deceit.
> > Moonlight and sun, once again constellations,
> > Soon they will reach their desired destinations,
> > Twilight and evening and fog in the night,
> > Great expectations and hopes burning bright.

Twilight is dropping its gossamer cover,
Venus has climbed to her throne in the sky.
Just one more hour! The trip will be over,
Those who had gathered will say their good-bye:
    Families wealthy, *gallants* and the bankers,
    Officers, councilman, prince and a scholar,
    Mingled with "gentry" a poet is found,
    Sweet little children with toys all around.

Darkness has now grown demonically thicker,
Lanterns are lit in the darkened coupées.
On and on on and on, axel sparks flicker,
Is that a signal up there far away?
    On and on on and on, what stands there waiting,
    Is this the goal we were anticipating?
    Stop stop stop stop stop the engineer cried—
    Another train smashes into its side.

Following day there is wreckage far scattered,
Rubble in heaps between charry remains,
Two empty spurs piled with ashes and battered,
Curling irons, stock receipts, watches and chains:
    Poetry: "Seraphic Music," and money,
    Sheet music: "My Dear Camena," and jew'lry,
    Lastly a doll which had burned in its bed,
    Drawn by a mule with a harness of thread.

TRANSLATED BY ADRIAN DEL CARO

## (90) Not worth mentioning

THEODOR FONTANE, Errors, Confusions

Theodor Fontane (1819–1898) spent his childhood in Neuruppin and Swinemünde. Like his father, he started out as a druggist. He was then attracted to journalism and went to London to work as a reporter. He subsequently reported from theaters of war during the Bismarck era and later worked as a theater critic. Only when he was older did he start to write novels. *Errors, Confusions* (1888) tells of a middle-class girl (Lene Nimptsch) who renounces her beloved (Botho von Rienäcker). Their class differences forbid their alliance; Botho marries a woman of his station; Lene a "regular man" of the people.

Botho wanted to go to Lene at once, and when he sensed that he did not have the strength, he wanted at least to write. But that didn't work either. "I can't, not today." And so he let the day go by and waited until the next morning. But then he hastily wrote.

"Dear Lene!
Now it has happened the way you told me yesterday: Farewell. And good-bye forever. I had mail from home which forces my hand; it has to be, and because it has to be, let it be over soon . . . . Oh, I wish these days were behind us. I will say nothing more, not even how I really feel . . . . It was a brief, beautiful time, and I shall forget none of it. About nine I will be with you, not sooner, because it must not take long. Good-bye, just one more good-bye. Your B. v. R."

And now he arrived. Lene stood at the gate and greeted him as usual; not the slightest sign of accusation or even of painful resignation showed on her face. She took his arm, and thus they walked up the front garden path.

"It's right, that you came . . . I'm glad you're here. And you must be glad, too."

With these words they had reached the house, and Botho looked as if he would enter the large front room from the hallway, as usual, but Lene led him along farther and said: "No, Frau Dörr is in there . . ."

"And is still angry with us?"

"Not that. I reassured her. But what do we need of her today? Come, the evening is so lovely, and we want to be alone."

He agreed and so they walked down the hall and across the yard to the garden. Sultan did not stir and only blinked after them, as they strode up the big middle path to the bench which stood between the raspberry bushes.

When they reached the bench, they sat down. It was quiet; from the field one could hear a chirp, and the moon stood above them.

She leaned against him and said softly, warmly: "So now this is the last time that I'll hold you hand in mine?"

"Yes, Lene. Can you forgive me?"

"You and your questions. What am I supposed to forgive you?"

"That I am hurting your heart."

"Yes, it hurts. That's true."

And now she became silent and looked up at the pale stars rising in the sky.

"What are you thinking about, Lene?"

"How nice it would be to be up there."

"Don't say that. You mustn't wish to be rid of your life; it's only one step from such a wish to . . ."

She smiled. "No, not that. I'm not like the girl who ran to the well and hurled herself into it because her lover danced with someone else. Do you remember when you told me about that?"

"But what does this mean? You're not the type to say something like this just to have something to say."

"No, I meant it seriously, too. And really [as she pointed upward], I would like to be there. There I'd have peace. But I can wait . . . And now come, let's go out into the field. I didn't bring a wrap and it's cold just sitting here."

And so they went up the same lane which had once led them along the first row of houses in Wilmersdorf. The steeple was clearly visible under a clear sky, and a thin veil of fog drifted over the meadow only.

"Do you remember," said Botho, "how we walked here with Frau Dörr?"

She nodded. "That's why I suggested it; I wasn't cold at all, or hardly. Oh, it was such a beautiful day then, and I was never so cheerful and happy, not before and not after. Even at this moment my heart laughs when I think back on it, how we walked and sang '*Denkst du daran.*' Yes, memory is a lot; it's everything. And now I have that and it will stay; it can no longer be taken from me. And I can really feel how it picks me up."

He embraced her. "You're so good."

But Lene continued in her quiet tone: "And because it makes me feel so good, I don't want to let it pass without telling you everything. It's really the same old thing I've been saying all along, even day before yesterday when we were out on that picnic that nearly fell through, and then afterward as we parted. I saw it coming from the beginning, and what's happening now must happen. When you've had a good dream, then you must thank God for it and not complain that the dream is over and reality begins again. It's different now, but all will be forgotten or will assume a friendly appearance. And someday you'll be happy again and maybe I, too."

"Do you think so? And if not, what then?"

"Then you live without happiness."

"Oh, Lene, you say that so casually, as if happiness were nothing. But it *is* something, and that's just what tortures me; to me, at least, it's as if I had done you an injustice."

"I absolve you of that. You did me no injustice, didn't mislead me and promised me nothing. Everything was of my own free choosing. I loved you from the bottom of my heart, it was my destiny, and if there was any fault, then it was *my* fault. And there is another fault. I have to tell you again and again, for which I am glad with my heart and soul, for it was my happiness. If I have to pay for it, then I pay willingly. You didn't offend, injure, or insult, or at most only that which people call propriety and proper etiquette. Should I fret about that? No. Everything will fall into place again, that, too. And now come, let's go back. Just look how the fog is rising; I believe Frau Dörr is gone now and we'll find the dear old woman alone. She knows everything and all day she's been saying the same thing over and over."

"And what is that?"

"That it's good this way."

Frau Nimptsch was in fact alone as Botho and Lene joined her. Everything was quiet and dusky, and only the fire from the stove cast a glow of light across the broad shadows which slanted diagonally through the room. The goldfinch was fast asleep in its cage, and one heard nothing but the occasional hissing of the water bubbling over.

"Good evening, little mother!" said Botho.

The old woman returned the greeting and wanted to rise from her stool, in order to offer him the large recliner. But Botho would not permit it and said: "No, little mother, I'll sit down in my old place."

And then he slid his stool near the fire.

A brief pause ensued; soon however he began again: "I 've come today to say good-bye, and to thank you for the kindness and goodness that I've enjoyed here for so long. Yes, little mother, I mean it sincerely. I was so glad to be here, and happy. But now I have to leave, and all that I have left to say is just this: It really is best this way."

The old woman remained silent and nodded approvingly. "But I'm not leaving the world," continued Botho, "and I'll never forget you, little mother. And now give me your hand. Yes. And now good night!"

Hereupon he stood up quickly and strode toward the door, while Lene clung to his arm. They walked together to the garden gate, without speaking another word. But then she said: "Be brief now, Botho! My strength won't hold out; it was too much for me after all, these two days. Farewell, my only, and be as happy as you deserve, and as happy as you have made me. Then you'll be happy. And don't talk about the rest anymore, it isn't worth mentioning. So. So."

And she gave him a kiss and one more and then she closed the gate.

As he stood on the other side of the street, he seemed to want to turn back again for another word, for another kiss with Lene, when he caught sight of her there. But she waved him away abruptly with her hand. And so he continued down the street, while she, supporting her head on her arm, and her arm on the gatepost, looked after him with eyes wide open.

Thus she stood for a long time, until his steps had echoed into the night's darkness.

TRANSLATED BY ADRIAN DEL CARO

## (91) What do you and your happiness matter?

Theodor Fontane, "Would There Be Something I'd Possibly Miss?"

Thomas Mann writes concerning the mature Fontane: "There is something absolutely charming about his style, especially in that of his last days, as is disclosed to us in the letters of the eighties and nineties. To me personally, at least, the admission may be permitted that no writer of the past or present awakens in me the sympathy and gratitude, this immediate, instinctive enchantment, this immediate cheerfulness, warming effect, and contentment that I feel in every verse of every line of his letters, of every fragment of dialogue. This luminous prose, even with all its comfortable breadth, is the result of its secret tendency toward the balladesque, and in its simultaneously attractive and verselike abbreviations. With seeming nonchalance it has an attitude and structure, an inner form that is only conceivable from extensive practice in writing poetry. In fact, it is much closer to poetry than its unceremonious modesty would seem to suggest. It has poetic conscience, poetic needs; it is written from the point of view of poetry and, like the verse from later years which is so concentrated and complete that it is immediately memorized, stylistically more closely approaches his prose. Hence the strange thing is that his prose is sublimated to the same degree to which it (permission for the word!) squanders . . . The drama offered by the mature Fontane, this drama of an elderly person that is a rejuvenation artistically, spiritually, humanly, this drama of a second real youth and maturity in advanced years does not easily find a counterpart in German intellectual history. 'With age I have become younger,' wrote the twenty-year-old youth to a friend, 'and the joy of life, which is actually youth's inheritance, seems to grow in me the longer the tangled thread becomes.' That is an early insight resulting from his vital uniqueness. He was born to become the 'old Fontane' who will live: the first six decades of his life were almost consciously merely a preparation for the two later decades spent amicably and skeptically in the growing shadows of the final riddle, and his life seems to teach that true maturity comes only with readiness for death. Ever freer, ever wiser, the unusual and charming personality matured toward the reception of the final answer. And in the literary remains of the immortalized was found the beautiful saying: 'Life: fortunate the person who has it/ Joy, children, daily bread,/ yet the best it sends/ is the knowledge that it ends/ is the exit, death.'"

Early today, having slept the whole night
I rose into the morning light.
Breakfast was ready and waiting for me,
The roll tasted fresh, and hot was the coffee,
I sat to read the paper then
(Promotions were being made again).
I stepped to the window and looked outside,
The city was starting to get into stride,
(At the butcher's) an apron hung over a stool
Little girls were out walking to school—
Everything friendly, everything gay
But if I had just stayed in bed the whole day,
Pretending to be unaware of all this,
Would there be something I'd possibly miss?

TRANSLATED BY ADRIAN DEL CARO

# THE DARK VISION

According to Hölderlin, the Germans were "poor in deed and rich in thoughts." At the end of the century Nietzsche spoke of the extirpation of the German spirit in favor of the German Reich, by which time the Germans had evidently become rich in deed and poor in thoughts. The titanic achievement of the German spirit, especially of idealism, consisted in answering, by means of a comprehensive system characterized by will and idea, the question of meaning. In doing so, however, the observer was exempt from reality—the world of ideas was what was actually true and real, while the human being as a spiritual creature had withdrawn to the needs of existence. Such "cerebral creations" proved to be a heroic deed: ideality was brought forward in an era of severe need and suffering and in the midst of the aridity of an era threatened by attack and danger.

A disintegration of idealism in the face of the pressing forces of the era characterizes the inner development of the German spirit in the last third of the nineteenth century. Instead of penetrating into the whole, all that remains is to maintain the position despite disintegration. Admittedly disintegration was also regarded as the necessary presupposition for overcoming an idealism that had become bourgeois and epigonal. In the sense of a materialistic interpretation of the world and conception of milieu, naturalism completed the "final reckoning" with the "great themes," seeking to concentrate on the moment and to portray what was momentary and relevant. This particularly included a portrayal of "natural" human existence, which was sought where the veneer of civilization and culture was either lacking or had sloughed off, such as in urban centers of misery where the wretchedness of existence provided the naturalists with the decisive truth about the human soul and its needs. In *Brutalities* (1886) Hermann Conradi asked where much-lauded and miserably maligned "idealism" was to be found:

Oh, well—ideals in abstractions, to be abstracted "just as life must be lived and death must be died. Our era as a whole has but little time for this act. For this reason, it is also so preeminently materialistic . . ." A younger generation of poets and writers are coming to the fore whose concern is to document ideal tendencies by analysis and to document temporally given realities by artistic expression—to the extent that each ideal is intensified into palpable plasticity when it anticipates a moment of the future that is conditioned by natural being and by the natural development of things. This, however, is only possible by energetically taking into consideration an utterly real substratum.

Naturalism implies a view of the world from below—social commitment and sympathy with the oppressed. Naturalism was, in addition, a technique of approaching reality, analogous to impressionism and to photographic technique. Momentary art was intended to arrest objectively each detail of an event, even the seemingly most unimportant and banal, to capture the smallest movement, the most trivial thought and to subordinate it aesthetically and poetically to this intention as a "documented" assertion, or as a fixing of reality.

Old art has nothing to report about the falling leaf except that it whirls around while falling to the ground. New art describes this event from second to second, describing how the leaf shines with a reddish hue on one side when the light falls on it, gray from the other side; the next second the situation is reversed, and it is shown how the leaf initially falls vertically, is then driven toward the side, and then again falls in an upright position . . . (Arno Holz)

Naturalism as a dark vision had its origin in the intimation of decline. "Am I surrounded by ghosts here?" asked the despairing John in Gerhart Hauptmann's tragicomedy *The Rats,* which was first performed in 1911. "The sun is shining! It is bright daylight! I don't know, though—I can't see! It's giggling, it's whispering, it's coming creeping along! But when I reach out for it, it isn't there." The insistently real event of the drama is that the servant Piperkarcka fights in vain for the love of her seducer and for the possession of their child whose birth had been kept secret and whom she has entrusted to Mother John, the wife of a mason. The realistic-naturalistic description of social conditions in the milieu of poor people and tenement houses where there are rats and other vermin has a second symbolic level: the rats are ciphers of an undermined and decaying society headed for decline.

Gottfried Benn portrayed the disintegration of the human body in the expressive melody of a still more exaggerated naturalistic directness (92). The eschatological mood of his writing, frequently presented with tragical snobbery and sentiments that are both elegiacal and melancholy, was an intimation of the chthonic ("earth is calling"). His work is laden with skepticism, cynicism, faithlessness. Only the poem is capable of providing some support—"nothing, but covered with glaze." Disintegration of reality ("The human—a conglomeration, the whole—teeth removed, tonsils removed, appendix removed, ovaries removed, fixed form that prophylactically fragments itself") is captured only by artistry. "Our order is the spirit, whose law is expression, form, style." Such "formalism," which no longer, as in Schiller's aesthetics, reconciles form and content with each other but only marks a position of "endurance," made it possible for Benn to look admiringly toward Rilke: "This meager figure and inspiration of great poets, who died of leukemia, buried between the bronze hills of the Rhone valley and in ground over which French lutes sound, wrote the verse that my generation will never forget: 'Who speaks of winning—to survive is everything.' "

If Baudelaire's definition of dandyism, that it is the last realization of heroism in eras of decay, is accepted, then Hugo von Hofmannsthal betrays "dandyist" traits. He was an aesthetic latecomer who from rejection of an ugly environment sought to establish a new inner aristocracy. Despite the "determined elegance" that characterized the poet's biography (from the mysteriously lyrical boy genius to the conservative *poeta ductus*), he manifests a particular ability for empathy with phenomena that were alien to his existence. The sight of a "scrap of world" such as a factory town, the "suffering ciphers of reality," filled him with horror. He could not endure human suffering "directly"; he repeatedly circled around it in often remote content, images, and similes in order to avoid an immediate confrontation.

The world as will and idea is a world conceived in and comprehended by language. That "cerebral creation," idealism, is an emanation from the depths of language. Self-discovery occurs in its essence as the exertion of the force of language, not in the sphere of force of action. Accordingly, for Hofmannsthal the disintegration of language implies a crisis in consciousness, a loss of identity (93).

Nietzsche greeted the waves of approaching nihilism as a natural process that swept away the old, outmoded, and brittle, and he was ecstatic, albeit with a trace of masochism, about the self-cleansing process of culture. Hofmannsthal, on the other hand, was characterized by a sensitive, resigned feeling of sadness. He recognized the dubiousness of old values but strove for no *tabula rasa* for a new mankind. He wanted the change to occur in a manner that preserved and passed on values (of the German spirit and the German language) in a more inward form.

"Incorporation" in an entirely different, revolutionary sense characterized expressionism's "Action Patricide" as described by Sigmund Freud in *Totem and Taboo*. "One day the banished brothers met, slayed, and devoured the father, thus making an end of the paternal horde. United they dared and succeeded in accomplishing what would have remained impossible for either of them alone."

The overwhelming power of the "father" was a problem of the century. Patriarchy culminated in the "ideas of 1914"; the virtues of obedience, submission, and fulfillment of duty reached a macabre highpoint. It is the origin of the era's "disdain for death." On the one hand, there is readiness of those equipped with rigorous force of command to sacrifice their fellowman; on the other hand, there is the willingness of those being sacrificed to accept their destruction completely.

The protest against the taboo of the ruler and against the ruler's power and grandeur could only occur when repressive conditions had deteriorated on their own, thus resulting in the destruction of the magical spell surrounding the greats and pillars of society. A generation now appears that passionately attempts to tear down paternal images, intending to realize the vision of the new man by an "attitude of brotherhood." The "sons" radically question a patriarchal social order that denies them any maturity. They do so at some times in a combination of enthusiasm and vagueness, at others in a combination of cynicism and aggression.

In the context of this new consciousness, when an awareness of being sacrificed began to dawn on the generation of the victims and when the credibility of command became subjected to attacks of doubt, the voices of the few protesters had become stronger. Meantime the applause of the ignorant, who had been seduced by society, became weaker, and at this point a peculiar, largely autobiographical literary document was made public. Seen within the framework of the collective subconscious the document can altogether be considered a symptom of the general situation. The work in question, Franz Kafka's *Letter to His Father*, was written in 1919 when the author was thirty-six, five years before his death. The father, ruler of the family's fate, was the superior in strength, health, appetite, temperament, powers of articulation, contentment, knowledge of the world and of people, endurance, presence of mind. The father's treatment of the anxious son reflects his mentality and is accordingly characterized by force, noise, and fury. Kafka goes to pieces from this overwhelming father (94).

> The son, however, sacrifices himself in boundlessly infatuated consciousness of guilt and innocence, in modesty and arrogance, in love that is hate, and in hate that is love. The order of the world is hopelessly perverted; it is the deadly truth of this letter that in itself is blinded. (W. Emrich)

The text appears to be focused on family matters. No notice is taken of the apocalyptic event of the war, and social reality is excluded. The religious dimension, however, is undeniable. The letter to the corporeal father is simultaneously a question to the heavenly father. Kafka's distress about the terrestrial world in which it is no longer possible to breathe derives from a destruction of immediately interpersonal relations. The lies in which all human forms of life and thought, including the legal order, are entangled, stem ultimately from the lies and deceptions that have become entrenched in the elementary emotional relations between fathers and sons, mothers and daughters, men and women. In addition, however, the question of metaphysical meaning is posed. Letter to the father—with no answer.

The dark vision that conjures up the deterioration of structure and existence, tradition and meaning, body and soul, language and spirit, connection and order, form and tradition, society and state—this end-of-the-world mood in which the inner history of the German spirit of the nineteenth century draws to a close is expressed in numerous symbols. Often the metropolis appears as the setting of mindless stumbling that is addicted to ruin (95). "The Tempest is At Hand" is the title of the poem written by Jakob van Hoddis two years before the outbreak of World War I (96). Looking back, the glow of the sun in the August days of 1914 was felt by many to be a simile. It was late for the gaudy happiness of the epoch's uncanny idyll. It was a Panic hour. Decades of stifled aggression exploded into the summer cheerfulness like a thunderstorm. The immature exaggerations of youthful credibility and conflict led into the hands of demagogues—and led astray. The end-of-an-era mood was misunderstood to be the mood of a new beginning, with no awareness that the enthusiasm was the dawning of death! The dreadful approaching catastrophe was suspected only by some socialists and artists. "Dying warriors, the wild lament of shattered mouths . . ." (97) Yelling death! (98)

The blood sacrifices demanded by the agitation of peoples fighting great wars are made in tragic, rueful enthusiasm, according to Franz Marc's obituary of the painter August Macke, one of the first victims of the war. Everyone extended hands in faithfulness, Marc continues, proudly bearing the loss among the sounds of victory. "The individual person who has lost the most precious human treasure in war chokes down the tears in silence. Grief creeps between the walls like a shadow."

Franz Marc's art reaches back to the Romantic view of the world. "Is there a more uncanny idea for the artist than that nature is surely reflected in an animal's eyes?" Novalis could have written such a sentence. Marc celebrates the animal as an artistic subject similar to Kleist's marionette. He yearns to be able to reenter the lost paradise from behind, through the aid of creaturely innocence that is exempt from human perversion. The animal perspective of his art signifies flight from the person and from human reality. It is a mystical world and proves to be a backward-directed utopia (99).

> If Marc had been somewhat more concerned with political and economic conditions, it would have occurred to him that the "European civil war," as he called it, was a statement of bankruptcy of the spirit in which he believed. This belief turned into a kind of living lie. It can no longer be denied that the content which is the vehicle for Marc's progressive artistic devices portrays the ideals of a lost era. Marc refused to admit that the blue flower of Romanticism had long faded before it was finally trodden to pieces under soldiers' boots. (Helmut Schneider)

Franz Marc volunteeered in 1914. Deceived, he believed that the war would clean "the stall of Augia," i.e., old Europe. Idealism in its deepest humiliation? Longing for death as the more complete purification and transition to longed-for pure being? Stupid foolishness that did not recognize the sign of dreadful reality and continues to dream of a lost paradise?

Franz Marc was killed on March 4, 1916, at Verdun—in France, a country he had often visited and where, as he wrote to his brother in 1903, he had wanted to live.

## (92) Decay.  Earth calls

GOTTFRIED BENN, "Man and Woman Go Through the Cancer Barrack"

Benn's first volume of poetry, *Morgue and Other Poems,* was published in 1912. "Macabre choice of content and a provocative tone based on a montage style that mixes poetic vocabulary with coldly scientific jargon and banal colloquial language to achieve crass alienation—this combination offered a shocking conception of the usual image of the doctor and the human being. Benn makes a 'clean sweep' of the 'ideal of the knight of the blue flower' [Ernst Stadler], juxtaposing the conventional promise and the flimsy progress of his era to the nothingness of death's public reality. Sickness, decay, death are the topics; the human being, 'the crown of creation,' 'the pig,' as Benn later adds (*The Doctor,* 1917), appears as a helpless animal, a pitiable object, as trash, lamentable, even contemptible. By linking apparently incompatible elements in crass images, by blending fixed areas of association Benn reveals the arbitrariness of value concepts that are generally regarded as binding. This principle of the fragmentation of illusion and destruction of mood, designated by the author in 1951 as the 'procedure of puncturing the context,' i.e., 'destruction of reality,' was again expanded by the use of harmonious montage by Benn on various topics in the rhymed verse of the 1920s. The clinical-nihilistic conception of the world ultimately yields, following Nietzsche's definition of art as metaphysical activity, to a Dionysiac view. 'Death' now means 'homecoming,' redemption, becoming one with the earth, with 'vegetable life,' and with the primordial womb." (Otto F. Best)

The man:
Here, this row is decaying wombs
and this row is decaying chests.
Bed stinks by bed. The nurse is changed each hour.

Come and just lift this cover here.
Look, once this lump of fat and foul saps
used to be something great for some man
and was his homeland and his ecstasy.

Come, look at this scar on the chest.
Do you feel the rosary of soft knots?
Just feel. The flesh is soft and doesn't hurt.

This one here, she bleeds like thirty bodies.
No human being has so much blood.
This one here,
they just sliced a baby from her cancerous womb.

They let them sleep. Day and night. The new ones
are told: You'll sleep your way to health. But Sundays,
they're kept a bit more wakeful for the visitors.

Not much of the food is eaten. The backs
are sore. You see the flies. Sometimes
the nurse washes them. The way you wash benches.

Here the soil is swelling around each bed.
Flesh levels off to land. Fire gives itself away.
Sap is about to run. The earth is calling.

TRANSLATED BY JOACHIM NEUGROSCHEL

## (93) The decay of language and thought

HUGO VON HOFMANNSTHAL, A Letter

The poet asserts that the *Letter* (1902) was directed by Lord Chandos, the younger son of
an earl of Bath, to Francis Bacon to apologize for having completely renounced literary
activity. In reality, what is involved is an extremely modern prose work on the topic of
the disintegration of identity. Diffusion of concepts, abstractions, and words—questions
everywhere, answers nowhere; the words lie, objects can no longer be grasped; nihilism is
spreading like "corrosive rust."

To sum the matter up: All existence seemed to me then, in a sort of
ongoing intoxication, to be one great unit. Spiritual and physical worlds
seemed to form no opposition, as little as did courtly and animal life, art
and barbarism, solitude and society. In all things I sensed the presence of
Nature, in the aberrations of folly as much as in the extreme refinements
of a Spanish ceremony, in the boorishness of young peasants no less than
in the subtlest allegories; and I sensed my own presence in all of Nature.
If, in my hunting lodge, I drank up the warm, foaming milk that some
unkempt person had squeezed into a wooden pail from the udder of a
beautiful, soft-eyed cow, it would be no different for me than if I lapped
up the sweet, foaming spiritual food of some folio read in the deep-set
window seat of my study. One was like the other; neither fell short of the
other, whether in its dreamlike, otherworldly quality, or in its physical

intensity. And so it went throughout my life, all about me; wherever I was I was in the center of life, never suspecting this to be an illusion. Or I divined that all was parable, and one being the key to every other; and I considered myself the one capable of seizing them all, or as many as possible, each by the tip of the other. Hence the title I thought of giving my encyclopedic work [*Nosce te ipsum*].

For someone susceptible of such notions, it may seem the well-appointed plan of divine Providence that my spirit had to plummet from such inflated arrogance into the depths of dejection and cowardice, now the permanent state of my soul. Yet religious views of that kind have no hold over me: they belong to those cobwebs through which my thoughts pierce, far beyond and into the void, while most of their companions get caught and come to rest there. For me the mysteries of faith have been condensed into a lofty allegory that spans the fields of my life like a splendid rainbow, at a perpetual remove, always ready to recede if it should occur to me to rush upon it and wrap myself up in the folds of its mantle.

But, my esteemed friend, in a similar way even worldly notions withdrew from me. How should I try to depict these curious intellectual torments to you; this recoil of the fruit bough from my outstretched hand; this ebbing away of the murmuring pool from my thirsting lips?

My dilemma, in short, is this? I have entirely lost the capacity to think or speak of anything at all coherently.

At first it became more and more impossible to treat some sublime or general theme and in the process assume the sort of language that men are accustomed to use automatically. I suffered inexplicable displeasure even in pronouncing the words "spirit" or "body" or "soul." I found it spiritually impossible to elicit any opinion whatsoever on the affairs of the court, the proceedings of Parliament, or whathaveyou. And not out of any sort of tact—for you know that my candor can sometimes border on thoughtlessness—but rather because the abstract terms one's tongue adopts as a matter of course, in order to utter any sentence at all, now crumbled in my mouth like rotten toadstools. And once, while scolding my four-year-old daughter Catherine Pompilia for a childish lie she had told, and seeking to impress upon her the necessity of always telling the truth, all the eloquent sentiments that were pouring into my mouth suddenly took on such shifting coloration and started to spill over so into one another, that I reeled off my sentences as best I could, spluttering at the end, as though suddenly ill and, literally turning pale, with a violent pressure on my forehead, left the child to herself, slammed the door behind me, and only by finding my horse and taking it for a good gallop through the empty pasture, began to recover somewhat.

Gradually, though, the assault spread like a corrosive rust. All the sentences of plain, familiar conversation, the ones recited easily, with somnambulistic assurance, now seemed to me so spurious that I had to cease taking part in any such discussions. With an unaccountable fury that I could necessarily hide only with great effort, I would hear such things as: Such-and-such affair had a good or bad outcome; Sheriff N. is a wicked man, Pastor T. a good one; poor tenant M., his sons are spendthrifts; lucky A., his daughters are thrifty; a certain family is rising in the world, another is going downhill.

All this seemed to me as indemonstrable, as fraudulent and faulty as could be. All things that arose in such discussions my mind now forced me to view with an uncanny closeness: just as I had once examined the skin of one of my fingers in a magnifying glass and discovered its resemblance to an open field full of pits and furrows, so I now viewed people and their acts. I could no longer regard them with the simplifying glance of habit. All crumbled into pieces, the pieces into still more pieces, and nothing would allow itself to be bound up in a concept any more. Lone words floated about me; coalesced into eyes that stared at me and made me return their stares: they are whirlpools it makes me dizzy to look into, they spin perpetually, and through them one enters the void.

TRANSLATED BY DAVID JACOBSON

## (94) Weighed down by your mere physical presence

FRANZ KAFKA, Letter to His Father

Franz Kafka, 1883–1927, was born in Prague. The poet published very little during his lifetime. Prior to his death he stipulated that his entire literary remains were to be burned. His friend, Max Brod, did not comply with his will, however, thereby rescuing an opus that is among the most distinctive and greatest achievements of the twentieth century.

The question of transcendence is decisive in Kafka's novels and stories. He describes the fragility of the world, the unknowable contexts of the cleavage, and society's "groundlessness." Kafka shows man in a paradox, an absurd situation between life and death. Released from all fixed terrestrial and supernatural order, man is disoriented and without a goal— without light (seen from the human standpoint) even when the presence of this light cannot be denied and redemption is expected. "To wait for the train, and then leave the tunnel even when the direction is unclear and the light perhaps comes from 'behind'; to hear the message even though it is not known whether the kings still live or whether the couriers merely whisper to each other the news that has long since become senseless. To look for the path even if repeatedly going astray in the thicket; to exist in the nameless and listen for the voice that sometimes whispers from far, far away: all of that makes clear the situation of a person who knows about the destination but does not know the way." (Walter Jens)

Your educational methods in the very early years I can't, of course, directly describe today, but I can more or less imagine them by drawing retrospective conclusions from the later years and from your treatment of Felix. What must be considered as heightening the effect is that you were then younger and hence more energetic, wilder, more untrammeled, and still more reckless than you are today and that you were, besides, completely tied to the business, scarcely able to be with me even once a day, and therefore made all the more profound an impression on me, never really leveling out into the flatness of habit.

There is only one episode in the early years of which I have a direct memory. You may remember it, too. One night I kept on whimpering for water, not, I am certain, because I was thirsty, but probably partly to be annoying, partly to amuse myself. After several vigorous threats had failed to have any effect, you took me out of bed, carried me out onto the *pavlatche,* and left me there alone for a while in my nightshirt, outside the shut door. I am not going to say that this was wrong—perhaps there was really no other way to getting peace and quiet that night—but I mention it as typical of your methods of bringing up a child and their effect on me. I dare say I was quite obedient afterward at that period, but it did me inner harm. What was for me a matter of course, that senseless asking for water, and the extraordinary terror of being carried outside were two things that I, my nature being what it was, could never properly connect with each other. Even years afterward I suffered from the tormenting fancy that the huge man, my father, the ultimate authority, would come almost for no reason at all and take me out of bed in the night and carry me out into the *pavlatche,* and that meant I was a mere nothing for him.

That was only a small beginning, but this sense of nothingness that often dominates me (a feeling that is in another respect, admittedly, also a noble and fruitful one) comes largely from your influence. What I would have needed was a little encouragement, a little friendliness, a little keeping open of my road, instead of which you blocked it for me, though of course with the good intention of making me go another road. But I was not fit for that. You encouraged me, for instance, when I saluted and marched smartly, but I was no future soldier, or you encouraged me when I was able to eat heartily or even drink beer with my meals, or when I was able to repeat songs, singing what I had not understood, or prattle to you using your own favorite expressions, imitating you, but nothing of this had anything to do with my future. And it is characteristic that even today you really only encourage me in anything when you yourself are involved in it, when what is at stake is your own sense of self-importance, which I damage (for instance by my intended marriage) or which is damaged in me (for instance when Pepa is abusive to me). Then I receive encouragement, I am reminded of my worth, the matches I would be entitled to make are pointed out to me, and Pepa is condemned utterly. But apart from the fact that at my age I am now almost quite unsusceptible to encouragement, what help could it be to me anyway, if it only comes when it isn't primarily a matter of myself at all?

At that time, and at that time in every way, I would have needed encouragement. I was, after all, weighed down by your mere physical presence. I remember, for instance, how we often undressed in the same bathing hut. There was I, skinny, weakly, slight; you strong, tall, broad. Even inside the hut I felt a miserable specimen, and what's more, not only in your eyes but in the eyes of the whole world, for you were for me the measure of all things. But then when we stepped out of the bathing hut before the people, you holding me by my hand, a little skeleton, unsteady, barefoot on the boards, frightened of the water, incapable of copying your swimming strokes, which you, with the best of intentions, but actually to my profound humiliation, always kept on showing me, then I was frantic with desperation and at such moments all my bad experiences in all spheres fitted magnificently together. I felt best when you sometimes undressed first and I was able to stay behind in the hut alone and put off the disgrace of showing myself in public until at last you came to see what I was doing and drove me out of the hut. I was grateful to you for not seeming to notice my anguish, and besides, I was proud of my father's body. By the way, this difference between us remains much the same to this very day.

In keeping, furthermore, was your intellectual domination. You had worked your way so far up by your own energies alone, and as a result you had unbounded confidence in your opinion. That was not yet so dazzling for me as a child as later for the boy growing up. From your armchair you ruled the world. Your opinion was correct, every other was mad, wild, *meshugge,* not normal. Your self-confidence indeed was so great that you had no need to be consistent at all and yet never ceased to be in the right. It did sometimes happen that you had no opinion whatsoever about a matter and as a result all opinions that were at all possible with respect to the matter were necessarily wrong, without exception. You were capable, for instance, of running down the Czechs, and then the Germans, and then the Jews, and what is more, not only selectively but in every respect, and finally nobody was left except yourself. For me you took on the enigmatic quality that all tyrants have whose rights are based on their person and not on reason. At least so it seemed to me.

Now, when I was the subject you were actually astonishingly often right; which in conversation was not surprising, for there was hardly ever any conversation between us, but also in reality. Yet this was nothing particularly incomprehensible, either; in all my thinking I was, after all, under the heavy pressure of your personality, even in that part of it—and particularly in that—which was not in accord with yours. All these thoughts, seemingly independent of you, were from the beginning burdened with your belittling judgments; it was almost impossible to endure this and still work out a thought with any measure of completeness and permanence. I am not here speaking of any sublime thoughts, but of every little childhood enterprise. It was only necessary to be happy about something or other, to be filled with the thought of it, to come home and speak of it, and the answer was an ironical sigh, a shaking of the head, a tapping on the table with a finger: "Is that all you're so worked up about?" or "Such worries I'd like to have!" or "The things some people have time to think about!" or "Where is that going to get you?" or "What a song and dance about nothing!" Of course, you couldn't be expected to be enthusiastic about every childish triviality, when you were in a state of fret and worry. But that was not the point. Rather, by virtue of your antagonistic nature, you could not help but always and inevitably cause the child such disappointments; and further, this antagonism, accumulating material, was constantly intensified; eventually the pattern expressed itself even if, for once, you were of the same opinion as I; finally, these disappointments of the child were not the ordinary disappointments of life but, since they involved you, the all-important personage, they struck to the very core. Courage, resolution, confidence, delight in this and that, could not last when you were against it or even if your opposition was merely to be assumed; and it was to be assumed in almost everything I did.

This applied to thoughts as well as to people. It was enough that I should take a little interest in a person—which in any case did not happen often, as a result of my nature—for you, without any consideration for my feelings or respect for my judgment, to move in with abuse, defamation, and denigration. Innocent, childlike people, such as, for instance, the Yiddish actor Löwy, had to pay for that. Without knowing him you compared him, in some dreadful way that I have now forgotten, to vermin and, as was so often the case with people I was fond of, you were automatically ready with the proverb of the dog and its fleas. Here I particularly recall the actor because at that time I made a note of your pronouncements about him, with the comment: "This is how my father speaks of my friend (whom he does not even know), simply because he is my friend. I shall always be able to bring this up against him whenever he reproaches me with the lack of a child's affection and gratitude." What was always incomprehensible to me was your total lack of feeling for the suffering and shame you could inflict on me with your words and judgments. It was as though you had no notion of your power. I too, I am sure, often hurt you with what I said, but then I always knew, and it pained me, but I could not control myself, could not keep the words back, I was sorry even while I was saying them. But you struck out with your words without much ado, you weren't sorry for anyone, either during or afterward, one was utterly defenseless against you.

But your whole method of upbringing was like that. You have, I think, a gift for bringing up children; you could, I am sure, have been of help to a human being of your own kind with your methods; such a person would have seen the reasonableness of what you told him, would not have troubled about anything else, and would quietly have done things the way he was told. But for me as a child everything you called out at me was positively a heavenly commandment, I never forgot it, it remained for me the most important means of forming a judgment of the world, above all of forming a judgment of you yourself, and there you failed entirely. Since as a child I was with you chiefly during meals, your teaching was to a large extent the teaching of proper behavior at table. What was brought to the table had to be eaten, the quality of the food was not to be discussed—but you yourself often found the food inedible, called it "this swill," said "that beast" (the cook) had ruined it. Because in accordance with your strong appetitie and your particular predilection you ate everything fast, hot, and in big mouthfuls, the child had to hurry; there was a somber silence at table, interrupted by admonitions:

"Eat first, talk afterward," or "faster, faster, faster," or "there you are, you see, I finished ages ago." Bones mustn't be cracked with the teeth, but you could. Vinegar must not be sipped noisily, but you could. The main thing was that the bread should be cut straight. But it didn't matter that you did it with a knife dripping with gravy. Care had to be taken that no scraps fell on the floor. In the end it was under your chair that there were most scraps. At table one wasn't allowed to do anything but eat, but you cleaned and cut your fingernails, sharpened pencils, cleaned your ears with a toothpick. Please, Father, understand me correctly: in themselves these would have been utterly insignificant details, they only became depressing for me because you, so tremendously the authoritative man, did not keep the commandments you imposed on me. Hence the world was for me divided into three parts: one in which I, the slave, lived under laws that had been invented only for me and which I could, I did not know why, never completely comply with; then a second world, which was infinitely remote from mine, in which you lived, concerned with government, with the issuing of orders and with the annoyance about their not being obeyed; and finally a third world where everybody else lived happily and free from orders and from having to obey. I was continually in disgrace; either I obeyed your orders, and that was a disgrace, for they applied, after all, only to me; or I was defiant, and that was a disgrace too, for how could I presume to defy you; or I could not obey because I did not, for instance, have your strength, your appetite, your skill, although you expected it of me as a matter of course; this was the greatest disgrace of all. This was not the course of the child's reflections, but of his feelings.

TRANSLATED BY ERNST KAISER AND EITHNE WILKINS

## (95) Smoke burns and blusters

GEORG HEYM, "The God of the City"

Georg Heym was born in Silesia in 1887. At the age of thirteen he went to Berlin where he later studied law. He drowned with his friend in January 1912 while ice-skating on the Havel.

> He broadly squats upon a block of buildings.
> The winds are seething black around his brow.
> He glares in rage at distant solitude,
> Where the last houses err into the country.

Baal's crimson belly glows with evening,
The giant cities kneeling all around him.
The enormous number of church bells surges
Toward him from a sea of ebony towers.

The music of the millions here is booming
Like Corybantic dances through the streets.
The smoke of chimneys, billows of the factory
Waft up to him like bluish incense fragrance.

The weather smolders in his eyebrows.
Evening darkness is numbed into night.
The storms are fluttering as they peer like vultures
From his head, and his hair bristles in anger.

He shoves his butcher's fist into the dark.
He shakes it and a sea of fire roars
Along a street. And the smoke burns and blusters
And eats it up, until the day dawns late.

TRANSLATED BY JOACHIM NEUGROSCHEL

## (96) The tempest is at hand

JAKOB VAN HODDIS, "World's End"

Jakob van Hoddis, pseudonym of Hans Davidsohn (1887–1942), studied architecture in Munich and classical philology and philosophy in Berlin. In 1909 he founded the "New" Club and the "Neopathetic Cabaret." In 1912 he experienced signs of schizophrenia and had to seek treatment. In 1915 he was given private care; after 1933 he lived in a sanatorium. As a Jew he was deported and murdered by the National Socialists. "The poem 'End of the World' in which the decline of the bourgeois world is portrayed as the beginning of the final catastrophe is extremely powerful, uniting vision, grotesqueness, irony, sarcasm, and melancholy." (Helmut Olles)

The hat flies off the burgher's pointed head.
The air resounds with something like a shriek.
Roof-menders fall to earth and come apart.
And on the coasts—we read—the tide is rising.

The tempest is at hand, the unruly seas
all hop ashore to smash the thickest dams.
Most of the people have a runny nose.
The railroad trains are dropping from the bridges.

TRANSLATED BY JOACHIM NEUGROSCHEL

## (97) All roads end in black decay

GEORGE TRAKL, "Grodeck" (Second Version)

Georg Trakl (1887–1914), proves to be a prophet of morbidity whose work is absolutely voluptuous and colorful, sensual and lyrical. Gladly following Baudelaire's addictive routes to future paradises, he was nourished by "a powerful pain." The title of his last poems, *Grodeck*, is the name of a place in former East Galicia. Grodeck is also the place from which a counteroffensive ordered by Conrad von Hötzendorf, chief of the Austrian general staff and a strong champion of the war, was begun in 1914, ending in renewed catastrophic defeats for Austria. The metaphors in *Grodeck* to a great extent crystallize the transition from the forms used in expressionist poetry to those of the plastic arts.

As a member of a medical battalion, Trakl had to attend the severely wounded in a barn beside the marketplace of Grodeck. Abandoned to the laments, cries of pain, and pleas for help in dying, he became insane and poisoned himself with an overdose of cocaine after being admitted to psychiatric treatment.

In the evening, the autumnal woods resound
With deadly weapons, the golden plains
And blue lakes, over them the sun
More grimly rolls; the night embraces
Dying warriors, the wild lament
Of their shattered mouths.
But silently at the meadow bottom
Red clouds, in which a wrathful god lives,
Gather the shed blood, moonly coolness;
All roads end in black decay.
Under golden boughs of night and stars
The sister's shadow reels through the silent grove
To greet the ghosts of heroes, the bleeding heads;
And softly in the reeds, the dark flutes of autumn are playing.
O prouder grief! You brazen altars,
The hot flame of the spirit is fed by more violent pain,
The unborn grandchildren.

TRANSLATED BY JOACHIM NEUGROSCHEL

## (98) Yelling death

AUGUST STRAMM, Two Poems

August Stramm, the son of a bureaucrat, was born in 1874. After attending the *Gymna-sium* he obtained a high position in the postal service, studied on the side, and graduated in 1909. He was killed in Russia in 1915. The point of departure in his poetry is natu-ralism. He later achieves a constructivist "compression style" that became characteristic of his writing. Reduction and abstraction ("technique of omission") were used to emphasize the single word. Feeling was delimited to a scream, or to "agglomeration."

| 92 | *Patrol* |
|---|---|
| 93 | The stones are foeing |
| 94 | Window grinning betrayal |
| 95 | Branches choking |
| 96 | Mountains shrubs leafing rustly |
| 97 | Yelling |
| 98 | Death |
| 99 | |
| 100 | *Guard* |
| 101 | A star scares the spire cross |
| 102 | The nag snaps smoke |
| 103 | Iron jangling sleepily |
| 104 | Fogs sweeping |
| 105 | Terrors |
| 106 | Staring freezing |
| 107 | Freezing |
| 108 | Caressing |
| 109 | Whispering |
| 110 | You! |
| 111 | |

TRANSLATED BY JOACHIM NEUGROSCHEL

## (99) The "pure" animal and the impious man

FRANZ MARC, Letters from the Field

Franz Marc (born in Munich in 1888; killed on the Western Front in 1916) originally wanted to become a minister, having been reared in French Calvinism, which was his mother's religious affiliation. He acquired an "endless number of theories and insights" after joining the circle of Kandinsky and Jawlensky in 1911. He writes that his paintings had never before succeeded so well and that it was possible to recognize in them the desire for religion. He considered himself a painter-emissary of a new faith at the center of which was animal symbolism. His two guiding principles were purity and feeling. "These goals became problematic in connection with the apocalyptic mood before the First World War, with expectations going beyond aesthetics and religion in the direction of world-historical change. The 'self-purification' the artist wanted to achieve with abstraction was supposed to be realized in world-historical terms by the war. This widespread madness was one of the tragic aspects of expressionism. Unintentionally this idealism served to justify and escalate an adventure whose real driving forces were power politics and nationalism. Even a person so gentle to people and animals as Marc championed the war as the purification that would free Europe from all 'self-centeredness' and materialism, which he considered basic evils, leading to an epoch characterized by pure spirit." (Eduard Beaucamp)

Hageville, Nov. 1, 1914

*Dear Maman:*

Today on "All Saints in the Field" I am sending you a little greeting from my garden, in which I now sit often and think and write. Now a real Indian summer, an "Old Wives' Summer" as we call it in Bavaria, has arrived, the days are of a melancholy silence and unspeakable mildness, only the eternal cannon thunder in the west and south (Toul-Verdun) rolling through. At night, too, the windows rattle incessantly. It is the heavy artillery before Verdun and Toul, which we recognize by the muffled rolling. Today was the first field mass which we experienced, outside of the open meadow near the artillery, since the church has been set up as a supply building. I often walk to the little cemetery, which is very similar to the one at Pippingen. It is so remarkable and touching to read all the strange French names, from the time of Napoleon I and earlier, with their old tombstones. I thought so vividly today about Papa's little grave, whose simple slab reminds me of these graves, and in my thoughts I laid a small bouquet on it. Our life here is unchanged; each day now I ride my horse 1 to 2 hours (a strong chestnut bay, which benefits greatly from the respite); otherwise I write and read and walk up and down in the garden for hours with my thoughts. I between there are days with guard duty, requisitions; recently I had to oversee road construction, etc. But there is not much duty. I now feel as strong as ever, only I'm not allowed to drink beer and must be cautious in general about eating and drinking. My intestine (or is it the stomach, I don't know?) has become remarkably sensitive; but I can maintain myself well here. With this little greeting, from the bottom of my soul, take a dear kiss from

*Your Franz*

Hageville, 11-11-14

*Dear Maman:*

Now the real autumn is beginning to come around, here too, cold and frosty. Ashamed, as we sit in our cozy quarters, we think about our comrades at the front, in the gun emplacements and the trenches. The only comfort for them, too, is that they are the victors, for even if it goes slowly, still the ring surrounding the enemy closes tighter and faster; at least here and in the Vosges they aren't charging ahead so madly anymore, as in September and August, in order to spare our precious manpower as much as possible. Now this dreadful war will be raging across all of Asia; Persia and China will be definitely dragged in, and I don't believe America will be able to avoid the fighting until the end. This world conflagration is certainly the most heinous moment of all world history. I often think how as a boy and a young man I grieved that I would not experience a great world historical epoch—now it is here and more horrible than anyone could dream. One becomes small in the face of the greatness of these events, and patiently submits to the place which is ordained by destiny. For a long time now I perceive of this war as a German affair no more, but as a world event. Certainly you are right that many will become aware of thoughts and religious feelings which they long believed were lost or overcome. It's the same with me. The monstrous spiritual shock makes us question our whole knowledge and our convictions down to the roots. Only I think that we cannot revert to old formulas of belief and habits if we really want to get a foothold in this sea of unrest and the turmoil of war; but I think new religious thoughts will arise, a whole new European empire. The religious sentiment always stays the same in man, but it expresses itself in ever new ways. The ancient Greeks were just as religious in their way as the Indians and Mohammedans and Christians, and the new Europeans of the 20th century will not perceive less religiously, only in a different way. I ponder this a great deal, whither, toward which goal and in which forms man changes and evolves. Europe *cannot* remain long as it has been, in no way after this monstrous war. As painful and melancholy as the separation from my home and my work is to me, still I am glad to be out here. I would feel depressed and ill at home. This way I live and experience everything. Hopefully, too, I will survive it all in good health. Here in H. we can gather strength. We are well supplied, no soldier suffers hunger or thirst here.———

4-12-15

*D[earest]:*

The more carefully and the more frequently I read your recent letters, the more compelling does their inner artistic logic seem to me. In the aphorisms I touched upon the truth everywhere, without ever saying the "real thing," what is essential; it means a total renunciation in the sense of the parable of the wealthy young man. Only when the renunciation has been carried out can one test whether the feelings which survive are worthy enough to be of meaning to others. With the great majority this will *not* be the case; their pictures would become quite unattractive or, on second thought, they would stop painting them. Consideration, healthy modesty and conscience would deter them from impure production. Measured against this noble standard there is *extremely little remaining* of all European art. The arrogant evolutionary spirit of recent centuries was all too unfavorable to art as we envision it. "Art only exists quite rarely." I contemplate my own art a lot. As a whole, instinct has not guided me poorly up till now, even if the works were impure; above all, the instinct which led me away from the sense of life in man to the sense for the animalistic, to the "pure animals." The impious man who surrounded me (above all the males) did not arouse my true feelings, while the animal's pristine sense of life made everything good ring out in me. And away from the animal an instinct led me to the abstract, which stimulated me even more; to a second vision which is quite Indian-untimely and in which the sense of life rings perfectly pure. Very early I perceived of man as "ugly"; the animal seemed more beautiful to me, purer, but even here I discovered much which was emotionally repulsive and ugly, so that my portrayals instinctively, from inner compulsion, became more abstract. Trees, flowers, earth, everything showed me uglier and more emotionally repulsive features year after year, until suddenly the ugliness of *nature* and its *impurity* completely dawned on me. Perhaps our European perspective has poisoned and disfigured the world, that's why I dream of a new Europe—but let's leave Europe out of it. The main thing is *my feeling,* my *conscience* as you say. My conscience tells me that before nature (in the broadest sense) I perceive perfectly correctly and cogently, and if I proceed from my sense of life, nature concerns me no longer, and stirs me like the scenes in a theater with which a work of fiction is draped. *Fiction* itself derives from quite different creators and basic motives, and if I were to express it as I feel it, I'm not allowed to work with scenes, but must seek a pure expression far from a theory of life. Whether there is such a thing?

Whether it will ever be discovered pure in painting? It has been found in music, there you are right, but how soon it was lost again! "We can't force anything with it," that is what I wanted to say. In that sentence I wanted to express the *relative lack of success* of that early triumph. _____ is undoubtedly close on the trail of that goal of truth; that is why I love him so. Maybe you are quite right in saying that as a person he is not pure and strong enough, so that his feelings are not generally valid but appeal only to the sentimental, sensuously nervous and romantic. But his striving is wonderful and full of lonely greatness. You must not conclude from the foregoing that now, after my old mistake, I am constantly dwelling on the possible, abstract *form;* on the contrary, I am trying to live very much *according to my feelings.* My outside interest in the *world* is very reserved and cool, very *penetrating,* so that my *interest* does not get entangled in it, and presently I am leading a kind of negative life in order to give pure feeling some room for breathing and artistic unfolding. I trust much in my instinct and instinctive production. I will only be able to do that again in Ried, but then it will happen, too. I often have the feeling that I have something secret, something happy in my pocket, which I'm not allowed to look at; sometimes I keep my hand on it and touch it from the outside.

What you say about _____ is very pretty.

*Your Franz M.*

3-14-16

D[*earest*]:

Just think: today I received a little letter from the people at my quarters in Marstadt (Lorraine), which contained your birthday letter! The woman had found it in one of the cartons in spite of my having looked for it! I was a bit ashamed but doubly glad that I have it after all, you have written so sweetly. Yes, this year I will return to my dear undamaged home, to you and to my work. Among the boundless horrible images of destruction within which I now live, this thought of homecoming bears a halo which is too lovely to describe. Just protect this, my home and yourself, your soul and your body and all that is mine, that belongs to me!

At the moment we are quartered with the column on totally devastated castle property, over which the erstwhile front lines of the French have passed. As a bed I have turned over a rabbit hutch, removed the bars and stuffed it with hay, then I set it into a room which is still rain-proof!

Naturally I have enough blankets and pillows with me, so that it's really quite comfortable to sleep in. Don't worry, I'll get through this all right, and healthy. I feel good and watch out for myself. Thank you much, very much, for the dear birthday letter!

*Fell the same day at 4:00 in the afternoon*

TRANSLATED BY ADRIAN DEL CARO

# BIBLIOGRAPHY
# OF GERMAN SOURCES

1. Friedrich von Hardenberg [Novalis]. *Hymnen an die Nacht.* In *Werke, Tage-bücher und Briefe Friedrich von Hardenbergs.* Ed. Hans-Joachim Mähl and Richard Samuel. Vol. 1. Munich-Vienna: Carl Hanser Verlag, 1978, pp. 149–155.

2. Joseph von Eichendorff. "Mondnacht." In his *Werke.* Ed. Wolfdietrich Rasch. Munich-Vienna: Carl Hanser Verlag, 1971, pp. 271–272.
Eduard Mörike. "Um Mitternacht." In his *Sämtliche Werke.* Ed. Herbert G. Göp-fert. Munich-Vienna: Carl Hanser Verlag, 1976, pp. 100–101.
Heinrich Heine. "Der Tod, das ist die kühle Nacht." In his *Sämtliche Schriften.* Ed. Klaus Briegleb. Vol. 1. Munich-Vienna: Carl Hanser Verlag, 1975, p. 149.
Annette von Droste-Hülshoff. "Durchwachte Nacht." In her *Sämtliche Werke.* Ed. Clemens Heselhaus. Munich-Vienna: Carl Hanser Verlag, 1974, pp. 272–275.

3. *Die Nachtwachen von Bonaventura.* Cologne: Bartmann-Verlag, 1955, pp. 73–76.

4. Jean Paul Friedrich Richter [Jean Paul]. *Blumen, Frucht- und Dornenstücke, oder Ehestand, Tod und Hochzeit des Armenadvokaten F. St. Siebenkäs.* In his *Sämtliche Werke.* Ed. Norbert Miller. Part I, Volume 2. Munich-Vienna: Carl Hanser Ver-lag, 1971, pp. 271–275.

5. Friedrich von Hardenberg [Novalis]. *Heinrich von Ofterdingen.* In *Werke, Tag-ebücher und Briefe Friedrich von Hardenbergs.* Ed. Hans-Joachim Mähl and Richard Samuel. Vol. 1. Munich-Vienna: Carl Hanser Verlag, 1978, pp. 241–244.

6. Johann Wolfgang von Goethe. "Urworte Orphisch." In *Goethes Werke. Auswahl in zwanzig Teilen.* Ed. Karl Alt. Vol. 1. Berlin-Leipzig-Vienna-Stutt-gart: Deutsches Verlagshaus Bong & Co., n.d., pp. 433–434.

7. Friedrich Hölderlin. "Hyperions Schicksalslied." In his *Sämtliche Werke und Briefe.* Ed. Günther Mieth. Vol. 1. Munich-Vienna: Carl Hanser Verlag, p. 229.

8. Wilhelm von Humboldt. *Bruchstücke einer Selbstbiographie.* Ed. Heinrich Weinstock. Frankfurt-Main: Fischer Bücherei, 1957, pp. 144–148.

9. Johann Wolfgang von Goethe. *Iphigenie auf Tauris.* In *Goethes Werke. Auswahl in zwanzig Teilen.* Ed. Karl Alt. Vol. 6. Berlin-Leipzig-Vienna-Stutt-gart: Deutsches Verlagshaus Bong, n.d., pp. 49–51.

10. Anselm Feuerbach. *Ein Vermächtnis.* Ed. Henriette Feuerbach. Berlin: Verlag Meyer & Jessen, 1912, pp. 160–163.

11. Leo Deuel. *Heinrich Schliemann. Eine Biographie. Mit Selbstzeugnissen und Bilddokumenten.* Munich-Vienna: Carl Hanser Verlag, 1979, pp. 191–194. (Original edition: *The Memoirs of Heinrich Schliemann.* New York: Harper & Row, 1977.)

12. Friedrich Schiller. "Nänie." In his *Sämtliche Werke.* Ed. Gerhard Fricke and Herbert G. Göpfert. Vol. 1. Munich-Vienna: Carl Hanser Verlag, 1979, p. 242.

13. Conrad Ferdinand Meyer. "Der römische Brunnen." In his *Gedichte.* Leipzig: H. Haessel Verlag, 1905, p. 155.

14. Rainer Maria Rilke. "Archaischer Torso Apollos." In his *Sämtliche Werke.* Ed. Rilke Archive, with Ruth Sieber-Rilke and Ernst Zinn. Vol. 1. Wiesbaden: Insel-Verlag, 1955, p. 557.

15. Stefan George. "Entrückung." In *Das grosse deutsche Gedichtbuch.* Ed. Carl Otto Conrady. Kronberg/Taunus: Athenäum-Verlag, n.d., p. 625.

16. Joseph von Eichendorff. *Das Marmorbild.* In his *Werke.* Ed. Wolfdietrich Rasch. Munich-Vienna: Carl Hanser Verlag, 1971, p. 1160 ff.

17. Friedrich Nietzsche. *Die Geburt der Tragödie oder Griechentum und Pessimismus.* In his *Werke in drei Bänden.* Ed. Karl Schlechta. Munich-Vienna: Carl Hanser Verlag, 1977, pp. 21–25.

18. Thomas Mann. *Tristan.* Stuttgart: Reclam, 1950, pp. 39–46.

19. Friedrich Schiller. *Ueber die ästhetische Erziehung des Menschen in einer Reihe von Briefen.* In his *Sämtliche Werke.* Ed. Gerhard Fricke and Herbert G. Göpfert. Vol. 5. Munich-Vienna: Carl Hanser Verlag, 1980, pp. 667–669.

20. Heinrich von Kleist. *Ueber das Marionettentheater.* In his *Sämtliche Werke und Briefe.* Ed. Helmut Sembdner. Vol. 2. Munich-Vienna: Carl Hanser Verlag, 1977, pp. 338–345.

21. Joseph von Eichendorff. *Aus dem Leben eines Taugenichts.* In his *Werke.* Ed. Wolfdietrich Rasch. Munich-Vienna: Carl Hanser Verlag, 1971, pp. 1144–1146.

22. Albert Leitzmann, ed. *Die Brautbriefe Wilhelms und Carolinen von Humboldt.* Leipzig: Insel-Verlag, 1921, pp. 381–387.

23. Adalbert Stifter. *Der Nachsommer.* Munich: Wilhelm Goldmann Verlag, 1964, pp. 31–35.

24. Johann Wolfgang von Goethe. *Wilhelm Meisters Wanderjahre.* In *Goethes Werke. Auswahl in zwanzig Teilen.* Ed. Karl Alt. Vol. 13. Berlin-Leipzig-Vienna-Stuttgart: Deutsches Verlagshaus Bong & Co., n.d., pp. 306–307.

25. Georg Wilhelm Friedrich Hegel. "Anrede an seine Zuhörer bei der Eröffnung seiner Vorlesungen in Berlin, am 22. Oktober 1818." In *Hegel.* Sel. and introd. Friedrich Heer. Frankfurt/Main-Hamburg: Fischer Bücherei, 1955, pp. 66–68.

26. Karl Marx. "Zur Kritik der Hegelschen Rechtsphilosophie." In *Karl Marx/Friedrich Engels. Studienausgabe in vier Bänden.* Ed. Iring Fetscher. Vol. 1. Frankfurt/Main: Fischer Bücherei, 1966, pp. 17–20.

27. Arthur Schopenhauer. *Die Welt als Wille und Vorstellung.* In his *Werke in zwei Bänden.* Ed. Werner Brede. Vol. 1. Munich-Vienna: Carl Hanser Verlag, 1977, pp. 34–35.

28. Arthur Schopenhauer. *Parerga und Paralipomena.* In *Arthur Schopenhauers sämtliche Werke in sechs Bänden.* Ed. Eduard Griesebach. Vol. 5. Leipzig: Verlag von Philipp Reclam Jun., n.d., pp. 107–108.

29. Bettina von Arnim. *Goethes Briefwechsel mit einem Kinde. Sein Denkmal.* Rev. and ed. Heinz Amelung. Berlin-Leipzig-Vienna-Stuttgart: Deutsches Verlagshaus Bong & Co., 1914, pp. 342–345.

30. Ludwig van Beethoven. *Das Heiligenstädter Testament."* In *Deutsches Lesebuch. Von Luther bis Liebknecht.* Ed. Stephan Hermlin. Munich: Carl Hanser Verlag, n.d., pp. 255–258.

31. Georg Friedrich Wilhelm Hegel. *Vorlesungen über die Philosophie der Weltgeschichte.* In *Hegel.* Sel. and introd. Friedrich Heer. Frankfurt Main-Hamburg: Fischer Bücherei, pp. 96–100.

32. Friedrich Schiller. *Was heisst und zu welchem Ende studiert man Universalgeschichte.* In his *Sämtliche Werke.* Ed. Gerhard Fricke and Herbert G. Göpfert. Vol. 4. Munich-Vienna: Carl Hanser Verlag, 1976, pp. 765–767.

33. Johann Wolfgang von Goethe. *Kampagne in Frankreich.* In *Goethes Werke. Auswahl in zwanzig Teilen.* Ed. Karl Alt. Vol. 19. Berlin-Leipzig-Vienna-Stuttgart: Deutsches Verlagshaus Bong & Co., n.d., pp. 41–43.

34. Karl Leberecht Immermann. *Die Epigonen.* In his *Werke.* Ed. Harry Maync. Vol. 3. Leipzig and Vienna: Bibliographisches Institut, n.d., pp. 135–136.

35. Jacob Burckhardt. *Weltgeschichtliche Betrachtungen.* Ed. Rudolf Marx. Stuttgart: Alfred Kröner Verlag, 1949, pp. 35–39.

36. Leopold von Ranke. "Wie der Begriff 'Fortschritt' in der Geschichte aufzufassen sei." In his *Geschichte und Politik. Ausgewählte Aufsätze und Meisterschriften.* Ed. Hans Hofmann. Stuttgart: Alfred Kröner Verlag, 1942, pp. 138–142.

37. Friedrich Engels. Brief an J. Bloch. In *Karl Marx/Friedrich Engels. Studienausgabe in vier Bänden.* Ed. Iring Fetscher. Vol. 1. Frankfurt/Main: Fischer Bücherei, 1966, pp. 226–228.

38. Karl Marx/Friedrich Engels. *Feuerbach.* In *Karl Marx/Friedrich Engels. Studienausgabe in vier Bänden.* Ed. Iring Fetscher. Vol. 1. Frankfurt/Main: Fischer Bücherei, pp. 109–110.

39. Freiherr von Stein. Denkschrift vom 24. November 1808 bei seiner Entlassung. In his *Staatsschriften und Briefe.* Munich, 1921.

40. Friedrich Hölderlin. "Gesang der Deutschen." In his *Sämtliche Werke und Briefe.* Ed. Günther Mieth. Vol. 1. Munich-Vienna: Carl Hanser Verlag, 1978, pp. 247–249.

41.    Friedrich Hölderlin. *Hyperion oder der Eremit in Griechenland*. In his *Sämtliche Werke und Briefe*. Ed. Günther Mieth. Vol. 1. Munich-Vienna: Carl Hanser Verlag, 1978, pp. 737–739.

42.    Heinrich Heine. "Nachtgedanken." In his *Sämtliche Schriften*. Ed. Klaus Briegleb. Vol. 4. Munich-Vienna: Carl Hanser Verlag, pp. 432–433.

43.    Heinrich Heine. *Deutschland, ein Wintermärchen*. In his *Sämtliche Schriften*. Ed. Klaus Briegleb. Vol. 4. Munich-Vienna: Carl Hanser Verlag, pp. 577–580.

44.    Jakob Grimm. "Meine Entlassung." In *Wissenschaft und Leben. Auswahl aus den Schriften Jakob Grimms für die Deutsche Bibliothek*. Ed. Alexander Eggers. Berlin, n.d., pp. 47–50.

45.    Fanny Lewald. *Erinnerungen aus dem Jahre 1848*. In *Spaziergänge und Weltfahrten. Reisebilder von Heine bis Weerth*. Ed. Gotthard Erler. Munich: Carl Hanser Verlag, 1977, pp. 359–363.

46.    Friedrich List. "Vom Nutzen der Eisenbahn." In his *Schriften, Reden, Briefe*. Vol. 3. Ed. Erwin von Beckerath and Otto Stühler. Berlin: Verlag Reimar Hobbing, 1929, pp. 347–349.

47.    Jean Paul Friedrich Richter [Jean Paul]. *Leben des Quintus Fixlein. Billet an meine Freunde anstatt der Vorrede*. In his *Sämtliche Werke*. Ed. Norbert Miller. Part 1, Vol. 4. Munich-Vienna: Carl Hanser Verlag, 1975, pp. 10–13.

48.    Karl Gutzkow. *Lebenserinnerungen*. In *Karl Gutzkows ausgewählte Werke in zwölf Bänden*. Ed. Heinrich Houben. Vol. 12. Leipzig: Max Hesses Verlag, n.d., pp. 44–48.

49.    Friedrich Hölderlin. "Hälfte des Lebens." In his *Sämtliche Werke und Briefe*. Ed. Günther Mieth. Vol. 1. Munich-Vienna: Carl Hanser Verlag, 1978, p. 344.

50.    Friedrich Hölderlin. "Abendphantasie." In his *Sämtliche Werke und Briefe*. Ed. Günther Mieth. Vol. 1. Munich-Vienna: Carl Hanser Verlag, 1978, pp. 237–238.

51.    Philipp Otto Runge. Brief an den Bruder Daniel, Dresden, den 9. März 1802. In *Künstler über Kunst. Briefe und Aufzeichnungen von Malern, Bildhauern, Architekten*. Sel. Hans Eckstein. Darmstadt: Stichnote Verlag, 1954, pp. 33–34.

52.    Franz Grillparzer. *Der Traum, ein Leben*. In his *Sämtliche Werke*. Ed. Peter Frank and Karl Pörnbacher. Vol. 2. Munich-Vienna: Carl Hanser Verlag, 1970, pp. 175–179.

53.    Johann Peter Hebel. *Kannitverstan*. In his *Werke*. Sel. Paul Alberdes. Munich-Vienna: Carl Hanser Verlag, 1960, pp. 48–51.

54.    Arthur Schopenhauer. *Die Welt als Wille und Vorstellung*. In his *Werke in zwei Bänden*. Ed. Werner Brede. Vol. 1. Munich-Vienna: Carl Hanser Verlag, 1977, pp. 363–365.

55.    Karl Immermann. "Goethes Haus am Frauenplan in Weimar." In *Goethe: Leben und Welt in Briefen*. Ed. Friedhelm Kemp. Munich-Vienna: Carl Hanser Verlag, 1978, pp. 490–493.

56.    Theodor Storm. Brief an Hartmuth Brinkmann, 28. September 1855. In *Briefwechsel zwischen Theodor Storm und Eduard Mörike.* Ed. Hanns Wolfgang Rach. Stuttgart: Verlag von Julius Hoffmann, n.d., pp. 78–83.

57.    Ludwig Richter. Jahreshefte und Briefe an seinen Sohn. In *Lebenserinnerungen eines deutschen Malers. Selbstbiographie nebst Tagebuchniederschriften und Briefen von Ludwig Richter.* Ed. Heinrich Richter. Leipzig: Max Hesses Verlag, n.d., pp. 595, 607–608, 612–613, 682, 686–687.

58.    Detlev von Liliencron. "Dorfkirche im Sommer" and "Bitte an den Schlaf, nach schwersten Stunden." In his *Gesammelte Werke.* Vol. 2. Berlin: Schuster & Loeffler, 1916, pp. 126–127, 392. Theodor Storm. "Abseits." In his *Sämtliche Werke. Neue Ausgabe in fünf Bänden.* Vol. 5. Braunschweig and Berlin, 1916, p. 11 f.

59.    Arthur Schopenhauer. *Parerga und Paralipomena.* In his *Werke in zwei Bänden.* Ed. Werner Brede. Vol. 2. Munich-Vienna: Carl Hanser Verlag, 1977, pp. 140–143.

60.    Johann Wolfgang von Goethe. *Faust. Part Two.* In *Goethes Werke. Auswahl in zwanzig Teilen.* Ed. Karl Alt. Vol. 8. Berlin-Leipzig-Vienna-Stuttgart: Deutsches Verlagshaus Bong & Co., n.d., pp. 299–302.

61.    Wilhelm Busch. *Herr und Frau Knopp.* In the *Wilhelm Busch-Album. Humoristischer Hausschatz mit 1500 Bildern von Wilhelm Busch.* Munich: Friedrich Bassermannsche Verlagsbuchhandlung, 1925, pp. 123–124, 166.

62.    Gottfried Keller. *Die Leute von Seldwyla.* In his *Sämtliche Werke und ausgewählte Briefe.* Ed. Clemens Heselhaus. Vol. 2. Munich-Vienna: Carl Hanser Verlag, 1979, pp. 9–12.

63.    Heinrich Heine. *Reisebilder.* In his *Sämtliche Schriften.* Ed. Klaus Briegleb. Vol. 2. Munich-Vienna: Carl Hanser Verlag, 1976, pp. 122–126.

64.    Wilhelm Raabe. *Die Chronik der Sperlingsgasse.* In his *Sämtliche Werke.* First Series. Vol. 1. Berlin-Grunewald: Verlagsanstalt für Literatur und Kunst/Hermann Klemm, n.d., pp. 8–11.

65.    Wilhelm Raabe. *Der Schüdderump.* In his *Sämtliche Werke.* Third Series. Vol. 1. Berlin-Grunewald: Verlagsanstalt für Literatur und Kunst/Hermann Klemm, n.d., pp. 1–5.

66.    Georg Büchner. *Lenz.* In his *Sämtliche Werke und Briefe.* Ed. Werner R. Lehmann. Vol. 1. Munich-Vienna: Carl Hanser Verlag, 1979, pp. 79–81.

67.    Adalbert Stifter. Vorrede zu *Bunte Steine.* In *Adalbert Stifters ausgewählte Werke in sechs Bänden.* Ed. Rudolf Fürst. Vol. 5. Leipzig: Max Hesses Verlag, n.d., pp. 3–8.

68.    Detlev von Liliencron. "Acherontisches Frösteln." In his *Gesammelte Werke.* Vol. 3. Berlin: Schuster & Loeffler, 1916, p. 98.

69.    Arthur Schopenhauer. *Die Welt als Wille und Vorstellung.* In his *Werke in zwei Bänden.* Ed. Werner Brede. Vol. 1. Munich-Vienna: Carl Hanser Verlag, 1977, pp. 356–359.

70.   Alexander von Humboldt. *Reise in die Aequinoktial-Gegenden des neuen Kontinents.* In *Deutsche Prosa. Eine Auswahl von Luther bis zur Gegenwart.* Wiesbaden: Dieterich'sche Verlagsbuchhandlung, 1949, pp. 261–263.

71.   Adalbert Stifter. "Bergkristall." In *Adalbert Stifters ausgewählte Werke in sechs Bänden.* Ed. Rudolf Fürst. Vol. 5. Leipzig: Max Hesses Verlag, n.d., pp. 133–138.

72.   Rudolf Virchow. *Vier Reden über Leben und Kranksein.* Berlin: Verlag von Georg Reimer, 1862, pp. 10–20.

73.   Georg Büchner. *Woyzeck.* In his *Sämtliche Werke und Briefe.* Ed. Werner R. Lehmann. Vol. 1. Munich-Vienna: Carl Hanser Verlag, 1970, pp. 174–176.

74.   Gottfried Benn. "Hirne." In his *Gesammelte Werke in vier Bänden.* Ed. Dieter Wellershoff. Vol. 2. Wiesbaden: Limes Verlag, 1968, pp. 13–19.

75.   Friedrich Hebbel. *Maria Magdalena.* In his *Werke.* Ed. Gerhard Fricke, Werner Keller, and Karl Pörnbacher. Vol. 1. Munich-Vienna: Carl Hanser Verlag, 1963, pp. 345–347.

76.   Friedrich Hebbel. *Tagebücher.* In his *Werke.* Ed. Gerhard Fricke, Werner Keller, and Karl Pörnbacher. Vol. 4. Munich-Vienna: Carl Hanser Verlag, 1966, pp. 531–536.

77.   Bettina von Arnim. *Dies Buch gehört dem König.* Berlin, 1852, pp. 594–597.

78.   Heinrich Heine. "Die schlesischen Weber." In his *Sämtliche Schriften.* Ed. Klaus Briegleb. Vol. 4. Munich-Vienna: Carl Hanser Verlag, p. 455.

79.   Georg Büchner. *Der Hessische Landbote.* In his *Sämtliche Werke und Briefe.* Ed. Werner R. Lehmann. Vol. 2. Munich-Vienna: Carl Hanser Verlag, pp. 34–40.

80.   Heinrich Heine. Brief an Karl August Varnhagen von Ense. In his *Werke und Briefe in zehn Bänden.* Ed. Hans Kaufmann. Vol. 9. Berlin: Aufbau-Verlag, 1962, pp. 215–217.

81.   August Bebel. *Aus meinem Leben.* Frankfurt/Main: Europäische Verlagsanstalt, n.d., pp. 56–60.

82.   Georg Herwegh. "Bundeslied für den Allgemeinen Deutschen Arbeiterverein." In *Das grosse deutsche Gedichtbuch.* Ed. Carl Otto Conrady. Kronberg/Taunus: Athenäum Verlag, 1977, pp. 509–510.

83.   Hugo von Hofmannsthal. "Manche freilich . . ." In his *Gedichte und lyrische Dramen.* Gesammelte Werke in Einzelausgaben. Ed. Herbert Steiner. Frankfurt/Main: S. Fischer Verlag, 1952, p. 19.

84.   Karl Otten. "Die jungen Arbeiter." In his *Die Thronerhebung des Herzens.* Berlin-Wilmersdorf: Verlag Die Aktion, 1918.

85.   Sigmund Freud. "Die 'kulturelle' Sexualmoral und die moderne Nervosität." In *Fragen der Gesellschaft. Ursprünge der Religion.* Sigmund Freud: Studi-

enausgabe. Ed. Alexander Mitscherlich et al. Vol. 9. Frankfurt/Main: S. Fischer Verlag, 1974, pp. 13–16.

86.   Arthur Schnitzler. *Jugend in Wien. Eine Autobiographie.* Afterword Friedrich Torberg. Vienna-Munich-Zurich: Verlag Fritz Molden, 1968, pp. 148–151.

87.   Friedrich Nietzsche. *Ecce homo. Wie man wird, was man ist.* In his *Werke in drei Bänden.* Ed. Karl Schlechta. Vol. 2. Munich-Vienna: Carl Hanser Verlag, 1977, pp. 1070–1073.

88.   Rainer Maria Rilke. *Die Aufzeichnungen des Malte Laurids Brigge.* In his *Prosa und Uebertragungen.* Ausgewählte Werke. Ed. Rilke Archive, with Ruth Sieber-Rilke, Carl Sieber, and Ernst Zinn. Vol. 2. Leipzig: Insel Verlag, 1938, pp. 8–11, 41–43.

89.   Detlev von Liliencron. "Blitzzug." In his *Ausgewählte Gedichte.* Berlin and Leipzig, Schuster & Loeffler, 1907, p. 11f.

90.   Theodor Fontane. *Irrungen Wirrungen.* In his *Werke, Schriften und Briefe.* Ed. Walter Keitel and Helmuth Nürnberger. Part 1, Vol. 2. Munich-Vienna: Carl Hanser Verlag, 1972, pp. 406–410.

91.   Theodor Fontane. "Würd es mir fehlen, würd ichs vermissen?" In his *Werke, Schriften und Briefe.* Ed. Walter Keitel and Helmuth Nürnberger. Part 1, Vol. 6. Munich-Vienna: Carl Hanser Verlag, 1978, p. 340.

92.   Gottfried Benn. "Mann und Frau gehn durch die Krebsbaracke." In his *Gesammelte Werke in vier Bänden.* Ed. Dieter Wellershoff. Vol. 3. Wiesbaden: Limes Verlag, 1960, pp. 14–15.

93.   Hugo von Hofmannsthal. *Ein Brief.* In his *Prosa II.* Gesammelte Werke in Einzelausgaben. Ed. Herbert Steiner. Frankfurt/Main: S. Fischer Verlag, 1951, pp. 10–12.

94.   Franz Kafka. *Brief an den Vater.* Afterword Wilhelm Emrich. Munich: R. Piper & Co. Verlag, 1960, pp. 10–16.

95.   Georg Heym. "Der Gott der Stadt." In his *Dichtungen und Schriften. Gesamtausgabe.* Ed. Karl Ludwig Schneider. Vol. 1. Hamburg and Munich: Ellermann Verlag, 1964, p. 192.

96.   Jakob van Hoddis. "Weltende." In his *Weltende. Gesammelte Dichtungen.* Ed. Paul Pörtner. Zurich: Verlag Die Arche, 1958, p. 28.

97.   Georg Trakl. "Grodek, 2. Fassung." In his *Dichtungen und Briefe.* Ed. Walther Killy and Hans Szklenar. Salzburg: Otto Müller Verlag, n.d., p. 94.

98.   August Stramm. "Patrouille," "Wache." In *August Stramm: Das Werk.* Wiesbaden: Limes Verlag, 1963, pp. 86, 99.

99.   Franz Marc. *Briefe aus dem Feld.* Berlin: Rembrandt Verlag, n.d., pp. 23–25, 62–64, 151.